FREE MONEY FREE STUFF

FREE MONEY FREE STUFF

The Select Guide to Public and Private DEALS, STEALS & GIVEAWAYS

Reader's Digest

The Reader's Digest Association, Inc.
Pleasantville, New York | Montreal

Staff

Project Editor Don Earnest

Project Designer Rich Kershner

Cover Design George McKeon

Editor Daryna Tobey

Associate Designer Erick Swindell

Copy Editor Jeanette Gingold

Indexer Nanette Bendyna

Illustrator Peter Hoey

Reader's Digest Books

Editor in Chief Neil Wertheimer

Managing Editor Suzanne G. Beason

Creative Director Michele Laseau

Associate Director, North America Prepress Douglas A. Croll

Manufacturing Manager John L. Cassidy

Marketing Director Dawn Nelson

President and Publisher, Trade Publishing Harold Clarke

President, U.S. Books & Home Entertainment Dawn Zier

The Reader's Digest Association, Inc.

President and Chief Executive Officer Eric Schrier

Text produced for Reader's Digest by

Gonzalez Defino

editorial and design services (www.gonzalezdefino.com)

Editorial Director Joseph Gonzalez

Editor Patricia Fogarty

Researcher/Fact Checker Hildegard B. Anderson

Writers Jennifer Block Martin, Stephen Brewer, Fred DuBose, Marie Hodge, Stephanie Johns, Fred Sandsmark, Mimi Torchin, Susan Wernert Lewis

Library of Congress Cataloging-in-Publication Data

Free money, free stuff : the select guide to public and private deals, steals and giveaways / [project staff, Don Earnest].

p. cm.

Includes index.

ISBN: 978-0-7621-0771-1 (hardcover)

ISBN: 978-0-7621-0903-6 (paperback)

ISBN: 978-0-7621-0919-7 (BAF edition)

1. Free material—Catalogs. I. Earnest, Don, 1938- II. Reader's Digest Association.

AG600.F65 2007

011'.03—dc22

2006032049

We are committed to both the quality of our products and the service we provide to our customers. We value your comments, so please feel free to contact us.

The Reader's Digest Association, Inc.
Adult Trade Publishing
Reader's Digest Road
Pleasantville, NY 10570-7000

For more Reader's Digest products and information, visit our website: www.rd.com

Printed in the United States of America

3 5 7 9 10 8 6 4 2 (hardcover)
1 3 5 7 9 10 8 6 4 2 (paperback)
1 3 5 7 9 10 8 6 4 2 (BAF edition)

Note to Readers

All information in this book has been carefully researched and fact-checked, and to the best of our knowledge, was accurate at the time this book went to press. However, the availability of the specific offers, giveaways, grants, loans, discounts, and other products and services described in this book cannot be guaranteed. Each is subject to being changed or discontinued, or having the requirements for availability changed, at any time at the sole discretion of the provider. Some offers listed in this book, especially those related to product samples, are temporary and identified as such; they are included solely as examples of the type of items that might be available. The names of, and contact information for, businesses, foundations, organizations, government agencies and programs, and websites are also subject to change. Neither Reader's Digest Association, Inc., nor Gonzalez Defino assumes any responsibility for a reader not being able to obtain any of the products or services described in this book

welcome to the great big world of bargains!

There are freebies, benefits, discounts, and other money-savers galore out there—more than enough for everyone. You just need to know how to find them.

FREE. IT'S ONE OF THE MOST POWERFUL words in the lexicon of business. Which is why you hear and see it all the time. "Buy one, get one free!" "Free shipping and handling!" "Free samples!" "Free gift!" "Free upgrade!" "Free consultation!" "Free estimate!"

In fact, "free" offers are so widespread, we consumers often scoff. Nothing is for free, says the skeptic inside us. For veteran shoppers, our hopes of a "free" offer delivering something of value have been dashed over and over. Yet look in many wallets, and you'll find at least one punch card for a favorite store that will grant you a "free" product after buying 10 or so. And when we see a "buy one, get one free" tag at the grocery store, our shopping carts quickly become a little more full. And who of us with business cards hasn't tossed one in a bowl next to a cash register at a store or restaurant in the hopes of winning a free item? Our minds may question the math of free offers, but our more hopeful hearts want to believe that free offers are at least sometimes for real.

We have good news.

For the assertive shopper or the savvy computer user, valuable free stuff truly does exist. You have to look for it, know the secrets, do a

By the **numbers**

5.5

The number of Web pages, in billions, listed by Google after a search for the word "free." Just proving where people's real interest lies, that's more than 100 times the number produced by a search for the word "sex."

little work sometimes. But for those willing to put in the effort, there are huge amounts of rewards to be had. Amounts that can honestly reach into the thousands of dollars.

How do we know? Because our team of experts spent months doing nothing but researching the world of free offers. We were motivated in part by our own curiosity, as well as the questionable advice we were encountering on the topic on TV, in magazines, and in books. Roughly 1,500 hours of research later, we're glad to report in detail what we found. To start, here are a few headlines from our research:

- A surprising number of companies seek new customers by offering them free products to try. The trick is to find out where and how they provide the service.
- Nearly every government body wants to help its constituents in some way, often by providing valuable services, products, or tax incentives. But you have to know whom to ask.
- Many nonprofit organizations, websites, and businesses thrive by serving as clearinghouses for free services or products.
- For certain groups—such as teachers, veterans, individuals with disabilities, seniors, the poor—there are many organizations dedicated to providing assistance at no or low cost.
- Most of all, there is a large marketplace of products that are sold at hefty discounts. Virtually every manufacturer routinely makes too many of a particular product. So what do they do? Either they sell it off at a huge bargain to customers, or sell it to other businesses for a song, and let them liquidate it.

A Note on Timeliness

We have made every effort to ensure that the offers, deals, and websites in this book are accurate and up-to-date. All quoted prices and offers were valid as of mid-2006. In some cases, we've included offers that are clearly temporary, in order to give you an idea of the *types* of freebies or discounts available from that source. But offers and websites do come and go. So we cannot guarantee that you'll find every offer available and every website up and running.

If a Web address is no longer functional, try typing the name of the company, organization, or program into Google or another search engine. That's likely to lead you to the right place. Whenever possible, we've also included toll-free telephone numbers and mailing addresses.

In the pages of this book, you'll find more than a thousand money-saving offers, all carefully researched and fact-checked for validity and accuracy. Each freebie or bargain is described in a short write-up that tells you all you need to know about that particular money-saver. Whether it's a coupon for a haircut or assistance paying for prescription drugs, we explain how it can benefit you, and how to take advantage of the savings.

We've also included brief special features that provide helpful related information. You'll learn, for example, how to be a good consignment shopper; how to navigate the Department of Veterans Affairs; what a social worker does; how to make the most of AARP; why it sometimes pays to travel abroad for surgery; and where to get free online calculators to help you determine your net worth or how much you'll need to save for your child's education.

For easy reference and access, we've arranged this wealth of information in handy sections and chapters that address the various areas and stages of your life, as well as the needs of special groups.

- In Part One you'll learn how to be a good bargain hunter and how to find even more discounts, freebies, benefits, and other money-savers. We also alert you to scams and cons, and tell you how to spot the difference between a trap and a bargain.
- Part Two is loaded with info on how to save on everything from food and household goods to health care and education, appearance, entertainment, and travel. You'll also discover how to get free job-search help, a low-interest loan for your small business, free money-management advice, a missing pension, or funding for your nonprofit.
- Part Three presents freebies and steep discounts targeted to specific groups: seniors, veterans and active-duty military personnel, people with disabilities, new mothers, and teachers and local government employees.

We hope that you will not only profit greatly from the offers, deals, tools, and information in this book, but also have fun doing it. We love bargains, too, and we take great pleasure in helping you find them. As you delve into our guide to the great big world of bargains, we wish you good luck and happy hunting!

—*The Editors*

contents

PART ONE

Something for Everyone

PART TWO

Low-Cost Solutions for Everyday Living

PART THREE

SUPER SPECIAL BARGAINS FOR SUPER SPECIAL PEOPLE

Part One

SOMETHING FOR EVERYONE

All About Bargains and How to Find Them!

• How to Spot Traps & Scams

CHAPTER 1

all about bargains and how to find them!

Ingenuity, resourcefulness, and sometimes a little boldness: That's what a great bargain hunter is made of. Do you have what it takes to seek and secure sales and steals? Read on.

By the numbers

13.08

Average percent interest, in September 2006, that Americans pay on fixed-rate credit cards. Want a better rate? Usually all it takes is a call to the credit card company (and maybe a threat to take your business elsewhere).

BARGAINS ARE ALL ABOUT SAVING MONEY, and you'll save lots of it with the freebies, discounts, tips, and information we've gathered for you in this book. In the chapters that follow, we tell you how you can save on everything from buying a house to prescription drugs, commuting expenses, and even frozen dinners. We tip you off to hundreds of ways to pay less for household items from food to face cream, along with techniques for finding bargains in just about every area of life, from low-cost travel to reduced-fee child care to cheap movie tickets and free advice for starting a business. We also provide plenty of info on lowering your expenditures on the big-ticket items, such as cars and even college educations for you or your kids.

But first, a review of the basics. In the first part of this chapter, we present nine simple rules that will make you a better bargain hunter, whether you're shopping for diapers or a used car. Then it's on to the where and how of finding bargains, benefits, and other money-savers. In the second half of the chapter, you'll find a baker's dozen of no-fail strategies for successful bargain hunting. Consider these to be your general instructions—practical, how-to techniques that will sharpen your consumer skills and help fatten your wallet.

9 Rules for Becoming a Better Bargain Hunter

1 Nothing is a bargain if you don't need it.

Consider whether you actually need and will use the item you are about to buy, even if you're parting with only a dollar or two. You've come across a beautiful set of antique andirons for next to nothing at a flea market? Wonderful, but remember, you don't have a fireplace. So you're not really getting a bargain at all—in fact, you're throwing away your hard-earned money. In your visits to the supermarket have you noticed that a gallon jar of mayonnaise costs only a little more than a quart jar? Seems like a bargain, no? You're on the right track, because buying in bulk is often a great way to save money. But if you live alone and that mayo's going to go bad before you have a chance to use all of it, you haven't saved any money—in fact, you've wasted some. By the way, you need to be especially cautious whenever you buy anything in bulk, because the low-cost-per-item come-on that many stores use can be especially deceptive. Ten legal-size writing pads aren't a bargain if you know in your heart of hearts that the day will come when you toss them out in a fit of spring-cleaning.

You'll be getting a true bargain if you buy something you need at a good price, or find it for free—like $1 off the price of a box of breakfast cereal, or some free samples of shampoo and conditioner, or a loan guaranty that allows you to buy a house without a down payment. You might not be as likely to show off the T-shirt you get for half price as you will be to brandish those "I got 'em for a steal" andirons, but actually you should be more proud of the shirt—you needed it and you saved money buying it, so that's the real bargain.

2 It pays to think outside the box.

A little creativity can save you an awful lot of money. You know those handy disinfectant wipes you use around the house? You pay about $0.13 apiece for them. Not a fortune, to be sure, but you can make your own simply by soaking paper towels with Lysol—for about $0.03. Do the math: You're saving $0.10 a wipe, and that adds up quickly, especially if you're a good housekeeper who enjoys having a house that sparkles. Looking for some inexpensive entertainment? Before you head down to the local cineplex, think about new ways to have some fun. Consider sitting in on a reading at your local bookstore, enjoying a band concert in the park around the corner, or taking in a free movie under the stars, something that many communities offer during the summer. Need to have major dental work done? This might seem really "out there," but would you entertain the notion of a trip to Hungary, the new "dental capital of the world"? High-quality work costs much less there than it does in the United States, and it's possible to arrange an all-inclusive trip that includes airfare, time in the chair, and accommodation for a price that will probably be less than the bill you'd get from your family dentist.

Companies charge more than you think to add a little "convenience" to their products.

Like most drivers, you'd probably be happy to save some money on gas. Have you thought about sharing the drive to work with a neighbor or two? Make the trip with one other person who shares the cost and you've cut your expenses in half. Add a third person and you're out only 33 percent of what you spend when you make the trip solo. How about taking the bus and enjoying some time to read the newspaper? Or biking to work a few days a week and adding a health-promoting workout to your commute? You get the idea. Be creative and see what money-saving techniques you come up with.

3 Discover all the saving benefits you're entitled to.

You're probably already aware that seniors, members of the military, and students are eligible for discounts at theaters, museums, amusement parks, and many other places, but did you know that in many cases veterans, educators, firefighters, and other municipal employees are also entitled to discounts on goods and services that range from cruises to hotel rooms, rental cars, and housing? Consider just a few of the many entitlements that might save you hundreds and, in many cases, thousands of dollars.

- Federal programs take a huge chunk off the mortgage bills of teachers, law-enforcement officers, firefighters, and emergency medical technicians by offering them government-owned homes in revitalization areas at half price.
- In New York City, students, teachers, union members, seniors, civil service employees, people on the staff of a not-for-profit organization, performing arts professionals, members of the armed forces, and the clergy are eligible for deeply discounted theater, dance, and music tickets provided by the Theatre Development Fund.

- If you're just leaving the service or have served in the past, you're entitled to a wealth of veterans benefits that include an education under the GI Bill and a home loan guaranty—a loan program that, in fact, can finance your retirement dream home the same way it helped you purchase your first house when you became a civilian again after serving your country.
- Many government programs and services from not-for-profit groups are geared to helping disabled persons. The NFB Newsline, run by the National Federation of the Blind, makes some 200 newspapers nationwide available via telephone. HIKE (Hearing Impaired Kids Endowment) provides free hearing aids to children. And some automakers hand out cash awards for outfitting a car with such adaptive devices as ramps, lifts, hand controls, and power assists that work with the driver's range of motion.

As you'll discover throughout this book, you may be entitled to more than you think you are. Make it a point to search out all the money-savers that are due you and take full advantage of them.

4 It never hurts to ask for a deal.

In many cases, the old saying "Ask and ye shall receive" really does pay off. If you're thinking about joining a gym, ask for a complimentary 10-day or two-week trial pass so you can get to know a club before you sign up. Or maybe a free or discounted health-club membership comes with your job, or maybe your local school lets neighborhood residents use its gym and pool for free. Just ask. You might be able to rack up substantial savings simply by inquiring about job-related discounts whenever you purchase a product or service. For instance, Walt Disney World Swan & Dolphin resorts offer varying discounts for local, state, and federal government employees, as well as members of the military. If you're a soldier in uniform, you should always ask about the discounts you deserve, because even places without an official policy might just decide to give you a treat.

Your membership in AAA and AARP comes with discounts at many hotels and car rental agencies. If you belong to one of these groups, never rent a car or a room without asking about discounts to which you might be entitled. Seniors should take advantage of the discounts at theaters and museums and on public transport that are theirs for the asking. You might be eligible for lower insurance rates if you take a driver's ed refresher course or install antilock brakes on your car; check with your insurance carrier. You could be making interest on your checking account; ask at your bank about its plans and fees to determine which will do the most for your bottom line.

5 Get in touch with your "master negotiator."

When you are bargaining, you don't always have to haggle like a camel driver, but a little crafty negotiating can save you lots of money. If you've ever bought a car, you've probably already earned your stripes matching wits with some of the craftiest sales folks on earth, and you probably didn't think twice about offering less than the asking price of your house. The same willingness to wheel and deal can come in handy in many other situations.

- In this age of skyrocketing medical costs, have you considered discussing the price of treatments, procedures, and prescriptions with your doctor or dentist and asking for a lower fee? You and your physicians can work together to find clinical trials that might cover treatment costs and to research generic medications that can save you a lot on prescriptions. Ask if you might be able to save money by ordering larger dosages than you need and cutting your pills in half.
- Nor should you reserve your negotiating skills for big-ticket items. You'll probably be surprised to learn how many freebies and deals are out there when you muster the courage to "talk turkey" and negotiate a better price. Repeat after me: Will you lower your commission rate on that stock transfer? Can't you do any better on that room rate? Would you bring me a half portion at half price? Do you have a nicer car available for the same low rate? Even in a locale as mundane as your local supermarket you might want to negotiate for discounts on items that are near expiration or overstocked.

6 Sometimes it pays to be a risk-taker.

Not that you should ever be reckless with your insurance protection and other tools that help keep you financially solvent, but sometimes you can save money in the long run by choosing what might seem to be the riskier option. For example:

- If you've never had an accident and only drive to church on Sundays, you may be better off opting for a higher deductible and lower monthly rates on your auto insurance. Increasing your deductible from $200 to $1,000 can slash the cost for collision and comprehensive coverage by up to 40 percent or more. Raising the deductible on a homeowners policy from $250 to $2,500 can cut premiums by 30 percent.

- You can enjoy similar savings by taking an educated gamble on how much long-term-care insurance you might need. A policy that covers care for a maximum of five years costs 50 percent less than one that guarantees lifetime care. Statistics are on the side of the risk-taker here—studies show that only 10 percent of claimants use these benefits for longer than five years.
- Taking all the insurance a rental car company offers may give you a sense of security, but one of your credit cards might provide some of the same coverage automatically. In fact, the extra amount you hand over to the rental car company might not provide one bit of extra protection—and usually adds a hefty sum to the cost of the rental.

7 A little common sense can save you a lot of money.

Saving money isn't rocket science. Sure, it pays to learn about discounts and other money-savers, as you'll do in this book, but sometimes you can save money just by taking the time to think. Consider, for instance:

- While we all like to patronize the gas station that charges less, you're not saving any money, and might be spending more, if you have to drive considerably out of your way to fill the tank. Likewise, you can cut your trips to the pump pretty dramatically just by combining errands and keeping the gas guzzler in the driveway more of the time.
- We all want to keep our cholesterol levels down, and we all know that egg yolks contain cholesterol. So, the answer is to buy egg substitutes, right? Wrong, because these products, most of which consist mainly of egg whites, are expensive. Instead simply separate the whites from the yolks yourself by straining the eggs through your fingers or using a low-cost egg separator—in other words, create your own cholesterol-free eggs.
- When you and your family dine out, you can take a pretty big bite out of the bill (and do your figure a favor) by asking for water with a slice of lemon instead of ordering calorie-laden soft drinks or alcoholic beverages.

Why buy pricey egg substitutes when you can separate the yolks from the whites yourself for free?

- That afternoon latte or fancy flavored coffee is a big pick-me-up, but did you ever consider how easy it is to make one at home? And how much you'd save if you did?
- The seasonal fruits and vegetables available at a farmers' market are likely to be less expensive than those you buy elsewhere, especially if you shop late in the day and snap up items as they're marked down.

Keep thinking along these same commonsense lines, and you'll probably come up with dozens of practical ways to save money.

8 Staying informed can lead you to big savings.

New federal, state, and local programs appear regularly, and the benefits they offer can change frequently. Likewise, new or amended laws and regulations can affect how much you spend for everything from interest on your credit card loans to your college education. Even a natural disaster can affect your household budget; if you're shopping for a car, for example, it pays to know that the market has been flooded with used cars that were damaged in Hurricane Katrina.

Keep informed to protect yourself against financial mishaps, and also to take advantage of opportunities. This might mean staying in touch with representatives from the U.S. Department of Labor's Career One-Stop Centers for leads on free job training or the National Association of Insurance Commissioners' Stop, Call, and Confirm program to protect yourself against the latest insurance scams. On the lighter side, Broadway Box (broadwaybox.com) keeps you posted on great deals on entertainment in New York, and lots of other websites provide breaking news on discounts for everything from restaurant meals to everyday household products.

One of the best ways to control your household finances? Watch the news.

You'll find tools and resources you can use to be a well-informed consumer throughout this book. The trick is to use them regularly so you don't miss out on new ways to save money.

9 Fools rush in, and you won't save if you are one.

Remember the andirons in Rule 1? Those would fall into the category of an impulse buy, snapped up without much thought about whether you really need it. If you make rash buying decisions, the consequences could be a lot more dire than a set of superfluous andirons. You could end up with features on a new car that you don't need and can't really afford, or an interest rate on a home loan that's much higher than your budget allows. That's why you should never simply hand over the cash or sign on the dotted line if you're feeling rushed or less than 100 percent sure of what you're doing. Take a time-out, do the homework you need to do, then proceed when you can do so confidently. Before taking the plunge, you should also take time to use the many free tools available to consumers on the Internet—two examples: calculators that help you determine the comparative costs of leasing versus buying a car or whether you'd be better off with a credit card that offers airline mileage or a low annual fee, and online guides that help you figure out the types of auto, home, health, and life insurance you really need.

13 Strategies for Great Bargain Hunting

STRATEGY #1

Let your websites do the searching.

You've heard it a million times: The Internet is a great resource for finding just about everything you need. And it is indeed handy for finding bargains. But let's be practical. You don't want to spend all your time clicking your way around cyberspace to find specials, giveaways, discounts, and other great money-saving offers. The solution is to use websites that round up information, so that what you need is just a click away. Many armchair travelers already know that it pays to make their first stop at the big online travel providers: Expedia.com (www.expedia.com), Travelocity.com (www.travelocity.com), and Orbitz.com (www.orbitz.com), for discounted fares on airlines, as well as good rates on hotels, car rentals, and vacation packages. Dealnews (www.dealnews.com) corrals compelling offers from major online retailers on computers and other electronics, games, office supplies, DVDs, and such; TheaterMania (www.theatermania.com) features a huge list of discounts for shows, concerts, and other entertainment and arts events in New York, Las Vegas, and London; and www.spoofee.com keeps track of hundreds of special offers from just about all the big-name retailers. Some of these roundup sites will save you money simply by providing free information that you might otherwise pay for. One such resource, www.worldwidewired.com, links readers to the online versions or websites of literally thousands of newspapers and magazines around the globe.

When you find a site that's especially helpful, bookmark it or put on your list of favorites and visit it as often as possible. Some sites make it even easier to keep up with discounts by saving you the trouble of checking in—instead, they reach out to you. Travelzoo (www.travelzoo.com) keeps an eye out for the best airfare, lodging, and vacation deals and publishes them in a newsletter zapped to your e-mail in-box free of charge every Wednesday. Dealnews and other sites will e-mail you when an offer that meets specific criteria you've established, such as a certain price for an HDTV, becomes available.

STRATEGY #2

Be a comparison shopper.

It doesn't matter if you're looking for a car, an insurance policy, or shampoo: You'll save money if you comparison shop, and the Internet makes it especially easy to do so. In the market for a new car? Click your way around www.cars.com for a survey of cars from nearly 10,000 dealers, as well as classified ads from across the country. You can do the same when shopping for insurance (at www.comparisonmarket.com) and for hotel rooms (at www.hotel discounts.com). At FramesDirect.com (www.framesdirect.com), not only can you can you choose from thousands of eyeglass frames at discounts of between 20 and 60 percent off; you can also upload your own photograph to see how the specs will look on your face.

STRATEGY #3

Take advantage of the freebies all around you.

You've probably munched your way through supermarket aisles, enjoying a snack or light lunch of free samples, and you may have walked out of the cosmetics section of a department store with a bounty of trial-size tubes and bottles of beauty products. But you don't even have to leave home to find samples like these—many companies and retail chains list the freebies they make available to consumers on their websites. Keep an eye out and you'll probably be amazed by the number of free samples that are available just for the asking. We've described hundreds of these giveaways for you; to find more on your own, simply go to Google or another search engine, type in "free ____," and see what you come up with.

Toothpaste, for free? At your dentist's office, it's usually yours for the asking.

STRATEGY #4

Accept a helping hand from those who care.

Your doctor, dentist, and other service providers can often help take the edge off their fees with giveaways and cost-saving programs. Your physician might be willing to give you samples of prescription drugs and vitamins, and your dentist probably won't give you the brush-off if you ask for complimentary toothbrushes, toothpaste, floss, mouthwash, and whitening product samples. You might also be able to net free drugs by taking advantage of the promotions that some pharmaceutical companies launch to introduce a new product. Many medical centers offer free treatment for a physical or mental condition to those who participate in a clinical trial, or you can take advantage of free cholesterol tests, skin-cancer screenings, blood-pressure readings, and other medical assessments. The family pet (and your pocketbook) can benefit from the reduced fees for injections and other routine care that humane societies and animal shelters often offer at specific times.

STRATEGY #5

Be on the lookout for free events.

Summer is an especially good time for free jazz festivals, stagings of the Shakespeare classics, and other events—just check with your local chamber of commerce. Free events aren't always splashy extravaganzas. On the annual Free Comic Book Day, participating comic book shops give away issues to anyone who comes into their stores. Many states have annual free fishing days when you can throw your line into the water without a license, on the chance that you just might become hooked on the sport. Sometimes these events are geared not to fun but to practical matters, like the Car Care Council's National Car Care Month (April), when you can have your car checked out for free. You can also schedule your own events, such as an annual insurance checkup, when you meet with your agent to review your homeowners and car policies and learn what new discounts might be available, or a free stem-to-stern Vessel Safety Check from the U.S. Coast Guard to make sure your boat is shipshape.

Bet you never thought you'd get good news from the IRS: It offers free advice on tax breaks and deductions.

STRATEGY #6

Clip your way to savings.

Generations of thrifty consumers have clipped coupons to save money, and these days the Internet makes the experience even more rewarding. Plenty of resources are available to help you make the most of this money-saving pastime, from websites that help you find coupons if you don't have time to linger over the Sunday papers to Web-based systems for organizing coupons. It might pay to become a regular visitor to the websites of the companies that provide many of the products we use in everyday life, such as the manufacturer Procter & Gamble or the mega-retailer Wal-Mart, for their most current crop of coupons. As you become a clipper, you'll discover some of the tricks of the trade, like using coupons even after they've expired and paying attention to special coupons at the checkout counter that cater to your specific buying habits. Coupons aren't just for shoppers anymore, either—smart consumers also save hundreds of dollars using dining-out and entertainment coupons.

STRATEGY #7

Don't forget the classifieds and other ads.

These old standbys at the back of the newspaper are still a treasure trove of savings, where you can find anything from a used sofa to the remaining months on the gym membership of someone who's moving out of town. The Internet makes searching through classifieds easier with websites that round up listings from around the country; www.careerbuilder.com, for instance, partners with newspapers in 200 cities to bring you classified job listings from all those areas. Your local newspaper is also still your best bet for info on free local events, for ads promoting sales at area stores, and for coupons. If you're setting off to see the world, browse the Sunday travel section—packagers and advertisers often advertise their low airfares and discounted resort and cruise packages on these much-read pages.

STRATEGY #8

Get a break with tax breaks.

Before forking over perhaps too much of your hard-earned income to Uncle Sam and his relatives at the state and local level, it always pays to check out the tax relief you might be entitled to. Federally mandated transit-commuter tax benefits can save you up to $105 a month; medical deductions allow you to write off the cost of prescription drugs and treatments that exceed 7.5 percent of your adjusted gross income; and many states offer tax breaks and other incentives to encourage business start-ups, as well as tax credits to small businesses. Need help sorting all this out? You can get plenty of free assistance from the Internal Revenue Service, state and local agencies, the Small Business Administration, and often, depending on such factors as income level or if you're a member of the military or another group, from private firms such as tax giant H&R Block.

STRATEGY #9

Ask Uncle Sam.

Your government works hard to provide free services, and you should take advantage of them whenever you can. Resources range from advice about keeping bugs off your rosebushes (from your local Cooperative Extension Service office of the U.S. Department of Agriculture) to help from the Federal Trade Commission in fighting identity theft. Federal grants provide free job placement and other assistance to those who have lost a job because of plant closings or mass layoffs and can't get a similar one, while federally funded Community-Based Job Training Grants train workers in high-demand, high-growth occupations such as nursing and automotive repair. The government also helps buyers purchase homes; provides a wealth of services to members of the military, veterans, and their families; guarantees loans to students and offers help in paying them back; lends a helping hand to small businesses ... you'll encounter the free help you can get from government programs in almost every chapter of this book, along with guidance on finding more on your own.

STRATEGY #10

Go back to school ...

... not necessarily as a student, but as a beneficiary of the services some schools provide. You might be able to get low-cost haircuts, manicures, and facials at many cosmetology and hairstyling schools, even a soothing rubdown for a great price at a massage school. Veterinary schools sometimes offer reduced costs when Fido and

Felix are cared for by supervised students. Business schools can be great sources of free help, along the lines of helping you develop a marketing plan for your small business.

Enrolling as a temporary student can save you money too: Depending on the state in which you live, taking a driver's safety course might lower your car insurance rates by 10 percent or more. Help is also plentiful if you decide to go to college or return to finish a degree or to take a course or two just for your own enjoyment, or are looking for ways to finance your child's education. Millions of dollars in scholarships are available to people with disabilities, to members of the military, their kids, and veterans, and to many others.

STRATEGY #11

Change your spending habits.

Saving money doesn't have to involve drastic changes. You can take quite a bit off your grocery bill simply by switching from name-brand products to the supermarket's own brands, or buying bread and other baked goods at your local bakery outlet. You'll probably see even more dramatic savings if you work with your pharmacist to buy generic instead of name-brand prescription drugs. Surely you'd welcome the chance to spend less on energy—the word alone conjures up images of dollar signs with wings. One surefire way to cut your gas bills is to keep the gas guzzler in the garage whenever possible and to use alternative modes of transport, including your own two feet or the bus. The Alliance to Save Energy, the American Automobile Association, and the U.S. Department of Energy are among the many organizations eager to help you spend less on energy, whether it's with information on installing energy-efficient windows in your home or an admonition to save money by keeping your foot off the gas pedal and driving at lower speeds.

STRATEGY #12

Get free advice.

There's plenty of free advice out there, and a lot of it is well worth heeding. The Federal Citizen Information Center (see page 53), for example, is a terrific source of free or low-cost information on a vast array of topics—from money matters and health issues to cars, travel, consumer protection, diet, work, federal benefits, and much more. With a few clicks you can access online brochures on vacation getaways from www.snowpak.com, on sun protection for kids from the Skin Cancer Foundation, on breast-feeding from breast-pump manufacturer Evenflo, on safe-driving techniques from the American Automobile Association, and on insurance from the industry-sponsored Insurance Information Institute.

The easiest way to spend less? Buy secondhand.

STRATEGY #13

Learn from the pros.

Some folks just love to shop, whether it's in a flossy boutique or a parking-lot flea market, and experienced, savvy shoppers know where the great bargains are. Follow their lead. Flea markets, yard sales, and consignment and secondhand shops are the favorite haunts of inveterate bargain hunters, and justifiably so—you can find used, nearly new, and sometimes new merchandise at very low prices, and these venues are often especially well stocked with clothing, household items, and DVDs, videos, CDs, and books. But "buying retail" is not necessarily off-limits for bargain-hungry shoppers. Many department stores periodically have sales with savings of up to 75 percent off regular retail price, and salespeople are usually more than eager to put you on mailing lists or to call you for backroom and sample sales. You might also ask a friendly salesperson at your favorite clothing shop about the possibility of getting a deep discount on merchandise that has been worn and returned for one reason or another and cannot be put back into stock.

Okay, now you have the basics—essential rules and proven tips and strategies to help you succeed as a bargain hunter. As you turn the following pages, you'll learn about the thousands of dollars' worth of free and discounted goods and services, grants, scholarships, and other savings that are out there waiting for you. We can tell you where to find them, but only you can take advantage of them. You'll start saving money the minute you do.

CHAPTER 2

how to spot traps & scams

Nothing in life is free—that is, when you're being conned and shaken down by scam artists. Here's how to keep from falling for those too-good-to-be-true deals.

By the **numbers**

26

Percentage of identity theft complaints that had to do with credit card fraud, according to the Federal Trade Commission's 2005 figures.

FREE MAY BE FABULOUS (heavily discounted isn't bad either!), but it isn't always what it's cracked up to be. While "If it's too good to be true ..." doesn't apply in all cases, there are definite telltale signs that an offer is more trap than deal. Bilkers and beguilers have been around forever; today, however, when scammers have computer technology at their disposal, the warning *caveat emptor* ("let the buyer beware") has never been more apt. Digital scammers dangle bait via e-mail, knowing that in the huge pool of potential victims there are plenty who are ready to bite. These hustlers also play on human greed, promising easy money through scams that redirect funds from victims' pockets to theirs.

Out-and-out cons aren't the only things you need to watch out for. Some legitimate businesses, service providers, and credit card companies have ways of subtly trapping you into paying a bit more on monthly bills than is fair. A classic example is a questionable service charge by your phone company, with the often dubious justification buried in the fine print in the flyers accompanying your monthly bill (the flyers that most customers never read!). This is less a true scam and more a failure to adequately disclose information to customers, but the net result is still your loss.

This chapter is all about outsmarting con artists and uncovering hidden consumer traps. We'll show you how to recognize those "bargains" that really are too good to be true and how to guard against scams big and small, from outright frauds to subtle price-gouging and fine-print ploys. Featured in our rogues' gallery are:

- Retail hucksters
- False investment gurus, financial flimflammers, and credit card con artists
- Shady house contractors
- Larcenous garage mechanics
- Fake job promoters
- "Free vacation" scammers
- Phony health insurers
- Modern-day snake-oil vendors
- The ever-growing numbers of identity thieves, Internet phishers and pharmers, and lowlifes who make a business of preying on seniors.

We'll advise you about asking the questions that need to be asked, focusing on the fine print, and keeping your antennae ever on the alert. Armed with this knowledge, you'll be able to take full—and safe—advantage of the wealth of freebies, bargains, and real deals we've compiled for you throughout this book.

Shopping Schemes

Bait-and-Switch Ploys

"Toddler togs 'n' toys closeout. Up to 80 percent off!" So says the newspaper ad from a store we'll call Kiddo World. You arrive at 11 a.m. on the day the ad appears, only to find that the sale items are four shorts-and-shirt sets (all in size XXL) and three stuffed animals. A salesperson says there was "a run on everything" when the doors opened, then directs you to a rack of irresistibly cute shirts. You buy two. As you walk out, you realize you were snagged by a great-sounding but nonexistent deal—and you're $50 poorer.

Safeguarding Your Identity

These days, "Someone's out to get you" often means, "Someone's out to become you." Identity theft has progressed from instances of innovative chicanery to an alarming epidemic. The practice of assuming someone's identity is hardly new, but computer technology has given identity thieves the ability to take control of their victims' personal information in ways their predecessors never could have imagined. As we accumulate account numbers, passwords, and PINs, scammers have all the more to work with. What's worse, it can take weeks for you to discover you've been had.

Computers are by no means their only ways to steal your identity. Just think of what interceptors can do with postal mail: tax documents and health insurance forms showing your Social Security number; credit card and department store bills with account numbers—not to mention your mailed payments, which provide your checking account number; even greeting cards that look as if they could include a check.

Then there are the "Dumpster divers" who sift through trash looking for credit card receipts and financial statements—anything that gives them data they can use. Pre-approved credit card applications are favorites because a thief can fill them out with your name and his or her mailing address. After receiving the card, the thief quickly maxes it out, tosses it, and sticks you with the bill.

Corrupt employees with access to checking account and credit card numbers—cashiers and waiters, for example—can use your personal data for their own purposes or feed it to identity-theft rings. Other identity thieves steal the old-fashioned way: by picking your pocket or snatching your purse.

Protect yourself:

- Keep telemarketers (most are legitimate, but some fish for personal info) at bay by registering with the Federal Trade Commission's National Do Not Call Registry at www.donotcall.gov or by calling toll-free 888-382-1222.
- Retrieve mail from your mailbox soon after it arrives.
- Find out whether your credit card issuers and any stores where you have a charge card will add your photo to the card.
- Do a thorough check of credit card and bank statements as soon you receive them. Review your bank transactions every few days online.
- Shred any about-to-be-discarded documents that reveal personal data.
- Leave your Social Security card and account PINs at home—they're a pickpocket's or purse snatcher's greatest prize.
- Never reveal your Social Security number to anyone you're not 100 percent positive won't misuse it.
- Consult the Federal Trade Commission at www.consumer.gov/idtheft or www.ftc.gov to learn about the latest scams.

In a typical bait-and-switch tactic, the salesperson says the store has sold out of the advertised item, then offers you a similar item at a higher price, or tells you the lower-priced product is of inferior quality and directs you to a pricier one.

Protect yourself: Check the fine print in ads offering great deals. If disclaimers like "limited quantities" or "no rain checks" appear, the store may be pulling a bait-and-switch. If you're ever scammed by a tactic like this, lodge a complaint with the Better Business Bureau (www.bbb.org).

Warranty Games

Ever wonder whether you're asking for trouble if you don't send in the warranty card packed with newly purchased appliances and electronics? Far from it. Your product already is under warranty for a designated period, and your receipt of purchase is the only documentation needed. Truth be told, warranty cards are a way for manufacturers to obtain personal information. When you fill out the "registration" form with details about your income, number of children, and interests, you're compiling a profile that will be sold to other companies.

Retailers love to sell you an extended warranty along with your purchase of a new appliance. The extended warranty is a "protection plan" that covers the cost of repairing or replacing a defective item for a period of time (typically one to four years) beyond the period covered by the manufacturer's warranty (typically one year). Retailers and salespeople tend to push extended warranties aggressively because, in fact, they are much more likely to benefit from this "extra" than you are.

Protect yourself: If you decide to send in a warranty registration form, provide only your name, address, and the date of purchase, and, if required, enclose a copy of the receipt. Ignore all other queries, and file away all receipts and service contracts in case you need to make a claim. Extended warranties are very profitable for stores and commissioned salespeople. Whether or not they're worthwhile for you is another matter. For a new type of product with an unproven repair rate, buying an extended warranty might make sense. But given the general reliability of appliances and electronics today, extended warranties are often a waste of money. A warranty that costs more than 20 percent of the purchase price of the item (or more than the cost of an actual repair) is certainly a bad investment. Don't succumb to on-the-spot sales pressure to buy a warranty (you often have 30 days to make up your mind), and check with your credit card company first to see if it offers similar protection—free—for products purchased with the card.

Costly "Freebies"

This book is packed with legitimate freebies and authentic deals. Unfortunately, freebie or mega-discount offers aren't always what they're cracked up to be, especially those offered on the Internet. Far too often, falling for such pitches means giving over the kind of personal information treasured by spammers and scammers. And sometimes the items turn out to be not so free after all, once you factor in add-ons such as excessive shipping costs, up-front fees, or purchase requirements buried in the fine print.

Protect yourself: Be suspicious of any freebie offers that go overboard with bells and whistles, ask for an up-front fee for a supposedly free item, or use high-pressure tactics. No matter how enticing or legitimate an offer seems, read the fine print carefully to make sure you're not paying too much for shipping and handling or agreeing to purchases you really don't want.

Shopping More Safely Online

Keep your guard up and learn how to spot the scammers. Be on the lookout for one or more of these red flags: The seller's website isn't in good working order or is badly designed; the site doesn't list a telephone number or postal-mail address; there's no sign of sales, return, and privacy policies. Another clue is the lack of a unique domain name and, instead, the use of a free website service such as Tripod.

If you're bidding in an online auction, always check feedback on the seller; eBay and most other aboveboard sites list positive and negative comments by bidders. If an auction site offers no feedback option, avoid it.

Before completing an online transaction, tally the cost. Then compare the total (merchandise plus shipping and handling fees) to that charged by competitors; websites like BizRate.com make it easy to compare prices.

Whenever you buy online, use a credit card or charge card, which means that the Fair Credit Billing Act protects your transaction—which in turn usually makes you liable for no more than $50 of an illicit transaction. (Don't use a debit or bank card! It doesn't offer the same protections.) Also make sure that your transaction is secure. Most websites use pop-ups to tell you when you're entering a secure page; another safety sign is a website address beginning with *https* (the "s" at the end stands for "secure").

Financial Flimflams

Advance-Fee Scams

A money-mooching plot of long standing is the advance-fee scam, which convinces victims that they must spend a little money to earn a lot. The best-known example is the Nigerian Letter. A "civil servant" from Nigeria or other distant nation proposes a confidential business transaction involving the transfer of millions of dollars (usually the surplus from a "double-invoiced" oil contract or some such) into a foreign account—yours. For your trouble, you'll get a nice percentage of the total. Oh, and you'll have to pay an advance fee of some sort—a "performance bond" perhaps, or a "transfer tax." If you pay, you'll likely be asked for additional fees due to "complications." In any event, you can kiss your money good-bye, since it's almost impossible to recover once it's on foreign shores.

Other advance-fee frauds include guaranteed loans pitched to those with low incomes, the creditless, and the unemployed. The catch is that you must pay a fee before receiving your funds—money that, by the way, you'll never see. Lenders who are strictly aboveboard sometimes charge for applications and credit reports, but they never demand advance payment before granting a loan. (For fake advance-fee credit card offers, see "Credit and Debit Card Cons," next page.)

Protect yourself: Walk away from any individual or company that promises something only if you make a payment up front. Then file a complaint with the Federal Trade Commission online (go to www.ftc.gov/ftc/consumer.htm and click on "File a Complaint") or by calling toll-free 877-FTC-HELP (877-382-4357). Many advance-fee scams carried out over the phone originate in Canada. PhoneBusters, Canada's national anti-fraud phone center, is a great resource on all sorts of phone scams and how to recognize, report, and stop them. To learn more, go to www.phonebusters.com/english/reportit.html; or call toll-free 888-495-8501.

Investment Frauds

So many investment scams, so little space to review them!

With *pump-and-dump schemes* fraudsters create a buzz about the innovative nature or unique products of a small public company in which they have bought shares. They often tout the stock as a new "best buy" through postings on Internet chat rooms and bulletin boards and e-mails to potential investors (the pump). Investors then rush to purchase the stock, which quickly increases in value. The fraudsters sell their shares at peak price (the dump), cease the hype, and watch the stock crash.

The *Ponzi scheme* is named for Charles Ponzi, who developed a type of pyramid scheme to cheat investors out of millions by promising them 40 percent returns on their investments in a postage-stamp speculation scheme. The scam uses money from new investors to pay previous investors until the pyramid collapses and the newest investors get crushed.

Oil and gas investment fraud scammers are inspired by high prices at the pump. Victims receive, from a distant drilling enterprise, sales materials that often include surveyor maps and letters from "geologists" claiming that the company's prospecting is almost certain to pay off. Getting a share of the action requires investing thousands of dollars—a classic example of money down the well.

With the *prime bank scheme,* promoters claim they'll give you access to "secret trading markets" of the world's top banks. You can supposedly buy guaranteed notes or debentures from these banks, then sell them for big-time returns. You're not only asked to sign a confidentiality agreement but are told that because these trades are normally for institutions that invest at least $100 million, small individual investors like you must pool their money for an accumulated trade. The pool in which you deposit your money is an offshore account. However, you'll never see said money again, because neither the high-yield notes nor the debentures nor the secret trading markets exist.

Protect yourself: A good resource for staying on top of the latest investment scams is the Fraud Center of the North American Securities Administrators Association (www.nasaa.org). Before making an investment, find out whether the seller is licensed in your state. Also demand written information that fully explains the investment, then contact your state securities regulator with questions about an investment product, broker, or adviser.

Credit and Debit Card Cons

A mailing from a credit card company announces, "You're preapproved!" When you contact the company, a rep says you'll receive a Visa or MasterCard with a $2,500 line of credit, regardless of your current credit rating. You're then asked to pony up a $150 fee. The package you receive contains not a Visa or a MasterCard but a charge card good only for ordering items from an accompanying

CASE STUDY The Credit Repair That Wasn't

Worried sick about the black marks on his credit record, Paul, a restaurant manager, took note of a newspaper ad placed by a company we'll call BalanceBusters, then set up an appointment with a counselor. Sue explained that the company's representatives spoke the credit bureaus' language and understood their regulations in a way that ordinary citizens cannot. The company would be able to see to it that certain debt citations in Paul's record were deleted. Indeed, a few weeks later Paul was shown a legitimate credit bureau report from which two of his long-standing debts had disappeared.

What Sue failed to tell Paul was that the credit bureau in question temporarily removes disputed debts as it investigates them, and that the report she showed him would soon revert to its former status. In the meantime, she presented Paul with a bill for the successful repair of his credit. BalanceBusters thus put itself in violation of the Credit Repair Organizations Act (see www.ftc.gov/os/statutes/croa/croa.htm): It billed Paul for services that were never rendered.

catalog. Your major credit card will arrive after you've bought $500 worth of catalog goods. What's more, your $2,500 line of credit applies only to the catalog charge card. Once you've ordered the amount of merchandise required (usually overpriced junk), you're sent a regular application form for a Visa or MasterCard, which means applying through the normal channels.

A ploy that's benign by comparison is the low-interest credit card offer. Mailings offering an 8.9 percent interest rate or lower may lure you into signing up for a card with a rate of up to 22.9 percent—something you may not discover until you get your first statement and notice that your finance charges are much higher than expected. That's because the company reserves the right to set any rate it chooses after reviewing your credit history; it said so in the original offer—but in the very small print. Likewise, any savings actually gained from "low introductory rates" can be canceled out by higher-than-average rates when the introductory period (usually three to twelve months) ends.

Debit cards are attractive to thieves because they're an easy route to quick cash. And foreign crime rings have become adept at cracking the codes on the cards and creating new cards bearing your encrypted account number. Finally, criminals are eager to steal either your credit or debit cards or their numbers.

Protect yourself: Unless you have a rock-solid credit rating, be very suspicious of "pre-approved" credit card offers, and check out the fine print carefully on low-interest offers. Carry your cards not in your wallet or purse but elsewhere on your person. Never leave them where anyone can see them, and never give a credit card number over the phone unless you've initiated the call. Check your credit and debit card and bank statements as soon as you receive them, and notify your bank immediately if you see any suspect charges; if you don't do so within 60 days, you may not be able to recover stolen money. For more ways to protect your card from fraudsters, see "Safeguarding Your Identity," page 28.

Scholarship Rip-Offs

Today's out-of-control college tuitions have given rise to a wave of unsolicited, and often bogus, scholarship and student loan offers. Be especially wary of any such offers that arrive via e-mail. Tip-offs include a request for an advance fee (any student loan source that asks for an up-front fee is illegitimate; real lenders deduct any fees from the disbursement check); claims that the scholarship is guaranteed; a request for your credit card or bank account number in order to hold the scholarship; and notification that you've been chosen as a finalist in a scholarship contest or that you "can't get this information anywhere else." Also, services that promise to apply for scholarships or loans on your behalf, sometimes in conjunction with financial aid seminars, can be a front to sell overpriced loans or glean personal info such as bank account or Social Security numbers.

Protect yourself: Always disregard a scholarship offer that involves paying a fee. To learn more, check the Federal Trade Commission website's page on scholarship scams: www.ftc.gov/scholarshipscams.

Phony Charity Solicitations

Many of the "charities" that solicit donations through e-mails, phone calls, or door-to-door solicitations are far from legit. Groups that support medical research or police or firefighters have long been fronts for fraudulent charities; thousands of bogus disaster-relief charities were set up in the wake of the tsunami in Southeast Asia in 2004 and Hurricane Katrina.

Protect yourself: Charity scammers are usually looking for more than just an immediate windfall; they often target personal data as well. The tip-off for the latter is a request for your bank account or Social Security number. Check the legitimacy of a charity by

Phishers and Pharmers

How ironic that two words for legitimate, beneficial human activities—fishing and farming—have been borrowed to describe electronic practices that set you up for a good fleecing! The first two letters of *phishing* stand for "password harvesting"; the term *pharming* is a play on "phishing" and "farming."

Phishers broadcast e-mail or pop-up messages that appear to be from a bank, credit card company, or other legitimate business—but aren't. The point is to make you reveal private information. Clicking on the link brings up a counterfeit website (a *spoof*) that looks identical to the site of a company or organization you do business with. You're then asked to update your password or verify Social Security and account numbers or PINs. Phishers use the purloined data to set up new accounts in your name, or keep you from accessing your accounts. They can not only cause you great inconvenience; they can ruin your credit.

Pharmers don't need to use e-mail as bait. These scammers do their mischief from within your computer. Pharming involves either the surreptitious installation of malicious software (or *malware*) in your computer or a tactic known as *DNS cache poisoning*, in which hackers exploit a vulnerability in Domain Name Service server software to redirect a legitimate website's traffic to a bogus facsimile website. (DNS servers are the computers that translate domain names to Internet protocol, or IP, addresses.) Either way, when you type a Web address into your browser or click on a bookmark, you wind up at a site that looks authentic but isn't. When you enter your user name, password, and other personal data at the fraudulent site, they—and potentially your entire identity—become the property of the pharmers. (For more on pharming methods, see www.pharming.org/index.jsp.)

Protect yourself:

- Communications from financial institutions often include a portion of your account number(s)—be wary when no numbers are shown.
- Remember that legitimate companies never ask for personal or financial information via e-mail.
- Watch for misspelled words or grammatical errors. Many phishing expeditions originate overseas.
- Most businesses you deal with greet you by name in e-mails or on their websites ("Hello, Peter DiMarco"). A generic greeting ("Dear BehemoBank customer") is a red flag.
- Change your passwords every two or three months at the least. Install anti-phishing software or a firewall.
- Check credit card and account statements as soon as they arrive, and report any unauthorized charges immediately.
- When an e-mail from a company you know directs you to its website, don't click the link provided; instead, access the site by typing its address into your browser. (This tactic is useless against pharming, as explained above.)

contacting your state or local consumer-protection agency. You can also consult the BBB Wise Giving Alliance; call 703-276-0100 or visit www.give.org, which lists and comments on authentic charities. Never give an unknown charity your credit card number.

Home and Auto Scams

Contractor Fraud

Some unscrupulous contractors inspect your house's foundation, plumbing, or chimney and "discover" problems that don't exist. They then make "repairs" that can leave your home in worse shape, often after charging exorbitant fees. Among the possibilities: You pay a remodeler to build a mudroom off your kitchen and he leaves town before completing the job. A chimney cleaner tells you that unless your chimney gets a new liner, noxious fumes could endanger your family; he then installs an inferior liner that really puts you in danger.

Other scammers use construction or repair work as a cover for outright thievery. A roofing contractor you've hired at a bargain price asks you to step outside and inspect the work. At the same time, one of his workers asks to use your bathroom and, once he's inside the house, pockets items of value.

Protect yourself: Be wary of any contractor who solicits your business through e-mail or fax, or by knocking on your front door. Always ask for full documentation of legitimacy, including license, bonding, insurance, and references. Don't allow yourself to be rushed into making a deal. Stay on top of potential contractor scams by consulting such websites as www.ownerbuilder.com and www.hadd.com, operated by the consumer-protection group Homeowners Against Deficient Dwellings.

Home Mortgage Rip-Offs

In a time when potential and longtime homeowners alike can find themselves financially strapped, scammers are all too quick to offer trusting consumers a quick bailout. Some shady mortgage brokers offer to refinance your mortgage at an unbelievably low rate but are actually more interested in the personal data they can mine; others may falsify signed documents or levy high "processing fees" for a loan that never materializes.

Protect yourself: Before doing business with a mortgage provider, always ask the state attorney general, housing department, or banking commission to verify the provider's legitimacy. Another protection against crafty mortgage brokers or lenders (and paying a higher interest rate than you should) is to learn your FICO scores (FICO is the Fair Isaac Corporation, which calculates the credit scores of individuals for the use of creditors). Scores usually fall between 300 and 850; knowing whether you fall within the "acceptable" range (660 and up) equips you to negotiate with lenders for the lowest rate. To obtain your scores and learn more, visit the FICO website (www.myfico.com) or call toll-free 800-319-4433. The fee you'll pay for your scores (about $43 per year as of mid-2006) can save you considerable money in the long run.

Hidden Car Costs

Some auto dealers are partial to piling hidden cost onto the price sheet of a car—charges ranging from delivery or document fees to "paint sealer" that's nothing more than car wax, and marked up many times over. Document fees are bogus because paperwork is a normal part of the selling process. So-called dealer preparation charges for things like waxing are dubious because carmakers usually reimburse dealers for doing whatever it takes to get a car shipshape before delivering it. And what about extended warranties? Be aware that they're always optional, not a part of the purchase price—no matter what the car salesman says.

Protect yourself: Do your homework to avoid paying hidden costs. Research prices beforehand on websites like Kelley Blue Book (www.kbb.com) and Edmunds (www.edmunds.com). Also learn how to avoid fine-print ploys that can add hundreds, even thousands, of dollars to the price.

Car Accident Scams

Staged auto accidents are often perpetrated by an organized crime ring. The fraudsters force you into a fender-bender (minor, if you're lucky), then file major insurance claims for auto damage and fake injuries. One method of choice is quickly swerving into your lane, then slamming on the brakes so you'll rear-end them. Another is slowing down and waving you forward as you merge into traffic, then ramming into your car and subsequently lying about signaling you. Yet another is deliberately sideswiping you at a car-clogged dual left-turn lane. Victims of staged accidents can be injured or

Q How can I tell if a website is secure?

A Even if you're positive that a website is authentic, make sure a given data-entry page is secure before inputting any personal data; on most sites a pop-up indicates that you're entering a secure page. Check the page's address to see if it begins with *https*—the "s" stands for "secure." Also look for a lock icon somewhere in the browser window. Test the lock's functionality by clicking or double-clicking on it; information about the site's security should pop up. Another security indicator is a prominently displayed site seal issued by an SSL Certificate vendor such as VeriSign or GeoTrust.

even killed, but those who remain unscathed hardly get off easy: Most not only watch their car insurance rise but also waste valuable time dealing with repairs, claims, and legal matters.

Protect yourself: First, don't tailgate. Keep a pen and paper and a disposable camera in your glove compartment to record essential information in case of an accident. If you are a victim, record the other driver's license plate number, insurance carrier, and the names, phone numbers, and driver's license numbers of any passengers in the other car; then snap a picture of the damage to both cars and of the other people involved. Even if the damage is minor, call the police immediately and get a police report, carefully checking it for accuracy.

Body Shop Rip-Offs

Beware of garage mechanics and body shops that are out to cheat you. Underhanded tactics range from short-sticking (pushing an oil dipstick only partway in to show that you need a top-up, then "refilling" the crankcase from an empty container) to stealing your airbags.

Protect yourself: To locate reliable garage mechanics, check www.trustmymechanic.com and the website of the National Public Radio show *Car Talk*, which has a database listing more than 16,000 mechanics recommended by the show's listeners (available at www.cartalk.com). For more information on auto rip-offs in general, consult the Coalition Against Insurance Fraud (www.insurancefraud.org) and the National Insurance Crime Bureau (www.nicb.org).

Business and Employment Gimmicks

Work-at-Home Schemes

Today's job seekers often post résumés on websites like Monster.com or Vault.com or pick up tips in chat rooms. Smart? Yes and no. Thanks to the personal information on résumés, the Web is a gold mine for con artists pitching work-at-home schemes.

One scam that predates the Internet is the envelope-stuffing "opportunity." The ads are everywhere. For a "small" fee, you'll earn hundreds of dollars a week at home stuffing envelopes with printed matter to be mailed in bulk. What you'll receive after paying

CASE STUDY Overseas Job Promise Equals Dashed Hopes

Polly, a public relations manager, dreamed of working in New Zealand. When she saw a newspaper ad headed "Overseas Job Opportunities," she called the advertiser—a company with the no-nonsense name of Foreign Job Placements, Inc.—to learn more.

The pleasant-sounding woman she spoke with explained that the company had relationships with many international businesses and a database of job openings that was updated daily. When Polly asked about New Zealand, the woman clicked away at a keyboard and came back with five PR job openings in Auckland, three in Wellington, and one in Dunedin. Polly's request for more details was met with, "We provide that information only to our clients." Becoming a client required registering online and paying a refundable $300 registration fee.

Polly signed up and paid, and the next day the company e-mailed descriptions of the New Zealand jobs. To Polly's surprise, only one was in public relations (three were at advertising agencies), and it was in a field she knew nothing about: pharmaceuticals. Realizing that FJP wasn't on the level, she requested a refund. The company responded with, "Because we fulfilled our obligation, no refund will be forthcoming."

Who got what? FJP: $300 straight out of Polly's pocket. Polly: the lesson that before sending money, one should always check a company's background.

the fee is a letter telling you to place the come-on ad in newspapers or magazines or to send it on to friends. If anyone responds, you collect the fee (becoming a scammer yourself), while the promoters of the scheme pay nothing. Can you spell pyramid scheme?

Another scam involves wiring money abroad. It begins when a scammer claiming to be a large overseas firm e-mails you to say it's looking to hire a "correspondence manager" or "financial agent" to process payments for the firm's U.S. orders—which means receiving checks, depositing them in your bank account, then transferring the check amount to the firm's account in a foreign bank, often in Africa or Russia. For each cleared check, you receive a commission of 5 to 15 percent. But guess what? The incoming checks are counterfeit, meaning you owe the bank the money you wired. (See also discussion of the Nigerian Letter, in "Advance-Fee Scams," page 31.)

Protect yourself: Be very leery of any offer that requires you to pay out money up front. And before sending any money, demand to know who will pay you, whether you'll be paid by salary or commission, what task you'll perform, and the total cost of supplies, equipment, and fees—in other words, what you'll get for your money. If the promoter is evasive, run the other way. As for electronic money transfers, unless you know the recipient personally or can verify his or her identity, don't do it.

Multilevel Marketing Frauds

Multilevel marketing businesses—Amway is perhaps the best known—aren't the big deal they once were; at one time, consumers who lived off the beaten path found MLM salespeople a godsend. Today, even people who rarely leave home are able to purchase almost any product online. Still, there are plenty of MLM employment opportunities out there—some legit; others designed to con you.

The foundation of any MLM program, whether it sells health and beauty products or cut-rate phone plans, is the recruitment of salespeople, either at a meeting advertised by the company or through an individual distributor of the company's products. Your earning power lies in both your sale of the products and your recruitment of other salespeople (your "downline"); as their "upline," you receive a portion of their income.

Protect yourself: To distinguish a legitimate MLM company from an illicit pyramid scheme—which may not even have a product to sell and just takes your "registration fee" and runs—watch for extravagant claims. Multilevel selling is hard work and rarely adds dramatic sums to one's bank account, so beware of MLM promoters who promise you'll get rich quick—particularly anyone who tells you that downline personnel will shoulder most of the work as you stroll along Easy Street. Most of all, don't get involved with MLM plans that require you to spend or invest money in order to earn it. And remember: If you become a distributor you can be held legally responsible for repeating any of an MLM company's false claims. Research the history of an MLM company before deciding whether to join; start with the Better Business Bureau (www.bbb.org), where you can check for complaints against a particular outfit. The Federal Trade Commission provides general information on MLM companies; visit www.ftc.gov or call toll-free 877-FTC-HELP (877-382-4357).

Mystery Shopping Scams

Major chains (retail, restaurant, fast food, hotel, theater, and such) hire "mystery shoppers" to visit their establishments and report on the quality of customer service, cleanliness of the premises, and so forth. In return, they are paid a flat fee and may be reimbursed for expenses. Mystery shopping (also called secret shopping, anonymous auditing, and spotting) is a legitimate business and a growing source of supplementary income for home-based workers; there's even a professional trade organization: the Mystery Shopping Providers Association (www.mysteryshop.org).

But not all solicitations aiming to enlist you as a mystery shopper are aboveboard. Bilkers operate scams as varied as fraudulent websites that charge a nonrefundable $30 to $60 for a directory of providers (almost always outdated) and fake mystery shopping companies that swear you can make easy money by wiring funds overseas for them (see "Work-at-Home Schemes," page 38).

Protect yourself: If you receive an e-mail, letter, or fax from a company trying to interest you in mystery shopping, beware if signing on requires you to pay a fee. (The same goes for any mystery

Seniors as Targets

Seniors are seen as potential gold mines because they're often homeowners, have solid financial assets, and maintain excellent credit. They may also be less likely to report a scam because they're embarrassed they fell for it or fear relatives may think they're no longer able to care for themselves. Investment and health-care scams are thrown at seniors right and left. To make sure they don't stick, follow these general guidelines:

- Be wary of unsolicited telephone calls and e-mails.
- Unless you've initiated a contact, do not offer personal information.
- Never fall for promises of huge, risk-free profits. "Experts" who tell you a stock or investment is "guaranteed" to double or triple in value are lying.
- Leave stock-buying decisions to a trusted broker or base them on research of your own—not on tips from an "insider," most of which are false.
- Think of the high-pressure tactics of people who urge you to "act now" as probable evidence that they're frauds.
- When you're solicited for a disaster-relief donation, ask for literature on the charity to be sent via postal mail; when (and if) it arrives, call the organization to take its measure.
- As soon as a caller trying to sell you goods or services starts behaving like an old friend, suspect that he or she is your worst enemy.
- Stand by the adage "If something seems too good to be true, it probably is."

shopping website you visit.) The Mystery Shopping Providers Association grants membership only to companies that promise never to charge up-front fees; e-mail the MSPA at info@mysteryshop.org to learn if it's safe to sign up with a company that seems suspect.

TRAVEL SWINDLES

"Free Vacation" Scams

Amid all the junk mail you receive is sometimes a postcard with happy news: "Congratulations! You've won a free vacation in the Bahamas!"—or Bermuda or Belize or any other faraway place that spells paradise. A call to the phone number on the card reveals the catch: You have to either pay a service charge or join a travel club—often to the tune of $200 or $300. If you pay up you'll receive a packet describing your vacation, along with lots of restrictions on when you can travel. You might also be billed for a $100 handling fee. The real clincher that you've been scammed comes when you end up taking the trip: Your hotel and most everything else in the package is substandard.

Protect yourself: Do a background check on companies offering "free vacations" by consulting the Better Business Bureau (www.bbb.org). Also search the Internet for reports of people's experiences with a certain company (type its name into a search engine). If you receive vacation offers by phone and the telemarketer pressures you, hang up. If you feel you've been scammed through the mail, submit a complaint to the U.S. Postal Inspection Service at www.usps.com/postalinspectors/fraud/mailfraudcomplaint.htm.

Questionable Time-Share Condo Offers

Consumers are usually lured to these offers with a heavily discounted or free hotel room, or a "prize" that turns out to have little or no worth. Once the scammers have your attention, high-pressure sales tactics for time-shares in Orlando or Palm Springs or similar playgrounds come into play. What the salespeople don't tell you is that once you buy, you may be permanently stuck with your slice of the property; time-shares are usually hard to unload.

Protect yourself: Think of a time-share as you would any other real estate investment, which means researching the market and the value.

CASE STUDY A Hoodia Whodunit

Doug was determined to lose 15 pounds but couldn't tame his addiction to starchy foods. Then the much-publicized appetite suppressant *Hoodia gordonii* (a cactus-like plant that grows in the Kalahari Desert) hit the market. Forking over a considerable sum, Doug bought a high-profile brand and prepared to wave his potato and pasta cravings good-bye. But after two weeks, he was as hungry as ever. Just another weight-loss scam, he thought.

Yet products with 100 percent hoodia really do work. Some manufacturers may sell fake versions, but others unwittingly market an ineffective product after being hoodwinked by hoodia brokers. Shady brokers may send a sample of genuine hoodia for testing, then fill the order with something else or cut real hoodia with fillers.

A recent test by Alkemist Pharmaceuticals of Costa Mesa, California, showed that only 6 of 17 tested brands—each allegedly containing 100 percent hoodia—were the real thing. Had Doug become an informed consumer, he would have known which brands to buy. Before making a purchase, smart users of dietary supplements browse the Internet for such reputable websites as the American Herbal Products Association (www.ahpa.org) and consult knowledgeable staff at well-established health-products stores.

Read the sales contract carefully and have it reviewed by a lawyer; if promises made by the salesperson are missing, don't sign on the dotted line. Ask the salesperson for references—and not just from former owners who were pleased; ask too for the names of any who were unhappy with the deal.

MEDICAL AND HEALTH RACKETS

Phony Health Insurance

Health insurance swindlers are selling gullible consumers bogus policies at up to half the normal cost. The warning signs of fraud are usually clear: The cost of the coverage is way below the norm; medical questionnaires or exams aren't required or number only one or two; a preexisting medical condition doesn't hurt your chances of gaining full coverage; or the agent claims that federal law exempts the plan from state licensing (there's no such exemption). Simply put,

99 percent of health plans that seem too good to be true are nonexistent. Signing up for one means you could be ruined financially.

Protect yourself: If the company's name is one you've never heard of, it probably doesn't really exist. If you suspect any health insurance agent of dishonesty, contact your state insurance department to find out if the company is licensed. Also check with the Better Business Bureau (www.bbb.org) for a history of complaints.

Dubious Alternative Health Treatments

Consumers fall for cure-all claims for everything from colonic irrigation to hydroelectric baths. Thousands of Americans travel to Mexico and other countries each year for unconventional treatments for cancer—yet most of the "clinicians" who treat these patients do little more than instill false hope and drain their bank accounts. Ads for weight-loss drugs sometimes make claims that defy belief. Controversy simmers over the efficacy of many herbal and other alternative remedies. How much faith should you put in these products? As with all manufacturers of consumer goods, some are upstanding in every respect and others are crooks.

Protect yourself: Trust your instincts. Common sense is your best first line of defense. Then, before undergoing an alternative medical treatment, do some research. Check with your state attorney general to make sure the practitioner is licensed. To gauge the efficacy and safety of herbal remedies, visit the websites of the American Botanical Council (www.herbalgram.org), the Herb Research Foundation (www.herbs.org), or the American Herbal Products Association (www.ahpa.org). Ask your doctor or pharmacist about possible interactions with prescription drugs. And use alternative medicines for serious health problems only under your doctor's supervision.

Online Pharmacies

Many Internet pharmacies flout state licensing requirements and standards. The worst of them may also commit crimes—including money-laundering, faking doctor approvals, and, once your personal data is in their grasp, identity theft. Your health could also be at stake when you order from an illegitimate online pharmacy, since its pharmaceuticals may be contaminated, diluted, or even counterfeit.

Protect yourself: Never buy prescription drugs online without checking the pharmacy for certification by PharmacyChecker.com or the Verified Internet Pharmacy Practice Sites program of the National Association of Boards of Pharmacy (www.nabp.net/vipps/intro.asp). For more, see "Buy Discount Drugs Online," page 90.

Part Two

LOW-COST SOLUTIONS FOR EVERYDAY LIVING

Home and Family • Your Appearance • Health • Entertainment
Travel • Education • Transportation • Employment
Small Businesses • Money Matters • Unclaimed Property
Community Nonprofits

CHAPTER 3

deals for your home & family

It costs a small fortune to keep the pantry full, the house clean, the kids entertained, and the whole family clothed. Here's how you can trim your costs without sacrificing taste, style, or sanity.

By the numbers

3.6

Amount, in billions of dollars, that Americans saved in 2000 by redeeming coupons. That number is not as big as it could be, considering that 330 billion coupons were distributed that year, and only 4.5 billion were actually redeemed.

EVER WONDER WHERE THE BULK OF YOUR MONEY is spent? Look no further than your own home sweet home. It's expensive enough to buy and run a home without children. Add kids to the equation and costs become stratospheric. It's estimated that raising a single child from birth through college graduation can take up to a million dollars, depending on where you live and the year of your child's birth.

Saving money on the costs associated with home and family has become more important than ever. Parents are looking for the best possible deals on everything from food and essential goods and services to pet care and fun activities for the kids. Home buyers and aspiring remodelers are searching for ways to make their dreams affordable.

Fortunately, there's tons of help out there, from federal, state, and local governments; nonprofit organizations; and manufacturers and retailers, big and small. All that's needed is a little bit of ingenuity to unearth the deals that will be most useful to you. In this chapter you'll find out how to:

- Develop strategies that can help you save big on food and groceries.
- Find legal, veterinary, and other services at low or no cost.

Always Buy Store Brands

You know that buying a supermarket's brand of canned vegetables or dish detergent is cheaper—but you hesitate. Will it be of the same quality? Never fear: When supermarkets develop their own "brands," they actually buy stock from the same national companies whose products are sitting right next to them on the shelves. All they do is change the packaging to reflect their own name and identity. If you want to know which national brand is likely to have supplied the store-sponsored version, check for clues: Coloring, typeface, and other packaging details often mimic those of the brand the item is identical to. Then stock up your cart with store brands and rack up your savings with confidence.

- Take the tedium out of clipping grocery coupons with a website that organizes them for you.
- Tap into the free money-saving information that's waiting for you around every bend, ready to be put to use to improve your lifestyle without breaking the bank.
- Keep the kids occupied and learning with free downloads and CD-ROMs that stimulate their imagination and sharpen their academic skills.
- Make the most of recycled bargains.
- Take advantage of federal, state, and local programs for homeowners and remodelers.

With the amount of money it takes to raise a family these days, you'll need every advantage you can muster. Check out the offers and opportunities in this chapter and start saving right now.

Everyday Savings on Food and More

Get to Know Your Supermarket Managers

You don't think of haggling at the supermarket, but if you get to know the managers in a few crucial departments, you can indeed get discounts on items that are near expiration or overstocked. (Think meat, bread, dairy products, and produce.) After all, they'd rather take less money for the item than throw it away as a total loss. And it's no hardship to buy about-to-expire hamburger meat when you're going to be cooking it the same evening. You can save as much as 50 percent if you're a good negotiator. Once the manager in each department gets to know you as a regular shopper, you may even get an early alert of bargains that are about to pop.

Are You Eligible for Food Stamps?

If your family or someone you know is having trouble putting food on the table, check out the U.S. government's Food Stamp Program to see the eligibility requirements for receiving assistance with grocery bills. The program is run by state and local agencies, but the central website operated by the federal government has a screening tool and other information that will give you a good idea of whether you qualify (restrictions typically pertain to the family's income, assets, and ownership of vehicles). For more information on the Food Stamp Program and to find an office near you, visit www.fns.usda.gov/fsp or call toll-free 800-221-5689.

Bakery Outlet Bonanza

If you've got a large family, keeping them in bread, crackers, cereal, chips, and cakes can cost a fortune. You can sweeten your bottom line by looking for a local bakery outlet, where such items are typically sold at discounts ranging up to 60 percent, even though the baked goods on sale are still well within their expiration dates. Interstate Brands Companies has 1,200 discount outlets nationwide, and many larger local bakeries sponsor their own thrift shops. To find an IBC outlet near you, enter your zip code on the Store Locator page of the company's website, www.bakeryoutlets.com.

All-Natural and Organic Discounts

Organic products have a reputation for being expensive, but it doesn't have to be that way. You can print a dozen or more online coupons ranging from $0.50 to $1 at the website of Stonyfield Farm (www.stonyfield.com), the environmentally conscious producer of all-natural and organic milk, yogurts, smoothies, and ice creams. Look for other offers on the site's "Contests, Steals & Deals" page, including an impressive discount on your first purchase of wine from the "earth-friendly" Organic Wine Company—as a new customer, you'll save $20 on any $60 purchase or a hefty percentage (it varies from 20 to 30 percent) on your entire order of more than $60.

Q How can I save money when shopping at farmers' markets?

A Farmers' markets typically offer just-harvested local produce that stays fresher longer in your fridge or pantry—a savings in itself—but there are other ways to stretch your food dollars there. For example, plan your menus to include whatever produce is in season and therefore most abundant at the market, then stock up on those fruits and veggies. More often than not, they'll be at the peak of both flavor *and* savings, since an abundance of any product tends to drive its price down. Also, if you arrive at a farmers' market near closing time, you may find prices further reduced in order to move items that haven't sold that day. To find farmers' markets in your area, go to the U.S. Department of Agriculture's state-by-state directory at www.ams.usda.gov/farmersmarkets.

Editor's Choice Online Meal-Planning Steals

Free Recipe Books

Figuring out which food companies or government offices offer free recipe books can be a daunting task—unless you visit www.cashwonders.com/recipes.html. There you can learn where to send away for approximately 75 free booklets, from the "Prize Winning Recipes" of Pillsbury in Minneapolis to the "Seafood Recipe Books" of the Maine Department of Marine Resources in Augusta.

Recipe Mix and Match

The next time you're faced with feeding dinner guests with diverse dietary requirements, look to Nestlé's www.meals.com. Click on "Advanced Search" and you'll be able to access thousands of free recipes in up to five categories. For example, ask for recipes that are Tex-Mex, diabetic-friendly, and take 30 minutes or less, and you'll get 12 mouth-watering options, from pork chops olé to black bean and veggie dip. (Try thumbing through the cards in a recipe box for that!) The site has other features too—such as recipes utilizing grocery-store brands and even the occasional coupon.

Your Cookbook, Your Way

Here's one cookbook that won't cost an arm and a leg, only to sit unused on your shelf. In the "My Cookbook" section of the Better Homes and Gardens website (www.bhg.com/bhg/mycookbook), you can compile your very own free cookbook, using the site's recipes, from appetizers to desserts, and/or your own time-tested favorites. Once you've completed the free registration, you can select a cover and style for your cookbook and then start adding recipes. You'll need Adobe Acrobat Reader (downloadable for free on the site) to view and download your culinary opus. You can also print it out and have it bound at a copy center (this, of course, will cost you). Other free offerings on the Better Homes and Gardens site (www.bhg.com) include more than 10,000 kitchen-tested recipes, a decorating gallery, more than 40 garden plans, and free newsletters on cooking, decorating, gardening, and more.

Surf to Save on P&G Brands

Procter & Gamble manufactures so many of the brands we purchase on a weekly or monthly basis that it's worth surfing the P&G website (www.pg.com) regularly for new product information and discounts. Savings come in different forms: Maybe you'll find a three-question survey you can fill out in exchange for a free Swiffer duster sample and a $2-off coupon. Or perhaps you'll see an offer to send in three proofs of purchase on bathroom tissue to get a free trial-size Cranium game for the whole family. You can also find out whether your local paper carries P&G's weekly coupon insert. Offers change often.

Make Your Own Wipes

Many families spend hundreds of dollars a year to buy cleaning products they can make for much less. You simply have to think creatively. For instance, disinfecting wipes for the bathroom can cost about $0.13 apiece at the supermarket. In her book *Everyday Cheapskate's Greatest Tips*, author, entrepreneur, and frugality expert Mary Hunt suggests a cheaper alternative: Take a roll of paper towels, separate and stack them in a plastic container with a lid, pour 3 cups of multi-purpose Lysol cleaner over them, and you've got the same effect for about $0.03 a wipe. Hunt's website (www.cheapskatemonthly.com) is a gold mine of cost-cutting ideas for house and home.

Homemade Lattes

Does anybody really need to spend $3 or $4 for a flavored cup of coffee with a fancy name straight out of the corporate marketing department? You can make your own fancy java at just pennies a cup—just make a strong brew, using a dark roast blend, and add a dash of almond, chocolate or vanilla essence, cinnamon, or other flavorings to the mix. Give the concoction a whirl in the blender, and you'll even get that neat foamy effect. It's a golden opportunity to experiment with different flavorings until you find the one concoction that best suits your palate. Savings on one cup a day over the course of a year? Somewhere in the neighborhood of $1,000.

Clipping Coupons

Reports of Expiration Greatly Exaggerated

Don't throw away expired coupons. Many grocery stores that don't double or triple coupon values make up for it by redeeming coupons that have expired, so watch for chances to "unload" your out-of-date discounts. Always ask about an expired coupon before discarding it. At Bed Bath & Beyond, which distributes countless 20 percent-off coupons through the mail and in publications, the coupons never expire, despite the date printed on the face. In fact, many people collect BB&B 20 percent-off coupons and use one for each of multiple purchases at the checkout (though in larger cities there may be a limit to how many coupons you can use at one time). Some customers never pay full price for anything in the store.

Editor's Choice

A Smart Source for Savings

Coupon sites are everywhere on the Web, but they're not all created equal. To save money with most of them, you have to answer a ton of survey questions—or even order other products! One of the best sites around is www.smartsource.com, operated by the company that provides coupons in Sunday newspapers and in those grocery-store coupon dispensers. You'll have to register on the site, but once you do, you'll start registering big savings at the store. Of 82 grocery coupons available recently, almost a third offered discounts of $1 or more. The site offers free samples of health and beauty products.

Check Out Register-Generated Catalina Coupons

Named for the St. Petersburg, Florida, marketing company credited with developing them, Catalina coupons are a type of promotional offer that's generated at many supermarket checkout counters based on items you've purchased. For instance, if you pick up an item and notice an offer of "Buy two, get one free on your next visit," the coupon for the freebie will be automatically generated at the checkout once the two items have been scanned. Or the offer might be for a free half-gallon of milk with the purchase of two boxes of a certain cereal; the coupon for the milk will be generated after the cereal boxes go through checkout. A competing manufacturer might use Catalina coupons to horn in on the action—you've bought a 2-liter bottle of Coke, so you're offered a discount on a 2-liter bottle of Pepsi. Because such coupons are targeted to the kinds of purchases you're apt to make, they're more likely than random coupons to meet your needs.

TIME IS MONEY **Tame the Coupon Monster**

You know the drill: The Sunday paper arrives, with pages and pages of coupons and grocery store specials. You put those sections aside, intending to browse them after you've digested the news, the funny papers, and the latest celebrity gossip. But by Sunday night it's time to help the kids with their homework, and you've never gotten around to checking what's available for the taking.

Stephanie Nelson knows you're out there. She's appeared on ABC's *Good Morning America* as the "Coupon Mom," explaining how to get $112 in groceries for only $1.95 after discounts and rebates. In her book *Greatest Secrets of the Coupon Mom*, Nelson laments that fewer than 2 percent of the $315 billion in grocery store coupons are used each year. If lack of time is keeping you from great savings, she's got a solution.

At www.couponmom.com, Nelson offers the Virtual Coupon Organizer, "the Dewey decimal system of grocery coupons." It works like this: Take your coupon and savings circulars from the paper, date them, and put them away. When it's time to shop, go to the organizer and type in your state. A list of current offers will appear, along with the date they appeared in your paper. Go back to your dated circulars and locate the coupon you want, cut it out, and take it shopping with you.

Two companies, SmartSource and Valassis, produce some 200 different versions nationwide of all weekly circulars. Nelson summarizes their offerings and generates a coupon overview for each state. The website contains printable coupons and links to other coupon sites, and you can also use it to find the best grocery and drugstore deals by state.

Editor's Choice Free Online Deal Tracker

Who can keep track of all the coupons and rebate offers from the big-box stores? Well, www.spoofee.com can. The site is a master tip sheet of hundreds of current coupons and special offers from just about all the name retailers, from Best Buy to 1-800-flowers.com. Typically, after you read about an offer, you follow a link to the vendor's website, where you can order directly from a page announcing the deal or punch in a coupon code that Spoofee has provided. In some cases, the store link takes you to a downloadable coupon that you can print out and take to the store's physical location. On the same day, you might be linked, for example, to a Kmart double offer of five Fruit of the Loom T-shirts for $10 plus a $10 gift card, an Amazon.com listing for a single-cup coffee machine with rebates that make it essentially free, and a KitchenAid mixer selling at Dillard's for half the usual price. Keeping track of all these deals on your own would be next to impossible. Readers post their own tips too.

Dining Out for Less

Eating out can take a bite out of your wallet, but if you plan properly, it may be no more expensive than gathering around the dining room table. At www.valpak.com, you can print out coupons for local eateries, from Domino's to higher-end establishments. Get a two-for-one entrée coupon and you cut the cost of your meal in half. If you and your dinner partner order a meal with large portions and take home half for the next day, you've just purchased four meals for the price of one. And for members' weekly coupon tips, which can't be beat, check out the Valpak blog at www.valpak.blogspot.com. Another great place to get dining-out coupons is the website www.restaurant.com; for details, see "Discount Dining Passes," on page 127.

Free Helpful Information

What's the 411?

The 411 on directory assistance is that it costs—up to $2.50 a pop. If you're willing to sit through a taped ad, you can get directory assistance free at 800-411-METRO (800-411-6387) or by calling 800-FREE 411 (800-373-3411). If you've got a computer handy, you can let your fingers do the walking—to free directory assistance websites such as www.anywho.com and www.superpages.com. At both sites, you can even do a reverse lookup to check whose number keeps showing up on your phone's caller ID. From your cell phone, you can also text Google—at 46645, or GOOGL—to get a free lookup, though you'll pay the usual texting rate.

Cheap Knowledge at Your Fingertips

You have access to hundreds of free or very-low-cost (many priced at just a dollar or two) publications on a wide range of issues, including cars, travel, business, money management, consumer protection, diet, health, work, federal benefits, and much more. All of this comes from the U.S. Federal Citizen Information Center, located in Pueblo, Colorado. It's easiest to browse their offerings on the Internet at www.pueblo.gsa.gov, a window onto an astounding world of useful information. You also can get a free copy of the catalog by calling toll-free 888-8-PUEBLO (888-878-3256).

Guzzle Less Gas

High gas prices emptying your wallet? Strike back by going to the U.S. Department of Energy's fuel-efficiency website (www.fueleconomy.gov). Because getting 30 miles per gallon versus 20 can save about $600 a year, the government offers free gas mileage tips (example: regularly replacing air filters can improve gas mileage by up to 10 percent) and a PDF list of estimated miles per gallon on all makes and models, from the current year back to 1985. Scan the charts, and you'll find that some models will set you back $1,000 more at the pump per year than others. As a bonus, you can link to sites with a sampling of gas prices in your neighborhood (see page 135) so you can buy where gas is cheapest. Another useful tip: Steer clear of gas stations at interstate exits; historically, they have charged their "captive" audience very high prices.

Watch the Birdie

You don't have to spring for a high-priced photography course to take smashing pictures of family events. Just go to www.kodak.com, click on "Consumer Photography" and then "Taking Great Pictures." You'll be directed to invaluable free tips on such topics as photographing people and animals (our favorite: how to avoid red eye), vacation and travel pictures that your friends will really enjoy seeing, snapping good candids at holidays and events, even how to get the most out of your camera phone. Once you've mastered the basics, you can go on to more advanced tips that just may result in photos that deserve a place on the wall and will be cherished by future generations.

Cooperative Know-How

Your local Cooperative Extension Service office, part of a nationwide educational network sponsored by the U.S. Department of Agriculture, is a terrific free asset for any homeowner. Staffed by one or more experts, each office typically offers a broad menu of services, information, and classes on the subjects of gardening, home management, money, and more. Check for the nearest office in your phone book, or visit www.csrees.usda.gov/extension.

CHILD'S PLAY

Is Your Kid Eligible for Free School Supplies?

Back-to-school supplies such as binders and backpacks can be prohibitively expensive for low-income families. In communities around the country, charitable organizations such as the Salvation Army hold giveaway days in which they provide free backpacks filled with school supplies for children from low-income families. Depending on the individual program, a child might qualify for the free goodies if he or she, for instance, receives school lunch for free. To check whether there is such a day planned in your area, and whether your child qualifies, check your local newspaper or online community calendar. You can also call your local chapter of the Salvation Army; if it's not sponsoring a giveaway day, it might know of an organization that does.

Geography Made Easy

Here's a way to make one school chore a lot more fun—and maybe prep your child for the National Geography Bee in the process. NATO's free online Map Game features 53 countries that are NATO members or affiliated with NATO. Kids learn which capitals and flags belong where by scrolling the map, zooming in and out with the mouse, and placing the flag or capital on the right country. You can order the game on CD-ROM or download it from www.nato.int./education/games.htm.

Q What is the best online resource for cutting energy costs?

A The Alliance to Save Energy wants to help you keep fuel bills down, so it has put together a website chock-full of tips on cutting home and car energy costs, info on programs offering energy assistance, breaking news about energy issues, and more. For instance, some homeowners could cut heating costs by at least $500 a year by upgrading to energy-efficient windows, and the website points the way to a program that helps finance the change. Power$mart, a booklet of tips, is downloadable. Go to www.ase.org and click on the "Consumers" link.

Free Rainy-Day Activities

Are you looking for indoor activities for your kids that won't break the bank? *Highlights for Children*, a magazine many parents remember fondly, offers a variety of puzzles, riddles, hidden pictures, and more at its website (www.highlightskids.com). For instance, your child can find objects hidden within pictures either by clicking with the mouse or by printing out a page and solving the puzzle by hand. In the website's story section, kids can personalize a tale by choosing whether, at crucial junctures, to heed advice from clueless Goofus or saintly Gallant. Online pastimes, which change periodically, are available free to all comers—no subscription or registration required.

Cheap Fun with Baking Soda

Anyone with a passing knowledge of household cleaning knows that baking soda is a wonder substance. So, as you might imagine, the Arm & Hammer Baking Soda website is full of useful tips, including downloadable PDF or Microsoft Word files on everything from stain removal to sensible septic tank care. And some of the PDFs involve fun crafts, recipes, and experiments for kids using baking soda—at pennies a pop. One in particular offers dozens of play clay crafts, made cheaply with baking soda, cornstarch, and water, that will keep kids occupied for hours. For a list of free online brochures for kids and their parents, go to www.armhammer.com/brochure.

Free Lego-Building Ideas

For many children, Legos are a passion—and a costly one at that, so they might as well enjoy it to the hilt. Your little Legomaniac can get a free two-year subscription to *Lego Magazine* at www.lego.com. At the site, you'll be prompted to download and mail in a form or call a number to get your subscription. The magazine is filled with clunky-cool Lego action figures and structures, lots of building tips, imaginative comic strip adventures, and readers' neat creations to whet your child's appetite. No need to register or sign in—everything is free.

Time Is Money

Find the Best Deal in a Jiffy

Looking for the best possible deal on a specific item, but have no time to run from store to store or even surf the Web? Dealnews (dealnews.com) categorizes the best deals on computers and other electronics, games, office supplies, DVDs, and such; corrals compelling offers from major online retailers; and provides lists of the best coupons and the most popular current deals. Plus you can register for free on the site and they'll keep an eye out for the product you want; when they find it, they'll tip you off via e-mail. A recent request for special deals on projectors yielded an e-mail alert every couple of days.

Free Spider-Man Comic

If your child's a Spidey fan and you want to instill good habits early, you can get a free Spider-Man comic with a strong antismoking message from the American Cancer Society. In this installment, Spidey and his friends set out to vanquish the evil villain Smokescreen. Call the society toll-free at 800-227-2345 to make your request—and while you're at it, you can ask about free adult publications covering the prevention and treatment of cancer.

Free Skin-Protection Games

No matter how old or young you are, excessive exposure to the sun increases your risk of skin cancer. The Skin Cancer Foundation is hoping to educate children about skin protection and provide a little fun, too, with a free kit called the "Sunny States of America." The kit contains background information, games, and puzzles, but the highlight is a map your child creates of good sun-protection practices in each of the 50 states. Write to the Skin Cancer Foundation, 245 Fifth Avenue, Suite 1403, New York, New York 10016. For more information and other goodies in the foundation's Children's Sun Protection Program, check the website at www.skincancer.org/children/index.php.

Goods and Services

Free Legal Assistance

You don't have to be rich to use the services of a lawyer. The U.S. government funds the Legal Services Corporation, which has hundreds of affiliates around the country that provide free legal help for people with low incomes. Call 202-295-1500 or visit www.lsc.gov; click on the state in which you live for local information. Many lawyers have a tradition of pro bono work, in which they donate some amount of legal services every year to people on limited incomes. To read about available pro bono programs, go to the website of the American Bar Association (www.abanet.org), click on "Find Legal Help," and then on your state and "Free Legal Help."

Free Phone Service

We don't need to tell you how much phone services cost. But if you're Internet-savvy, there are several sites where you can download programs that make your calls to like-minded folks free. At www.skype.com, you can install a program that lets you make free calls from your computer to other Skype subscribers—a great deal if you're making daily calls to, say, the computer of your child who's away in college. Also check out www.efonica.com, which offers free calls among member subscribers, using either computers or landlines (with adapters) and an Internet code. With a little investment of time, you can save on many of your most expensive calls.

More Help with Phone Bills

If you're having trouble getting phone service or paying your bills, there are two federal programs that can help. Lifeline Assistance provides income-eligible phone subscribers with discounts of up to $10 a month on basic monthly phone service at the user's primary residence; Link-Up America pays half of the initial hook-up fees up to $30. Why? Because the federal government considers phone service to be a necessity of modern life, and so requires all interstate telecommunications companies to contribute money to a fund to support low-income phone users. Eligibility requirements and the size of discounts vary by state. Native Americans living in tribal communities may qualify for even greater funding. To find out if you qualify for these programs, and if so, how to apply, visit www.lifelinesupport.org or call your local telephone company.

EDITOR'S CHOICE **Great Discounts on Overproduced Items**

Manufacturers are forever overestimating how much stock they'll sell of a certain product, which is good news for those who frequent the website www.overstock.com. The company running the website purchases overproduced items and sells them directly to consumers at 40 to 80 percent off. It's not uncommon to save 70 percent on an Egyptian cotton 400 thread-count sateen sheet set, or 48 percent off leather dining chairs. Never fear about shipping costs; even with larger items, your order is sent for $2.95, and if you subscribe to the free e-newsletter, you'll get frequent offers of free or $1 shipping.

Low-Cost Help for Your Four-Legged Friends

As much as we love our pets, their food and upkeep can cost a fortune. Below are some resources that will help you find the right pet, and rein in its maintenance costs. Your local animal shelters and pet shops can also be great places to find free advice and low-cost pet care.

Which websites can help me locate pets that need loving homes?

- Shelters and rescue organizations for dozens of breeds are listed at The Pooka (www.thepooka.com/rescue.html).
- Shelters run by the American Society for the Prevention of Cruelty to Animals (www.aspca.org) and humane societies (www.americanhumane.org and www.hsus.org) as well as local organizations have animals of all kinds in need of loving homes.
- Petfinder.com (www.petfinder.com) matches homeless creatures with animal lovers nationwide.
- The Utah-based shelter Best Friends Animal Society (www.bestfriends.org) rescues dogs, cats, bunnies, birds, farm animals, and more.

How can I save money on veterinary costs?

A dog or cat can cost you up to $15,000 during its lifetime—and a huge chunk of this goes to veterinary care. But less expensive options are usually available. Humane societies and animal shelters often offer clinics at specific times, with greatly reduced fees for injections and other routine care. Veterinary schools may offer reduced costs as supervised students learn from treating your pet. Many PetSmart stores periodically provide a veterinarian who gives low-cost injections; check with your local store to see what's available.

Where can I find free information that can help me choose a pet?

The American Humane Society offers free tips on adopting and caring for an animal. Go to www.americanhumane.org and click on the "How Do I . . .?" link for answers to prospective pet owners' most common questions. Once you've decided to go ahead and adopt a pet, there's no need to spend big bucks on even a pedigreed dog or cat.

How can I provide for my pet after I'm gone?

The Humane Society of the United States offers a free kit to help you plan for your pet's care after you are gone. "Providing for Your Pet's Future Without You" contains a six-page fact sheet, wallet alert cards, emergency decals for windows and doors, and caregiver information forms. Send an e-mail to petsinwills@hsus.org and check the Humane Society's website (www.hsus.org) for other information and goodies.

Free Spreadsheets

Buying Microsoft Excel or one of its competitors for your home office computer can set you back $85 or more. But if your spreadsheet needs are simple, you may want to use Google's free version at spreadsheets.google.com. Once you sign up for a Google account (it's free), you can create a spreadsheet for the kids' soccer team roster or your household budget, or import one you've already created elsewhere. You can edit and store the data online, and even view or edit the data simultaneously with someone on another computer—great for working on a shared project. For more free Google services, see page 229.

A Low-Cost Capitol Flag

An American flag can cost up to $50 or $60. But for between $13 and $28 (depending on where you live and the flag you choose), you can receive one that has flown atop the Capitol Building in Washington. With eight weeks' notice, you can even get a flag that has flown on a date you've specified, such as a family birthday or anniversary. You'll need to contact one of your senators and make a written request. Within weeks after it's flown, the flag will be mailed to you, along with a certificate from the Architect of the Capitol stating that the flag was flown on the date requested. For more information, go to www.usflag.org/capitol.flag.html; there you'll find a link to the page on the U.S. Senate's website listing senators' contact information.

Free King James Bible

Getting a free copy of the Bible is hard to argue with. The Church of Jesus Christ of Latter-Day Saints (the Mormons) will give you one just for the asking. If you live in the United States or Canada, you can get the King James version of the Christian holy book by filling out a form at their website (www.mormon.org/holybible) or by calling 800-796-1441. You'll be asked if Mormon representatives may visit you, and you're free to accept or decline.

Print Your Own Free Greeting Cards

Everyone loves a card for a special occasion. But with prices climbing to $3, $4, and beyond, the cumulative costs of greeting cards are getting out of hand. One way to save is to print out free cards and similar products at www.freeprint.com. For the price of paper and the ink in your printer's cartridge, you can get free holiday and

Q Besides hitting the clearance sales, how else can I save money when clothes shopping?

A You can save a lot by asking the manager at a favorite local clothing shop whether it sells "used" or "debit" merchandise—items that have been worn and returned for one reason or another and cannot be put back into stock or sent back to the manufacturer.

Depending on whether the item has a defect, such as a stain, you can often bargain to buy the item for up to half off the tag price. A small dry cleaning bill may be the only additional expense. Of course, as many savvy dressers know, thrift shops and consignment shops are filled with great "pre-owned" bargains.

birthday cards, business cards, calendars, gift tags, and more. Click on "Birthday Cards," and you'll be redirected to a site where you can choose from a thousand different styles—no registration required.

Rewards for Creative Moms

Mothers with an artistic bent can use their talent to win cash prizes in the Alice Abel Competition, sponsored by American Mothers, Inc., an interfaith, nonprofit, nonpolitical organization that works to strengthen the "moral and spiritual foundations of the family and the home." (It's also the official sponsor of Mother's Day.) The awards categories include art, literature, vocals, and instrumentals, and the prizes range from a few hundred dollars to $1,000. For

Savings for Savvy Readers

If you and your children are bookworms, your collective reading habit may be costing you dearly. Your first recourse, obviously, is the public library. But what if your branch does not have the books you want or there are long waiting lists for them?

Two good alternatives have the added advantage of recycling books and saving a few trees in the process. At www.paperbackswap.com, you list nine books you no longer want and get three credits to order any three books from a member database of nearly 6 million titles. If someone requests a book you've listed, you mail it at media rate, usually $1.59 per paperback. When that volume is received, you get another credit for a free book, sent to you free. Each time you spend $1.59 to ship a book to someone, you get your own book shipped free. Books must be respectable and in good shape, but otherwise just about anything qualifies. Don't let the site's name fool you; books are of all sorts, including hardbacks and tapes. While you may have trouble finding the latest bestsellers, you'll find past bestsellers and perennial favorites on the site.

A different philosophy governs www.booksfree.com, which operates much like a DVD service such as Netflix. It charges a fee, which can range from $8.49 a month for "renting" two books at a time to $34.99 for twelve at a time—from a database of more than 87,000 books and tapes. The books are sent and returned to Booksfree at no cost to you, so your total payout each month depends solely on how many books you want in your home at one time. Considering the price of books when they're bought new, the savings can be literally thousands of dollars a year.

competition rules, information, and applications, go to www.americanmothers.org/aliceabelcompetition.cfm.

Recycled Bargains

Tax Write-Offs on Old Equipment

If you're looking to get rid of technology you don't need—computers, fax machines, printers, and the like—you may be able to take them as a tax deduction. The National Cristina Foundation (call 203-863-9100, or visit www.cristina.org) will pair your donation with nonprofit organizations, schools, and public agencies that train people with disabilities, students at risk, and economically disadvantaged people. You can deduct the fair market value of the item, plus shipping costs, if the foundation can use it. Just be sure to use the Cristina website links to wipe information from computer hard drives before you send them off.

Bargain Lawn Mowers

In the market for a lawn mower? A good electric one can set you back $200 or more. But you can save considerably by purchasing a reconditioned model from your local lawn-mower repair shop. If it's a reputable outfit, you can be reasonably sure the staff have done a good job in the reconditioning process—and if anything goes wrong, they'll know how to fix it.

Try Freecycling

Want a piano for free? How about a slightly used television, furniture, camera, or mini-fridge? The Freecycle Network (www.freecycle.org) is a grassroots, nonprofit organization made up of groups across the globe that are giving (and getting) stuff for free in their own hometowns. Membership is free. Go to the site, locate your community (or one nearby), and sign up; after your membership goes through, you can check out what's available that you'd like to own. Simply respond to a member's offer, and you just might get it. It's up to the "giver" to decide who receives the item and to set up a pickup time. Everything posted must be free, legal, and appropriate for all ages—but be sure to grab it fast, because the hot stuff goes quickly.

Q Where can I get free stuff for my garden or lawn?

A If your yard is filled with trees and flower beds, keeping the soil cool, fertilized, and weed-free can be costly. Many counties and towns pick up residential lawn trimmings and leaves and turn them—along with Christmas tree pickups and park tree trimmings—into compost or mulch that's available free to anyone who will pick it up. Call your local government to find out if and where such a service is available. Take along your own shovel and containers for carrying the mulch.

When mixed with other mulching materials, such as grass clippings and leaves, used coffee grounds are a great fertilizer for acid-loving plants; the grounds are also great for speeding up the compost process. Under Starbucks' Grounds for Your Garden program, you can get a free five-pound bag of used grounds just by asking. Call your local Starbucks to see if it participates in the program.

Mortgage Matters

Free Home Down Payment

Are you making enough money to qualify for a mortgage, but lack the ready cash for a down payment or closing costs? The solution may be a down payment assistance program. AmeriDream, Inc., is a charitable, nonprofit organization that promotes homeownership by providing qualified buyers up to 10 percent of a home's cost as a down payment—with no repayment required! The offer is open to low- and moderate-income families; the ceiling on the price of a home is the Fannie Mae single-family home limit of $417,000; and you have to purchase from a builder or homeowner enrolled in the pro-

Federal Programs for Homeowners

If you're in the market for a home, need help with a down payment or closing costs, or want to remodel, Uncle Sam has a program—most likely, more than one—that meets your needs. While some programs are geared to low- or very low-income people, others are available to individuals at a moderate income level (those whose income is no more than 115 percent of the median level for the area where they live).

If you belong to a special group—Native Americans, the elderly, military families, minorities, those with chronic diseases, those who want to live in an urban setting or in a rural area—there may be a federal program designed specifically for you. Some are administered by the U.S. Department of Housing and Urban Development (HUD), others (particularly in rural areas) by the U.S. Department of Agriculture (USDA). Still others are administered locally through community development block grants.

Finding and applying to the best program can take patience. For a one-stop-shopping location that provides information on all federal domestic assistance programs, go to the Catalog of Federal Domestic Assistance (www.cfda.gov). There you can read about types of assistance and the steps to take to apply, browse a list of the newest and most popular programs, and learn more.

Once you find the programs that you're interested in, speak to the local office of the agency or authority that administers them for more information about how to apply, your chances of being accepted, and whether there is a more appropriate program that you've overlooked. Across the nation, HUD operates housing counseling agencies that advise on everything from buying a home to arranging a reverse mortgage; to locate the agency nearest you, visit www.hud.gov/offices/hsg/sfh/hcc/hcs.cfm.

gram. To find out more about AmeriDream and to register for its free online Homebuyer Education workshop, go to www.ameridream.org.

Local Help with Down Payments

Don't stop at nonprofits when you're looking for help with your down payment or closing costs. Contact your city, county, and state housing offices—find the numbers and addresses in the blue pages of your phone book—to see what kind of assistance is available. The requirements vary, but here are some examples: In Oregon, low-income first-time buyers can get loans up to $10,000 for a down payment and closing costs, with no interest until the property is sold or otherwise disposed of (www.ohcs.oregon.gov). In Baton Rouge, you can get a $10,000 loan with no interest and no payments for 20 years if you continue to live in the house (www.brgov.com/dept/ocd/housing/housing.htm).

Home Remodeling Aid from HUD

If you're buying or refinancing a fixer-upper, the typical process involves a high-interest interim loan to purchase the home—since the lender isn't likely to give a permanent mortgage until the house is repaired—followed by a remodeling loan, then a long-term mortgage. Section 203(k) of HUD Program 14.108, Rehabilitation Mortgage Insurance, saves you time and money by encouraging lenders to give you an all-in-one loan. Your planned improvements to the property must cost at least $5,000, and they can include such projects as adding or replacing plumbing, roofs, and gutters; landscaping; and energy conservation. To prove eligibility you must show that you can make the monthly mortgage payments. Check www.hud.gov/ll/code/llslcrit.html for a list of approved lenders.

Spruce Up Your Digs for Less

If you need cash to repair and remodel that deteriorating homestead, you might have to pay (as of June 2006) a 7 percent or higher interest rate on a loan. But many states, counties, and local governments offer grants, low-cost loans, and other assistance for just that purpose. For instance, in Hampton County, Virginia, the Hampton Redevelopment & Housing Authority will provide 3 percent loans for repairs and improvements, in amounts ranging from $1,000 to $25,000, depending on the homeowner's income and equity. Look in the blue pages of your telephone book to find the housing authority in your locale and check to see what help is available.

CHAPTER 4

improving your appearance

As the Billy Crystal saying goes, "It's not how you feel, it's how you look!" Here are our tips for looking *mahvelous* without spending a million bucks.

By the **numbers**

16

Percentage of women who think of themselves as attractive, according to a Harvard Medical School study. Another 72 percent think that their looks are just average; 13 percent say that they are less physically attractive than others.

AFTER EARNING A LIVING AND TAKING CARE of our families, looking good is high on most of our priority lists. We all know there are many ways to spend big bucks on looking good. What you may not know is that there are plenty of ways to look (and feel) great for free or for much less than "retail."

In the beauty and cosmetics world, sampling is a tried-and-true marketing technique, one that benefits both consumer and manufacturer. Most people are thrilled to try out a sample of something for free, and if they like it, they could become customers for life. Cosmetics brands' websites, lifestyle magazines, and in-store promotions are all great places to find free samples. To take advantage of online offers, you'll probably have to sign up and become a member, but it's a small price to pay. Beauty brand sites are also filled with tips and expert advice.

As always, when completing an online questionnaire, be careful about the information you share. Check the site's privacy policies to make sure your information won't be sold to a third party. Also, check the conditions of the offer to see if you have to pay shipping costs. And remember, almost all offers are for limited time periods and the content on websites changes frequently, so check back often with the sites you like.

Flea markets, street fairs, and catalog companies are good (and fun) places to find all kinds of new clothing items at deep discounts. All you have to do is love to shop. If you crave designer clothes but hate designer prices, there are many ways to get that label for less. Store sales, closeout stores that sell overstock at season's end, and consignment shops are great resources for high-end clothes at lower prices.

Fitness and diet are big parts of looking good, and there are a variety of ways to save on exercise and healthy food. Of course, you have to make commitments, but that's your responsibility! We've included a few websites that provide information and tools to encourage the kind of well-being that shows.

There's an important lesson to be learned from this chapter: You don't have to be wealthy to make a good appearance.

Offers and Giveaways

Finding Deep-Discount Coupons

You probably already receive Valpak coupons in the mail, with offers for free teeth whitening, tanning sessions, trial gym memberships, and more. But you can also visit Valpak's website to print out additional coupons or check out offers in nearby neighborhoods. At www.valpak.com, type in your zip code and click on "Fitness & Beauty," "Health & Medical," or a number of other categories. In mid-2006 Valpak.com deals included a free feet and toes package with purchase of any leg-hair removal package from American Laser Centers, which has locations in nearly 29 states, and offers savings of up to 75 percent on products like Brush-On Gold Beads from the Body Shop. You print out the coupons directly from the website or from the manufacturer's or store's site. Enter other zip codes in your area to view different offers. Finally, you can sign up to receive e-mail savings alerts when new offers or promotions in your area are posted.

Free Stuff from Wal-Mart Online

On its site (www.walmart.com), Wal-Mart posts free samples and special offers for products like shampoo, aftershave, and skin-care items. Look under "In Stores Now" and click on "Free Samples." When you see a sample you like, click on "Learn More," then on

Take Caution!

Visit General Freebie Sites with Caution

There are many websites full of free stuff of all kinds (www.freebiefanatic.com, www.mysavings.com, and www.actual-freestuff.com, for example), but you may have to kiss (or click on) a lot of frogs to find a prince of a product. Still, it's probably worth your while to check out these and other freebie sites on the Internet. In mid-2006 Actual Free Stuff offered samples of Nivea body lotion, Tag body spray, Nautica cologne for men, and an anti-aging skin-care cream, among many others.

EDITOR'S CHOICE In-Store Giveaways and Makeovers

Cosmetics counters of large department stores can be gold mines of free products and services. Don't be shy about asking for samples of even the most expensive perfumes, moisturizers, and body lotions. Clerks will be happy to demonstrate the products on you, and even give you a full makeover with cosmetics, with no obligation to buy anything. If you do make a purchase, ask if it comes with any gift packs. Clinique is famous for its free gifts with purchases, offering customers makeup bags filled with mini-mascaras, nail polish, lipstick, and other trial-size goodies. Check www.clinique.com (click on "Stores and Events," then on "Bonus Now") to register for e-mail alerts about when and where the company will be giving away gifts in your area during its periodic Clinique Bonus Now promotions.

"Free Sample." You'll sign up to have one sent to you or be directed to print out a coupon for in-store retrieval. Not all offers are available at all stores. For example, a free sample of Night & Day contact lenses would be found only at Wal-Marts that have a Vision Center (the "Store Finder" near the bottom of the home page notes the services offered by each store).

No-Cost Perfume and Cologne Samples

Are you a woman searching for a spicy floral fragrance composed of a rich blend of essential oils? Or maybe you're a man seeking a warm and spicy scent. Boudreau's Fragrances is offering no-obligation samples of its men's colognes and women's perfumes. Visit www.madameboudreau.com, fill out a brief form with your name and address, and Madame Boudreau will send you a free sample of either For Woman "A" or For Man "A." The company promises that no salesperson will contact you. If you have a question about perfumes, you can even "Ask Madame Boudreau" and she'll e-mail you an answer.

More Lower-Priced Internet Goodies

If you buy your health and beauty products online, look for sites that offer free shipping as well as samples and specials. Drugstore.com, for example, frequently waives the charge for shipping if you spend a certain amount. The site also commonly features a variety of buy one, get one free and other offers—as does Avon.com and MaryKay.com. Avon frequently has sales on cosmetics and skin-care products with savings of between 20 and 75 percent. You can register with Avon.com to receive notices of special online sales and free shipping offers (and sometimes you may even receive surprise trial-size product samples with your orders).

Get a Virtual Makeover Free

Ever wonder what you'd look like with a different hair color or style? How would you look in that bright red lipstick Scarlett Johansson is so fond of? You can try out hairstyles and colors, cosmetic colors, glasses, hats, and even eye colors (those colored contacts, you know) on your computer using iVillage's (www.ivillage.com) Makeover-o-matic feature. Just go to the site, click on "Beauty and Style," then on "Get a Virtual Makeover" under "Hot Stuff." You can upload your own photo or choose one of the twelve models provided. In addition to different hair colors and styles, you can "try on" lipstick, blush, and eyeliner. The name and brand is listed next to each color (though there's only one color from each company). You can mix and match and change your mind without wasting a penny on colors that don't work.

SKIN-CARE BARGAINS

Deals from L'Oréal

L'Oréal is the world's largest beauty-products company, and its website (www.lorealusa.com) provides links to all of its brands, including L'Oréal Paris, Biotherm, Kiehl's, Lancôme, Redken, Maybelline New York, Matrix, Biotherm, Skinceuticals, and many others you probably didn't know L'Oréal owned. Each brand's website has different special features, such as sampling or gifts with purchase, and all supply a plethora of beauty information. For example, visit Maybelline New York's "Makeup Studio" and get a virtual makeover or watch videos of the pros giving makeup tips. Redken has sweepstakes and personalized hair-product recommendations. If you join My Lancôme, you'll get product samples, special deals, and personalized beauty consultations. L'Oréal Paris also has retail stores in Los Angeles at the Beverly Center (310-360-6555) and in Farmington, Connecticut, at the Westfarms Mall (860-561-0220) that are makeup playgrounds where you can try every product in the line, get samples and free makeovers, and participate in special events.

Free Beauty Products

It isn't easy (or cheap) being beautiful, which is why you should take full advantage when your favorite beauty brands are handing out freebies like coupons and new product samples. Below are some examples of just how generous your favorite makeup companies are being—and how little you have to do to reap the rewards! Just remember that offers, especially those on the Internet, change frequently.

BRAND/WEBSITE	WHAT'S OFFERED	WHAT YOU HAVE TO DO
Color Me Beautiful www.colormebeautiful.com	Discounts of 50 percent or more on selected items.	Nothing—just log in
Dove www.dove.us	Free product samples, free gifts with purchases, and expert skin-care tips.	Provide your mailing address, and fill out a short survey about your use of Dove products.
Olay www.olay.com	Coupons and product samples; selection changes regularly	To get free samples, simply provide your contact information and answer a few questions about the skin products you use. Club Olay members get even more perks, but you have to create a free member account and fill out a longer survey.
Vitabath www.vitabath.com	Free samples of Vitabath Gelee	Join the print catalog mailing list or agree to receive special offers and notifications via e-mail.
Vital Radiance www.vitalradiance.com	Coupons and customized cosmetics samples	Fill out a questionnaire about your skin tone and type.

No-Cost Info on Cosmetics Safety

Ever wonder about the safety of that lipstick, foundation, or sunscreen you're about to apply? The U.S. Food and Drug Administration's Center for Food Safety and Applied Nutrition offers a wealth of free information on the safety of cosmetics, skin creams, hair dyes, and sunscreens on its website: www.cfsan.fda.gov. To access fact sheets on such topics as "What Are Hypoallergenic Cosmetics?" and "Are Cosmetic Products Containing Alpha Hydroxy Acids Safe?" go to the site and click on "Consumer Advice and Publications." After you've boned up on cosmetics safety, test your knowledge by taking the site's "How Smart Are You About Cosmetics?" quiz.

Free Skin-Care Guide

Beauty is as beauty does, they say, and keeping your skin healthy is a key ingredient in looking and feeling your best. The National Women's Health Resource Center's free, 26-page booklet "Women, Skin Health & Beauty" contains a wealth of information on keeping your skin in top form in all seasons and at all stages of life. Topics include protecting your skin from the relentless rays of the sun, facts and fallacies regarding makeup and skin-care ingredients, how to choose the right products for you, and other skin-care resources. You can order the booklet online at the NWHRC website (www.healthywomen.org; scroll down on the home page); write to the NWHRC at 157 Broad Street, Suite 315, Red Bank, New Jersey 07701; or call toll-free 877-986-9472.

Hair Care

Free Samples and Tips from Pantene

Become a Pantene Insider and receive personalized hair solutions, advice from the pros, free product samples, sneak previews of new products, sweepstakes entries, and a variety of other offers. In exchange for filling out a short survey, you could receive shampoo and conditioner samples in the mail from Pantene's new Full & Thick Collection. Go to www.pantene.com and click on "Get Profiled." As on all websites, the available product samples are always changing, so check back often.

Free Hair Stuff from Goody

Battle that next bad-hair day head-on. In addition to quality brushes and fashionable hair accessories, Goody offers a newsletter filled with tips on how to get the latest looks and styling solutions. You'll also get free goodies like bobby-pin trial packs. To sign up for the newsletter and free stuff, go to Goody's website (www.goody.com), click on "Sweepstakes," then on "Freebies" (and while you're at it, check out the current sweepstakes offers).

Free Dandruff Shampoo Sample

Those unsightly white dandruff flakes don't do much for a clean and inviting appearance, not to mention how uncomfortable and distracting all that scalp scratching can be! You can try out one or more of the Head & Shoulders dandruff shampoos by going to www.headandshoulders.com and clicking on "Special Offers." The offers change often (in mid-2006 it was a free sample of one of six different shampoos) and sometimes include free samples of related

Editor's Choice

Free Samples for Cheerleaders

Any girl who's a member of a cheerleading squad, a gymnastics team, or a dance troupe knows how important is it for every girl to have a unified look. BA Star, makers of cosmetics for performers, offers free team samples of its products at www.bastar.com. To sign up for the samples and to receive e-mail offers and company news, click on the "Free Samples" link and fill out the simple questionnaire, which asks for, among other things, contact information for the adult studio owner, teacher, or dance coordinator and your team or costume colors. A team must have at least 12 members to qualify.

Procter & Gamble products, such as Clairol's Natural Instincts Shine Happy. There is also a lot of information on maintaining a healthy scalp and keeping hair of all types clean, shiny, and healthy. Just click on "Scalp Care" or "Beautiful Hair" on the home page.

More Free Hair-Care Samples

Calling all redheads, blondes, and brunettes! Sign up to receive a sample collection of John Frieda's Radiant Red, Brilliant Brunette, or Sheer Blonde products. Each hair-care line has been specially developed to address the needs of these hair colors. You'll also receive the latest news and tips from the John Frieda hair-care professionals, as well as news about upcoming promotions and contests. For more information, go to the company website at www.johnfrieda.com and click on "Promotions."

More Free Haircuts

Be a hair model and get your locks cut for free. Bumble and Bumble University in New York City conducts advanced cutting and styling training for hairdressers from the top salons in the country under the guidance of the company's master stylists. As part of this program, it is constantly looking for hair models. No modeling experience is necessary, but you must be open to a style change and be available for the 90-minute to two-hour appointment. Apply on the site at www.bumbleandbumble.com, call toll-free 866-7-BUMBLE (866-728-6253), or send an e-mail to model@bumbleandbumble.com. The company may also ask you to try out some of the products it is currently developing.

No-Cost Hair-Product Samples and Demos

Give your hair a fresh change of pace. Visit the Garnier Fructis U.S. website (www.garnierfructisusa.com) for free hair product samples and other good stuff. Just click on "Get Lucky," fill out the short survey, and you'll be sent whatever is being offered, while supplies last. (Available in mid-2006 was a sample of Body and Volume Shampoo and Conditioner.) You can also sign up for e-mails about free samples, sweepstakes events, and other special offers. For some entertaining and useful information, check out the 25 or so styling-tips videos that show you in a few seconds how to use Garnier Fructis products for optimum results; among the categories covered are curl control and adding texture and volume. Or take a short

Q What's a good way to save money on haircuts?

A When you sign up for the free Haircut Alert e-mails at www.supercuts.com, you'll not only receive e-reminders about when you're due for a trim—you'll also receive a $2 coupon good toward any adult haircut at any Supercuts location nationwide. With every Haircut Alert after that, you'll get an additional $1 coupon. Check out the site periodically for sweepstakes offers. And when you're in the mood for a new 'do, or just feel like having fun with hair, go to the site's free "Style File" for 360-degree views of the latest Supercuts styles for men, women, and kids.

quiz that will help you decide what products you need, all by Garnier Fructis, of course!

Get Hair Therapy for Free

Do you need a little therapy for your hair? Just request free samples of Sunsilk shampoo, conditioner, and styling products at www.gethairapy.com. In mid-2006 you could choose among five popular product lines: Anti-Flat, De-frizz, Hydra-TLC, Anti-Poof, and Straighten-Up. You can also sign up to receive e-mails with product updates, samples, and special promotions. Check out the site's product info, lifestyle Q&A topics, and hair-care tips too. If you don't have a computer and are interested in receiving free samples and coupons for Sunsilk lines or other Unilever brands like Pond's, Dove, or Rexona Deodorants, call 800-298-5018 and follow the voice prompts to speak to a customer service representative who will be happy to sign you up on the phone.

Uncle Sam Wants You ... to Look Good!

Apparently, the government cares about the way you look. Its Consumer Information Catalog offers the following booklets (all free but the last one). To order, write to the Federal Citizen Information Center, Consumer Information Catalog, Pueblo, Colorado 81009, call toll-free 888-8PUEBLO (888-878-3256), or visit www.pueblo.gsa.gov. Most of these publications are also available to read or download, for free, on www.pueblo.gsa.gov (under "Online Shopping," click on "Item # Listing").

- The four-page "Cosmetic Laser Surgery: A High-Tech Weapon in the Fight Against Aging Skin" (#542L) explains how laser surgery can help remove facial wrinkles and lines, how to tell if it's right for you, what the risks are, and more.
- "Tattoos and Permanent Make-Up" (#651M) describes in two pages the types of tattoos, the risks involved in getting one, and ways to remove them.
- "Losing Weight: More Than Counting Calories" (#523M) tells you, in six pages, how to learn whether you're overweight, develop healthier eating habits, increase your physical activity, and create a successful weight-loss plan.
- "Fever Blisters and Canker Sores" (#386K) explains the causes of, treatments for, and research on these mouth infections. This booklet costs $0.50.
- "Cosmetics" (#541N) is a two-page fact sheet about using cosmetics safely, and "Clearing Up Cosmetic Confusion" (#639M) gives you five pages of facts on cosmetic terms as well as advice on how not to misuse makeup.

Low-Cost 'Dos at Beauty Schools

Cosmetology, hairstyling, and barber schools can be great sources for free or low-cost haircuts, manicures, and facials. Check the phone book for one near you. Some schools may ask for a small fee or a tip for the trainee; others may offer free cuts at certain times of the year, or request only certain types of hair, such as long and straight or curly. For example, the Cosmetology Training Center (www.cosmetologytrainingcenter.com) in Mankato, Minnesota, offers hair, nail, and skin care at discounted prices, as well as birthday party makeovers for girls ages 12 and younger. Call your favorite salon and ask when it will be training students.

Dental Care

Discounts from Colgate

Colgate is one of the most trusted names in dental products, especially toothpaste. If you already use a Colgate product or are interested in trying one, go to www.colgate.com, click on "Oral Care," then "Special Offers," and sign up for rebates or print coupons for toothpaste, toothbrushes, Listerine mouthwash, and more. Subscribe to receive the Colgate SmileTalk newsletter by e-mail every other month; you'll get dental-care tips and savings on products not included on the site. Answer a short survey and include the ages of your kids to receive information regarding their age-specific oral-care needs—for example, what to consider when they are teething, getting permanent teeth, or considering braces.

Free Denture Cleaner Sample

Cascade Dental Products Company has developed a powerful cleaner used by professionals for cleaning full dentures, partials, or retainers. For your free sample of Sparkle Denture Cleaner, go to www.cascade-dental.com and either fill out the online form or print the mail-order form. You can also call toll-free 800-939-9926, or send an e-mail to info@cascade-dental.com for more information.

Free Aquafresh Samples

Even though teeth are its game, Aquafresh knows where consumers' hearts are: in their pocketbooks, especially where a good bargain or

Beauty Steals for Women of Color

It's only been over the past decade or so that beauty and cosmetics companies really started paying attention to women of color's very specific hair and skin-care needs.

Companies like those mentioned below sell products specially designed to match this slice of the population; larger cosmetics companies are now following suit, too, and are producing makeup shades in varying skin colors, and hair products for a variety of hair textures.

Makeup counters at department stores can be great places for women of color to get free goods and advice: Complimentary mini-makeovers are usually yours for the asking, and you'll be able to find out firsthand whether a brand's products are right for your skin type.

Free Hair-Care Product Samples

Got a few minutes to spare, and hair that needs repair? For minimal effort (like filling out brief surveys, or signing on as a site member), these sites will send you samples of hair-care products designed specifically for women of color.

- **Crème of Nature** (www.cremeofnature.com)
- **Tress Tranzitions** (www.tresstranzitions.com)
- **Motions** (www.motionshair.com)
- **Namasté Laboratories** (www.organicrootstimulator.com)

Cosmetics and Skin-Care Bargains

Nia Enterprises is a minority-owned company that conducts market research on the buying habits and preferences of African American women; Nia consults with Fortune 500 companies on its findings. If you sign up for its Simple Sampling Consumer Advisory Panel at www.niaonline.com and provide feedback and opinions on beauty products, you'll receive samples from companies like Revlon and Johnson products.

Supermodel Iman's Bargains and Free Samples

One of the world's most beautiful women, supermodel Iman has developed a medium-priced cosmetics and skin-care line for women of color. Her website (www.imanbeauty.com) offers, in addition to individual products for sale, around a dozen special-value packages in a variety of a fashion bags or cases. Summer 2006 offerings included the Glitz and Glam grouping, with four full-size products packaged in a black evening bag—a $75 value for $20—and the Beauty Bazaar, with 12 products (some promotional size, some full size) in a bamboo serving tray—a $137 value for only $35. You can also subscribe for free to the newsletter *Beauty Noir* and receive specials not found anywhere else; if you don't have Internet access, call toll-free 877-367-4626. You'll find the same sort of great values on collections of Flori Roberts cosmetics at www.floriroberts.com, as well as free samples with every purchase.

Editor's Choice

Ask Your Dentist for Free Samples

Your local dentist is a good stop on your hunt for free stuff. During your next appointment, ask for complimentary toothbrushes, toothpaste, floss, mouthwash, and whitening product samples. More often than not, dentists are happy to give these away; many do so even without your asking. For patient literature on teeth whitening or to find a cosmetic dentist near you, ask your regular dentist or visit the American Academy of Cosmetic Dentistry's website: www.aacd.com.

a freebie is concerned. When you go to the Aquafresh website (www.aquafresh.com), all the current free samples are right there on its home screen. (Should that change in the future, click on "Savings and Special Offers.") In mid-2006 you could get two product samples (White & Shine and Extreme Clean), three free music downloads with a purchase, several printable coupons for a variety of products (such as Tartar Control toothpaste, Sensitive Toothpaste, and Toothbrush Twin Pack), and a free Dr. Seuss book with the purchase of two products. Aquafresh's site has great tips on good dental hygiene and a special "Kidzone" with special information on tooth care for children and dental products especially for kids, such as Dr. Seuss toothbrushes and toothpaste.

Eye Care

Designer Frames for 60% Off

Eyeglasses are expensive—and designer-name frames can take a huge bite out of your budget. Many brick-and-mortar stores, including Costco and other "warehouse" operations, offer discounts on eyeglasses. For greater selection, you can turn to the Internet, but if you shop online you can't always try on frames before purchasing them. What you can do is go to a store, try on some styles, and write down the brand of the frames you like and, if possible, the style number. Then go to a website like www.go-optic.com, which has hundreds of designer frames and sunglasses to choose from, many discounted as much as 60 percent. When you've chosen your frames, type in your prescription (or fax or mail it in) and Go-Optic will call your doctor to ensure that it's correct. It takes about 10 days to get your glasses, and all work is guaranteed. For more information, visit the site or call toll-free 877-634-2020.

Try on Half-Price Frames Online

At FramesDirect.com (www.framesdirect.com), one of the biggest names in online eyewear, you can choose from thousands of frames at discounts of between 20 and 60 percent off (most are around 55 percent off) retail prices—*and* you can see how lots of them will look on your face with their FrameFinder Virtual Try-On technology. Upload your own photograph or use one of FramesDirect's face models to try more than 65,000 eyeglass images from hundreds of designers worldwide. There are many lens types to choose from, including tints and coatings, all at about half the cost of retail. For more info or to order by phone, call toll-free 800-248-9427 (in Houston, call 713-914-0011, or visit them at 3100 South Gessner, Suite 329, Houston, Texas 77063). You can also get live support online. FramesDirect.com and GO-Optic.com (see "Designer Frames for 60% Off," opposite) also sell contacts.

Clothing Bargains

Get Deep Discounts at Retail Outlets

If you use shopping as "therapy," buying at retail outlets doesn't have to be bad for your pocketbook. Many department stores periodically have sales with savings of up to 75 percent off regular retail price. You can often get high-quality items for the same prices as lower-quality or used clothing. Check your favorite stores frequently for sale dates, and ask salespeople to put you on mailing lists or to call you for back-room and sample sales, which are a great way to acquire discounted designer clothes. Shop at upscale off-price stores like Loehmann's to find seasonal overstock from designers and lots of special purchases at deep price cuts. Then log on to your computer for even more deals. Sites like www.Bluefly.com sell designer clothes at heavily discounted prices, and www.DailyCandy.com sends out e-mail alerts for sample sales in major U.S. cities.

Low-Priced Duds from Chadwick's

Chadwick's is a mail-order and online shopping outlet that sells well-made, mostly casual clothing and shoes at bargain prices all the time. But when it has its several-times-a-year seasonal sales, the company practically gives the stuff away. You'll often receive special additional savings online or, if you spend a certain amount (usually \$50), when you shop through the catalog. Occasionally the company also offers a free gift, like a cotton sweater, with a purchase of \$50 or more. If you had shopped the catalog during the "Red Hot Summer Sale" in 2006, you could have bought all-cotton T-shirts in four styles and 14 colors for \$6.99 each. A linen zip-up hoodie in seven colors was on sale for \$9.99, down from \$24. Online, there

Editor's Choice Get a Free T

The T-Shirt Outlet (www.petrix.com/shirt) provides a way for manufacturers to distribute promotional T-shirts with printing errors or imperfections. They're still usable for promotional purposes, but because they aren't perfect, the companies that ordered them prefer not to give them to their customers. The T-Shirt Outlet says that there are always shirts available, though the logos change. You have to take what it offers, usually one size and one color only. In most cases you don't even have to pay shipping. As of mid-2006, the company didn't ship to all parts of the country but noted it has plans to expand its distribution. Meanwhile, just fill out a short form with your name and address to receive your free shirt.

were savings of up to 85 percent. Most dresses, pants, and jackets also come in tall and petite sizes, and many items are available in plus sizes. Shop online at www.chadwicks.com, or call for a catalog toll-free at 800-525-6650.

Half-Price Jeans (and More) at the Gap

Everybody loves jeans, but good ones can be expensive—unless you know where to look. Gap has always had terrific in-store sales, but don't forget about its website (www.gap.com), which presents jeans (and other) bargains in a well-organized fashion. Go to Men, Women, GapBody, or GapMaternity and check out the sales. Or click on "Sale" for an overview of clearance products. You can also click on a specific item like "Jeans" and take a look at the clearance merchandise in that category. In summer 2006, the site featured a big selection of $49.95 jeans on sale for between $14.99 and $19.99. Big sales tend to occur at the middle or end of a season, with much merchandise discounted far more than 50 percent, though there's always a good selection of merchandise on sale anytime.

Learn to Tie a Tie for Free

We live in a casual age. But that doesn't mean that dressing well is obsolete. Some professions and many occasions still require a suit and tie. Many men have never tied a tie or, when forced to wear one, press their moms, wives, or girlfriends into service to tie it for them. But who says women are experts in this sartorial art? For a hand in tying a tie, with step-by-step drawings, go to the website www.tie-a-tie.net, created just for guys and gals who want to know all about Windsor knots and the like. If you're really serious about the subject, you can download a video series for $13.95. But, in general, everything you need to know is on the site for free.

Gently Used Bargains at Consignment Shops

The clothes found in charity-run thrift stores have been donated. Consignment shops differ in that people expect to be paid money if the goods they place there are sold, and you can usually find great-quality used clothing and accessories at these relatively upscale stores. Though some charities operate consignment stores featuring a variety of bargain-priced merchandise, most are privately owned, and some even sell pre-worn designer or celebrity clothing. As a rule, consignment shops won't accept merchandise unless it looks new, has a recognizable label, and is less than two years or two seasons old (unless it's "vintage"). Items that have been worn only

Seven Tips for Better Consignment Shopping

Fashion expert Raya Premji, who owns Rodeo Drive Resale (see "Bargain Duds Worn by the Rich and Famous," page 78), shares insider info that will help you become a world-class bargain shopper.

- **Know your price range before shopping.** Consignment shops offer different price ranges, so have your budget in mind as you pick a store. If the shops don't use print ads or have a website, call the store to inquire about its price range.
- **Reputation counts.** Many resale stores sell fakes and may not even know it, so make sure the store has a 100 percent authenticity guarantee.
- **Only buy items that are in like-new condition.** Always examine an item carefully before purchasing it. Never buy items that have holes or stains or that are damaged in any way.
- **New items come in daily**, and some don't make it onto the rack. If you're serious about consignment shopping, visit your favorite shops at least once a week.
- **Never go by the size on the label.** All designers size their items differently, so always try everything on before buying. (Rodeo Drive Resale not only gives the size but also exact waist and chest measurements.) You should also find out what the store's returns policy is.
- **Sign the stores' guest books** and personal shopper lists, and make friends with the salespeople. Most stores will call you when your listed item comes in.
- **Don't rush.** Consignment stores generally have a lot of merchandise to choose from. But unlike department stores, there is usually just one of each item, so take your time going through the racks.

once, such as wedding gowns, tuxedos, and prom dresses, are consignment shop mainstays. Find consignment stores in your yellow pages; www.consignmentshops.com provides some listings by state.

The Coolest Used-Clothing Store on the Planet

Buffalo Exchange does more than just sell great used clothes. What makes it unique is that clothes and accessories are bought, sold, and *traded* directly with store customers. You can sell clothing you're tired of from last season (or the 1960s!) for cash, or trade it instead for someone else's old favorites. Buffalo Exchange buys high-quality items to resell, and the eclectic inventory includes vintage clothing, designer wear, jeans, leather, basics, one-of-a-kind items, and more. The stores also sell new merchandise and accessories, and almost everything is at bargain prices. The first Buffalo Exchange opened in Tucson in 1974. There are currently more than 30 stores in cities across the country, including Austin, Boulder, Las Vegas, Los Angeles, New York (Brooklyn), Philadelphia, San Francisco, Seattle, and Tucson. To scheck out sales and special events, and find a store near you, go to the store's website: www.buffaloexchange.com.

Bargain Duds Worn by the Rich and Famous

Rodeo Drive Resale is on Ventura Boulevard, not Rodeo Drive, which is good news for bargain hunters. Because the store is in

Off Their Star-Studded Backs

You might buy the dress Meryl Streep wore to the Golden Globes or Jon Stewart's Oscar tux *and* help children at the same time if you place the winning bid at a Clothes Off Our Back (www.clothesoffourback.org) online auction. The Clothes Off Our Back Foundation hosts Internet charity auctions featuring attire worn by stars at awards shows like the Golden Globes, the Academy Awards, the Daytime and Primetime Emmys, the Grammys, the Sundance Film Festival, and other high-profile celebrity events. Proceeds benefit children's charities that have included UNICEF, the Children's Defense Fund, and Cure Autism Now. The idea was the brainchild of actors Jane Kaczmarek and Bradley Whitford who, with the help of scores of big-name celebrities and designers, have improved the lives of children around the world. Check the site immediately after major award shows and periodically at other times for auctions, added merchandise, and information.

Sherman Oaks rather than Beverly Hills, even regular folks can afford some high-end, gently worn (and sometimes new) designer duds and accessories. Rodeo Drive Resale gets its used merchandise from Hollywood stylists, celebrity closets, television and movie studios, and some of the world's best-dressed women, and the shop also buys extra stock from expensive boutiques. Every item is guaranteed to be authentic, not a knockoff. Among the many designer names often available for 25 to 90 percent off retail are Versace, Chanel, St. John Knits, Marc Jacobs, Jimmy Choo, Pucci, Gucci, Dolce & Gabbana, Blue Cult (jeans), Prada, and Manolo Blahnik. You can shop in the store (13727 Ventura Boulevard, Sherman Oaks, California) or online (www.rodeodriveresale.com). For more information visit the website or call toll-free 888-MY-RESALE (888-697-3725). Even used, designer goods aren't cheap, but considering their quality and cachet, they're definitely a bargain.

Staying in Shape

Free Weight-Control Program

When you keep track of your daily nutrition, you're more likely to reach your diet and health goals, and doing that is the basis for a trimmer, more glowing you. So learn what your ideal calorie intake is and be mindful of the number of calories, protein, carbohydrates, and fat you consume. Allurelle's Weight Loss Program, a free software program (for Windows only) that is downloadable from www.allurelle.com, helps you become aware of your eating habits. The food diary allows you to keep track of your eating, and to look back and see how things have changed over time. It may take a little while for you to become comfortable recording everything you eat and drink, but the results when you look in the mirror should convince you that it's worth the effort.

Track Your Food Intake for Free

Shape magazine features a weight-loss diary at www.shape.com. This no-cost, accurate, easy-to-use tool allows you to keep track of your daily food intake, and you don't have to write anything down or look up calories or fat grams—the computer does all the math for you and can calculate your body mass index. You'll have access to

Time Is Money

Free Personal Shoppers

It sounds like something out of our grandmothers' time, but even in this hurly-burly world the personal shopper still exists at major department stores. Macy's by Appointment, for example, is a free personal-shopping service tailored to each customer's needs. Its personal-shopping staff will help with things like developing a more professional style to buying a complete, all-purpose wardrobe. You can shop in person or consult over the phone, by e-mail, or even fax. Call your local Macy's or go to www.macys.com, click on "Shopping Services," then "Personal Shoppers" — the contact information will be at your fingertips.

Customers using this service also receive advance notice of exclusive events and promotions. Bloomingdale's and Neiman Marcus also provide this free service.

healthy recipes, as well as information about 16,000 foods and beverages and the basics on eating for weight loss. Unfortunately, you can't save your daily food totals; you have to print out your information to keep it.

Stay Trim with Free Nutrition Info

The website www.nutritiondata.com is a terrific source of nutritional information if you're dieting or just want to eat healthy. You can get complete nutritional analysis of almost any food item, including specific brand-name products, by entering it in the website's search field or by clicking on areas like "50 Most Popular Foods" or "Fast Food Facts." There's general nutrition information, as well as an area where you can have your recipes' nutritional content analyzed (and improved), get an estimate of your daily nutritional needs, find foods that match specific nutritional criteria (for example, those that are high in iron or low in carbohydrates), or explore a variety of specific topics, such as the Glycemic Index, Secrets of Weight Loss, and Food Additives. You can also sign up for Nutrition Data's free Update Newsletter explaining how to use new features on the site.

Half-Price Massages

Need a massage but don't want to pay big bucks for it? Check your yellow pages for a massage school near you. Such schools periodically offer special student training clinics, and your participation gives the students an opportunity to practice their new skills—

EDITOR'S CHOICE Analyze Your Exercise for Free

My-calorie-counter (www.my-calorie-counter.com) is a free, comprehensive food and activity search engine, with instant information on more than 45,000 different activities and brand-name, fast-food, and generic foods. The information available includes calorie content (for foods) and calories burned (for exercise), carbs, proteins, sugars, and other nutrients. Among the activities included for analysis are tennis, walking, gardening, kick-boxing, home repair, washing dishes, and yoga. You choose an activity, enter your weight, and find out how many calories you'll burn in an hour. For example, a 150-pound person burns 157 calories washing dishes for an hour—now you have an incentive to roll up those sleeves! If you don't have a computer and want further information on this service, you can call toll-free 800-507-2557.

sometimes under the supervision of an instructor and sometimes alone—while you get a wonderful treat at a great price. For example, the Lauterstein-Conway Massage School in Austin, Texas, offers one-hour Swedish massage sessions for half the cost of a comparable massage at a spa, with no tipping permitted; the appointments are with students completing their state-mandated, 50-hour supervised internship. Ask if your local clinic will schedule small groups, such as bridal parties, sports teams, and work groups, or if it offers additional discounts for seniors.

Bargain Shape-Up Program

For a food journal that gives you recommended daily calorie intakes and allows you to save your entries from day to day, check out the custom weight-loss system from *Shape* magazine at iShape.com. It costs $29.99 for 12 weeks, a fraction of the cost of most diet programs, and is delivered to you in daily e-mails. The program provides you with meal plans designed for your food preferences, recipes, exercises (cardio and strength), and online support. With iShape's 10-day free trial, you'll get a good idea if it works for you.

Cosmetic Procedures

Free Information on Plastic Surgery

The decision to undergo any type of cosmetic surgery should not be taken lightly. You need to do your research first. An excellent place to start is www.plasticsurgery.org, the website of the American Society of Plastic Surgeons, founded in 1931 and the world's largest plastic surgery specialty organization. Click on "Procedures" to read (and print out, for free) general information, including psychological issues and insurance coverage, and descriptions of procedures from dermabrasion to liposuction. There is a section on reconstructive surgery that, for example, can eliminate scars and repair breasts, as well as before-and-after photos for some of the most popular procedures. Go to the site's "News Room" section to read society press releases and back issues of articles from the newsletter *Plastic Surgery Today*, with news, advice, and information targeted to consumers.

Q I want to try a weight-loss program before I commit to it. Do any of the major programs offer trial periods?

A Weight Watchers lets prospective members go to a meeting at no cost. Just visit www.weightwatchers.com, click on "Visit a meeting for free," and type in your zip code to find a meeting location and time convenient for you—no appointment necessary. At the site you can also sign up for a free e-mail newsletter containing recipes, inspirational success stories, and weight-loss tips and secrets. As another benefit of signing up, you'll receive periodic updates about other Weight Watchers services, products, and events.

Work Out for Less

Looking to get in shape? Here are ways to make joining a gym or health club less of a workout for your wallet.

- Ask for a complimentary 10-day or 2-week trial pass so you can get to know a club before you join.
- Check craigslist.org and local classified sites for people selling their memberships for less than the regular fee. Before you buy, make sure the gym will accept a transferred membership.
- Get in on a discounted charter membership when a health club first opens. You may get a free gym bag, water bottle, or T-shirt, too.
- If you're also looking for a job, you should know that many gyms give their employees (including accountants, salespeople, child-care providers, and front-desk clerks) free memberships.
- If you live near a school with a gym, ask if it offers free use of gym facilities to people in the neighborhood; if there's a fee for use, ask about a neighborhood discount.
- Always inquire about special rates for seniors, students, and disabled persons, and whether there are cheaper rates if you use the gym during lower-volume hours.
- When you join, be sure to ask if the club offers free personal training sessions and introductory spa treatments.

No-Cost Info on Tattoos and Piercings

If you're serious about getting a tattoo or a piercing, first visit the American Society for Dermatologic Surgery's website (www.asds-net.org) and check out the printable "Tips to Consider When Obtaining a Tattoo or Piercing" (click on "Patients," then "Do's and Don'ts"). If you decide that the tattoo was a mistake or if you have problems, the site gives names of qualified dermatologic surgeons in your area. There's also information on skin care at various ages, fact sheets about dermatological procedures (including tattoo removal), and before-and-after photos for a variety of procedures (including tattoo removal).

Deep-Discount Products and Cosmetic Enhancement Tips

New Beauty magazine is a niche publication featuring beautifully photographed, in-depth articles on all forms of cosmetic enhancement. It covers a wide range of procedures in cosmetic dentistry, plastic surgery, dermatology, and more. The magazine's website (www.newbeauty.com) is filled with info on these topics and has two programs that provide freebies, discounts on treatments, and information from experts in return for your feedback. Sign up for the Test Tube program and receive three tubes a year filled with beauty products and brochures. Send in your feedback, and in a couple of months another Test Tube is delivered to your door. Each Test Tube will cost you $25, but in August 2006, the first one was filled with $205 worth of products, including a $20 gift card for luxury skin-care products from SpaLook.com. Become a member of *New Beauty's* BeautyPass, fill out a brief online questionnaire, and you'll receive coupons worth hundreds (maybe thousands!) of dollars in beauty treatments and procedures, invitations to beauty events, and a newsletter filled with info and expert advice on the latest in cosmetic enhancement. Just for joining, you'll get a $20 gift card from SpaLook.com.

CHAPTER 5

cures for the high cost of health care

Nothing depletes a hard-earned nest egg more quickly than medical expenses. Here's how you can keep those costs in check, and get a few freebies in the process.

By the numbers

11,000

Average amount, in dollars, that a family of four spent on health insurance costs in 2005.

A RECENT HARVARD UNIVERSITY STUDY revealed that medical bills are responsible for half the personal bankruptcies in America. Ouch. The same study showed that people with health insurance spend an average of $13,000 for out-of-pocket costs in medical emergencies. Double ouch. Even if health costs haven't forced you into bankruptcy, most likely they make up such a major part of your budget that doing *anything* to lower them can save big bucks.

Everyone loves discounts. This chapter will tell you how to get everything from medical care to prescription drugs to dental work for less. Learn where to buy contact lenses at discounts of 50 percent or more, and how to save even more by purchasing generic drugs and using online pharmacies. Discover how to combine pleasure travel with high-quality medical treatment abroad. Find out about low-cost virtual trainers that are sometimes even better than the real thing.

Discounts are great—but freebies are even better. Do you know how to get free medications? Free transportation or lodging when you face a serious medical situation? Free hearing evaluations? Free hotline advice? This chapter will tell you how.

You'll also learn about some innovative medical assistance programs. It's a common misconception that such programs are only for poor people. Not true. Though some programs exclude individuals and families living above the poverty level, others offer welcome aid to anyone in need. Patients suffering from a debilitating disease can get help with drug co-payments or an attorney to help them battle insurance companies. Free or low-cost blood tests, support groups, health and fitness classes, even swimming programs and tai chi are offered across the country.

Especially in medical matters, knowledge is power. These days it is absolutely critical to partner with your physicians and pharmacists to find out about the best treatment options. That's also true if you want to keep your medical bills from skyrocketing. How can you find out about clinical trials that will cover your treatment costs? Which of your pills can be split in half? When can you substitute a generic medication? The pages that follow will help answer these questions, and more.

Ultimately, the best way to pare medical bills is to take good care of yourself. Free online checkups—including one that estimates your longevity—can suggest how to live a longer, healthier life. "Quitmeters" and other tools make it easier to stop smoking, monitor blood pressure, and boost fitness. Paying for health care will never be easy, but we guarantee that this chapter will remove some of the pain.

Q How can I keep my out-of-pocket medical expenses low?

A Except in an emergency situation, always ask your doctor or dentist how much a treatment will cost before you give the go-ahead. If you have insurance, ask your provider how much it will pay for the treatment. If you find out that it will cost more than the insurer will pay for—or if you have no coverage—ask for a lower fee. It may seem less forbidding to ask the receptionist instead of the doctor, or to write a letter instead of making the request in person. However, you are more likely to be successful if you do it face to face—and in advance, not when the bill comes through.

General Medicine

Co-Pay Assistance

If you have health insurance and suffer from certain life-threatening or debilitating diseases, you may be eligible for financial assistance to help offset out-of-pocket treatment expenses. The Patient Advocate Foundation recently began the Co-Pay Relief program for patients with autoimmune diseases, diabetes, macular degeneration, and certain kinds of cancers. Other medical conditions are likely to be covered in the future. To find out more about the program, call toll-free 866-512-3861, or read about it at www.copays.org. Telephone counselors will help you apply.

Help for the Hospital Bound

Having a serious illness that requires a hospital stay is stressful enough on its own. Add to that the burdens of having to fly long distances to receive your treatment, and trying to find a place to stay for an extended period of time. These programs offer free services that will put you on a speedy road to recovery.

Free Air Transportation

People with compelling needs, such as specialized medical evaluation, diagnosis, or treatment, may be able to arrange for free air transportation through Angel Flight America. Though sometimes the organization can help with commercial flights, most of the free flights are handled by volunteer general aviation pilots, who fly small privately owned planes. Angel Flight America asks for five working days' notice when you need to arrange a flight. Evidence of financial need, such as a letter from a social worker or clergyman, is required. Passengers must be mobile, and a companion can go along for free. Request flights toll-free at 877-621-7177, or enter your zip code at www.angelflightamerica.org.

Cancer patients who have to travel by air for diagnosis or treatment can get help through the Corporate Angel Network, an organization that arranges free travel on corporate jets for cancer patients, bone marrow donors, and bone marrow recipients who are traveling to or from an approved cancer treatment center. More than 500 corporations participate in the program nationwide. Travelers must be able to walk up and down the steps to a private plane without assistance and not require supplemental oxygen, an IV, or any other life support during the flight. Patients can take along one companion for free; two adults can accompany a child with cancer at no cost. To request a flight, register within three weeks of the appointment date by calling the Corporate Angel Network Patient Line, toll-free 866-328-1313. Requests can also be e-mailed to info@corpangelnetwork.org. Although flights are arranged for about 50 percent of the people who qualify, travel is not guaranteed; travelers should always make backup arrangements.

Temporary Housing for Young Patients' Families

Ronald McDonald Houses are comfortable, supportive, temporary residences for families whose children are receiving medical treatment at a nearby hospital. Families are asked to donate a small fee, usually in the range of $5 to $25 a night. If they can't afford it, the stay is free. Guests can stay just one night or as long as several months—sometimes even a year or more, depending on the duration of medical treatment. Ronald McDonald Houses have opened in nearly every state. Florida has twelve, California nine, New York seven. Find locations at www.rmhc.org.

Discount Dental Plans

Joining a dental plan can cut costs by up to 50 percent or more, depending on the plan you choose, your geographical area, and the work being done. Dental plans are not insurance. Participants pay an annual fee of $100 to $150 and receive reduced-rate services from participating dentists. There are no monthly premiums, deductibles, co-pays, annual limits, or claim forms. Some plans cover cosmetic procedures and orthodontic work in addition to routine and surgical services. Compare discount plans offered for your zip code at www.dentalplans.com. Before you sign up, call the dentist you plan to use to verify his or her participation.

Half-Price Overseas Dental Work

Thanks to a large influx of patients seeking high-quality dental work at a lower cost, Hungary has become the dental capital of the world. Posh Journeys, a Reno-based travel operator, arranges treatment with an English-speaking dentist at a Hungarian hot-springs resort. Patients stay about 10 days—a week for the dental procedures and a few extra days to make sure all has gone well. Treatments cost about half as much as in the United States. Day trips to Budapest and Vienna are an added incentive. Find out more at www.poshjourneys.com, or call 775-852-5105.

Free Magazine from the NIH

The nation's leading medical research agency—the National Institutes of Health—has launched an attractive consumer magazine to publicize new research findings and other important health information. Published quarterly, the 32-page *NIH MedlinePlus Magazine* covers such topics as high blood pressure, seasonal allergies, and breast cancer therapy. Each issue features an in-depth interview with a celebrity or other individual who is coping with a serious health problem (Lance Armstrong was profiled in the premiere issue). To receive free printed copies by mail, fill out the subscription form at www.nlm.nih.gov/medlineplus/magazine.html. Issues can also be downloaded from the website.

More Free Health Information

One of the best sources of free health publications in the United States is the Federal Citizen Information Center. Some of its material is quite short, though still very useful. Free print publications that offer more depth include *Arthritis and Rheumatic Diseases; Eating*

TAKE CAUTION!

Beware of Modern-Day Snake Oil

It's not easy to ignore the hoopla around the latest miracle cures, wonder drugs, and newfangled gizmos that claim amazing health benefits. But are heavily hawked health-care products worth buying, or do they boost only corporate profits, not individual health? Quackwatch (www.quackwatch.com) and the National Council Against Health Fraud (www.ncahf.org) monitor the marketplace for you for free. Check their websites before you shell out big bucks.

Disorders; Handout on Health: Back Pain; How to Find Medical Information; Joint Replacement Surgery and You; Lupus; Osteoarthritis; Questions and Answers About Fibromyalgia; Rheumatoid Arthritis; and *Your Pharmacy Benefit: Make It Work for You!* To obtain a complete list of publications, go to the website www.pueblo.gsa.gov. You can order FCIC publications through the website or by calling toll-free 888-878-3256 (a $2 service fee is added to each telephone order, regardless of size; the service charge is waived for online orders.) You also can download FCIS publications at no cost.

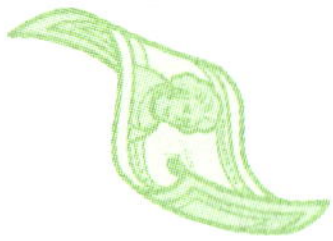

Free Clinical Trials

If you want free treatment for a physical or mental condition, consider participating in a clinical trial—a carefully designed research study that uses human volunteers. Interventional trials assess the safety and effectiveness of experimental treatments. Other trials are observational only—for example, comparing health in people who use vitamin E regularly with those who do not. Your physician may know about clinical trials for your condition, or you can look them up at www.clinicaltrials.gov. You can also find information on clinical trials—but only those that are industry-sponsored and actively recruiting participants—at www.centerwatch.org. Would-be participants should be aware that in some studies only the experimental group receives an active drug or experimental treatment; people in the control group may get a placebo—a "dummy" medication or treatment. Participants are never told which group they have been assigned to, as it might skew the results. If you have questions, ask the trial's clinical coordinator. Participants can withdraw at any time, but be sure to consult your physician before signing on.

Online Health Courses for Free

About U. offers dozens of free health-related courses. The 12 Weeks to Weight Loss class provides weekly nutrition assignments, workouts (including cardio, strength, and flexibility training), and logs to track progress. Heartburn 101 gives all the basics about chronic heartburn and acid reflux—both surgical and nonsurgical treatments are covered—in 10 daily, information-packed e-mails. Meditation 101 is a nine-day e-course to help integrate the health-giving technique into your life. Living a Low-Stress Lifestyle offers 10 weekly lessons on stress management with worksheets to see how you are doing. You'll find the full list of courses—and links to each—at u.about.com (click on "Health & Fitness").

Group Deductions in One Year to Save

Deductible medical and dental expenses include only what you paid out during the calendar year, regardless of when the services were provided. If you are about to reach the threshold for deductions (7.5 percent of adjusted gross income), or think you might do so in the following year, it is perfectly legitimate to shift appointments and payments from one year to the next. To make sure a payment falls in the tax year you intend it to, don't make payments around the end of the year. If you pay medical expenses by check, the day you mail or deliver the check generally is the date of payment. If you use a "pay-by-phone" or online account, the date is the one reported on the financial institution's statement showing when payment was made. If you charge expenses, they are deductible in the year the

Deducting Health Costs from Your Tax Bill

If your year was filled with horrendous medical bills, you may be pleasantly surprised at tax time. Granted, you can't deduct unreimbursed medical and dental payments unless the year's total exceeds 7.5 percent of your adjusted gross income. But deductible expenses add up—if you know what they are. Keeping good records is a must.

According to the IRS, you can deduct co-payments or other costs for prescription drugs, lab fees, prescription eyeglasses and contact lenses, laser eye surgery, hearing aids, false teeth, bandages, crutches, in vitro fertilization and other fertility procedures, vasectomies, guide dogs, smoking-cessation programs (but not nicotine gum or patches), and weight-loss programs for obesity or other doctor-diagnosed diseases.

Visits to doctors, dentists, chiropractors, psychiatrists, psychologists, acupuncturists, therapists, and Christian Science practitioners are covered—but not over-the-counter drugs, health-club dues, or most cosmetic surgery. (In the case of the latter, surgery to correct congenital abnormalities or after an accident or a mastectomy are among the exceptions.) Costs for health-related transportation, such as doctors' appointments and hospitals, are deductible, as are premiums for health insurance, accident insurance, and certain long-term care policies.

For more information, consult your tax professional or the IRS Web page on medical and dental deductions (www.irs.gov/publications/p502/index.html). During the tax season, live telephone assistance is available toll-free at 800-829-1040.

charge is made, not when you pay it. If you overlooked certain expenses that would have been deductible in an earlier year, you can file an amended income tax form for that year claiming the deduction using Form 1040X, Amended U.S. Individual Income Tax Return. In general, you can't file for more than three years back.

Medication Matters

Free Web Drug Reference

The PDR—*Physicians' Desk Reference*—is one of the most trusted and frequently consulted sources in any doctor's library. Use the free, consumer-friendly, online version (www.pdrhealth.com/drug_info) to look up the latest on the side effects, drug interactions, and other information on just about any drug. Prescription drugs, over-the-counter medications, herbal medicines, and nutritional supplements are all included.

Buy Discount Drugs Online

Though the process may seem complicated at first, it is actually surprisingly simple to buy prescription medications over the Internet. You can comparison-shop among both Web-based businesses, such as www.drugstore.com, and the online divisions of larger operations, such as www.costco.com and www.cvs.com. Generally, the larger the quantity purchased, the bigger the discount. Savings may top 40 percent on certain drugs. Be sure to check shipping costs before you finalize your purchase; pharmacies may waive them on orders that exceed a certain amount or if customers opt for standard delivery. To check the legitimacy of an Internet pharmacy, look for the Verified Internet Pharmacy Practice Sites (VIPPS) seal or certification by PharmacyChecker.com. All reputable sellers require a written prescription from a physician. Make sure that a pharmacist is available to answer questions and, if you expect your health insurer to pay for the medication, that the pharmacy accepts your plan.

Free Arthritis Drug Guide

Do you know how frequently you can safely take your preferred arthritis medication? Or which ones *don't* cause constipation or some

Q What are the benefits of ordering generic rather than brand-name medications?

A Buying generic instead of branded drugs can result in big savings. Generic drugs, which become available as patents expire on the branded versions, have the same active ingredients as their brand-name cousins, but they cost significantly less. At one online supplier, the generic blood-pressure drug quinapril costs 45 percent less than the brand-name product (Accupril). The branded antidepressant Paxil sells for triple the price of paroxetine, the generic form. Go for the generic even if your health insurer picks up your prescription drug costs; co-payments for branded drugs can be five times or more higher than co-payments for generics. Occasionally, as a drug comes off patent, an insurer may even waive the co-payment or offer some other incentive to encourage switching to the generic version.

other nasty side effect? The free Arthritis Foundation drug guide, prepared by top rheumatologists and updated annually, covers dosages, side effects, and other essential information. You can order the latest edition of the guide online at www.arthritis.org/conditions/drugguide, or call toll-free 800-568-4045 to place your order by phone.

Are You Eligible for Prescription Drug Assistance?

Many drug companies and other groups have patient assistance programs (PAPs), which provide certain medications at little or no cost to people without prescription drug coverage. Which companies offer what drugs to whom can get *very* complicated. To find programs you might be eligible for, consult the Partnership for Prescription Assistance (PPA), which serves as a clearinghouse, matching patients to programs through its website (www.pparx.org) or toll-free number, 888-477-2669. Most, but not all, PAPs have strict financial eligibility requirements. For example, your income must be less than 200 percent of the Federal Poverty Level to qualify for most of Pfizer's programs.

Free Drug Samples

Drug promotions come and go. You may find new offers at any time, especially if an expensive medication for a common health condition has just come on the market. If you're interested in trying new products, keep an eye out for print advertisements, and check manufacturers' websites (you'll find a full list at www.drugs.com/manufacturers.html). Over-the-counter samples may come in the mail, but prescription drugs require taking a prescription as well as the coupon or voucher to the pharmacy. The offers listed below were all valid as of mid-2006:

- To control attention-deficit/hyperactivity disorder (ADHD): coupon for free 30-day supply of Adderall XR; prescription required to pick up sample; see www.adderallxr.com/resource/adhd_coupon.asp.
- To promote cardiovascular and bone health: two free Nature's Bounty Omega-3 fish oil softgels; the site is www.naturesbounty.com/fishoil/fishoil.aspx.
- For pain relief: two free half-ounce samples of Sore-No-More; visit www.sorenomore.com/sample.html or call toll-free 800-842-6622.

Editor's Choice

Split Pills for Large Savings

You might think that a high-dose pill would cost more than a lower dose of the same medication. But a pill's ingredients make up such a small fraction of the cost that most pills are priced pretty much the same regardless of dose. Splitting pills seems such an easy way to cut medication costs that occasionally health insurers have required patients to buy certain drugs in higher dosages and cut them in half. However, pill splitting must be done wisely. Never split a medication without asking your doctor whether doing so is safe. If your doctor okays the split, cut tablets with an official pill splitter, available at most drugstores.

Doing Without Drugs

Before you rush off to fill a new prescription or to alleviate a chronic condition with over-the-counter drugs, ask your doctor whether you should first try lifestyle changes.

If you can do without the medication, so much the better for your wallet—and you'll be spared any side effects the medication might cause.

A word of caution: If you already take medications, do not stop them on your own. Consult your physician, set up a plan for trying out lifestyle changes that might help your condition, and get appropriate follow-up care to see whether the condition has improved.

To Cut High Cholesterol...

- Eat less saturated fat (major culprits include red meat and whole-milk products) and trans fats (found in crackers, candies, cookies, snack foods, fried foods, and baked goods). Consult food labels before buying—saturated and trans fats must now be listed.
- Eat nuts, garlic, soy, and lentils and beans.
- Lose weight, exercise, and if you smoke, stop.

To Lower Blood Pressure ...

- If you're overweight, shed the excess pounds. For every two pounds of weight lost, blood pressure falls one point.
- Follow the DASH (Dietary Approaches to Stop Hypertension) diet, which emphasizes fruits, vegetables, whole grains, and low-fat dairy products. For details, go to www.nhlbi.nih.gov/health/public/heart/hbp/dash.
- Cut your salt intake.

To Relieve Insomnia ...

- Reduce your intake of alcohol and caffeine, even early in the day.
- Get more exercise.
- Avoid large meals late in the day.
- Take a warm or hot bath at night.
- Go to bed at about the same time every night, get up at the same time, and don't take naps.
- Practice meditation or another relaxation technique regularly.

- For heartburn prevention: free Maximum Strength Pepcid AC tablet; go to www.pepcidac.com (click on "Special Offers").
- Sleep aid: four free Lunesta tablets to help you sleep better, with a prescription from your doctor and a voucher you can print out at www.lunesta.com.

Pfizer Pfriends Discounts

One prescription drug assistance program without financial eligibility requirements is Pfizer Pfriends, which offers discounts on more than 80 medicines purchased at retail pharmacies to anyone without prescription coverage regardless of income. (Applicants must be legal

U.S. residents and over 18 years of age.) The size of the discount depends on family income and is best for lower-income families. It is relatively small (an average of 15 percent) for families earning more than $45,000 a year, but it beats paying full price. For more on the program visit www.pfizerhelpfulanswers.com/pfizerpfriends.aspx.

Emergency Help

Free Vital Information Supplies

A nationwide free program run by the nonprofit organization Vial of Life helps emergency personnel locate personal health information they need when they arrive at a home. The recommended place to put information on medications, emergency contacts, and such is on the refrigerator door, using a form supplied by Vial of Life. Some people use official Vial of Life plastic-bag containers for the forms (call your local hospital or fire department to see who distributes them in your area). Or download forms and information for making your own container at www.vialoflife.com/vial_works.html; you can also print out a decal for your front door that tells responders where to look for the information. Make sure that every member of your extended family has a system like this to help emergency personnel help you. It can save a loved one's life.

Poison Information Free

Call the National Poison Control Center hotline toll-free at 800-222-1222 with any poison-related question, at any time of the day or night. If you call about a possible poisoning, be prepared to tell the operator the victim's age, weight, existing health conditions, type of substance, mode of contact (swallowed, inhaled, splashed into the eyes, and so on), and whether the person has vomited; all calls are confidential. Although young children are at greatest risk for accidental poisoning—top culprits are cosmetics and other personal-care products, household cleansers, and analgesics—poisoning problems can occur at any age. Anyone might take the wrong medication in the middle of the night; adolescents may be poisoned by alcohol or drugs; wild-food foragers may try toxic mushrooms or other plants. Learn how to prevent poisoning at the National Poison Prevention Week Council website (www.poisonprevention.org/faq.htm).

Lifesaving Wallet Cards

Get these free pocket-sized lifesavers for every member of your family. If you print them out yourself, you may want to cover them with clear packing tape or have them laminated at a copy shop or printer. Show cards with medication information to your doctor or pharmacist before starting a new drug.

Although not a wallet card, the handy stroke information brochure offered free by the National Institute of Neurological Disorders and Stroke can also be a lifesaver. *Know Stroke. Know the Signs. Act in Time.* covers the causes, risk factors, warning signs, and treatment of stroke. Order it at https:// ice.iqsolutions .com/ninds/strokepubs.asp. You can also get a free bookmark listing stroke risk factors and symptoms.

CARD NAME	DESCRIPTION	AVAILABILITY
Act in Time to Heart Attack Signs	What to look for and what to do.	Call 301-592-8573 or visit www.nhlbi.nih.gov/health/public/heart/mi/wallet.htm.
Diabetes Check-up Wallet Card	Keep track of test results and other personal information	Print out the card at www.diabetes.com/diabetes_management.html.
Medical ID Alert Wallet Card		Print it out at www.medids.com/free-id.php
Mind Your Meds Wallet Card	Record the names and dosages of your drugs and supplements	Print out the card at www.condell.org/health-information/medication.php.
My Blood Pressure Wallet Card	A record of blood pressure readings, medications, and such	Call 301-592-8573 or visit www.nhlbi.nih.gov/ health/public/heart/hbp/hbpwallet.htm.

Free Organizing Tool for the Sick

Lotsa Helping Hands provides a free, easy-to-use online system to organize volunteer help after a heart attack, broken leg, or some other crisis. You choose one or more coordinators from among your friends, relatives, neighbors, and colleagues. After the coordinators register, they set up a private group calendar to arrange help with food shopping, meal preparation, child care, transportation, and other tasks. The system automatically sends out e-mail messages about the needs listed by the coordinators. Group members volunteer for the tasks and activities they want to be involved in and receive automatic confirmations and reminders of their commitments. Set up the calendar at www.lotsahelpinghands.com.

Free Nurse Hotlines

In a life-threatening emergency, call 911 or get to a hospital emergency room right away. But in a less serious situation—say, a tick bite, splinter, or rash—calling your doctor's office or a nurse hotline may be all that's needed, and it may spare you a doctor or hospital visit, and the bills that follow. Staff members at hotlines are trained to differentiate between questions they can answer safely and those that require a physician to see the patient. Examples of toll-free local hotlines include Florida's Englewood Community Hospital (888-685-1598), Kingwood Medical Center in Texas (800-258-5064), and Holzer Medical Center, which services southeastern Ohio, West Virginia, and Kentucky (800-462-5255 in Ohio and West Virginia; 740-446-5000 elsewhere). Call your health insurer, health department, or nearby hospitals to find out about the availability of free nurse-staffed hotlines. Health plans—among them Aetna, Blue Cross, and Melaleuca—often offer free hotlines, and the Yale-New Haven Hospital Nurse Advice Line, toll-free 877-688-1101, will answer questions from anywhere in the country. Keep your hotline information near your phones and in your wallet or purse.

EDITOR'S CHOICE

No-Cost/Low-Cost Help from Hospital Social Workers

Hospital social workers are a little-known fount of wisdom on free or low-cost community services. Inpatients or their families can ask them about such topics as crisis counseling, local or other rehab facilities, substance abuse counseling, clergy resources, eldercare attorney referrals, and Medicare/Medicaid restrictions. Ask your nurse case manager to put you in touch with a social worker. For more about these invaluable professionals and the work they do, see page 350.

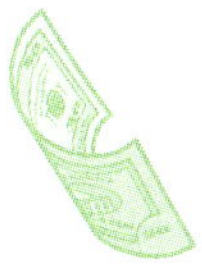

HOSPITAL HELP

Hospital Freebies for the Community

Many hospitals offer free cholesterol tests, skin cancer screenings, wellness seminars, and other free or low-cost programs and services at their main and satellite locations. Although some events may be restricted to people who have joined a particular program (programs for seniors are especially widespread), most are open to all. Call area hospitals to learn about community health events, or look up their calendars online. Check the MedlinePlus hospital directory (apps.nlm.nih.gov/medlineplus/directories) for contact information, directions, and websites for hospitals throughout the United States.

Check and Double-Check Hospital Bills

Nearly all hospital bills contain errors, usually in the hospital's favor. And they are often for substantial amounts, giving, for example, the full "list price" of a procedure rather than the lower price negotiated by your insurer or Medicare. The most common mistakes are charges for services a patient never received (one heart patient was charged for use of the delivery room) and double billing for the same item. Hospital patients should ask the billing office for an itemized printout of charges on a daily basis, so that questionable items can be challenged right away. Check over the final bill when you are discharged, and compare it with statements from your health insurer as they arrive by mail.

Keep a Record of Your Hospital Treatments

While in the hospital, keep a notebook beside your bed, and make a brief written record whenever you are examined or treated. If you aren't able to do it yourself, ask a friend or relative—even a member of the hospital staff—to do the record-keeping. Your "diary" will help enormously when it comes time to check your bill and will usually save you lots of money.

Surgery Abroad at 75% Off

Tummy tucks in Thailand? Gastric bypass in Argentina? A growing number of Americans are traveling abroad to take advantage of significantly lower surgery costs. Some of these patients have no health insurance. Others want procedures that are not covered by insurance, such as hair implants, cosmetic surgery, or corrective eye surgery.

Facilities that attract patients from abroad have internationally trained physicians and state-of-the-art technology. For example, Bumrungrad Hospital in Bangkok, Thailand, treats more than 350,000 foreign patients a year. Treatments there cost a quarter or less than they would in the States. And post-surgery patients may opt for a relaxing, recuperative vacation on the beach.

Travel agencies or tour operators make the arrangements, but prospective clients should research *everything* thoroughly. Find out about down payments, physician training, possible post-surgery complications, mortality rates, and other potential problems. Here are four leading "medical tourism" service agencies (telephone numbers are toll-free):

- Medretreat sends patients to Brazil, South Africa, Turkey, and other countries. Call 877-876-3373 or visit www.medretreat.com.
- Planet Hospital works with hospitals in Belgium, Costa Rica, India, and other countries. Call 800-243-0172 or go to www.planethospital.com.
- Plenitas specializes in medical travel to Argentina. Call 800-761-5795 or check out www.plenitas.com.
- VisionQuest International arranges surgery in Thailand. Call 866-365-6900 or go to www.visionquestintl.com

Help for Chronic Conditions

Free Magazine for Stroke Survivors

Stroke survivors have a slow road to recovery—and a very useful free magazine to help them along. *Stroke Connection* is the 36-page bimonthly publication of the American Stroke Association. Offering information and inspiration for stroke survivors and their loved ones, it features new treatment options, assistive aids, useful tips for daily living, and real people's experiences with strokes and their aftermath. A recent issue included caregiving advice, guidelines for preventing another stroke, new directions in rehabilitation, and recently approved devices for dealing with foot drop. For a free mail subscription, call toll-free 888-478-7653, and ask for the Stroke Family Warmline, or fill out the online form at www.strokeassociation.org/strokeconnection.

Low-Cost Arthritis Aquatics

The Arthritis Foundation runs a gentle, low-cost, warm-water exercise program that improves functional ability and range of motion. Programs are run in the Greater Chicago area, San Diego, Tulsa, and many other locations. Find out whether one is offered in your region by calling toll-free 800-283-7800, or enter your zip code at www.arthritis.org and click on "Programs and Events." The foundation may offer other appealing free or low-cost programs in your area, such as support groups and tai chi classes.

Free Diabetes Library Box

The National Institute of Diabetes and Digestive and Kidney Diseases publishes a set of 10 brochures called the Diabetes Library Box, which covers such topics as diabetes medications, eating and diabetes, and care of the feet, heart, eyes, kidneys and other parts of the body that can be affected by the disease. To order a Diabetes Library Box, go to the NIDDK website at catalog.niddk.nih.gov and click on "Diabetes Materials." A single copy is free; each additional set costs $10.

Free Info to Help Kids with Diabetes

The American Diabetes Association's cleverly designed Wizdom kit makes juvenile diabetes a little less daunting. The free kit contains

Q Are there resources online that can answer my questions about pain management?

A Which pain medications won't make you sleepy during the day? How can you relieve toothache—fast? What can you do about shoulder pain? An army of medical professionals, including pain doctors, pharmacists, and anesthesiologists, await your questions at the "Ask the Pain Doctor" section of www.pain.com. Send in your questions by e-mail, or look up archived responses to the questions of fellow sufferers. Related websites give research news and help you find a local pain clinic or specialist.

Free Disease-Help Organizations

Are you suffering from arthritis? Depression? Diabetes? Hereditary hemorrhagic telangiectasia? Nearly every health condition, physical or mental, has at least one organization devoted to it. Although the missions of such groups vary, most provide free online information and inexpensive or free print publications on diagnosis, treatment, and current research. Some also offer information-sharing message boards for people affected by the disease.

The National Library of Medicine has compiled a comprehensive listing of organizations with toll-free phone services. The database, which can be found at the website healthhotlines.nlm.nih.gov, provides phone numbers, websites, and other contact information for hundreds of groups. Major disease-help organizations that you may find particularly useful include the ones listed below.

NAME	PHONE NUMBER	WEB ADDRESS
American Chronic Pain Association	800-533-3231	www.theacpf.org
American Diabetes Association	800-DIABETES (342-2383)	www.diabetes.org
American Heart Association	800-242-8721	www.americanheart.org
American Lung Association	800-548-8252	www.lungusa.org
Arthritis Foundation	800-283-7800	www.arthritis.org
Asthma and Allergy Foundation of America	800-7-ASTHMA (727-8462)	www.aafa.org
Food Allergy and Anaphylaxis Network	800-929-4040	www.foodallergy.org
American Cancer Society's National Cancer Information Center	800-ACS-2345 (227-2345)	www.cancer.org
National Eating Disorders Association	800-931-2237	www.nationaleatingdisorders.org
National Headache Foundation	800-843-2256	www.headaches.org
Thyroid Foundation of America, Inc.	800-832-8321	www.allthyroid.org
Us TOO International, Inc (prostate cancer)	800-80-US-TOO (808-7866)	www.ustoo.org

one book for kids and one for parents—each filled with information on managing this chronic disease. To order the box, go to www.diabetes.org/for-parents-and-kids/wizdom-kit-disclaimer.jsp. The organization also offers a free e-mail newsletter for parents.

Free Psoriasis DVD

My Skin's on Fire is a documentary film that chronicles the lives of people with psoriasis, a chronic, noncontagious skin disease that affects more than five million people in the United States. Order the free DVD at the website https://www.beyondpsoriasis.com/about_skin_on_fire_film.jsp.

Free Headache Diary

Headaches have many triggers—among them, aged cheeses, chocolate, onions, eyestrain, fatigue, and stress. Doctors encourage people who suffer from frequent headaches to record when they occur in a headache diary so they can identify personal triggers. Download the monthly diary form at www.houstonheadacheclinic.com/diary.html.

CANCER CONNECTIONS

Free Breast Exam Shower Card

The Susan G. Komen Breast Cancer Foundation recommends that women begin performing breast self-exams monthly by age 20. The foundation offers a free instruction card to keep in your shower as a reminder of the proper technique. Order at www.komen.org/bci/shower-card.asp?nodeId=458.

Talk to a Fellow Patient

If you have been diagnosed with cancer and would like to be in contact with someone who has lived with your kind of condition, call the R. A. Bloch Cancer Foundation, Inc., toll-free at 800-433–0464, or go to its website (www.blochcancer.org) and click on the "Info for Patients" link. The service is free. The organization, established by a co-founder of H&R Block, also offers three free books—*Fighting Cancer*, *Guide for Cancer Supporters*, and *Cancer … There's Hope*. Call the toll-free number to order.

Gilda's Clubs for Cancer Patients

No one should face cancer alone. Gilda's Clubs—named for Gilda Radner, the *Saturday Night Live* comedian who experienced a tremendous outpouring of support after her ovarian cancer diagnosis—are homey meeting places for men, women, and children living with cancer and their loved ones. The clubs run networking and support groups, lectures, workshops, and social events. Membership and events are free. Seattle members, for example, can participate in

Q What options are there for cancer patients seeking low-cost outpatient housing?

A Hope Lodge offers free temporary housing to outpatient cancer patients and their companions. About two dozen lodges have opened in the East and Midwest, including facilities in Worcester, Massachusetts; Nashville, Tennessee (Vanderbilt University); and Rochester, Minnesota (Mayo Clinic). Hope Lodges have kitchen facilities and other amenities, and provide transportation to and from the cancer centers. Referrals and support services are also offered. Most houses have a three-day minimum stay. Find out specific details by calling the American Cancer Society toll-free at 800-227-2345, or enter "Hope Lodge" in the search field at www.cancer.org.

a half-marathon training program, family art therapy, Chinese cooking lessons, yoga sessions, meditation workshops, several book clubs, a young adult networking group, a "football 101" clinic with a Seattle Seahawks player, and many other activities, or they can go to the clubhouse just to talk or relax. There are about 20 Gilda's Clubs across the country, including Chicago, Detroit, Fort Lauderdale, Milwaukee, and New York City (which has two). The map at www.gildasclub.org/wheretofindus shows all locations.

Free "Looking Better" Help for Chemo Patients

Any female cancer patient who is undergoing radiation or chemotherapy can join the free "Look Good … Feel Better" program, which provides videos, pamphlets, and classes focusing on makeup, nails, and hair. Women who attend a class get a free makeup kit with products from leading cosmetics companies that donate more than a million items every year. For more information, call the "Look Good … Feel Better" toll-free number (800-395-5665) or your local American Cancer Society office, or check the website www.lookgoodfeelbetter.org. Men with cancer can use the same channels to get the free *Look Good … Feel Better for Men* self-help brochure. And call the same toll-free number for details on the special teen cancer program; teenage patients can also look up information on appearance, peer pressure, and adolescence-related issues at www.2bme.org.

Free Prostate Cancer Support

Sponsored by the American Cancer Society, the Man to Man program provides information and support to men with prostate cancer and their loved ones. Local programs vary but may include monthly

EDITOR'S CHOICE No-Cost Legal Advice for Cancer Patients

Cancer patients may experience difficulties with insurance coverage, employment discrimination, government benefits, guardianship and custody problems, and other issues that can have a legal dimension. The Cancer Legal Resource Center, based at the Loyola Law School in Los Angeles, provides free telephone counseling, cancer rights workshops, and, if necessary, volunteer attorneys for people with any kind of cancer. About a third of the calls concern insurance. For more information about the center's services and workshop schedule, call toll-free 866-843-2572 between 9 a.m. and 5 p.m. Pacific time. You can also write to the Cancer Legal Resource Center, 919 Albany Street, Los Angeles, California 90019. There are no financial eligibility requirements for the center's services.

meetings, one-on-one visits, and quarterly newsletters. Wives or partners sometimes attend meetings, or participate in a separate group program called Side by Side. For more information, contact your local American Cancer Society or call the national toll-free helpline (800-227-2345). Another helpful resource is the Prostate Cancer Foundation, which publishes a free monthly e-mail newsletter called *Newspulse*. Go to www.prostatecancerfoundation.org and click on "Publications" to subscribe.

Eyes and Ears

Contact Lenses for Up to Half Off

Depending on the brand, you can save as much as 50 percent or more by getting contact lenses through the mail. You'll receive precisely the same product you get from your current source—only for less money because of the high sales volume. The biggest supplier is 1-800-Contacts, which sells about two tons of lenses every day. Call its toll-free number or consult online at www.1800contacts.com. Other popular online sellers include Vision Direct (call toll-free 800-847-4663 or go to www.visiondirect.com) and Lens.com (toll-free 800-536-7266 or www.lens.com). All contact lens orders require a valid, detailed prescription. Don't accept substitutes for the contacts you are currently wearing unless your eye-care practitioner approves. Consult your practitioner regularly to make sure your eyes are in good health and your vision has not changed.

No-Cost Hearing Evaluation for Costco Members

Costco offers members a free, no-obligation hearing evaluation performed by a licensed hearing-aid dispenser. Current hearing-aid wearers are invited to schedule a free hearing-aid checkup that includes a cleaning and a new battery. Call toll-free 800-774-2678 for an appointment at more than 100 locations. The centers will only test people over age 18.

Free Eye Exams for Infants

InfantSEE provides a free, comprehensive eye assessment for infants up to 12 months old. The honorary chair is former President Jimmy Carter, who has two grandchildren with amblyopia (lazy eye). One of them wasn't diagnosed until well into grade school, when classroom difficulties made the condition disturbingly apparent. Early diagnosis is the best, which is why more than 7000 optometrists have volunteered for the nationwide program. Find one in your area at www.infantsee.org.

EDITOR'S CHOICE

Free Online Hearing Test

Anyone can try the free hearing test at www.freehearingtest.com. The test, which involves adjusting the volume on your computer and then listening for six differently pitched tones, is intended to help people figure out whether they should consult a hearing professional—not to provide an official diagnosis. The website also gives valuable information, including an animation sequence, on how hearing works.

PREVENTION—THE BEST DEFENSE

No-Cost Walking Program

Brisk walking makes people look and feel better—and saves money too. According to a survey published in *The Physician and Sportsmedicine*, brisk walking or other physical activity performed for at least 30 minutes three or more times a week saves hundreds of dollars a year in doctors' bills and other health-care costs. To turn walking into a regular habit, participate in About.com's free, 10-week walking program, available online at walking.about.com/od/walkoflife. The website provides daily walking assignments (except for one rest day each week), motivational tips, diet and exercise advice, even recipes. Beginning and advanced walkers receive different assignments. If you prefer, you can sign up to have the material e-mailed to you instead of having to remember to go to the website every day.

Low-Cost Virtual Trainer

A personal trainer can help you boost fitness faster, but an hour-long session can cost up to $100 or more. Some gyms let people double up and split the fee. To save even more, consider using an online training program, such as those offered at www.myexerciseplan.com or www.efitness.com. With virtual trainers, you pay to use the service for a specified time period (myexerciseplan.com costs about $40 for the first six months). At the beginning of a typical program, you decide on a goal (say, weight loss or endurance), complete a health assessment, and consult with a trainer over the phone. Then you start a personalized exercise program involving workout reminders, training logs, motivating messages, nutritional advice, exercise demonstrations, and online consultations. Online programs can work especially well for road warriors who aren't home enough to benefit from a real-life trainer, or for well-motivated people who don't like someone watching over them during workouts.

Free "Quitmeter" Programs

Kicking the smoking habit is deadly serious—but tracking your progress with a quitmeter can make the journey fun.

- Quit Keeper is a free PC program from Dedicated Designs, a Web design firm. It allows you to track how long you have been smoke-free, how many cigarettes you have not smoked, and how much money (and how much of your life) you have saved by not smoking. Quit Keeper has a hotkey to send your quitting data to other people. Download the program at www.dedicateddesigns.com/qk/.
- Quitometer, a free Mac program from SV Macintosh Consulting, automatically calculates the number of minutes, hours, days, weeks, months, and years since you stopped smoking. It also keeps a record of all the money you have saved. Download it at www.svmac.com/pages/sw.html#qt2.

A great motivational tool, a quitmeter lets you see how far you have come. Why not use one to spur yourself on?

Detailed Nutritional Data at No Cost

Are you staying up at night because of hidden caffeine in your food or drink? Do you want to boost your intake of cancer-fighting lycopene, or cut blood cholesterol levels by eating more fiber? A free USDA database gives the nutritional composition of hundreds of prepared and raw foods; go to www.nal.usda.gov/fnic/foodcomp/search. Click on "Nutrient Lists" to find foods that have large amounts of a particular nutrient. Tomato paste is tops for lycopene. Canned clams offer the most vitamin B_{12}. Amazingly, some enriched cereals have even more calcium than milk does—and that's *before* you mix them with milk.

Cutting the Cost of Weight Watchers

Excess weight means higher medical costs because of the increased risk of heart disease, diabetes, and other chronic ailments. No one says that losing weight is easy, but many people find that joining a support program speeds the process. The Weight Watchers program is highly rated and frequently offers special money-saving promotions, such as waiving the registration fee or allowing overweight

EDITOR'S CHOICE Free Pedometer

Walking 10,000 steps a day is a popular goal these days—and deservedly so. Especially if walks are brisk (or stairs are involved), all that movement will boost health. Recording the number of steps you take every day can turn plain old walking into a delightfully motivating game. Most people use pedometers to do the counting. As part of the "My Heart Now" program, pharmaceuticals giant Pfizer is giving away a free pedometer to anyone who participates in a survey on heart health. Answer its questions at www.myheartnow.com/content/index.jsp—then start your walking program even before your pedometer arrives.

kids to attend weekly meetings for free. Members can also cut costs by paying for the meetings in advance. One further incentive: People who reach their goal weight and stay there become lifetime members and get free maintenance support. To find out about current promotions, call toll-free 800-651-6000, or visit the Weight Watchers website www.weightwatchers.com. For more on Weight Watchers and how to attend a free introductory meeting, see page 81.

Reduced-Cost Gym Membership

If you live near a hotel or resort, call the manager and ask whether you can buy an inexpensive "membership" that allows you access to the swimming pool, sauna, fitness center, or tennis courts. Unless business is truly booming, resorts and hotels are often happy to strike such deals. While traveling, find out whether the places where you are staying offer free use of an on- or off-premises gym.

LOOK IT UP ONLINE

Free Info from the Merck Manual

Instead of buying the 1,900-page print edition of the *Merck Manual of Medical Information, Second Home Edition*, you can consult this comprehensive reference work online—for free. Both the print and Web versions cover medical conditions, diagnoses, and treatments, but the one on the Internet boasts audio, video, animations, and photos the print edition doesn't have. The online edition won the Webby Award (the "Oscar of the Internet") as the best health website of 2005. Check it out at www.merck.com/mmhe/index.html.

Store Your Health Records Online Free

Patients today can't assume that their physicians communicate with one another or that they know—or check—their patients' full medical histories. Keeping your own health records is key to preventing unnecessary medical tests, dangerous drug interactions, and other problems. Now you can compile and store health records on the Web for free. Medem, a leading physician-patient communications network, provides one of the most widely used record-storage services. Its iHealth Record allows you to store insurance information as well as medical records. Your records are kept secure and confidential, but you can call them up anywhere in the world, and grant access to a family member or physician. Sign up at the website www.ihealthrecord.org, or check with your health insurer to see whether it offers a similar free service. It can be a true lifesaver for people who have a medical emergency away from home.

Free Online Health Calculators

What is your heart disease risk? How much fat should you eat? What is your BMI (body mass index)? The University of Maryland Medical Center offers 24 free, online calculators to evaluate your health—and to learn how to improve it too. To access the calculators, go to www.umm.edu/healthcalculators.

"Fab Four" Free Government Websites

Don't get caught up in Internet "information" that is outdated, misleading, or just plain wrong. Find facts fast at the four very comprehensive websites run by federal health agencies and departments.

AGENCY	DESCRIPTION	WEB ADDRESS
Centers for Disease Control and Prevention	Information on infectious diseases—including bird flu and West Nile virus—and other current health threats.	www.cdc.gov
Healthfinder	A drug database, a chronic disease library, directories of organizations and providers, dozens of online checkups, and 12 weekly newsletters.	www.healthfinder.gov
MedlinePlus	A medical encyclopedia and dictionary, interactive tutorials, videos of surgical procedures, news highlights, and resource lists.	www.nlm.nih.gov/medlineplus
PubMed	A medical research database that provides free abstracts (summaries) of articles in professional journals. Sometimes the full studies are free, or public libraries may be able to retrieve them from subscription-only databases.	www.ncbi.nih.gov/entrez/query.fcgi

Free Help for Quitting Smoking

There is certainly no shortage of organizations that can help you stop smoking for free.

- The American Lung Association runs Freedom From Smoking Online, a program that helps formulate a quitting plan, and provides strategies for maintaining a smoke-free life. Smokers decide when to quit and use the message boards to say a special good-bye to their cigarettes. Enroll in the program at www.ffsonline.org or call toll-free 800-586-4872.
- Smokefree.gov, a program created by the Tobacco Control Research Branch of the National Cancer Institute in collaboration with the CDC and the American Cancer Society, offers several smoking-cessation tools. Call its "quitline" (877-448-7848) to order printed information, receive referrals to other resources, and get real support from a real person. Go to www.smokefree.gov/guide to download the quitting guide; you can order a free print copy there, too. If you do instant messaging, use the National Cancer Institute's live-chat service to receive information and advice about quitting; click on "Instant Messaging" at www.smokefree.gov.
- The American Cancer Society offers phone counseling (800-227-2345) and other resources. One innovative feature is an e-card that you send to friends and relatives to announce your quit day. The ACS's website is www.cancer.org.

No-Cost Calculator of Mercury Levels

Mercury-contaminated fish can be a serious health threat, especially to children and pregnant women. Use the National Resource Defense Council online calculator, (www.nrdc.org/health/effects/mercury/index.asp) to calculate the likely amount of mercury in your blood. You'll also learn what to do if you have too much, and which kinds of fish pose the greatest risk. The NRDC also has an online guide to home water filters; find out which type best suits your needs at www.nrdc.org/water/drinking/gfilters.asp.

Estimate Your Longevity Free

Estimate how long you will live by answering questions on health habits, seat belt use, and other topics. Accompanied by animated graphics and sound, the Longevity Game is fun to play, but its message is an important one. The game, produced by the Northwestern Mutual Financial Network, a financial and insurance group, makes it very clear how changes in lifestyle can affect longevity. Play the game at www.nmfn.com/tn/learnctr--lifeevents--longevity.

CHAPTER 6

economical entertainment

Who says you can't be frugal and also keep up with the latest movies, books, and Broadway shows? Follow these hints to stretch your "fun" dollars to the max!

ONE OF THE GREAT THINGS about entertainment is that it's absolutely everywhere. It's also totally subjective: One person can have as much fun watching a bird build a nest in his backyard as someone sitting in an expensive seat, center orchestra, at a big, splashy Broadway musical.

And the truth of the matter is that you can have that night on the town without spending an arm and a leg. All it takes is knowing where to find the best deals, a little research, flexibility, and an adventurous spirit—including the willingness to take a chance on something new or unexpected.

If you have a computer and Internet access, you never have to leave home or pay an extra penny for endless free entertainment. The Internet is not only the greatest source of free information since the establishment of the first public library—it's also a bottomless source of free entertainment right at your fingertips! Listen to music; watch videos (long and short on every conceivable subject); read books and periodicals; play games; watch movies, movie trailers, television shows, and clips; look at photographs; take virtual museum tours—it's impossible to list all the categories of entertainment that are available on the World Wide Web.

Check the websites of your favorite restaurants for discount coupons and other money-saving offers. Check other sites to find

By the numbers

7,767

Number of times (as of September 12, 2006) that *The Phantom of the Opera* has been performed on Broadway. The show now holds the record for Broadway's longest-running show; the previous record holder, *Cats,* was performed 7,485 times.

bargains on entertainment offerings of all kinds, from Broadway plays to ballet. If you're not Internet-savvy but have access to a kid who is at least ten years old, he or she can probably teach you what you need to know. And surfing the Internet works much better and faster with a cable or DSL connection than with dial-up, but dial-up is doable. If you don't have a computer or Internet connection at home, go to your local public library, which does.

Your local newspaper and community access television channel list many of the events that happen daily in your town—lots of them free, especially if you live near a college or university or in a resort area. Check out the yard sales and flea markets in your paper's classified ads. Not only are they fun in and of themselves, especially for inveterate browsers, but you can also find very inexpensive used and nearly new DVDs, videos, CDs, audiocassettes, books, boom boxes, television sets, games, sports equipment, and much, much more.

Does the park around the corner have a band shell? Then it's likely that a local group provides free summer concerts. Bookstores feature no-cost lectures and book signings by renowned authors. Galleries charge you nothing to look. Reacquaint yourself with your public library, which, if it's like most, offers many more products, services, and events than it did a couple of decades ago.

If you use such resources, plus your brain and a little imagination, you'll never run out of free or inexpensive ways to entertain yourself and your family indoors and out, day or night. Have a ball!

Movie Bargains

See Films for Free

Movie tickets cost a bundle, but there are several ways to get free passes to special, usually advance, screenings to big Hollywood movies. The four movie websites www.freemoviescreenings.net, www.iscreenings.com, www.campuscircle.net/filmscreenings, and www.wildaboutmovies.com provide information about and access to major studio screenings across the country. You either enter lotteries to win tickets, print out passes online, or find store locations to pick up free tickets. Most sites feature movie reviews and other movie-related info. Wild About Movies has celebrity interviews,

Sit Among the Stars for Free

Have you ever dreamed of sitting in the audience at the Golden Globes, the Emmys, the Grammys, or any number of other glamorous, celebrity-filled awards shows and events? Most "civilians" can't even buy tickets to these televised industry shows, which cost hundreds of dollars if they are even open to the public. But as a "seat filler" you can attend them for free and rub elbows (literally) with the biggest stars in the entertainment world. Seat fillers ensure that there are no empty spots when the camera pans the audience; when Gwyneth Paltrow gets up to powder her nose or present an award, a seat filler moves in to take her place. The downside is that when she gets back, the seat filler gets up. Still, it's an adventure and an insider encounter with an exciting, star-studded world. For the scoop on the ups and downs of seat filling, go to www.seeing-stars.com/showbiz/seatfillers.shtml. To try for one of these coveted spots, sign up at seatfiller.com or at www.audiencesunlimited.com/seatfillers.htm. To be considered, you'll probably be asked to supply a photograph for its files. Events are mostly in Los Angeles, with a few in Las Vegas and New York. A lot of people are eager to play this game of celebrity musical chairs, but why shouldn't you be one of the lucky ones? What a story to tell your colleagues around the water cooler on Monday morning!

movie news, contests to win free DVDs, and video trailers for every current and many future releases. The blog site Movie Lovers (fxblader.wordpress.com) functions as a clearinghouse for numerous free movie sites and offers. You have to check these sites often, a ticket doesn't guarantee seating (the screenings are intentionally overbooked to assure a full audience), and you usually have to stand in a long line. But, hey—it's free! Be sure to arrive early.

No-Cost Summer (Movie) Camp for Everyone!

Everybody loves the movies, and there's nothing like experiencing them in a theater on a big screen, the way they're intended to be seen. Some kids don't get the chance that often, but AMC Summer MovieCamp is a super opportunity for youngsters and adults alike to enjoy free G- and PG-rated Hollywood movies on the big screen every Wednesday morning at participating AMC/Loews theaters. The perfect way to spend a rainy morning (or even a sunny one, for movie lovers), AMC Summer MovieCamp simulates a fun-filled, summer camp-like atmosphere in theaters. Check the AMC Theatres website (www.amctheatres.com) for information on current summer MovieCamp dates and to find a location near you.

Get a Free Video Rental on Your Birthday

Some locally owned video stores give you a free rental on your birthday if you're a member. It's not worth buying a membership for a free movie once a year if you aren't going to take advantage of the discount prices on rentals for members. But if you rent movies often, you might as well get a freebie with your membership. Ask about it at your neighborhood video emporium.

More Free Summer Movies for Kids and Parents

At selected Clearview Cinemas theaters in New York, New Jersey, and Pennsylvania, you and your children can enjoy a movie a week for eight weeks with Clearview's Kid's Club free summer movie series. The schedule usually starts in July, and movies are shown on Thursday mornings at 10:30. In 2006 Kid's Club screened such acclaimed family films as *Curious George*, *Nanny McPhee*, *Madagascar*, and *Wallace & Gromit in The Curse of the Were-Rabbit*. Start checking www.clearviewcinemas.com in June for information.

Free Classic Movies Under the Stars

It's one of New York City's most popular summer pastimes, and it's free! At the HBO Bryant Park Summer Film Festival (on Avenue of the Americas between 43rd and 44th Streets, behind the main branch of the New York Public Library), movie lovers watch classic films (think *To Have and Have Not*, *The Birds*, *High Noon*) on a large screen at dusk on Monday nights from June through August. Access to the grass to put down your blanket and set out your picnic begins at 5 p.m., but it's probably best to line up by 4:30 because the relatively small park fills up pretty fast. The rain date for all shows is Tuesday. For more information and the schedule, call 212-512-5700 or check www.bryantpark.org and click the "Calendar" link.

Free Film Oldies Downloads

Entertainment Magazine (emol.org) is a cool website that has extensive entertainment news in all categories and a few great freebies, including free legal movie downloads. As of mid-2006 the site offered about a hundred films, all in the public domain, mostly from the 1930s, '40s, and '50s, with a few from the '60s. Some of the movies are obscure; others are well-known classics. Featured categories include action/adventure, comedy, drama, family, horror and sci-fi, international, newsreels, and westerns. The films open quickly; the screen size is pretty small, though it can vary, depending on your computer memory, modem, and the kind of file you choose. You can watch the movies directly on the site (no special software required, and picture quality is good), or, depending on your computer setup, you can download many to your hard drive to watch later or upload them to your iPod or MP3 player.

Watch New and Old Trailers for Free

Some people like the coming attractions better than the movies themselves. And it's no wonder; trailers are a unique and compelling art form. There are many sites on the Internet where you can view trailers for new movies, older movies, and really old classics.

- Yahoo Movies (movies.yahoo.com) is a great resource for trailers of new and upcoming features and those from the past few decades, as well as show times, reviews by major critics, and fan reviews.
- The Trailer Park (www.movie-trailers.com) has a huge archive of all kinds of trailers.
- Turner Classic Movies (www.tcm.com) has a super collection of old movie trailers, rare short features and interviews, and clips from and about such great classics as *Casablanca*, *Grand Hotel*, *Gone with the Wind*, *Meet Me in Saint Louis*, and hundreds more.
- The Internet Movie Data Base (www.imdb.com) is the "go to" spot on the Web for just about everything about almost any movie, including trailers.

EDITOR'S CHOICE

What's on TV? Free Listings

Want to know what's on TV anywhere you happen to be? Go to Zap2it.com (www.zap2it.com/tv), click on "TV Listings," enter your zip code, choose your cable or satellite provider, and voilà—the current program listings (you can browse through the whole week). The site is also filled with the latest TV news stories, best bets, ratings, and gossip. There are also movie listings, reviews, and news, but the site's real ace in the hole is its great, comprehensive TV listings keyed to your locale.

TV Deals

Free Tickets to Live Television Tapings

Sit in the audience at live tapings of your favorite television talk shows, game shows, and sitcoms! Most shows are shot in Los Angeles, and a few in New York, Chicago (*Oprah*), and Las Vegas. You can get free tickets to see, among others, *The Late Show with*

David Letterman (taped in New York), *The Tonight Show with Jay Leno*, and *Wheel of Fortune* by checking the show's website or that of its network; typically, you can write in for tickets (the address for tickets frequently appears as part of a show's closing credits) or make the request online or by telephone. For game and talk shows taped in Los Angeles, check out www.tvtix.com. Audiences Unlimited (www.audiencesunlimited.com) provides tickets to sitcoms like *Two and a Half Men*, *The King of Queens*, and *All About Jim*, and for the *Poker Dome Challenge*, shot in Las Vegas.

The Best and Oddest TV Clips Online ... for Free

It's the hottest spot on the Internet to watch clips of classic television moments, hilarious home videos, music videos, obscure foreign video clips and commercials, stupid pet tricks, and subjects you've never even thought of watching, like someone named Jane talking about phobias or Bulgarian Theatrical Dancers, well, dancing. It's a website called YouTube (www.youtube.com/index), and its subtitle says it all: Broadcast Yourself. YouTube has gone from being a renegade community site (users remain the major contributors and post their own videos and favorite clips) to an acknowledged marketing tool for the networks, record labels, and movie studios. It's a classic case of "if you can't beat 'em, join 'em," and the public is the beneficiary. You can search the site by category, most-viewed, top-rated, most-discussed, and more. Some clips are fantastic, fascinating, and professional; others are outrageous and incomprehensible. Warning: You're likely to spend more time on YouTube than you should!

Free Fun from the Networks

If you love television, the major broadcast networks, as well as most of the cable networks, have websites filled with free clips, previews of new shows, games, show downloads (some charge a small fee), interviews and special features, cast lists and bios, story synopses, ticket information for live tapings, message boards, and a lot more. NBC (www.nbc.com), CBS (www.cbs.com), ABC (abc.go.com), Comedy Central (www.comedycentral.com), BBC America (www.bbcamerica.com), and Turner Classic Movies (www.tcm.com) are just a few of the dozens of broad-based or special-interest network websites filled with info and activities for TV addicts and aficionados.

Theater, Dance, Music, and More

Culture for Five Bucks for Teens

High 5, a nonprofit organization that provides $5 tickets to teens ages 13 to 18 (or those currently enrolled in middle or high school) is one of the lowest-cost ways for young people to attend hundreds of New York City theater, music, and dance events (including Alvin Ailey, New York City Ballet, New York City Opera, and numerous other first-class offerings), as well as most museums and some films. For each ticket bought by a teen, an extra $5 ticket may be purchased for an accompanying adult, thereby making anyone eligible for this terrific program. High 5 tickets to participating museums are two for $5 every day, and there's also a buy-five-get-one-free admissions offer. There's nothing to join, no lines to stand in, no applications to fill out—and nothing costs more than $5! All that's needed is a student ID. For more information and a list of events, go to www.highfivetix.org, or call 212-445-8587.

See Plays and More Free by Ushering

Become a volunteer usher and attend plays and concerts for free at your local theaters. The work isn't difficult, the schedules are flexible, you're often doing a service for your community, and it's fun. If you live in or near Washington, D.C., for example, the historic Ford's Theatre hires volunteer ushers; go to www.fordstheatre.org and click on a home-page link to fill out a form you can submit by

Editor's Choice **Discount Theater Tickets Online**

One of the best online sites for discount theater and other entertainment events is TheaterMania (www.theatermania.com), which lists productions in Austin, Boston, Chicago, the D.C. metro area, Las Vegas, London, Los Angeles, New York, Philadelphia, San Francisco, and other major metropolitan areas. Although not everything listed is discounted and the deals vary from around 20 percent to 70 percent off, it's one of the few theater discount sites that covers cities other than New York. The site also includes theater news and reviews, listings for cabarets and nightclubs, video clips, restaurant guides, and notices of future openings. Your best bet is to join (online) the TM Insider Club; it's free and gives you broader access to discounts and a complimentary subscription to the *TM Insider*, a newsletter that features the latest information about shows and deals.

Broadway for a Song!

It's unheard-of to visit New York City without taking in a Broadway show, but the costs of entertainment on the Great White Way are ever increasing. In the 2004-05 season, the average Broadway ticket price was over $66—and that's including the ones purchased at discount outlets! The following tips can help you get to the theater on the cheap (and if you don't plan on visiting New York, so much the cheaper for you—the road versions of Broadway shows cost about $15 less, on average, than their Broadway counterparts).

Broadway Bargains

You'll find the best theater deals on Broadway on the day of the performance, often as late as an hour before the show begins. For the cheapest last-minute deals (generally between $15 and $25, even for shows with a top ticket price of more than $100), try for tickets classified as:

- **Rush:** These are unsold seats or a few that are set aside for release about an hour before curtain.
- **Student:** Admission at student rates requires a valid student ID.
- **Lottery:** Some theaters offer a limited number of tickets for which you throw your name into a hat.
- **Standing room:** You view the show from behind the orchestra section; some theaters routinely offer standing-room tickets, others only if the show is sold out.
- **Obstructed view:** The nature of the "obstruction" varies; generally you can see most of the stage most of the time.

All of these options involve standing in line at the box office with no guarantee of a ticket, though if you get there early and close to the front of the line, your chances are good. For a complete listing of the theaters that offer these deals, go to www.talkinbroadway.com/boards. It's a good idea to call the box office of a show you're interested in to confirm details of its policy.

Kids' Night on Broadway

The best way to keep the theater alive is to encourage children to grow up to be theatergoers. To help this process along, Madame Tussauds New York sponsors Kids' Night on Broadway, a once-a-year-event for children ages 6 through 18 to attend participating Broadway shows for free when accompanied by a full-paying adult. Kids' Night on Broadway also includes family-friendly restaurant and parking discounts and a free pre-theater party at the famed Madame Tussauds interactive wax museum in Times Square. Some Broadway touring companies in cities other than New York also participate in the program. For information on these and the next Kids' Night on Broadway, go to www.kidsnightonbroadway.com.

Discounts for Broadway and Beyond

Pick your price at Broadway Box (broadway box.com), a terrific website that provides a huge list of discounts for Broadway and off-Broadway shows, as well as concerts and other entertainment and arts events in New York, Las Vegas, and London. Discounts can be up to 50 percent off, but most save you around 25 percent. Broadway Box often lists several different offers for the same show, and all listings include codes you must reference when you order by phone or online; or you can print coupons at home and take them to the box office. The site is free and easy to use. Listings change often, but on any given day there are around 180 discount offers to choose from. Peruse the list, choose your show and the deal you like, click on the coupon, and you're all set! You can also sign up for weekly free e-mail alerts with new and updated offers.

Special Deals for Special Folks

The Theatre Development Fund (www.tdf.org) in New York City is the country's largest not-for-profit service organization for the performing arts. One of TDF's core initiatives is its membership program, which makes 70,000 arts lovers eligible for deeply discounted theater, dance, and music tickets. The following groups are eligible for membership: students, teachers, union members, seniors (62 or over), civil service employees, people on the staff of a not-for-profit organization, performing arts professionals, and members of the armed forces or clergy. Apply in one of three ways:

- You can apply online and start buying tickets immediately but must send in proof of eligibility within 30 days.
- Write to TDF at Theatre Development Fund, 1501 Broadway, 21st Floor, New York, New York 10036, Attention: TDF Membership (enclose a self-addressed stamped envelope) for an application form.
- Go to the website, print and fill out the form, and send it in with proof of eligibility (proof of membership in a union, copy of your student ID, a pay stub from a nonprofit organization, and such).

For membership and to receive the TDF mailing list, there's an annual fee of $25.

TKTS, Broadway's Best Bargain

Perhaps the most popular service of the Theatre Development Fund is the sale of discount tickets to New York City events at the TKTS booths in Times Square and at the South Street Seaport. At these two locations, TDF sells tickets to Broadway, off-Broadway, dance, and music events at 25 percent to 50 percent off full price (plus a $3 per ticket service charge). All tickets are available on the day of performance only, except for matinee tickets at the South Street Seaport, which must be purchased the day before. Available shows are posted on boards outside the booths and can change from minute to minute. Check www.tdf.org/tkts for operating times, locations, and restrictions, and for shows that were available the previous week. At Times Square, the ticket windows open at 3 p.m. for evening performances, but lines start forming in the morning; however, unsold tickets are released to TKTS as late as 7 p.m., so you can often get a seat for a big show after the rush, when lines are short. Note: Payment is by cash or traveler's check only.

mail, e-mail, or fax. The North Shore Music Theater in Beverly, Massachusetts, uses more than 300 ushers in its volunteer program; for information, call Diane Ogiba at 978-232-7253 or e-mail her from the site (www.volunteersolutions.org/neu/org/215112.html). Call nearby theaters for their policies and to find out how to participate, or visit their websites. Once the theater gives you a little training, you'll be good to go!

Listen to Great Opera for Free

You don't have to travel to New York City and buy a ticket to hear a glorious opera performed live at the Metropolitan Opera House. Instead, you can listen to more than 20 operas annually for free right in your own home (or car!) thanks to the live Saturday afternoon Metropolitan Opera Radio Broadcasts. The longest-running classical music series in American broadcast history, the Met programs present world-renowned operatic performances, plus live interviews with singers, designers, and directors during intermission. The program is heard on more than 300 radio stations in the United States, Canada, and Europe. At www.operainfo.org you can locate a station in your area, request a free illustrated broadcast brochure, read synopses and casting information, and hear audio samples. The site offers a wealth of background information about the operas and the performers, curriculum materials for teachers, and current opera news.

Seeing the Sights

Theme Park Discounts for Local Residents

If you live near a big theme park, take advantage of the steep discounts on ticket packages and annual passes that the parks make available to local residents. The most popular vacation times are usually "blacked out," but you'll be able to save a bundle by taking your family out for a day of fun when the out-of-town tourists aren't filling the park. ThemeParks.com (www.themeparks.com) publishes a comprehensive list of ticket prices, including resident passes, for major parks like Walt Disney World, SeaWorld, Busch Gardens, Universal Parks, and Cedar Point. If you want specific information about the parks, the site provides phone numbers. Be prepared to prove your residency when you purchase tickets.

Q How can I find out about free or low-cost performances of Shakespeare's plays?

A Many people consider Shakespeare the greatest playwright who ever lived. Maybe that's why so there are so many summer Shakespeare festivals around the country, many of which are absolutely free. Among the best known is New York's free program Shakespeare in the Park (www.publictheater.org), in which famous actors star in the Bard's masterpieces in Central Park's outdoor Delacorte Theater. Cleveland (www.cleveshakes.org), San Francisco (sfshakes.org/park), Princeton, New Jersey (www.princetonrep.org), and Louisville, Kentucky (www.kyshakes.org) are some of the other major cities where companies present free Shakespeare. For cultural listings in your area, check the calendar sections of local newspapers and your Chamber of Commerce.

Editor's Choice The Ultimate Entertainment Discount Book

The Entertainment Book, which has a more than 30-year track record, is available for 159 cities in the United States and several foreign locations. Although it costs an average of $30 (some of which goes to support schools and other nonprofit groups if you buy the book as part of a fundraiser), it offers thousands of dollars in discounts, including two-for-one dining at dozens of restaurants, half-price tickets to movies, sporting events, and museums, reduced-fee golfing, and a huge variety of other deals, mostly at 50 percent off. Just present the book's coupons at participating businesses. People who purchase the book also get a card for 20 percent discounts at restaurants, hotels, and other venues not included in the book; members have access to the book's website, which provides additional printable, mostly 50 percent-off coupons and shopping discounts. The Entertainment Book includes many high-profile merchants who typically don't discount; it's a great incentive to try new restaurants in your area. The more coupons you use, the more of a bargain the book becomes. For more information and to purchase the book, go to www.entertainment.com.

Free Galleries and Art Show Openings

Art galleries can be as appealing as museums, and most cities and even small towns have several featuring all kinds of art. Watch your local newspaper or put your name on your favorite gallery's mailing list for opening receptions where you can mingle with other art lovers in a party atmosphere, meet the artists, and usually have a free glass of wine or two, possibly along with some fruit and cheese. It's an interesting way to have an evening out and to meet people without spending any money—and you may just see some great art, too!

Half-Price Admissions with CityPass

New York, Boston, Philadelphia, Chicago, Southern California (including Los Angeles, Hollywood, and San Diego), San Francisco, Seattle, and Toronto all have CityPass programs offering substantial savings on the price of admission to major museums and attractions. If you visit most or all of those included, you'll pay well below half price for each; for example, Boston's CityPass is $39 for six museums, including the New England Aquarium, which normally costs $18 for adults. Your CityPass will also allow you to avoid main entrance ticket lines at most attractions. CityPass booklets contain actual tickets; when you visit a participating attraction, the agent removes that attraction's ticket, and you're in. Purchase your CityPass at any of the participating attractions, online at www.citypass.com, or from many

U.S. travel agents. It's valid for nine consecutive days from the first day you use it (two weeks in Southern California). See page 145 for information on similar passes in cities outside the United States.

Q Is it true that some museums offer discounted admission passes, and some don't charge admission at all?

A Museums offer entertainment options for almost every taste, and very often you can enter for free. Some major venues, like the Metropolitan Museum of Art in New York, ask for a suggested donation rather than a set price, and paying what you can is totally acceptable in most cases. Many museums have a free night or charge nothing at all, ever; admission to the Smithsonian museums in Washington, D.C., for example, is always free. Also, several large cities have bargain-priced "city passes" that let you visit many of their major museums and attractions for one reduced price (see "Half-Price Admissions with CityPass," page 117). Check the Museums of the World website (www.museum.com), for information, entrance prices, and admission policies for thousands of museums and art galleries worldwide.

Book Bargains

Free Romance

Well, actually, free novels and gifts from Harlequin, the publisher of romance fiction. To encourage you to subscribe to series like Harlequin Intrigue or Silhouette Desire, Harlequin will send you two free books and two surprise gifts for each series you order (large-print books are available in some series). You can end the subscription at any time, even before it begins, by writing "cancel" on the bill included with the books and sending it for receipt by Harlequin within 30 days of the invoice date. (If you opt to continue the subscription, you'll receive monthly shipments of four books at a small discount off the regular cover price.) To subscribe to the world of Harlequin romance, go to store.eharlequin.com/t5_free_books.jhtml. Other goodies on the eHarlequin.com site include free book excerpts, book chats, and a bargain book outlet offering a 40 percent discount on limited quantities of selected titles.

Free Classic Literature on the Internet

Project Gutenberg (www.gutenberg.org) is the Internet's best source for free e-books, with, in mid-2006, more than 18,000 titles in its catalog. The books are free to download because their copyrights have expired, so you won't find the latest Stephen King or Dan Brown thrillers. However, thousands of books, for every taste from Jane Austen to Emile Zola, are available. Selections of public domain sheet music, mostly classical chamber pieces, have been digitized and can be downloaded, and audio books are also available. The site offers a variety of options for downloading books to your hard drive or for burning to a CD or DVD for reading later, offline.

Yard Sales and Flea Markets

It's amazing what great stuff people want to get rid of! Your newspaper's classified section and your local penny saver are the places to look for listings of weekend yard sales, flea markets, swap meets,

Free Factory Tours and Samples

From first steps to finishing touches, factory tours offer fascinating insights into how everyday items are made. Described below are a few of the many factories that offer tours for free or a nominal charge. Many send you home with free samples and valuable coupons. Call or check the website of a factory that interests you to see if it offers tours. (Check age restrictions as some have minimums.)

NAME	LOCATION	LENGTH OF TOUR	DESCRIPTION	CONTACT
Jelly Belly candy factory	Fairfield, California	40 min	Explains why it takes more than a week to make a single jellybean! The factory whips up more than 150 sweet treats, and you can taste any of them at the Sampling Bar at tour's end.	Call 800-953-5592 or visit jellybelly.com and click on "Fun"
Kohler Company	Kohler, Wisconsin	3 hrs	Visit buildings—Pottery, Brass Building, and Foundry—where everything from china bathroom sinks to huge cast-iron tubs are created.	Call 920-457-3699 or visit www.destinationkohler.com and click on "Plan Your Experience"
Celestial Seasonings	Boulder, Colorado	45 min	Takes you along on the journey from plant to teapot. You'll also be treated to a tea tasting from among 50-plus varieties, a stroll through the fragrant herb garden, and a visit to the sinus-clearing mint room.	Call 303-581-1202 or go to www.celestialseasonings.com/whoweare/tour/index.php
Miller Brewing Company	Milwaukee, Wisconsin	1 hr	Guides visitors through Miller's history and brewing process with a three-screen video and an up-close look at the brewhouse, packaging center, and caves that kept the beer cool before refrigeration was invented. At tour's end guests 21 and older can enjoy a frosty sample.	Call 414-931-2337 or toll-free 800-944-5483 or visit www.millerbrewing.com and click on "Beers and Breweries"
Steinway & Sons Pianos	Long Island City, New York	2 hrs	Creating these magnificent instruments is an amazing art form. Walks you through each step as 300 craftsmen bend wood, create soundboards, string instruments, form felt hammers, and perform all steps down to the last tuning	Call 718-721-2600 or visit www.steinway.com/factory

and crafts fairs that are entertaining in themselves just for browsing but have great bargains (frequently prices of a dollar or less at yard sales!) in used books, as well as audiocassettes and CDs, sporting equipment, and movies. You'll also find TVs, stereos, boom boxes, board and video games, collectibles, and all kinds of fun stuff you won't even know you want until you see it! Go early—the best things go fast, especially at yard sales; on the other hand, prices usually drop on what's left later in the day. Flea markets often have new but inexpensive items as well as antiques and used items. If your newspaper has a "Bargain Box" section, you can often find a lot of "entertaining" items offered free for the asking.

Meet the Author for Free Erudition

If books are your passion, you probably already know that free readings and lectures by famous authors take place every week in bookstores across the country—both large chain stores like Barnes & Noble (www.barnesandnoble.com; www.bn.com) and small,

The Greatest Bargain Bookstore on Earth!

Amazon.com is one of the best and most reliable Internet shopping sites for bargains on books, music, movies, and consumer electronics. Nearly every product Amazon sells is already discounted between 10 percent and 40 percent every day. But there are other reasons to check out Amazon.

- Its Bargain Books section features myriad titles discounted a minimum of 50 percent and as much as 80 percent, even for hardcover, blockbuster bestsellers from the world's most famous authors. Don't expect to find Patricia Cornwell's or Elmore Leonard's latest mystery entries, but in mid-2006 you could get Cornwell's 2003 thriller *Blow Fly* in hardcover for $7.99 (70 percent off the regular cover price).
- Browse through "Books under $5, $10, or $20" in online remainder "book bins." (The lists of available bargain books change frequently as supplies shift.)
- Check out the "buy four books get the lowest priced book free" deals.
- For big savings on items other than books, visit Amazon's Outlet store (click on "Directory of All Stores" at the bottom of any Amazon page to find this or any category of store on the site).
- Almost any product Amazon offers, including the most recent versions, can be purchased used from mostly private vendors at huge savings, though you'll have to pay for shipping (see below for free shipping on direct purchases from Amazon).
- Read book, movie, album, and product reviews by pros and other customers.
- Look inside books and read excerpts. Listen to snippets of music from almost any artist whose CDs are sold on Amazon.com.
- Shipping for all purchases over $25 is free.
- As of mid-2006 there was no sales tax on any item sold by Amazon itself (but note that several of its merchant partners like Target, Adorama Camera, J&R Music and Computer World, and other chains and stores do charge shipping and sales tax).

independently owned shops. Bookstore lectures are a great way to "meet the author" and spend an entertaining hour or so among people who share your love of books—all at no cost to you.

Free Comic Book Day

You don't have to be a kid to love comics, and that's one of the things this promotion is out to prove. As the name implies, Free Comic Book Day is a single day when participating comic book shops across North America and around the world give away comic books absolutely free to anyone who comes into their stores. Don't expect to get one of these freebies at the corner convenience store; only independent comic book stores (of which there are thousands) participate. Special comic books are distributed, and each store decides how many each person can have. For information on the next (or past) Free Comic Book Day, to find participating stores, and to sign up for an e-mail notice about the next event, go to www.freecomicbookday.com.

Gently Used Book Bargains

If you want to own rather than borrow used books, CDs, vinyl records, videocassettes, and DVDs, you can usually find fantastic bargains at thrift shops sponsored by charitable organizations. The Salvation Army and Goodwill are two charities that operate such outlets nationwide. Local organizations that sponsor thrift shops typically include hospital auxiliaries, PTAs, and a variety of community service and religious groups. Check your local yellow pages for listings.

Media Online

Get "All the News That's Fit to Print" Free Online

Almost every newspaper and magazine has an online version you can read for free; just Google the periodical you're interested in and see if it's on the Internet. This wealth of electronically available news, entertainment stories, reviews, lifestyle features, celebrity interviews, recipes, video reports, movie trailers, and more includes the contents of *The New York Times* (www.nytimes.com), the daily many consider the national newspaper of record. Sign up and it's all

Editor's Choice

Still the Greatest Free Resource of All

Hardcover bestsellers, literary masterpieces, reference works, and almost any book you'll ever need, all for free! Free blockbuster movies, classic films, festival and foreign favorites on DVD and videocassette! Free music CDs of all kinds! Free newspapers and magazines! Free Internet connection and computer use! All this can be found under a single roof in practically any city in the country. It's called the public library, and anyone with proof of residency is eligible for a library card. Most libraries also offer lectures, book clubs, and children's programs. If you don't have a card, visit your local library or branch and get one.

Q How can I avoid paying $4 or $5 per issue for my favorite magazines?

A If you like to read your magazines in paper form rather than on a computer screen, there's no reason to pay those hefty newsstand prices, and for most publications you don't have to pay top subscription prices either. Many subscriptions available at Magazines.com (www.magazines.com) and Magazines 4 Cheap (www.mags4cheap.com) will save you more than 50 percent off the newsstand price. Some of the subscriptions save you less, but others are at discounts of as much as 90 percent; prices vary depending on the site and when you check. And it's not a bad idea to visit the website of the magazine itself: Sometimes its introductory offers are the lowest of all; sometimes it allows you to receive several free issues to see if you like the publication.

free, except for access to high-profile columnists and a few other special features; for that, readers subscribe for a yearly fee to Times Select, which also lets you download 100 archived articles a month, going back as far as 1981. But if you can live without a few opinions and free archives, access to the rest of this fantastic newspaper costs nothing!

Online Celebrity Gossip at No Cost

Pop culture and entertainment junkies can learn the latest about their favorite stars, films, television shows, and sports personalities in online versions of *People* (people.aol.com), *TV Guide* (tvguide.com), and *Entertainment Weekly* (www.ew.com), among other celebrity-oriented publications. *EW* has online movie trailers and often posts opportunities for advance free movie screenings. All three sites provide video clips and celebrity photos, as well as text. And they're not above dishing a little gossip!

Free Your Brain for Free

If you're interested in articles with more gravity or intellectual content, *The Atlantic Monthly* (www.theatlantic.com) has an excellent site filled with fascinating articles from the magazine, as well as interactive features and selected archival information. The monthly *Opera News* (www.metoperafamily.org/operanews) is the premier publication for opera lovers; the online version includes interviews, news, and features, though much of the content is available only to subscribers to *Opera News* or members of the Metropolitan Opera Guild; if the limited content intrigues but doesn't satisfy you, the site offers a pretty good deal on a subscription. Or check out NewsDirectory.com (newsdirectory.com) for hundreds of online versions of magazines listed by topic, including scientific and medical journals; you can also search by subject or keyword for thousands of articles.

Free Games and Puzzles

If you like video games, especially not very complicated ones, dozens of websites let you play arcade-style and card games, work puzzles, and indulge in video poker, among many other pastimes—absolutely free! Some sites require memberships, but others, such as Dyno Downloads (www.dynodownloads.com), ArcadeGamesHome.com (www.arcadegameshome.com), and the aptly named Free Online Games (www.freeonlinegames.com), let you click on any game and play. Some games come with instructions, while others make you

Editor's Choice Free Media from Around the World

One of the most comprehensive media sites on the Internet is www.worldwidewired.com, which links readers to the online versions or websites of literally thousands of newspapers, magazines, and radio and television stations around the globe. Newspapers as diverse as *The Laredo* (Texas) *Morning Times* and the *Sydney* (Australia) *Morning Herald* are among the hundreds you can access from this site and read online for free, as well as online versions of hundreds of magazines from the United States and Canada, Europe, South America, Africa, Asia, and Australia. World Wide Wired also airs live radio broadcasts from around the world. For example, go to the listings of UK radio stations (www.worldwidewired.com/radio_europe.htm), choose any of the six BBC stations, and listen to live programming, replays of recent broadcasts, archived programs, or podcasts. You could spend the rest of your life on this site and never even scratch the surface of what it makes available.

fend for yourself. Free Online Games also offers humorous video clips, optical illusions, jokes, and other funny stuff.

Listen to Free Music at Napster

Napster (www.napster.com), which began as a controversial music file-sharing website, has made legal arrangements with the music industry and gone legit. That means you can choose from thousands of music tracks to listen to for free on your computer without paying a dime or breaking the law. The catch is you can play the same song only five times. If you want to download tracks for unlimited listening you'll have to subscribe to Napster for $9.95 a month; transferring those songs to a compatible MP3 player (which doesn't include iPods) will cost you $14.95 a month for unlimited downloads. But there's still a lot of music available for free; it's a great way to get to know new artists because you can hear complete songs instead of the usual 30-second excerpts you get on most sites that want you to buy the songs. Also Napster's no-cost music "encyclopedia," n.archive, is a fascinating, ever-growing, user-contributed archive of bios, photos, forums, and music.

Have Free Fun Just Browsing

There are hours of free fun and entertainment to be had and knowledge to be gleaned simply by browsing websites like Amazon.com, Barnesandnoble.com, and iTunes.com. You can listen to snippets of thousands of pieces of music; read excerpts from thousands of books; read critical, editorial, and customer reviews of books, movies, CDs, games, and more (on Amazon and Barnes & Noble); see lists of favorite books, music, and films compiled by other customers who share your passions (on Amazon); and read biographical information on thousands of authors, musicians, photographers, and other artists whose work is sold on these sites.

Trade in Old, Unused Electronics

At the rate entertainment and computer technology becomes obsolete these days, most of us have a lot of unused equipment lying around gathering dust. How about trading in your old electronic equipment for a Circuit City Gift Card? Circuit City gives you a way to lower the cost of new home-entertainment electronics and dispose of your old equipment—computers, camcorders, digital cameras, car audio systems, game systems, mobile phones, and iPods—in an easy and environmentally friendly way. Go online to cc.eztradein.com and fill out a form about the item you want to trade. You'll get an

A Passion for (Mostly Free) Podcasts

Although podcasts were conceived as programming to be uploaded to iPods, you don't have to own an iPod to enjoy the thousands of podcasts available on iTunes and elsewhere on the Internet; iTunes comes loaded on all Mac computers but can be accessed, at iTunes.com, on your PC in Windows format too. Podcasts are (mainly) radio-type shows that are downloaded over the Internet, almost always for free. As short as a couple of minutes or as long as an hour or more, they're produced by networks and big companies with something to promote or by a guy with a tape recorder—the quality and content vary enormously. Browse titles in categories that interest you in the iTunes podcast directory, and click on the one you want to hear. If you subscribe (it's free) to a podcast, new episodes will be added to your podcast playlist automatically. Among the myriad categories are movies and TV, news and politics, comedy, sports, music, food, arts and entertainment, and technology. You'll find scores of podcasts on your favorite TV shows, usually in the form of commentary. But the soap operas *As the World Turns* and *Guiding Light* rebroadcast each day's episode in audio format. Free video podcasts in 2006 included *ABC World News Now*, *Vintage Tooncast*, and *NIKE Football Videocast*. The world of podcasts isn't yet as user friendly as it will probably become, but it's worth delving into for the hours of free entertainment and information it provides. You can learn enough to get started at www.apple.com/itunes/podcasts.

estimate and a free shipping label for sending in the product. After Circuit City receives it and checks it out, you'll get your gift card. To start the process or for more information, go to the site or call Dealtree at 949-305-6600. You won't make a fortune, but it's easier than selling it on eBay!

Outdoor Fun

Free Info on Boating

If you've ever dreamed of owning a boat and experiencing the "life aquatic," there's valuable information, at no cost, to help you make that dream a reality. At www.discoverboating.com/marketing/dvd you can sign up for the free DVD "How to Get Started in Boating." The Discover Boating site itself (www.discoverboating.com) is filled with useful information to help you decide if this is an activity for you, including a quick overview of boat types and how they work, where to go for boat safety classes, a marina locator, and an interactive "boat selector" and price estimator to help you find just the right craft. Boating can be thrilling fun or a relaxing way to get away from it all. But it's a big commitment, and there's a lot to learn before buying a boat. This is a good place to start.

Free or Cheap Summer Swimming

There's no reason to swelter in the hot summer sun when you could be swimming in a cool pool. Many cities have free municipal swimming pools. For example, the St. Louis Department of Parks, Recreation and Forestry has eight free pools (stlouis.missouri.org/citygov/parks/recreation_div/pools.html). The New York City Department of Parks and Recreation (www.nycgovparks.org) has 51 free outdoor pools. The San Antonio Parks and Recreation Department (www.ci.sat.tx.us/sapar) operates 25 free pools. The Los Angeles Department of Recreation and Parks (www.laparks.org) or call 323-906-7953) offers swimming at 59 pools, 10 lakes, and a beach (12 operate year-round), and charges only $1.50 for adults 18 to 64 (admission is free if you're under 18, over 64, or disabled). Call your parks department or check online for public pools in your city.

Free License to Fish

Fishing is a passion that encompasses everything from expensive sport fishing on a specialized boat in the middle of the ocean to dropping a line attached to a stick into the creek "out back." If you're going to fish in a public area, however, most states require a license for each category of fishing. License fees vary widely, from about $6 to $700 (for a combined fishing and hunting license). But every state also has several annual free fishing days when license requirements are waived to enable people interested in taking up the sport to try it before buying a license. At www.takemefishing.org you can click on your state and see the free days for the various kinds of fishing. The site also has the lowdown on all things piscatory, including how and where you can borrow free gear.

Entertainment Alfresco for Free

Many parks in the United States conduct free or inexpensive activities geared toward nature and sports, especially in the summer. Besides hiking, biking, tennis, bird watching, nature walks, lectures, and zoos, your local parks often provide free live entertainment. For example, in Virginia, the Fairfax County Park Authority (www.fairfaxcounty.gov/parks/performances) presents a summer-long calendar of free shows, concerts featuring local professional musicians and vocalists, and drive-in movies. Chicago's Grant Park (www.chicago-downtown.com/events) is the venue for a panoply of outdoor summer music festivals, such as the annual Chicago Blues, Gospel Music, Country Music, and Jazz festivals, which are all free and attended by millions of fans. Toward the end of June the week-long event called Taste of Chicago offers food sampling and gourmet goodies from scores of the city's most popular restaurants, booths with cooking demonstrations, and musical entertainment on four stages. Check your city's parks department for a schedule of events in your area.

Borrow Nature Videos Free

Are you interested in mushrooming, our national parks and forests, fishing, Komodo dragons, eagles, wild mustangs, forest genetics, or any number of other subjects on the wonders of nature? The U.S. Department of Agriculture's Forest Service has a video lending library with hundreds of titles that are entertaining, educational, enlightening, and entirely free to the public except for the cost of return postage. The videos are of varying lengths—some as short as four minutes, others as long as an hour. You can request up to 10 titles at a time. For information on how to borrow the videos, listings of categories and titles, and descriptions of the videos, go to www.fs.fed.us/video/library.

Play Ball for Free or a Small Fee

Almost every city parks department provides—for free or a minimal registration fee—facilities, clinics, and sometimes equipment for playing tennis, baseball, basketball, soccer, and golf, among other sports. Call your local parks department or check its website for complete listings of facilities, times, and fees, if any. Some localities feature activities during the winter, but summer is really a bonanza for low- or no-cost sports in the parks.

> **EDITOR'S CHOICE**
>
> **Happy-Hour Dining Discounts**
>
> Make a note of nearby restaurant-bars that offer a happy hour in the early evening, hoping to attract the after-work crowd for dinner. You'll be able to buy a discounted drink or two and feast on a variety of free hors d'oeuvres. When you get home, a simple salad or an omelet, or maybe just a dish of ice cream for dessert, will be all you need for dinner. It's a good way to meet people too!

EATING OUT

Discount Dining Passes

If you're looking for deals on meals, Restaurant.com (www.restaurant.com) offers $25 dining coupons for $10 or, in a few cases, $10 certificates for $3 that can be used at more than 6,000 restaurants around the country. Check the site by city and neighborhood for the restaurants in your area that accept these coupons or to see if a particular restaurant you're interested in is listed. The site is user-friendly: Click on a restaurant to get dining information, to see any restrictions on the offer, in some cases take a virtual tour of the restaurant, and make online reservations. Most restaurants accept only one certificate per party, and certificates usually have to be presented before ordering. If you have questions or problems, Restaurant.com has friendly and helpful toll-free customer service at 800-979-8985 (9 a.m. to 5 p.m. CST, Monday through Friday), and satisfaction is guaranteed. Bon appétit!

Pre-Theater Dining Bargains

Restaurants in big cities like New York, Los Angeles, and Chicago have "pre-theater" menus that usually have a limited selection but offer a three-course meal (appetizer, entree, and dessert) for about the same price as the main course alone later in the evening; some even include a glass of wine or another beverage. Restaurants post these menus in their windows or out front, or you can check the websites of establishments you'd like to try. (You don't really have to go to the theater!) And even in many smaller towns, many restaurants likewise offer "early bird" specials (usually before 6 p.m. or 7 p.m.) at a substantial savings over the regular à la carte menu.

Free Birthday Meal

Ask at your favorite restaurants, especially those in your neighborhood, whether they offer a free meal on your birthday. Many do, and you'll want to make note of them before the big day. Check the websites of several eateries for this policy (and other moneysaving offers that might show up there!). Who knows, you might get breakfast, lunch, and dinner—all for nothing!

Discount Fast Food

Want to get a 20 percent discount every time you eat out for breakfast, lunch, or dinner? If you eat at fast food outlets several times a week, this could be a great deal for you. For a fee of $7.87 per month, you can join the Fast Food Diet Meal Club and become eligible to download one meal coupon per day worth 20 percent off the final bill (up to $25). You can also download a two-for-one meal coupon twice each month. Coupons are good at more than 155,000 restaurants, mostly fast food outlets, nationally. There's a three-day free trial so you can sample membership without risking a cent. Go to www.thefastfooddiet.com and click on Free Meal Coupons. The site also provides free practical tips on losing weight, better nutrition, and improving your health (new content everyday) from their resident expert, Dr. Stephen Sinatra, a cardiologist and certified nutritionist who has written several health books.

CHAPTER 7

top savings tips for travel

Are you yearning to visit Yellowstone, or dying to go to Disney? Here's how to get the best airfare prices, hotel room upgrades, and meal bargains on your next vacation.

WHETHER YOU WANT TO SEE the great wide world or simply get away from it all, travel can be one of life's great pleasures. But these days, steep airfares, high gas prices, and the rising cost of just about everything make travel seem increasingly out of reach. Well, take heart: With some savvy shopping and occasional wheeling and dealing, you can travel well, live it up a bit, *and* stay well within your means.

You can begin saving even before you hit the road. Navigate websites and scour newspapers for cheap airfares, check the prices of hotels and car rentals, shop for sightseeing passes, visit tourist offices online. As you do, and once you leave home and get out into the world, keep the following in mind.

- **Be thorough**. See a great airfare? Good for you … but keep looking, because you might find a better one with one more phone call or click of the mouse. Shop for the best-priced hotel room, then explore ways to get a better rate. Determine how much you will spend to visit the museums that interest you and how much you will or will not save by purchasing an all-inclusive museum pass. Compare the price of flying to taking the train. The more you learn, the more you'll save. After shopping around for a while, you'll come to know a good deal when you see one—and when you do, snap it up.

By the numbers

2,200

Amount, in dollars, that the average family spends per year on an extended vacation. About a quarter of that figure is spent on lodging.

EDITOR'S CHOICE Research Costs Nothing, Pays Big

Go native even before you leave home. Learn as much as you can about the places you plan to visit, keeping an eye out for deals and bargains. Guidebooks are a good place to start, and many include money-saving tips in their coverage. The big guns—Frommer's, Fodor's, Lonely Planet, and TimeOut, among others—all have free online editions that are great sources of information and travel planning advice. Check with tourist offices and chambers of commerce to see what free information they provide, either online or through postal mail. Keep an eye out, too, for city magazines—these are often loaded with news of free and low-cost events as well as dining and sightseeing discounts, and many are available online. If you're up for a little Web browsing, go to your favorite search engine and type in the name of the place you plan to visit plus the word "guides" and see what pops up.

- **Be flexible.** Changing your flight from a Monday to a Tuesday can save hundreds of dollars, and moving your Caribbean trip from March to June may save even more. You might want to move up your dinner hour to take advantage of early-bird specials, consider becoming a courier to save on airfare, take a bus instead of a taxi, or forgo your preference for hotels and sign up with a home-stay program that matches up hosts and travelers. Being flexible puts you in a better position to take advantage of travel bargains.
- **Be bold.** Ask and ye shall receive: Is that really the best you can do on a room rate? Would you bring Junior a half portion of pasta—at half price? Is there any way I can get a free upgrade on your flight today? Can I bring my own bottle of wine to dinner? Do you have a nicer car for the same low rate? You'll probably be surprised to learn how many freebies and deals are out there when you just muster the courage to ask for them.
- **Be nice.** Yes, it can be as simple as that: As treacly sweet as the sentiment may sound, you'll get a lot further with a smile than you will with a frown. Hotel clerks, airline agents, and other hard-working travel professionals are used to dealing with sourpusses. They might so appreciate your pleasant attitude that they'll lower the price, give you a better room, hand out an upgrade, or refill your glass at no charge.
- **Enjoy.** Travel is what you make of it: fun, exciting, adventurous, relaxing, eye-opening—and it's all the more rewarding when you know you've saved money with a good deal!

Planning Your Trip

Free Travel Info from Uncle Sam

The U.S. government dishes up plenty of sound travel advice in booklets that you can read for free on the Federal Citizen Information Center website (www.pueblo.gsa.gov). Especially useful are "A Safe Trip Abroad," with suggestions on such typical travelers' concerns as what to pack and how to avoid being the victim of crime, and "Fly-Rights," with the low-down on how to avoid airline scams, what your rights are if a flight is canceled, and much more. You can also print out all or part of them. Or you can order print versions of the booklets, which range in price from $1 to $4, plus a $2 service and shipping charge; write to the Federal Citizen Information Center, P.O. Box 100. Pueblo, Colorado 81002, or call toll-free 888-878-3256.

Free Scenic America Map Offer

Explore America's scenic byways with a free illustrated map from the U.S. Department of Transportation. Featured byways include the Natchez Trace Parkway, the Coronado Trail, the Pacific Coast

Which Discounts Are You Eligible For?

Discounts for travelers are fairly plentiful and often yours for the asking. Many are geared to seniors (see Chapter 15), and folks of any age can take advantage of the reduced rates and fares offered by other groups. Membership in the American Automobile Association (www.aaa.com) entitles you to discounts on airlines, car rentals, lodging, and more. Students (see also Chapter 8), children, and active members of the armed forces get free or reduced admissions to museums and other attractions, and kids can stay and eat for free at many resorts. You may be entitled to discounts you might not even know about. Airlines will take 50 to 70 percent off the price of a ticket booked at short notice for family members flying to a funeral; before opting for one of these bereavement fares, though, make sure that you can't do even better buying a discounted ticket through an online travel provider or elsewhere.

Your church or community service organization may have arrangements with members in other parts of the country to host travelers. A resident of a resort community can often stay for free or at very low cost in other facilities managed by the same company around the country. If you belong to any sort of organization, check on travel benefits that might come with membership—and never plunk down the money for a plane, bus, or train ticket, hotel room, museum admission, or other travel-related expenditure without first asking which discounts are available.

EDITOR'S CHOICE

3 Easy Ways to Cut Your Airfare Costs

A little strategizing can help you save big on airfares:

- **Buy early.** Standard airline practice is to offer the lowest fares with an advance purchase of at least 21 days.
- **Shop around.** Check out such online travel providers as Travelocity, Orbitz, Hotwire, and others; the fares they offer can vary considerably. Also look at airline websites.
- **Be flexible.** Changing your travel dates can often save money (fares are usually lowest for Tuesday, Wednesday, and Thursday), and so can switching airports—if you live near more than one airport, check fares to and from all of them.

Highway, and other routes—126 in all—that the department has singled out for their natural beauty and historic relevance. For your free map, visit www.byways.org; write to the U.S. Department of Transportation, Federal Highways Administration, National Scenic Byways Program, HEPN-50, Room 3232, 400 Seventh Street SW, Washington, D.C. 20590; or call toll-free 800-429-9297 (press Option 3).

Free Travelers' Health Updates

The U.S. Centers for Disease Control helps send you off with peace of mind by providing loads of free info on travelers' health. Experts weigh in with advice on everything from how to spare your infant a bout of diarrhea to how to avoid illness on a cruise. Browse through these tips at www.cdc.gov/travel, where you will also find the latest updates on bird flu and other health issues of concern to travelers.

Bargain Bags

You'll begin saving even before you leave home when you gear up for your trip at online luggage discounters. The largest, eBags (www.ebags.com) routinely offers discounts on bags and such handy accessories as flat toiletry kits, and throws in free shipping on orders of more than $35.

GETTING THERE

Last-Minute Bargains for Flexible Fliers

Are you the type of eager-beaver traveler who always has his bags packed, ready to go just about anywhere at short notice? Sign up with the major airlines for their weekly e-mails listing last-minute fares on select routes. Airlines usually send these e-mails on Tuesday. You must purchase tickets online no later than Friday for departures the following Friday or Saturday and returns on Monday or Tuesday. Tickets are nonrefundable and carry hefty change fees, but it's hard to beat some of the fares—sometimes less than $200 from coast to coast, and as low as $500 from New York to Tokyo. Keep in mind, though, that airlines offer these deals on limited routes and offers vary from week to week, so it's quite unlikely that a fare to a specific destination of your choice is going to be available at a time

Maximize Your Frequent-Flier Miles

Two rules to help you make the most of your frequent-flier miles:

- **Consolidate.** Try to earn your miles with one airline, so you'll rack up free travel quickly, and choose the airline with the most flights from your local airport, so you can use your miles easily.
- **Get the most bang** for your buck. If you redeem 25,000 miles for a trip that would cost $250, you're getting one cent for every point you've earned; if you redeem 25,000 miles for a trip that costs $500, you've doubled the value of your points. For more tips on using frequent-flier programs, check out the sites frequentflier.com and insideflyer.com.

you want. These programs work best for really flexible travelers. To sign up, browse the e-mail programs on airline websites.

Visit Travelzoo for Low Prices

Angling for low airfares causing you angst? Haggling for hotel deals a hassle? Then check out www.travelzoo.com, a one-stop Internet source. Staff experts round up the best airfare, lodging, and vacation deals and publish them in their Top 20 newsletter, delivered to your e-mail in-box free of charge every Wednesday. You can also sign up to have Travelzoo Newsflash E-mail Alerts zapped to you as soon as they are announced. You pay no add-on commission fee to use Travelzoo; when you want to book, Travelzoo links you directly to the airline, car rental agency, hotel, or other outfit offering the deal.

Get Upgraded for Little or No Cost

Being upgraded—moved out of coach into a higher class of service—puts the pleasure back into flying and, given the price of a business- or first-class ticket, is one of the biggest travel bargains around. Here are three strategies for getting these perks:

- **Join a frequent-flier program** with one airline and use it whenever possible. When you've acquired enough miles, you'll be awarded elite status, which on most airlines entitles you to free upgrades when they are available.
- **Buy an upgrade.** Some airlines sell upgrades (often at check-in) when business and first-class seats are not filled, and the combined costs of the economy ticket and the upgrade will probably be a fraction of the cost of a business- or first-class ticket.

Q What are the best online resources for planning a vacation with kids?

A If you're planning a family vacation, you have a wide choice of family packages, kids-stay-free programs, and other deals to consider: Interested in a stay at a San Diego hotel with free tickets to the city's acclaimed zoo? Accommodation and admission to Hershey Park, Pennsylvania, at one low cost? A midweek bargain on a room in a historic Charleston, South Carolina, inn and a tour of Fort Sumter? An Alaska cruise that invites you to bring the kids along for free? A four-star New York City hotel that lets children share their parents' room at no extra cost and gives them breakfast as well? Two websites that work hard to keep up with the best family-friendly options out there are Family Travel Forum (www.familytravelforum.com) and We Just Got Back.com (www.wejustgotback.com).

- **Redeem miles for upgrades.** With most frequent-flier programs, upgrades require fewer miles and are easier to get than free flights.

Discover Deep Discount Airfares

Dig a little deeper to unearth the best airfares. Discount, no-frills airlines, such as Europe-based Ryanair (www.ryanair.com) and EasyJet (www.easyjet.com), can fly you around the Continent and beyond for a song, but they're not on the radar screens of most Internet travel providers (one exception worth checking out is LowCostAirlines at www.lowcostairlines.org). Consolidators, also known as bucket shops, buy seats in bulk at a discounted rate and pass some of the savings along to customers; look for their ads in the Sunday travel sections of such large-circulation newspapers as *The New York Times* and the *Los Angeles Times*; many also show up on the website www.cheapflights.com.

Fly Courier for Half the Bargain Price

Courier travel is an oft-romanticized way to see the world on a shoestring. And, no, sunglasses and a trench coat are not required. Couriers are ordinary travelers who accompany time-sensitive cargo that needs to get somewhere fast on a commercial flight to make sure it reaches the other end and clears customs. You must have the flexibility to travel when and where packages need to go and be willing to travel lightly (the company uses your allotted space in the cargo hold for its shipment, so you can bring only carry-on luggage). Your payoff is a fare that's usually about half of other bargain fares. Groups such as the International Association of Air Travel Couriers (www.courier.org) and the Air Courier Association (www.air-courier.org; toll-free 800-282-1202) post courier flights available to their dues-paying members (annual dues run about $40).

Package Deals Cut Costs Dramatically

The term "package tour" may conjure up images of traveling in a pack of camera-toting loudmouths, but give the concept a second thought. Package tours that combine airfare and a hotel room for one price can save you big bucks. Because tour packagers get bulk rates on airplane seats and hotel rooms, you often wind up paying just a bit more for an airfare and hotel package than you would for airfare alone. The vacation pages of airline websites and the travel sections of Sunday newspapers are good places to begin shopping for packages. Don't snap up a package without doing a little homework, though: Price the cost of buying airfare and hotel separately; check out the accommodations so that you don't get stuck in an undesirable outlying hotel; and make sure you're not paying for sightseeing, fiesta nights, and other extras you might not want.

Traveling in Packs for Group Discounts

Many hotels and cruise lines offer discounts to guests who book a block of rooms or cabins. In fact, many large hotel chains and most cruise lines have group travel departments whose mission it is to reel in guests for family reunions, shipboard weddings, and other events, and even small hotels are usually happy to book blocks of rooms at a discount, especially when business is slow. What constitutes a group varies considerably, but as a rule of thumb, whenever you require more than two rooms, ask for a group discount. And book early—eager to fill space, hotels and cruise lines will be more receptive to giving group discounts if you reserve well in advance.

Free Gas-Price Check

Setting out on a road trip? Worried about the cost of topping up the tank? Check in at www.gasbuddy.com, a handy website that shows you where you'll find the cheapest gas in any part of the United States and Canada. Type in a U.S. zip code or click on the name of a Canadian province, and up comes a listing of what service stations

Getting Bumped: Is It Worth the Bother?

Some frequent travelers regularly net free tickets by getting bumped from flights. "Bumping" is airline slang for "denied-boarding compensation" and refers to the practice of asking a passenger to give up a seat on a plane that's been overbooked in return for a voucher for free travel and/or cash, along with passage on the next available flight. You're most likely to be bumped from flights that are heavily booked, such as those before major holidays, or those on which other passengers are less willing to give up their seats—business travelers on their way home for the weekend, for instance, or vacationers flying to Miami or another port to board a cruise ship. To learn more about denied-boarding compensation, visit the U.S. Department of Transportation's website (www.dot.gov) or call 202-366-4000. Also ask airlines about their policies, which vary considerably.

in that area are charging for gas—just like driving around looking for the lowest price, only you're not wasting gas to do it! GasBuddy also provides some genuinely helpful fuel-saving tips.

Scoring the Best Cruise Bargains

As you would with airfares, employ a few tried-and-true techniques to get the best cruise deals:

- Be flexible with dates, because rates vary with bookings—if a cruise is heavily booked on the dates you want, you will pay more than if you wait for a time when the ship is not full.
- Stick to well-traveled routes, such as the Caribbean, because cruises to these competitive markets are generally less expensive than those to less-traveled places.
- Do some research before signing up for an air/sea package—you might get a better airfare if you book it separately.
- Book early, because cruise lines almost always offer the best deals three to six months in advance.

Accommodations

Comparison Shop for Lower Hotel Rates

Hotel rates, even for the same room, can vary wildly, and some savvy comparison shopping can save you a lot of money. The best prices often turn up on websites, so click your way through www.hoteldiscounts.com, as well as Travelocity, Orbitz, Hotwire, Cheap Tickets, and other online travel services. Browse through the websites of individual hotels, too, because the lowest rates sometimes show up there. If you find a deal that seems attractive, don't grab it right away. Instead, call the hotel, say what you've found, and ask if a better deal might be available—you might be told that the Web offer can't be topped; on the other hand, you may learn that a little human-to-human wheeling and dealing can outperform the sites.

It Pays to Book Early

If you're planning to travel in high season, book as early as you can. You probably won't get a discounted rate—after all, hoteliers in the Caribbean and at ski resorts can fill their rooms in the winter and won't be offering deals. But you might avoid paying top dollar, as you'll do if you wait until the last minute and are forced to snap up any vacancy you can find.

Finding Newspaper Discounts

Check newspapers regularly. Even in the age of the Internet, many hotels, tour operators, and other tourist-oriented businesses still reach out to travelers with print ads. You'll probably find the best deals on travel to places that are especially popular with readers in the region the paper serves—in Minnesota, to Florida and other winter escapes; in California, to Hawaii, Baja California, and other West Coast getaways. The travel sections of these newspapers may also run articles on discount travel to these places. So no matter where you live, you might want to consult newspapers around the country, which are often available in libraries.

Factor Location into a Hotel's Price

The old maxim "location is everything" can in fact steer you to savings. Even if you pay more to stay in a center-city hotel, you might recoup the extra expense in what you save in transportation costs getting to and from the places you want to go. Before booking, do the math. Say you're drawn to an outlying hotel that offers attractive rates. What will it cost to get to and from the sights you want to see? Will you need to drive and pay to park? If you're a family of four and paying $2 a head each way to travel by bus, any round trip is going to clock in at $16. Make two trips a day and that's $32, plus time and inconvenience. Does the lower room rate compensate for these considerations? You can plot the location of hotels in relation to sights and attractions at MapQuest.com or by just using a map in a guidebook.

Consider Downgrading to Save

You may have tried to upgrade to a nicer hotel room for free, but have you ever thought of downgrading to an inferior room that costs less? When booking, ask if any rooms have been removed from service because of minor damage (perhaps torn carpeting or wallpaper hasn't been repaired yet). Are there old rooms in a hotel with a new wing, or rooms in a recently refurbished property that have not yet been renovated? Are there rooms without private baths? If you're doing this sort of negotiating on the spot, ask to see the accommodation where you'll be roughing it to make sure you'll be comfortable—you shouldn't have to suffer to save money.

Q What's the single best secret to getting unadvertised hotel deals?

A One word of advice for hotel guests trying to get the most value for their dollars: Ask! How much is a room and can you do better than that? Do you have a nicer room for the same price? Do you have a smaller room for a much lower price? A double for the price of a single? Large rooms for families? Special rates for kids? Which extras are included—free parking and breakfast? Discount in the hotel dining room? If the hotel is hosting a convention and filled to the rafters, you'll probably just elicit a bemused smile. But if the place is half empty, you might be surprised at how genuinely accommodating a hotel staff can be.

EDITOR'S CHOICE

Beware the Minibar

Don't even open it! In-room drinks and snacks are among the many high-priced amenities with which hotels tempt you. Other typically expensive extras are telephone calls, as much as $1 for local connections, and laundry services. When looking for a hotel, keep an eye out for such money-saving conveniences as in-room fridges or kitchenettes, on-premise Laundromats, free or inexpensive parking, free or reasonably priced telephone service, and free e-mail or Wi-Fi connections.

Money-Saving Hotel Packages

When shopping for a hotel, look for special packages. Business hotels often lower their rates, sometimes to half price, for two-night weekend stays; some resorts that do a good weekend business have midweek getaway packages; hotels with restaurants sometimes offer good-value, all-inclusive bed, breakfast, and dinner rates. Make a list of the places you'd like to stay, then look for money-saving deals on their websites (often the only places these offers appear).

Overnight Travel Savings

Sleeping on an overnight train or boat to save money on a hotel room might take you back to your youth, but a bargain is still a bargain. About $160 can get you a berth on a night train from Paris to Rome; around $130 buys passage and a bed on a ship from Venice to Patras, Greece. For a cost comparison, you might want to check the prices of a flight on a budget airline and a night's stay in a hotel, but depending on where you're traveling, chances are you'll do better with the overnight travel scenario. Besides, you'll probably find the experience to be as enjoyable now as it was years ago.

Be a Guest in Someone's Home

Staying with friends is an age-old way to save money, and usually includes a nice dose of hospitality. You can enjoy similar perks even if you don't know anyone in the places you plan to visit—through networks that match up hosts and travelers. Welcome Traveller (www.welcometraveller.org) charges a flat $10 per person per night for accommodations that can range from a room with private bath to a couch in someone's living room. The site GlobalFreeloaders (www.globalfreeloaders.com) asks you to give back what you receive—you host a traveler for as many nights as you've stayed as a guest in someone else's home. Friendship Force International (www.friendshipforce.org) arranges home stays of five to seven days with host families who act as local guides, and usually tacks on an optional land tour for a relatively low fee.

Home Swaps for Great Savings

A home exchange is an arrangement in which you stay for free in the house or apartment of someone who stays for free in yours at the same time. The deal saves you the cost of a hotel and comes with all sorts of other cost-saving benefits, including a chance to cut down on restaurant expenses and sometimes free use of a car. Of course, there are risks to home-swapping: Is your co-swapper going to take good care of your place? Is the house where you stay going to be as clean and comfortable as yours? Sharing photos, speaking with references, and some frank discussion about how to handle emergencies and other matters can cut down on potential hazards. Several companies publish print and online directories of home exchanges. Expect to pay from about $40 to $60 a year to list your home with such well-established firms as the International Home Exchange Network (www.ihen.com; 386-238-3633) and Home Exchange.com (www.homeexchange.com, toll-free 800-877-8723).

Getting Around

Take the Train to the Plane

You've gone to the trouble to get the best airfare, so why squander the savings getting to and from the airport when you can use public transportation? More and more cities are expanding subway and bus lines and other transport links to serve airports, providing much lower-cost alternatives to taxis. To learn about the public transportation options for the airports you will be using, just type the name of each airport into a search engine along with the words "ground transportation." Too much luggage to cope with public transport? Check out SuperShuttle (www.supershuttle.com). This shared van service usually clocks in at about half the price of a taxi ride and provides door-to-door service in some 20 U.S. cities.

See the U.S.A. . . . on Amtrak

Amtrak's North America Rail Pass allows you to travel anywhere you want to go in the United States and Canada within a 30-day period. If you're simply making one round trip, even cross-country, you're probably better off purchasing a regular ticket. But since the combined network covers more than 28,000 miles and serves more than 900 cities and towns, the pass is a good deal if you plan on making multiple trips and want to cover a lot of ground. You'll save more if you travel off season, from mid-October through mid-May, when the pass costs considerably less. For more information on the North America Rail Pass and other Amtrak discounts and deals, go to www.amtrak.com.

Go Greyhound and Save

The long-haul bus is the workhorse of the cheap travel circuit, and if you're traveling by Greyhound, a little advance planning can save you even more money. Many of the bus line's money-saving deals (see www.greyhound.com) are available only when purchased at least several days before travel. A companion, of any age, gets a 50 percent discount if you buy your tickets at least three days in advance. You can travel anywhere you want to go within certain distances (300 miles, 500 miles, and so on) for set, low-cost Go Anywhere Fares—provided you purchase your ticket at least seven days in advance.

Subway/Metro/Tube Discounts

Next to walking, public transportation is the least expensive way to get around a city, and all the more so when you take advantage of visitor travel cards and other multiple-ride discounts. In Paris, La Carte Visite entitles you to unlimited rides on the metro and buses and costs €8.35 ($10.40) a day, and you can save €3 ($3.75) when you buy a carnet of ten single tickets for €11 ($13.75). In New York, a seven-day Metrocard is good for unlimited rides on subways and buses and costs $24. Before you plunk down your money, calculate how much traveling you are going to do. In London, where a single tube ride is £2 ($3.70), an off-peak one-day travel card for £4.30 ($7.95) becomes a deal—and a darned good one—when you use it for three or more trips.

Rent-a-Car Savings Strategies

Some wise navigating can bring down the costs of car rentals:

- Check the major car-rental companies first, because volume allows them to offer some of the best deals.
- Look for discounted weekend rates and other specials.
- Consider extending your rental to a week to get the most value; in fact, you might pay less for a weekly rental than you would for a rental of a few days.
- Be prepared to drive a stick shift in Europe and other parts of the world where most cars are equipped with manual transmissions; you can save hundreds of dollars on even a weekly rental.
- To save money on gas, rent the smallest car in which you'll be comfortable.

TAKE CAUTION!

Eurailpass Pros and Cons

The many different kinds of rail passes for travel throughout Europe can save you money, but think about how often you'll be riding the rails and how far you want to go before you purchase one. If you're going to be hopping on and off trains every day and making some long-distance trips, the $600 Eurailpass, good for 15 days of unlimited, first-class travel, might be a good deal. But if you're planning to make only a few trips, you'll probably spend a lot less buying second-class tickets as you go. Map out your itinerary, then visit www.railpass.com and www.raileurope.com, where you can calculate the cost of tickets for individual trips and read about passes and their costs.

- Rent from a downtown location rather than an airport, because most airports tack on usage fees that can add quite a bit to the cost.

Free Rental Car Upgrades

When you reserve a rental car, request the least expensive model available. That will probably be a small economy car, but you may end up behind the wheel of a larger, snazzier car anyway: Since it's hard for agencies to know in advance what cars they are going to have on hand, they may not be able to match your request and will have to upgrade you to a larger car for free. Think twice before snapping up the offer, though—if you drive away in an SUV or another gas guzzler, your upgrade could end up costing quite a bit extra.

Consider Car Sharing for Quick Trips

If you're visiting a city and decide to pay a quick visit to a hard-to-reach outlying spot, car sharing might be a good alternative to a trip on public transport, which can take hours out of a sightseeing schedule, or a car rental or taxi ride, which can put big dents in your vacation budget. Typically, car-sharing companies operate in the

Go Online for Travel Savings

The personal computer is probably the biggest innovation to shake up the travel industry since the jet airplane. We armchair travelers now have vast resources at our fingertips. The first online stops when looking for good deals should be the big online travel providers: www.expedia.com, www.travelocity.com, and www.orbitz.com. All provide discounted fares on airlines, as well as good rates on hotels, car rentals, cruises, and vacation packages; prices can vary quite a bit, so always shop around. Some smaller sites that you should also include in your searches are www.cheaptickets.com, www.sidestep.com, and www.cheapflights.com.

With so-called opaque services, such as www.priceline.com and www.hotwire.com, you plunk down your money without knowing the name of the airline, time of the flight, name and exact location of the hotel, and other details; Priceline adds a little more gamesmanship to the experience by asking you to name the price you want to pay. In return for playing along with these smoke-and-mirrors routines, you get some of the lowest prices you are likely to find.

Q Do I really need to buy additional insurance when I rent a car?

A Save some money on a rental car by checking with your insurance and credit card companies to determine exactly what coverage they provide for rentals. Then don't pay the rental-car company for insurance you already have. The company that issues your car insurance, for instance, may or may not provide personal liability insurance when you drive a rental car, and many credit cards automatically cover collision insurance on rental cars.

same way as rental-car agencies, except they supply cars by the hour, at hourly rates that range from $8 to $10 and that include gas, mileage, and insurance. So a short-term rental will usually cost quite a bit less than a standard daily car rental. Companies offer a wide variety of deals that usually include a one-time application fee and a monthly membership fee or commitment. Even so, if you use a plan with some frequency, the savings over standard car rentals can add up quickly. Not-for-profit CarSharing.net provides info on car sharing, with links to many programs in North America and Europe.

Dining

Save with Early-Bird Specials

Some of the world's finest restaurants are taking the early-bird-special concept to new heights and offering good-value, prix-fixe menus before the evening rush, often until about 7 p.m. Select some restaurants you'd like to try and call or check the Web to see what low-cost menus might be available for early diners, or at lunch. To whet your appetite, Zagat.com reviews restaurants in cities around the globe, and a one-year subscription ($19.95) costs about the same as an early-bird special in a good restaurant.

Cut Your Drink Tab to Save

Keeping an eye on the liquor tab will also help you stay within your allotted travel budget, and you needn't become a teetotaler to do it. Since you pay a lot less for liquor in a shop than you do in a restaurant, buy a bottle and enjoy a drink in your hotel room before dinner, or find a restaurant that has a "bring your own bottle" policy. House wines are often excellent and very fairly priced, and many bars, especially in resorts, lure customers with two-for-one happy hours. Of course, the simplest strategy is simply to drink less—order two glasses or a half carafe of wine instead of a bottle—to spend less.

Kid-Friendly Dining Deals

Are the little ones taking a big bite out of your vacation dining funds? Click your way to www.kidseatfree.com to find the places around the country that feed youngsters for free. At Holiday Inns, guests 12 and under dine for free in the chain's restaurants at all

Talk to Other Travelers to Find Bargains

You can't beat the advice of travelers who've been there, done that, and know the great inexpensive hotels and the best places to dine on a shoestring. If you find that your friends and acquaintances are coming up short in this department, start visiting online travelers' forums, where globetrotters swap advice. On most, you post a question—Does anyone know of a cheap hotel in Bangkok?—and other members will post a response. You can also browse through the notices that other travelers have exchanged, usually handily organized by subject. Some good places to begin your exchanges with other travelers are the forums at Frommer's Travel Guides online (www.frommers.com); Fodor's (www.fodors.com); and www.tripadvisor.com.

meals, seven days a week (as long as they are accompanied by a paying guest); many other places offer kids-eat-free deals one or two days a week. There's no need to pay a lot at other times, either. As any parent knows, a lot of restaurants have kids' menus that offer small portions and low prices to match, but those that don't aren't necessarily "kid unfriendly"—wherever you dine, ask if you can get half portions, preferably at half price, for your children.

Vary Your Routine to Halve Food Costs

Straying from your regular dining routines can add some spark to your travels and save you money in the process. Enjoy your largest meal at midday; in many restaurants the tab for a full meal at lunch is about half the price of a full meal at dinner. Consider alternatives to restaurants; you'll probably find that you can dine quite well for less in cafés, coffee shops, wine bars, pizzerias, museum cafeterias, and other casual eateries. Order two appetizers instead of an appetizer and a main course—you'll have plenty to eat and will shave several dollars off the bill—and try to forgo desserts, as those empty calories tend to be expensive. In parts of the world where tap water is safe to drink, spare yourself the expense of bottled water.

Cheap Eats

Creative foraging can cut down on the cost of meals and provide good entertainment too. At town fairs, church fish fries, and PTA potlucks you'll eat well and inexpensively and rub elbows with locals. You can find listings for some of these affairs at tourist offices; to do some advance planning, step into your library and consult *Chase's Calendar of Events* (published annually by McGraw-Hill) for listings of festivals, observances, and other events around the United States, and browse through travel guides for listings of seasonal happenings in foreign destinations.

Seeing the Sights

Take Free Self-Guided Tours

Don't sign up for costly sightseeing tours—you can usually see as much without them. Tourist offices in many towns and cities distribute itineraries and maps, free or at low cost, for self-guided walking or driving tours you can follow at your own pace. Many offices also provide free or low-cost tours on which a knowledgeable guide will introduce you to the sights, usually with a good measure of local color.

City Sightseeing Bus Bargains

Hop-on, hop-off sightseeing buses ply the streets of cities and towns around the world and can provide an economical way to see the sights. To get the most value from a hop-on, hop-off ticket (most cost in the neighborhood of $20), do a little strategizing:

Editor's Choice **Freebie Bonanza at Tourist Offices**

Whenever you arrive in a city or town anywhere in the world, head straight to the tourist office. Some tourist offices are not much more than souvenir shops, but others are well stocked with free maps and handouts on local attractions and are staffed by knowledgeable and helpful locals happy to dispense advice, find you accommodations, and be helpful in other ways. Also look for postings for festivals, concerts, and other events that are often free. You can check out tourist offices before you get to town by visiting their websites, which you'll find in the Tourism Offices Worldwide Directory (www.towd.com), a comprehensive listing of tourist offices, chambers of commerce, and other organizations that provide free and unbiased information to the public. To order free brochures from visitor centers throughout the United States, go to www.24-7vacations.com.

- Most companies sell tickets that are good for 24 hours, so extend your touring over two days (when you buy the ticket at noon, you can use it the following morning as well); you'll probably end up seeing more than you would if you try to cram all your sightseeing into one day.
- Determine if you really need to travel by bus to reach the places you want to see. If a town is small, with few outlying attractions, the answer is probably no.
- Concentrate on far-flung sights and attractions to save the cost of reaching these places on your own. City Sightseeing (www.citysightseeing.co.uk) operates hop-on, hop-off bus tours in cities around the world, and Viator (www.viator.com) offers many hop-on, hop-off tours from other operators.

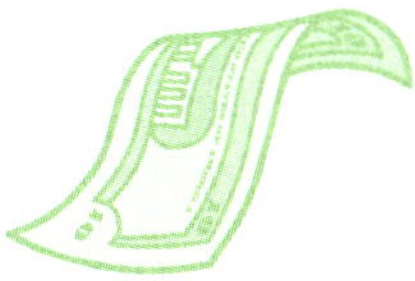

Make the Most of Museums

The Getty in Los Angeles, the collections of the Smithsonian Institution in Washington, D.C., and the National Gallery in London are not only some of the world's top museums; they are also among the many that do not charge entrance fees (the Getty does charge a parking fee of $7). Museums that do charge an admission fee often open their doors for free at least once a week; many offer gallery tours, lectures, and kids' programs for free or at a very reasonable cost. Ask the tourist boards in the places you plan to visit for information on local museums. Museum.com and Artcom.com are useful Internet resources, with links to museum websites.

Bargain Admissions with City Passes

The sightseeing passes available in many cities promise admission to major sights and attractions for one all-inclusive fee and may add up to big savings—but do some research before purchasing one. Does the pass include all of the places you want to visit? What is the cost of individual admission fees versus the cost of the pass? You might find that the Paris Museum Pass, priced at €30 ($37.50) for two days of admissions to more than 60 museums, earns its value even if you just want to visit the Louvre, the Musée d'Orsay, and a few other big collections. On the other hand, the London Pass, £29 ($53.65) a day, lost a lot of its punch when England's state-financed museums began offering free admission. A one-stop shop for passes is Viator.com, where you can find info on sightseeing passes in cities around the world.

EDITOR'S CHOICE

Reduce the Sting of ATM Fees

You might be surprised at how expensive it can be to get your hands on your own hard-earned money when traveling. Your bank will probably charge a fee when you use a different bank's ATM, the bank that administers the ATM will charge a fee, and when traveling abroad, you may pay an extra exchange fee to convert the dollars in your account into a foreign currency. To cut down on ATM fees, make withdrawals in large sums (but only if you feel comfortable carrying a lot of cash) and pay with a credit card (which also usually gets you a favorable exchange rate), check, or debit card when possible.

Save If You're Visiting a Lot of National Parks

In the United States, National Parks Passes help ensure that expense doesn't keep you from enjoying the great outdoors. As with any pass, though, do a little research before purchasing one. A pass, available for $50, admits a vehicle where a vehicle fee is required or a family where a per-person entrance fee is charged to any national park for one year. Given the fact that parks like Yellowstone and the Grand Canyon charge a $25 per vehicle fee for seven days, that's a savings only if you plan on visiting at least three national parks or make several visits to one of them. If you are an outdoors enthusiast and will make good use of the pass, consider paying an extra $15 for a Golden Eagle hologram, good for admission to sites managed by the U.S. Fish and Wildlife Service, the U.S. Forest Service, and the Bureau of Land Management. Buy a National Parks Pass in any national park where an entrance fee is charged or at bookstores affiliated with the National Park Service; online at www.nationalparks.org; or by calling toll-free 888-GO-PARKS (888-467-2757). If you are over 65, get a lifetime Golden Age pass for $15 (see page 302).

MORE SAVINGS STRATEGIES

Stop at State-Line Visitor Centers for Bargains

When traveling in the United States, don't speed by the visitor information offices that greet you at state lines. They are treasure troves of discounts. Most stock booklets on dining, lodging, shopping, and entertainment that are filled with coupons and special offers—$15 off the price of a double room, two meals for the price of one, a 10 percent discount at a local retailer. Since these offers are from local businesses, you won't find them elsewhere, and these booklets are usually not included in online resources or in the information packets that visitor information offices mail out.

Discounts at Disney Parks

You can save a lot of money if you look for bargains when taking the kids to visit Disney World theme parks, Epcot, Animal Kingdom, and those other ever-so-popular and ever-so-expensive Florida attractions. Make your first stop the Walt Disney World website (http://disneyworld.disney.go.com), where you can order a free vacation planning kit with good tips on special offers on theme park admissions and lodging and other deals. Then visit the websites www.mousesavers.com and www.allearsnet.com, where you can browse through offers on discounted tickets and other money-savers, such as shopping coupons, and 99-cent meal deals for kids.

Popular Sites Are Often Cheaper

Some of the most popular vacation spots are also the least expensive. Las Vegas, Nevada, and Branson, Missouri, depend entirely on tourists and lure them throughout the year with big discounts on hotels, restaurants, theaters, clubs, and attractions. To find out what savings await you in these places, check first with the Las Vegas Chamber of Commerce, at 702-641-LVCC (702-641-5822) or www.lvchamber.com, and the Branson Chamber of Commerce at 800-296-0463 or www.bransonchamber.com.

Controlling Cell Phone Fees

Extra charges like roaming fees can inflate your cell phone bill when you travel. Check with your provider to see just how much it will cost to make calls from where you are going—and with typical rates of about $1 a minute or more when calling from abroad, be prepared for sticker shock. You might be able to bring calling rates down considerably by having a cheap, prepaid SIM card (a removable computer memory phone chip) installed in your phone. To learn more about inexpensive options for international cell phone usage, check out Cellular Abroad; call toll-free 800-287-5072 or visit www.cellularabroad.com.

Remember Your VAT Refund

If you shop in Europe, don't forget to pick up your VAT (value-added tax) refund on your way home. Throughout the European Union, taxes of 17 percent and more are added to the price of most goods. As a nonresident, you are entitled to a refund of this tax when you spend the equivalent of about $175 in any one store. Spend $200, and you can get $34 or more back—well worth the small effort you'll make to retrieve it.

Editor's Choice

Phone Home from a Booth

You'll pay a lot less to use a public phone than you will to use the one in your hotel room. That's because hotels often tack exorbitant service charges onto telephone calls. Your cheapest options are usually to buy a discounted, prepaid calling card or, perhaps cheaper yet, take advantage of the reduced rates most telephone networks put in place for long-distance calls at certain times of the day or week; ask the local operator how much a call you plan to make will cost and when the lowest rates are in effect.

CHAPTER 8

cutting the costs of education

When you get beyond the basics of reading, writing, and 'rithmetic, education costs soar. Want to know how to get that diploma without going into debt? Read on.

By the
numbers
16,950

Median annual cost, in dollars, of 2005-06 school year tuition at a four-year private college in the United States. Tuition at Yale University was $31,460 that same academic year.

ARE YOU A COLLEGE-BOUND STUDENT—or the parent of one—searching for relief from the high price of higher education? Or maybe you're the kind of person who thinks education doesn't end when you graduate? If education is your passion and saving money is your game, this is the chapter for you.

It's best to begin your quest for saving money on education at your local public library, where you have free access to information about financial aid for students in publications and on the Internet. While you're there, be sure to inquire at the main desk; there's a good chance your local librarians will know about scholarships and grants offered by businesses and organizations in your hometown. You have a better chance of winning a scholarship from a club or a group whose members know you or your family.

Even if you receive a full-tuition scholarship from the college of your choice, you'll still need considerable funds for room and board, transportation, books, lab fees, supplies—the list can seem endless. We'll show you how to trim the cost of many of those so-called extras.

Start by saving money on prep courses for entrance exams and learn how you can lower the costs associated with the college application process. Next, we'll introduce you to the Free Application for Federal Student Aid form. Filling it out is a time-consuming chore, but to qualify for federal aid, it's absolutely necessary; the FAFSA form is required by almost every college as part of the process of applying for need-based grants.

Do you think you or your student won't qualify for a need-based scholarship? Even if you don't have a 4.0 GPA or exhibit winning moves on the basketball court, there are hundreds of scholarships available for "average" students with special interests, special needs, and links to special-interest groups. We've compiled dozens of national, state, and regional scholarships and grants. If a scholarship program described in this chapter is of interest to you but located in another state, don't despair. Chances are your state, or state university, offers something comparable. The same is true of other special scholarships. Be resourceful and diligent as you research local opportunities, and remember: It never hurts to ask.

We've tried to give you a sense of how much money scholars and even average students can apply for—on the federal and state levels, for training in particular occupations, and for students with special interests. It can be grueling to apply for multiple scholarships, but the payoff is worthwhile. Applying generally doesn't cost anything, and you could reap thousands of dollars in free cash.

Discounts for Students

Save on Sales Tax

Want to make back-to-school shopping less "taxing"? Put those backpacks and sneakers on layaway until your state's tax amnesty days roll around. If you live in Washington, D.C., or one of a dozen states that exempt purchases from sales tax during the weeks before

Recycle Printer Cartridges to Get Money for Your School

Recycling is a good thing, but earning money by recycling is even better. You can save the planet *and* earn $3 for your school for every eligible ink or toner cartridge you collect under the Staples Recycle for Education program. Sign up using your school's tax ID at staplesrecyclefored.com. You'll get a free starter kit, collection boxes, and prepaid UPS mailer labels. It couldn't be easier to turn trash into cash, and Staples even pays for shipping.

students head back to school, you can save between 5 and 9 percent, depending on the tax rate. Some states, such as Georgia and Missouri, extend the tax exemption to computers and computer-related accessories (with maximum costs ranging as high as $3,500 in North Carolina), while other states, such as Connecticut and Iowa, exempt only items you can wear. For an annually updated list of state tax holidays, go to the Federation of Tax Administrators website: www.taxadmin.org.

Refurbished Computers for Even Less

Want a deeper discount on a computer? Consider buying a refurbished one. Dell holds an online auction for refurbished laptops and desk models, and some computers come with warranties; learn more—and bid—at dellauction.com. To find the best deal, compare prices before you bid, read the fine print, and be flexible about the bells and whistles you think your new machine really needs.

Beating the High Cost of Textbooks

It happens every semester. You want to buy a used textbook at your campus bookstore, but they're all out. What do you do now?

- To avoid paying top dollar, shop early—check the bulletin boards at the student union, dorm, and library. Cut out the middleman (your college textbook retailer) and find other students who are selling their texts.
- If you come up empty-handed, turn to the Internet before you head to the bookstore. Put aside any preconceived notions about which stores and which Internet sites are the cheapest—used book prices can be all over the lot, and sometimes a brick-and-mortar store will have the best deals. Compare prices on new and used textbooks by entering the book's International Standard Book Number (ISBN) on Amazon.com, Ebay.com, Half.com, Abebooks.com, Campusbooks.com, Barnes & Noble (bn.com), and other sites that sell books.
- When you're ready to sell your old textbooks, check the price differential between buying a used textbook and what a site is willing to pay for that same used volume. We checked prices for a calculus textbook that retails for $120. The cost for a used copy ranged from $48 to $170, but bn.com offered a used copy for only $20.

Whether you're selling or buying, do your research, and post lists in your dorm and on community bulletin boards—you may get the best deal by selling or buying student to student.

Study Aids

No-Cost Access to Expensive Journals

Ever found yourself working on a science term paper and desperately needing a journal article that is available only to subscribers? Before you pay big bucks (up to $20 or $30) to access that content, try your college library, which can probably give you online access to hundreds of scientific and literary journals. No online library at your college? Ask your local public librarian about online access to such searchable databases as EBSCO or ProQuest. Such electronic resources give you ready access to millions of documents originally published in magazines, newspapers, and journals. And if EBSCO or ProQuest is not available through your local branch, there's still hope. Some reference librarians will arrange for you to get faxed copies of the full text of scholarly articles or arrange interlibrary loans; ask at the main desk. Check out all your options before you opt to pay for articles you can get without opening your wallet.

Free SparkNotes Study Guides Online

Q. What do you call a tooth in a glass of water?

A. A one-molar solution.

If you don't get the joke, you can brush up on chemistry at the SparkNotes website: www.sparknotes.com. In addition to chemistry, the site offers free online study guides for math, biology, and physics, as well as practice tests and quizzes for advanced-placement subject exams and a variety of vocabulary-improvement aids, such as free SAT Vocabulary Novels that feature 1,000 of the most frequently tested words used in context, with links to their definitions. You can read the novels, free, on the website: www.sparknotes.com/satfiction. Or delve into the site's numerous study guides and discussions about great films, economists, and philosophers. All this and more is available at no charge at the SparkNotes site.

Free CliffsNotes Summaries on the Web

Didn't have time to read *Moby Dick* over summer vacation? Need to know the name of the ship that rescues Ishmael at the end of the novel? You can read summaries of each chapter, learn more about the book's major themes, take a mini-test, and read a complete analysis of more than 200 other classic novels, short stories, and plays, online—for free—at the CliffsNotes website: www.cliffsnotes.com. Whether you're looking for character analyses, tips on mastering the

Editor's Choice

Discounts for Students

Some of the best deals on computers and software are available to college students through their on-campus bookstores. But Apple retail stores also give discounts to students who show a school ID and a driver's license, or you can shop online at store.apple.com (click on "Education Store" to find discounts available for students at your school). And when you need software for that new machine, head to your college bookstore. Most campuses offer discounts of 50 percent or more on brand-name software, including expensive Microsoft products such as MS Project and FrontPage.

five-paragraph essay, or ways to make the most of your study time, CliffsNotes has dozens of online links to help you become a better student and tackle tales of whales and other literary beasts.

Planning Ahead

Save for College as You Shop

Even if your uncles aren't rich, they can still contribute money to your college education. When you open a Upromise College Fund savings plan (see page 375), you can register the supermarket club cards and credit cards of your rich (or poor) relatives, and between

Editor's Choice Tomorrow's Education at Today's Rates

State Education

College costs are expected to rise 7 or 8 percent per year for the next ten years. You can combat future inflation by locking in today's prices with a prepaid-tuition plan. Such plans are related to state-run 529 college-savings plans, named after the IRS code that allows you to save for college in a tax-deferred investment. Eighteen states currently offer different types of prepaid-tuition plans. In plans like Maryland's Prepaid College Trust (www.collegesavingsmd.org), you buy a contract based on today's tuition rates (plus a premium) that obligates the plan to pay your child's tuition for a given number of semesters 10, 15, or 20 years from now. In a "guaranteed savings" plan, such as Washington State's Guaranteed Education Tuition program (www.get.wa.gov), you buy tuition "units" redeemable in the future to pay for tuition and state-mandated fees. Although usually designed for use at in-state public colleges and universities, most plans allow students to attend out-of-state or private institutions. Prepaid tuition plans tend to work best for middle-income families with younger children. To see if prepaid tuition plans are available in your state, go to www.college savings.org/locator/index.htm.

Private Education

A private school plan, known as the Independent 529 Plan, covers prepaid tuition at more than 250 participating colleges and universities, including Amherst, Smith, Stanford, Tulane, Notre Dame, and Princeton. Because of disparities in tuition costs among colleges, the certificate you purchase might pay for 50 percent of the tuition at one college but only 20 percent of the tuition at a higher-priced university. And be advised that paying in advance is no guarantee of admission: Your student still must meet academic entrance requirements. However, if he is rejected by the college of his choice, you can get a refund, but you will have to pay taxes and a penalty. Learn more about these plans at the website www.independent529plan.org.

Tax-Free Gifts to Your 529 Tuition Plan

Got a rich uncle who wants to give you some money for college? Thanks to section 529 of the Internal Revenue Code, that rich uncle can contribute $11,000 in one year (or up to $55,000 pro-rated over a five-year period) to your (or your child's) 529 savings plan without incurring any gift taxes or reducing his federal unified estate and gift tax credit. Funds in a 529 plan grow free of federal income taxes, and may be free of state income taxes as well, depending upon the state you live in. This money can be used to pay not only for tuition, but also for fees, room and board, books, computers, and other supplies at accredited public and private colleges, universities, graduate schools, community colleges, and most vocational and technical schools. For more information on 529 plans, visit the U.S. Securities and Exchange Commission's online primer at www.sec.gov/investor/pubs/intro529.htm.

1 and 8 percent of the amount they spend on groceries, travel, restaurant dinners, and so on, at participating Upromise companies will be rebated to your or your child's 529 education account. Interest accumulates tax free, and you don't pay tax when you take the money out for educational expenses. For more on Upromise College Fund savings plans, go to www.upromise.com.

Become a Resident and Get Half-Price Tuition

If you live in the same state where you want to attend college, you can reap significant savings on your tuition. In Texas, for example, your tuition fees as a resident would be about 40 percent of what you'd pay as an out-of-state student—a difference of approximately $7,500 per semester. But let's say you live in Oklahoma and want to attend the University of Texas at Austin to study at the College of Pharmacy. It might pay for you to become a resident of the Lone Star State. But how do you qualify? If you can't convince your parents to move before your senior year of high school, you could live and work in Texas for a year after high school graduation. According to Texas Education Code Sec. 54.052 (e), any individual 18 years of age or over who is "gainfully employed in Texas for a 12-month period immediately preceding registration in an educational institution shall be classified as a resident student as long as he continues to maintain a legal residence in Texas." Be advised that an Oath of Residency may be required. Check out the rules for determining resident status in Texas at: www.thecb.state.tx.us/reports/pdf/0183.pdf

College Prep for Pennies

It costs parents tens of thousands of dollars a year to send a student to college—and that's just for public school fees! Though tuition payments may be just around the corner, pre-college application and preparation costs don't have to run you an arm and a leg. From test prep to waived application costs, here are a few ways for would-be university students (and their parents) to save big.

Free Test Prep for SAT Exams

Scoring well on the SAT (formerly called the Scholastic Aptitude Test) college entrance exams can give you an extra edge when applying to schools. But tutors and test-prep courses are expensive—as much as $900 for six weeks of practice sessions. You can prepare for the SAT free of charge by visiting the College Board's official website (www.collegeboard.com), where you can take a free, full-length practice test, and receive a free skills report and detailed explanations for all test questions. Want even more practice to help improve your scores? The College Board offers an online self-study course for $69.95 for four months, with numerous practice tests, explanations, score reports, and suggested areas for improvement. That's not cheap, but it's much less than the cost of courses from Kaplan or Princeton Review.

Free Test Prep for ACT Exams

Most colleges and universities will accept scores from either the SAT or the ACT (once known as the American College Test). The ACT has four subject areas—English, mathematics, reading, and science, plus an optional writing test. Unlike the SAT, which is designed to measure skills needed for academic success in college, the ACT is an achievement test that measures what a student has learned through grade 11. Another difference between the two tests: Your ACT score is based on the number of correct answers, without any penalty for incorrect answers, while the SAT downgrades your score for every incorrect guess. You'll find free sample ACT tests at www.actstudent.org/sampletest. Want more practice? The ACT offers an online course that's triple the duration of the SAT's official online course for less than one-third the price. Pay only $19.95 for a full year's access. For more information, visit the ACT website (www.act.org); or call 319-337-1270.

Fee Waivers for the ACT and SAT

Can't afford the fees to take either the ACT or SAT college entrance exam? If you're a high school junior or senior with financial hardship, you can register for fee waivers to cover the cost of testing. You must visit your high school guidance office to obtain an online fee-waiver identification number for the SAT, or official fee-waiver forms for the ACT (you can't request a waiver directly from ACT online). Funds are limited for ACT fee waivers; once they are depleted, requests for waivers are denied, so be sure to apply early. Students who qualify for SAT fee waivers may also be eligible for application fee waivers at some colleges. For more information on colleges that offer application fee waivers, check the 2005–2006 Directory of Colleges Cooperating with the SAT Program Fee-Waiver Service online at www.collegeboard.com. Students who use SAT fee waivers are eligible to receive up to four Request for Waiver of College Application Fee forms.

Fee-Free College Applications for Everyone

Paper or electronic? The choice is yours, but when you choose postal mail to send your paper application to Smith College, for example, you must include a check for as much as $60. However, if you apply online—using the Common Application (www.commonapp.org)—Smith's fee is waived. More than 90 colleges and universities, including Colgate, Hobart & William Smith, Albright, DePauw, and Marquette, are so eager to have prospective students send electronic applications that they let them apply free of charge even if they don't meet the stringent income requirements for waived application fees. So when you apply to college, save a stamp, save some trees, and, best of all, save between $25 and $60 on every college application you submit by using the online Common Application form.

Free and Bargain Campus Tours

Checking out colleges on the East Coast when you live in, say, San Francisco can be prohibitively expensive, especially if you're traveling with a parent. You can save money on train travel with Amtrak's Campus Visit Discount program, which allows students to take a parent along for free; check it out at www.campusvisit.com. And a "virtual college visit" will save you money *and* time by bringing the campus to you. To open your portal to hundreds of college campuses in the United States, visit the websites campustours.com and ecampustours.com. You'll find alphabetical lists of colleges, or you can search by state and preview dozens of campuses, from coast to coast, in a single afternoon.

TAKE CAUTION! Not All Scholarship Applications Are Free

"The more the merrier" may not be true when it comes to all scholarship applications. If you're a cash-strapped student, you'll want to apply for numerous scholarships to better your odds of receiving aid, but choose wisely before you apply. Some private schools and scholarship organizations will ask you to submit a CSS/Financial Aid PROFILE (a fee-based service of the College Board). The CSS form solicits financial information not reported in the Free Application for Federal Student Aid (see "What You Need to Know Before Applying for Federal Student Financial Aid," page 159) and may set you back $23 for your first application and $18 for each additional one, if you don't obtain a fee waiver. More than 600 colleges, universities, and scholarship programs, including the United Negro College Fund, the Mexican American Legal Defense Fund, and the NAACP Scholarship Fund, use the information collected on the CSS PROFILE to determine your eligibility for student aid. For more information, visit https://profileonline.collegeboard.com.

STATE INCENTIVES

Seek Out Deals for State Residents

Not eligible for federal education funding? Your state may offer special residents-only scholarships, financial aid programs, or grants. To find what's available in your state, contact its commission on higher education. The fastest and easiest way to find contact information for your state's commission on higher education (which may have a slightly different name in some states) is to search for "student aid" and your state's name in Google or another search engine.

Florida's Lotto-Funded Scholarships

If you play Lotto or another Florida lottery game, chances are about 22,957,480 to 1 that you won't win any cash for your college education bill, but part of your purchase will go toward funding resident students' postsecondary educations through Florida's Bright Futures Scholarship Program. Winners of the program's Florida Academic Scholars awards receive 100 percent of tuition and fees at Florida public institutions (including lab fees up to $300 per semester, and $300 per semester for college-related expenses) or a comparable amount toward tuition at a private institution. Winners of the Florida Medallion Scholars awards receive 100 percent of their tuition and fees for college credit courses leading to an associate's degree at one of 28 Florida community colleges. Each award has its own academic and other eligibility requirements. For additional information, see the Florida Bright Futures Scholarship Program homepage (www.firn.edu/doe/brfutures); or call the Bright Futures Hotline toll-free at 888-827-2004.

Oklahoma's Promise Scholarships

Lottery losers in Oklahoma can take some solace in the fact that their losses are helping to fund higher education. About 45 percent of the $37 million in scholarships awarded by the Oklahoma State Regents for Higher Education comes from lottery and casino gaming revenues, and an estimated 15,000 students will have received Oklahoma's Promise scholarships in 2006–2007. The "promise" begins as early as the eighth grade. Students promise to prepare academically for college and stay out of trouble—they are required to take specific courses and keep up their grades—and the state of Oklahoma promises to help pay their college tuition. To qualify for free tuition at Oklahoma public institutions or partial tuition at Oklahoma private schools, you must live in Oklahoma and your family income must be less than $50,000. Get the details at www.okhighered.org/ohlap/about.shtml.

Free Tuition for County Residents

Residents of Garrett County, Maryland, may qualify for the Garrett County Commissioners Scholarship Program, which provides eligible graduating high school seniors with a tuition-free education at Garrett College. (The scholarship fills the gap between the full cost of tuition and fees at the two-year college and any other federal, state, or private aid for which a student qualifies; for details, visit garrettcollege.edu/csp/index.html.) And lucky Tennessee students who graduate from the city of Kingsport or Sullivan County high schools and whose parents have been county residents for at least one year may qualify for the Kingsport/Sullivan County Educate and Grow Scholarship, which gives qualifying graduates two years' free tuition to Northeast State Community College. For information, write to NSCC, 2425 Highway 75, P.O. Box 246, Blountville, Tennessee 37617; or call 423-323-3191.

Tuition Breaks for Kalamazoo Residents

Are you a resident of Kalamazoo County, Michigan? You may qualify for a tuition scholarship for up to four years at any Michigan public university or community college. The Kalamazoo Community Foundation Scholarship program (www.kalfound.org/page10933.cfm) rewards the talents and achievements of students graduating from Kalamazoo public high schools. The amount of the tuition benefit is based on time spent in Kalamazoo public schools, and although most of the scholarships are for graduating high school seniors, some funds are available for students already enrolled in college. A similar program is available for students who graduate from high school in Newton, Iowa. Funding depends upon a student's years of residency and the total number of grades completed at Newton Public Schools. For details, visit newtonpromise.com.

Credit Union Scholarships in Virginia

If you live in Virginia and are a member of the Virginia Credit Union, you might qualify for a scholarship of up to $2,500. The VCU's Dorothy J. Hall Scholarship Program awards some 25 scholarships to VCU members enrolled at an accredited college or university who are taking at least nine semester hours. High school students who themselves are members of a Richmond, Virginia, area credit union or whose parents are members may be eligible for a Richmond Chapter of Credit Unions Scholarship. For details about both the VCU and Richmond scholarship programs, visit www.vacu.org/about/scholarships.asp.

Occupation-Specific Scholarships

Florida Scholarships for Future CPAs

Love numbers? Scholarships for accounting students are available through the Florida Institute of Certified Public Accountants' Educational Foundation. And if you're a minority student who wants to be a CPA, there is a special fifth-year minority scholarship program that offers a total of $100,000 per year in scholarships. If you meet the requirements—which include financial need; ethnicity, gender, or racial minority status; and scholastic ability and the intention of sitting for the CPA exam—you could receive a scholarship of $3,000 per semester for a maximum of two semesters. For more information about the Educational Foundation, contact the Florida Institute of

Q Is it true that attendance at colleges like West Point and the Naval Academy is free?

A Not only do the United States Service academies—West Point, and the Coast Guard, Air Force, and Naval academies—offer free tuition, room, and board; they also provide free medical and dental care and a salary. At West Point, cadets pay for uniforms, textbooks, a personal computer, and incidentals from their monthly pay. Of course, admission is highly selective, and there is a catch: To receive that free education all cadets are obligated to serve five years of active duty in the U.S. Army after graduation, plus three years in the reserves. For more information, visit the academies' websites: West Point (www.usma.edu); the Naval Academy (www.usna.edu); the Air Force Academy (www.usafa.af.mil); or the Coast Guard Academy (www.uscga.edu).

What You Need to Know Before Applying for Federal Student Financial Aid

Educational aid comes in many forms. Your total financial aid package may include grants, loans, scholarships, and work-study programs from federal, state, and private sources. To qualify for financial aid, you must complete the Free Application for Federal Student Aid issued by the U.S. Department of Education. The FAFSA determines the federal aid (grants, loans, and work-study programs) students are eligible to receive based on their Expected Family Contribution (EFC), the amount of money a family should be able to pay for college tuition based on income and assets. Apply at www.fafsa. ed.gov. Don't type www.fafsa. com—that website, a private enterprise not affiliated with the Department of Education, charges new applicants $80 for a service that is free at www.fafsa .ed.gov.

Grants to students, unlike loans, do not have to be repaid. Grants may be provided by individual states or the federal government.

- *Federal Pell Grants* are the most common form of financial aid provided by the federal government. They are need-based and awarded by individual schools to low-income undergraduates.
- *Federal Supplemental Educational Opportunity Grants* are awarded to Federal Pell Grant recipients with the greatest financial need and the lowest EFCs.

Loans to students must be repaid with interest, even if you do not complete your education. There are three federal loan programs:

- *Federal Perkins Loans* have the best terms, but the loan amounts are small. Perkins loans, funded by the federal government and awarded by the college, are generally reserved for students with serious financial need.
- *Federal Stafford Loans,* obtained through a bank, credit union, or the government, come in two forms: subsidized and unsubsidized. The loan of choice is a subsidized Stafford Loan—the government pays the interest while you are in school. If you do not qualify for a subsidized loan, interest starts accumulating on your loan while you are still in school, although you may postpone payment of both interest and principal until after graduation.
- *Federal PLUS Loans* are available for parents of undergraduate students. A credit check and credit history are required, and repayment begins within 60 days after funds are received.

CPAs at 850-224-2727 or toll-free (in Florida only) at 800-342-3197, ext. 200; or visit the institute's website: www.ficpa.org (go to "FICPA Educational Foundation" under "Special Programs & Events"). For an application, write to the Florida Board of Accountancy, 240 NW 76th Drive, Suite A, Gainesville, Florida 32607.

ROTC Scholarships

If you can't attend one of the military academies, you may qualify for an Army ROTC scholarship (www.goarmy.com/rotc/scholar ships.jsp). Some scholarships pay full-tuition or provide living allowances of up to $500 per month for upperclassmen. Army National Guard Scholarships and Guaranteed Reserve Forces Duty scholarships, which pay up to $20,000 for tuition and fees, are awarded based on merit and grades, not financial need. Like the service academies, these Army programs require that you accept a commission and serve in the Army on active duty or in the U.S. Army Reserve or Army National Guard. To learn more about the ROTC program, write to the U.S. Military Academy, West Point, New York 10996; or call 845-938-4011. You can also consult your guidance counselor or your college's military science department.

Firefighter-Related Scholarships

Dozens of local squads, state associations, and national organizations provide scholarships for firefighters or the children of firefighters. The National Burglar & Fire Alarm Association Youth Scholarship Program awards $6,500 for first-place winners and $3,500 to second-place winners in an annual contest open to the children of police and fire officials. Awards are based on academic achievement, test scores, extracurricular participation, and an essay explaining "How Your Father, Mother or Guardian Helps Us Secure Our Community." For more information, visit the NBFAA's website (www.alarm.org; go to "Consumer Information" and click on

EDITOR'S CHOICE Free Tuition at Cooper Union

The Cooper Union for the Advancement of Science and Art, in New York City, was established in 1859 by Peter Cooper, the designer and builder of America's first steam railroad engine. It is the only private, full-scholarship college in the United States dedicated exclusively to preparing students for the professions of art, architecture, and engineering. If you apply to Cooper Union, you must submit a CSS Profile (see "Not All Scholarship Applications Are Free," page 156), but it could be the best $23 investment you'll ever make. At Cooper Union, every student receives a tuition scholarship worth more than $30,000 per year. Competition for admission is fierce—only 300 students are admitted, and typical SAT scores are high (1260–1460). For more information, write to the Cooper Union for the Advancement of Science and Art, 30 Cooper Square, New York, New York 10003; call 212-353-4120; or visit www.cooper.edu.

State Firefighter Scholarships

Even if your grades and test scores are not top-notch, there are still hundreds of firefighter scholarships available. The following are typical of what might be available in your state:

- The Illinois Fire Chiefs Association (P.O. Box 7, Skokie, Illinois 60076; toll-free 800-662-0732) awards more than 70 scholarships of up to $2,000 for active members of recognized fire departments in Illinois. Apply online at www.illinoisfirechiefs.org.
- If you live in Virginia, the International Association of Fire Chiefs Foundation (4025 Fair Ridge Drive, Fairfax, Virginia 22033; 703-273-0911) offers scholarships for Explorer Scouts, volunteers, and career firefighters for the study of fire sciences and related academic programs. Check out the requirements on its website: www.iafcf.org/html/scholhome.html.
- Members of the South Carolina State Firefighters' Association are eligible to apply for $1,000 scholarships, awarded each academic year, to cover tuition and the cost of books. Application forms are available at scfirefighters.org.

"NBFAA Youth Scholarship Program"); or call 888-447-1689. More firefighter-related scholarships are detailed in "State Firefighter Scholarships," above.

Veterans and Survivors Scholarships

American Legion Scholarships for Vets' Children

Are you the child or grandchild of a U.S. wartime vet? If so, Samsung may have a scholarship for you. The Samsung American Legion Scholarship Program was established with a $5 million endowment to show appreciation to U.S. veterans of the Korean War. Eligibility is limited to high school juniors who have participated in or completed the American Legion Boys State or Auxiliary Girls State program, and who are direct descendants (a child, grandchild, great-grandchild, or legally adopted child) of a U.S. veteran who served on active duty in the Korean War or any other eligible conflict from World War I through the Persian Gulf War. For full details, write to the American Legion, P.O. Box 1055, Indianapolis, Indiana 46206; or visit the

American Legion's website: www.legion.org (click on "Scholarship Information" under "Useful Links.")

More American Legion Scholarships

Make sure to check out the other scholarship opportunities described on the American Legion's website (www.legion.org; click on "Scholarship Information" under "Useful Links"), including the Eagle Scout of the Year award (one $10,000 scholarship, with three runners-up scholarships of $2,500 each); the American Legion National High School Oratorical Contest (an $18,000 scholarship for the first-place winner); and the American Legacy Scholarship fund, which benefits the children of active duty U.S. military, Guard, and Reserve personnel who died on active duty on or after September 11, 2001.

Armed Forces Line-of-Duty Scholarships

The children of Americans who served in the armed forces and died or were permanently disabled (100 percent disability) in the line of duty or who are certified as prisoners of war or missing in action are eligible to apply to the Freedom Alliance Scholarship Fund. To receive a one-year scholarship, which can be renewed for full-time students who maintain an acceptable grade point average, you must be a high school senior, a high school graduate, or a registered undergraduate under the age of 26; your parents' income cannot exceed $75,000 annually. For complete information, write to the Freedom Alliance Scholarship Fund, 22570 Markey Court, Suite 240, Dulles, Virginia 20166; call toll-free 800-475-6620; or visit the Freedom Alliance website: www.freedomalliance.org (click on "Scholarship Fund").

NYS Police and Firefighters Line-of-Duty Scholarships

Most states have memorial scholarship funds for the children of police officers and firefighters who died in the line of duty. In New York State, the Higher Education Services Corporation's Memorial Scholarships are available to eligible children, spouses, and financial dependents of deceased firefighters, volunteer firefighters, police officers, peace officers, and emergency medical service workers. The award is equal to the applicant's actual tuition cost or the State University of New York undergraduate tuition, whichever is less. (Students must be New York residents and full-time undergraduates at approved programs to qualify.) For detailed

EDITOR'S CHOICE Elks Scholarships

With more than one million members in more than 2,100 local lodges, the Benevolent and Protective Order of Elks of the U.S.A. is one of the world's largest and most active fraternal organizations. Each year it awards more than $3 million in college scholarships to graduating high school seniors. Legacy Awards and Educational Grants are available only to children of Elks, but Most Valuable Student, Eagle Scout, and Girl Scout Gold Award scholarships are open to any graduating high school senior. The application process and deadlines vary by program, and most applications must go through a local Elks Lodge before reaching the Elks National Foundation office. For more information, consult your high school counselor, contact your local Elks Lodge, or visit the Elks website: www.elks.org (click on "Scholarships").

information, go to the HESC website (www.hesc.com; enter "Memorial Scholarships" in the search field); call toll-free 888-697-4372; or write to the NYS Higher Education Service Corporation Memorial Scholarship Fund, Education Department, 99 Washington Avenue, Albany, New York 12255.

ORGANIZATION AND FOUNDATION SCHOLARSHIPS

Union Scholarships for Working Families

The AFL–CIO's Union Plus Scholarship Program was established in 1992 to assist students of working families who want to begin or complete their college educations. The program database describes more than $4 million in union-sponsored scholarships, with details about eligibility, application deadlines, and contact information. While the database doesn't list all of the scholarships available from 38,000 local unions in the United States, it does include the major programs and is a great place to start a search for free scholarship money. To access the database, go to unionplus.org/benefits/education/scholarships/up.cfm (from the home page, click on "unionscholarships.com").

New York State Carpenters Scholarships

When you're searching for scholarship money, it pays to explore family connections. If one of your parents is a member of the Empire

State Regional Council of Carpenters, you may be eligible to apply for one of eight scholarships awarded by the Council each year on the basis of SAT scores, grades, teacher recommendations, and extracurricular activities. The scholarships consist of annual stipends of $2,000 for four years. For more details, visit the council's website: empirestatecarpenters.org (click on "Scholarship Information").

Science Scholarship for Upperclassmen

If you didn't receive any scholarship help as a college freshman, don't fret. There are plenty of opportunities for upperclassmen, especially those with excellent academic credentials. Among the most prestigious awards for upperclassmen is the Barry M. Goldwater Scholarship, granted to outstanding sophomore and junior students pursuing careers in mathematics, the natural sciences, and engineering. More than 300 scholarship recipients are typically chosen from a field of more than 1,100 nominees. Each scholarship covers eligible expenses for undergraduate tuition, fees, books, and room and board, up to a maximum of $7,500 annually. For more details, go to www.act.org/goldwater; or call 703-756-6012.

Political and Environmental Sciences Scholarships

Interested in foreign affairs? Check out the Thomas R. Pickering Foreign Affairs Fellowship, administered by the Woodrow Wilson National Fellowship Foundation. The program recruits talented students in the areas of international affairs, political and economic analysis, and science policy. Awards include tuition and room and board during the junior and senior years of college and the first year of graduate study. For more information, visit www.woodrow.org/public-policy/undergraduate.php. The Morris K. Udall Foundation awards approximately 80 scholarships of up to $5,000 to sophomore- and junior-level college students who are interested in careers related to the environment, and who are Native Americans or Alaska Natives with an interest in pursuing careers in either tribal public policy or Native health care. Find out more at www.udall.gov (click on "Morris K. Udall Scholarship" under "Our Programs").

Jack Kent Cooke Scholarships for Undergrads and Grads

The Jack Kent Cooke Foundation awards some 35 Undergraduate Transfer Scholarships to help students of exceptional promise transfer to four-year institutions. Each award covers a portion of educational expenses, including tuition, living expenses, fees, and books for the final two to three years of the baccalaureate degree, up to $30,000 per year. The same foundation grants Graduate Scholarships to 65 outstanding college seniors and recent grads who plan to attend graduate school for the first time. The maximum amount of each award is $50,000 per year; the maximum length is six years. For more about these scholarships—as well as the Foundation's Young Scholars program for high-achieving youth with financial need and its September 11 Scholarship Fund for spouses and dependents of 9/11 victims—go to the website www.jackkentcookefoundation.org (click on "Scholarships").

Wal-Mart Scholarships for Employees and Community

The Walton Family Foundation and the Wal-Mart Foundation support a variety of scholarship programs. The Higher REACH Scholarship (up to $2,000 per year) and the Associate Scholarship ($2,000 per year) are both for employees of Wal-Mart Stores, Inc.; the $10,000 Walton Family Foundation Scholarship is for children of full-time Wal-Mart Associates. The $1,000 Sam Walton Community Scholarships, however, are available to the general public. For details, including eligibility requirements, go to www.walmartfoundation.org (click on "Education," and then on "Scholarships").

Unusual Scholarships

David Letterman Scholarships

To win the David Letterman Telecommunications Scholarship at Ball State University in Muncie, Indiana, you don't need a 4.0. Grades are not the issue—creativity is. Ball State's most famous alumnus (class of 1970), Letterman established the scholarships in 1985 for students (first-quarter juniors through first-quarter seniors) majoring or minoring in telecommunications. The scholarships are awarded on the basis not of grade point averages or SAT scores, but rather on the merits of a "creative endeavor"—a written work, research effort, audio or video project, film, or presentation. The first-place scholarship is for $10,000, with runner-up awards of $5,000 and $3,333. For more information, go to www.bsu.edu/ccim/tcom/scholarships.htm, or write to Dr. Wes Gehring, Department of Telecommunications, Ball State University, Muncie, Indiana, 47306.

Scholarships for Duct-Tape Tuxes and Prom Gowns

Formal prom attire is expensive. So save your cash, and make your own prom tux or gown—with duct tape. Yes, duct tape. Not only will you save money by not renting or buying formal wear, you'll also have excellent odds of winning the Stuck at Prom Duck brand duct tape scholarship contest. Only 233 couples entered the 2006 contest and vied for 13 prizes totaling $20,000. But the best part of this scholarship contest is there's no essay to write and no application to fill out. All you have to submit is a photo of you and your date at the prom wearing your duct tape finery, and your signed release forms. Each first-place winner receives a cash scholarship of $3,000—that's $6,000 per couple. And the school that hosts the winning couple's prom also receives a cash prize of $3,000. Second-prize winners take home $2,000, third-prize winners get $1,000, and ten "best in class" award winners receive $200 each. Check out the rules and previous winners at www.stuckatprom.com.

Scholarships for the Tall and Big

Here's a pair of scholarships for the tall and plus-sized:

- Guys 6'2" or taller and gals who are at least 5'10" are eligible to vie for $1,000 Tall Clubs International Scholarships. You must be sponsored by a local TCI chapter, be under 21 years of

EDITOR'S CHOICE Scholarships for Left-Handers

Sometimes a tiny detail in your background can bring on a scholarship bonanza. Southpaws at Juniata College, in Huntingdon, Pennsylvania, are eligible to apply for the Frederick and Mary F. Beckley Scholarship, worth $1,000 to $1,500 a year to studious, left-handed Juniata students. The scholarship fund was established in 1979 by a former Juniata student with a bequest of $24,000. Dozens of left-leaning students have taken advantage of this award, which is open to Juniata sophomores, juniors, and seniors with financial need and good grades. For more information, write to the Office of Student Financial Planning, Juniata College, 1700 Moore Street, Huntingdon, Pennsylvania 16652.

age, and write an essay on "What Being Tall Means to Me." Download a brochure from the TCI website: www.tall.org.

- Write an essay on the importance of fat acceptance, fat activism, or how the National Association to Advance Fat Acceptance has changed your life, and you could win a $1,000 or $500 merit scholarship. Founded in 1969, the NAAFA works "to eliminate discrimination based on body size and provide fat people with the tools for self-empowerment through public education, advocacy, and member support." The scholarship contest is open to NAAFA members studying at a community/junior college, college, or university. For more on NAAFA, visit www.naafa.org. For details of the 2006 contest, go to www.naafa.org/new events/meritaward06.html.

Two-for-One Scholarships for Twins

Twins may double the fun—until it comes time to pay for college tuition. If you have a twin, Lake Erie College, in Painesville, Ohio, has a deal for you: a special Twins Scholarship. You pay full tuition and your twin gets a full scholarship—a savings of nearly $22,000 per year. For more information, write to Lake Erie College, 391 West Washington Street, Painesville, Ohio 44077; or call 440-296-1856.

Half-Price Tuition for Second Sibling

George Washington University, in Washington, D.C., offers half-price tuition for the younger sibling of a student, as long as the two are enrolled concurrently. The GW Family Grant is not available to students charged a discounted tuition or if either sibling is enrolled in the Seven-Year Integrated B.A./M.D. or the Integrated Engineering and Medicine Programs. For full details, go to gwired.gwu.edu/finaid (click on "New Undergraduate Students," then on "Family Financing," and scroll down to "GW Family Grant").

Special-Interest Scholarships

Awards for Environmental Scholars

Planning to study ecology? Is *Silent Spring* one of your favorite books? Chatham College, in Pittsburgh, Pennsylvania, offers a

Q Are there any special scholarships for students who study foreign languages?

A If you have a knack for languages, specifically Urdu, Pashto, Korean, Farsi, Hindi, Dari, Chinese, or Arabic, the National Security Agency offers up to $25,000 per year for students in the last one or two years of a graduate degree program through the new Pat Roberts Intelligence Scholars Program for highly qualified students. As one of the nation's largest employers of language professionals, NSA offers competitive language scholarships to applicants who demonstrate foreign language proficiency in reading and listening skills on NSA tests. For more details, go to www.nsa.gov/careers/students_4.cfm (scroll down to the PRISP section). You can also call toll-free 866-672-4473; or write to the National Security Agency, 9800 Savage Road, Suite 6779, Fort George G. Meade, Maryland 20755.

$1,000 Rachel Carson Book Award for excellence in science and writing to high school juniors with an interest in environmental issues. For more information on the award, visit the website www.chatham.edu/admissions/scholarships.cfm. Cal State Fullerton offers a $400 Rachel Carson Scholarship to returning students studying conservation biology; find out more at the site biology.fullerton.edu/scholarships/bio-scholarships.pdf.

Scholarships for Landscapers

Like sinking your hands into the dirt? Check out the scholarships available for landscape architecture students from the Leadership in Landscape Scholarship Program of the Landscape Architecture Foundation. Your odds of striking "pay dirt" with this application are high. In 2006, only 112 applications were received, and a total of $66,500 was awarded to 21 students (that is, 19 percent of the applicant pool). For more information, contact the LAF, 818 18th Street NW, Suite 810, Washington, D.C. 20006. You can also call 202-331-7070 or visit the foundation's website: www.lafoundation.org (click on "Scholarships").

Scholarships for All Things Polish

If you're an American student of Polish descent on your way to graduate school, you may be eligible for a Kosciuszko Foundation Tuition Scholarship of between $1,000 and $7,000 per academic year. Kosciuszko Foundation Scholarships support:

- Graduate studies in the United States in a variety of fields (from art, architecture, and accounting to law, music, Polish studies, and social science)
- The one-year master's program at the Center for European Studies at Jagiellonian University in Cracow, Poland
- Programs at English-language schools of medicine in Poland.

Even if you're not of Polish descent, you may be eligible for foundation support if you will be pursuing a full-time graduate program in Polish studies. Awards are based on academic excellence and interest in Polish subjects or involvement in Polish American community affairs; financial need is considered. For more information, go to www.kosciuszkofoundation.org/EDScholarships_US_Tuition.html; call 212-734-2130; or write to the Kosciuszko Foundation, 15 East 65th Street, New York, New York 10021.

Diversity Scholarships in Chemistry

Interested in science? The American Chemical Society wants to be a catalyst for underrepresented minority students seeking to pursue undergraduate degrees in the chemical sciences. Since 1995, some 1,700 minority students have benefited from the ACS Scholars Program, which awards scholarships to and provides mentoring for African American, Hispanic/Latino, and American Indian students. For information, write to the American Chemical Society, ACS Scholars Program, Department of Diversity Programs, 1155 16th Street NW, Washington, D.C. 20036. You can also call toll-free 800-227-5558 (ext. 6250) or send an e-mail to scholars@acs.org.

Latino Legal Defense Fund Scholarship

If you're a Mexican American law student with a passion to serve the Latino community as a lawyer, you may be able to tap into the Mexican American Legal Defense and Educational Fund. The MALDEF Law School Scholarship offers matriculated law students annual awards of up to $7,000 per student. In addition to being of Mexican descent, you'll have to demonstrate involvement with and a commitment to serve the Latino community, financial need, and academic achievement. For more information, visit the MALDEF website (www.maldef.org; click on "Education Department," then on "Scholarship Programs"); or write to MALDEF, 634 South Spring Street, 11th Floor, Los Angeles, California 90014.

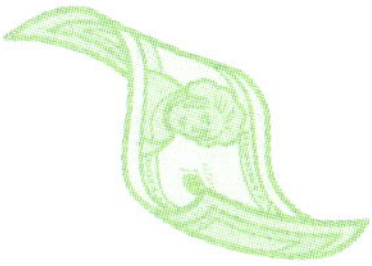

Adult Education

MIT for Free for Self-Learners

You may not have the credentials to attend Massachusetts Institute of Technology, but you can learn with the best. The OpenCourse Ware project (ocw.mit.edu/index.html) is a Web-based electronic publishing initiative that provides free, searchable access to MIT undergraduate and graduate course materials for students, teachers, and self-learners everywhere. No registration is required, and you won't earn credit, but you can choose from more than 1,400 courses in science and the humanities. Do it for the love of learning, or to get a better understanding of courses you're taking in college. MIT's

Editor's Choice

No-Cost Online Learning at Free-Ed.Net

Yes, it does sound too good to be true. But Free-Ed.Net offers online courses and tutorials in more than 120 different disciplines, all free of charge. Never finished high school? You can prepare for a high school equivalency diploma. Interested in the building trades? There are courses in masonry, electrical construction, and professional carpentry that cover all the basics. Computer geeks can learn the fundamentals of Visual C++, Java, and HTML. Links to a collection of free online textbooks (located at www.samspublishing.com) complement the course offerings. Find free online learning at www.free-ed.net.

EDITOR'S CHOICE

Fun Learning Free at Barnes & Noble U

Don't know much about history? Barnes & Noble offers a wide range of free online reading groups led by book authors and experts. Barnes & Noble Book Clubs offer groups studying and discussing books on everything from mysteries and classic novels to how to use Photoshop Elements. New discussion groups are added monthly; check out the latest offerings at bookclubs.barnesandnoble.com.

OCW concept is also expanding. As of mid-2006, Johns Hopkins Bloomberg School of Public Health (ocw.jhsph.edu), Tufts University (ocw.tufts.edu), and Utah State University (ocw.usu.edu/Index/ECIndex_view) offer similar programs, as do dozens of universities in China, Japan, and France.

Cheap College Credits Through Exam Program

Put all that free online learning to good use by getting college credits for what you know via the College-Level Examination Program. Once reserved for older students, CLEP now enables students of any age to demonstrate college-level achievement through a program of exams based on undergraduate college courses. CLEP exams are accepted for credit and/or advanced standing by 2,900 colleges. The exams, which are administered through the College Board, are not free, however. You'll have to pay $60 for each one you take—but compared to the cost of tuition, the fee is a veritable bargain. If you are enlisted in the military, CLEP exams are free, and military veterans can seek reimbursement from the U.S. Department of Veterans Affairs for CLEP exams and fees. For more information, visit the CLEP section of the College Board's website: www.collegeboard.com/student/testing/clep/about.html.

Free Online Business Courses

Getting ready for the real world and a real job? Before you enter the occupational arena, boost your skills by taking Procter & Gamble's free online business courses. All of P&G's topics are chosen to help you make the most of your career opportunities. There are courses to assist you in mastering Excel, MS Project, and PowerPoint, or in learning the ins and outs of business etiquette and teamwork. Visit P&G's virtual campus at pgvirtualcampus.com to find current courses, including Improving Communication: Say What You Mean; if you've ever become tongue-tied when it was time to negotiate a price or ask for a raise, this course can help you say what you mean so that you get what you want.

CHAPTER 9

lowering the cost of transportation

With these free auto safety sources, gas conservation tips, rebate offers, and more, commuters will be on the road to savings in no time.

IF YOU'VE FILLED THE TANK RECENTLY, or had your car repaired, or shopped for auto insurance, or ... well, there's really no point in telling you how expensive it is to own and operate a car. On average, our car habits cost us anywhere from $7,000 to $10,000 a year, more than many households spend on food. It's enough to make you give up the gas guzzler and just walk or ride a bike—which is what many folks are doing, with encouragement from their employers and even the government.

Now, the good news: There's a lot you can do to keep transportation costs down, from bargaining for a lower finance rate on your car loan to using public transportation to carpooling (which can cut your commuting costs by 50 percent, 75 percent, even more).

As you read on, remember that saving money on transportation costs requires a concentrated effort on your part. You need to:

- **Be bold.** Mustering the courage and endurance to bargain with a car salesperson will pay off if you get a lower price, some free accessories, maybe even a good deal on an extended warranty. Similarly, you'll be well rewarded for fighting for Guaranteed Ride Home programs, tax-free transportation benefits, and other workplace perks.

By the numbers

11,904

Number of miles that the average American drives per year.

- **Be flexible.** Taking the bus may not suit your "tiger in a Mercedes" image, but it will save you a lot of money. Likewise, while sharing the trip to work as a carpooler may deprive you of some solitude, you'll find solace in your end-of-month accounting.
- **Be meek.** On the road, that is. Using a lighter touch on the gas pedal, avoiding sudden braking, and visiting your mechanic for frequent checkups and tune-ups can save you a small fortune in gasoline expenditures. Taking a refresher driver's course can cut insurance costs.
- **Be alert.** There's much to think about, whether it's finding ways to refinance your car for a lower interest rate, discovering shorter routes to work, or keeping your van pool full for maximum cost effectiveness. You'll save money if you stay open to the many options you can explore.

Finally, take pleasure in your efforts to find alternative means of getting around. Rediscover the joys of cycling and walking, and delight in the fact that you're reaping health benefits. Be proud that with every mile you don't drive, you're helping the environment. Enjoy the camaraderie of a car pool or daily bus ride. And keep track of the money you save—you'll be pleasantly surprised.

Maintaining and Driving Your Car

Free Auto Checkup

April may be tax time, but on the plus side of the ledger, it's also National Car Care Month, and that's when you can have your car checked out for free. The Car Care Council, a national nonprofit organization that promotes the benefits of proper vehicle care, works with repair facilities and auto-parts stores around the country to sponsor free inspections of fluid levels, tires, lights, and other system components. You may need this freebie more than you think you do: The council reports that in past years 85 percent of all vehicles inspected required repair or maintenance; 30 percent had low or dirty engine oil; 27 percent had inadequate cooling protection; 24 percent had dirty air filters; 26 percent had low or contaminated brake fluid; and 19 percent needed new belts. To find out more about National Car Care Month, visit the Car Care Council website at www.carcare.org.

To Save, Calculate Your Driving Costs

Do you have any idea how much you pay to drive your car every year? Well, brace yourself: If you're the average American, you shell out $7,967 for fuel, routine maintenance, tires, insurance, license and registration, loan finance charges, and depreciation costs annually. If you drive an SUV, you pay even more ($9,800), and even if your car is a small Honda, the total still comes to $6,300 a year. You can comb through cost breakdowns and other details in *Your Driving Costs*, compiled annually by the American Automobile Association; it's available at club offices and downloadable for free at www.aaapublicaffairs.com. Worksheets will help you determine your actual driving costs. Who knows? That might be all the inspiration you need to start driving less and cutting your car costs any other way you can.

Don't Let Your Auto Battery Cost You a Bundle

You might not lie awake at night worrying about your car battery, but maybe you should. A little vigilance can help you get the most life out of your battery and save you a lot of money. Did you know, for instance, that hot temperatures can make a battery deteriorate quickly by causing water to evaporate from the electrolyte (battery acid) solution? You will after a visit to www.autobatteries.com, where Johnson Controls, a battery manufacturer, explains batteries in plain language. Included are useful tips on buying, storing, and recharging your car battery, and a health checkup that helps you determine when it's time to replace it—this could save you a tidy sum, sparing you the high price you'll pay if your battery dies unexpectedly while you're on the road.

Free Online Car-Care Tools

Keeping your car in roadworthy shape not only ensures a safer ride but also helps prevent major and costly breakdowns later on. The Car Care Council (www.carcare.org) provides handy tools to help you keep your car in good running order. The Service Interval Tool asks you to input the model and year of your car and the number of miles since it was last serviced, then tells you exactly what needs to done—engine oil filter replaced, links and hoses inspected, body

Getting the Best Extended Warranty

Still reeling from your last auto repair bill? Then you may not need much convincing to consider an extended warranty to cover repair costs on the next new or used car you buy. Considering the high cost of auto repairs, an extended warranty—which will probably cost several thousand dollars—can be a real money saver, but do a bit of careful navigating before settling on one of these policies that extend the warranty offered by an automobile manufacturer.

- To get the most value, buy an extended warranty as soon as you purchase your car. The cost of extended warranties keeps going up, and so does the cost of repairs, so paying now means you'll save when the coverage kicks in.
- Compare plans offered by dealers and those provided by reputable companies like www.warrantydirect.com. Dealers often provide a plan from one of the companies you can find on your own, but they tack on an extra middleman fee.
- Read carefully before signing on the dotted line, because a warranty contract can be full of loopholes. Find a "bumper to bumper" warranty that covers the most parts, and make sure the warranty covers wear and tear, overheating, and other common problems that can require costly repairs.
- Make sure the warranty covers towing, rental car, overnight accommodation, and other expenditures you might face when your car breaks down.

components lubricated, whatever. A Service Interval schedule tells you which components should be checked when—tires monthly, automatic transmission fluid every three months, brakes every year.

Is Your Car Eligible for a Free Recall Repair?

You might know from experience just how big a dent car repairs can put in the budget. There's a chance, though, that some maintenance may be covered by mandated repairs, called recalls, that manufacturers are required by law to offer for free. You can check to see if your vehicle is eligible for one of these repairs at Carfax (www.carfax.com); click on "Recall Check" under "Free Services," then type in the vehicle identification number (VIN) to find the recalls in effect for the make, model, and year of your car. The Office of Defects Investigation at the National Highway Traffic Safety Administration (www-odi.nhtsa.dot.gov) also provides recall alerts; just follow the instructions and type in the make, model, and year of your car to see notices of the repairs to which you may be entitled—for free.

EDITOR'S CHOICE Take Safety Courses to Lower Insurance Costs

Parking your pride and taking a driver's safety course helps make you a better driver and, depending on the state in which you live, might also lower your car insurance rates by 10 percent or more. Check with your insurance provider or your state DMV to learn about courses that may entitle you to a reduction. In many states, these include the Defensive Driving Course from the National Safety Council; state agencies sometimes offer classroom versions of the course, which is also available online at www.nscddconline.com for $41.25. AARP's Driver Safety Program, a classroom refresher course that's taught around the country to educate participants on the effects of aging on driving, may also entitle you to a reduction. The course costs AARP members just $10; an online version is available ($15.95 for AARP members and $19.95 for nonmembers). For information on the classroom course and to find sessions near you, call toll-free 888-AARP-NOW (888-227-7669) or go to www.aarp.org/families/driver_safety; to learn more about the online course, go to dsop.aarpdriversafety.org.

Use Common Sense to Save Cents

Driving is such a part of everyday life that we seldom slow down and think about ways to save money doing it. Consider these no-brainers:

- Run-of-the-mill license plates are not as snazzy as vanity plates, but in many states a set of standard plates costs as little as $5, while adding a witty acronym or a picture of an emblem of your local sports team greatly increases the price.
- Need to run certain errands regularly? Make a game plan that combines as many stops as possible into one outing. You may be able to shave miles off your weekly driving routine.
- Drive less. You might be surprised at how easy it can be to keep the car in the driveway. Stock up on groceries so you don't make a daily trip to the supermarket, hitch a ride with a friend rather than taking two cars to the same place, shop online instead of driving around town.
- If you have more than one car, use the one that's most fuel efficient whenever possible.

Free AAA Safety Info

You can't put a price on safety, nor will you pay a penny for the useful videos and brochures from the nonprofit AAA Foundation for Traffic Safety (www.aaafoundation.org). Easy to download PDF versions of eight brochures cover such topics as handling distractions while driving, cutting down on glare from headlights at night, and steering clear of aggressive-driving incidents. You'll find these in "Free Materials" under "Products"; you'll also come across quizzes you can take to rate your driving skills and, in the "Resources" section, detailed research reports on such issues as teen driving and booster-seat safety.

Fuel Costs

Calculate the Real Value of That Cheap Gas

Finding a gas station where you can fill up for less will save you money, right? Well, not necessarily. If you have a small tank and drive out of your way to buy cheaper gas, you may actually be spending more by the time you factor in the cost of making repeat visits to the bargain pump. You can find out if the trip is worth it with the gas calculator at www.bankrate.com. Go to www.bankrate.com/brm/calc/gasPrice.asp and enter the capacity of your car's gas tank and the car's fuel efficiency (miles per gallon). Then enter the distance you drive to a gas station near your home or office (the primary gas station) and the price you pay for a gallon of gas. Next, enter the distance you drive to a secondary station that charges less and the cost per gallon there. The calculator will tell you how much you save or waste making the trip for cheaper gas.

Gas Rebates with Credit Cards

You don't get much of a break at the gas pump these days, but the Visa credit card available with no annual fee to members of the American Automobile Association helps stanch cash flow a bit. Cardholders get a rebate of up to 5 percent on gas purchases—not a fortune, but over the course of a year the savings will probably cover the basic AAA membership fee (around $50 a year) and a tank of gas. For details go to www.aaa.com or call toll-free 800-545-7899. Also check with banks and major gas companies to see what sorts of gas rebates their credit cards offer. Be careful, though—the come-on of a rebate on gas purchases could end up costing you money if you pay an annual fee for the card or carry a balance and pay interest.

Time Is Money

Automatic Toll-Collection Systems

E-ZPass, the electronic toll-collection system used widely on bridges and highways—and FasTrak, the system used in California—not only saves you time, but often money as well. E-ZPass uses an electronic transponder that you stick to the windshield of your vehicle; each time you pass through a toll, the appropriate amount is automatically deducted from your debit account. E-ZPass members often get discounts simply for using the system, and additional discounts might apply for driving at off-peak hours, carpooling, and using one toll road or bridge regularly. You'll find links to the state transportation departments, highway and bridge authorities, and other agencies that handle E-ZPass accounts at www.e-zpass.net.

Gas Rebates to Attract Tourists

Finding cheap gas can seem like real detective work, but here's a clue—look for businesses that try to rope in motorists with gas rebates. These giveaways are not always available, and amounts and terms vary considerably from season to season. These offerings were available in mid-2006:

- At www.hotels.com, the online reservations service: a $30 gas rebate to guests presenting gas receipts from dates corresponding to stays of two or more nights.
- 100 members of www.bedandbreakfast.com, a national network of small inns: gas rebates typically amounting to $25 or more.
- The Branson, Missouri, Tourism Center (www.bransontourismcenter.com): for eligible customers residing 100 or more miles away, coupons for 20 cents a gallon off gas purchased at a local service station.

Track Your Gas Consumption to Save

Just as you need to monitor your spending to stay within the household budget, keeping an eagle eye on the amount of gas you use will help you save. To keep tabs on your gas consumption, use the free, downloadable Fuel Purchase Records form at www.fueleconomy.gov.

Holding Down Auto Insurance Costs

Insurance payments add a lot to the cost of owning and driving a car, so do what you can to lower them. Here are some approaches:

- **See what discounts you might be entitled to.** Some insurers offer discounts to teachers and other professionals they assume to be low-risk drivers. Membership in the American Automobile Association and other organizations might also help you nab a lower rate, as can having certain safety features on your car, such as antilock brakes and side-impact air bags.
- **Shop around.** Insurance is a competitive business, and rates vary considerably. The Internet makes it easier to be a comparison shopper—for example, the website www.comparisonmarket.com rounds up rates from different insurers for you.
- **Be a risk-taker.** Not on the road, but in your coverage. If you've never had an accident and only drive to church on Sundays, you may be better off opting for a higher deductible and lower monthly rates.

Getting Better Mileage from Your Car

One surefire way to spend less money on gas is to use less. Here are some ways to be a gas miser:

- Avoid rapid braking and acceleration. At highway speeds, driving at a steady pace improves gas mileage by 33 percent.
- Slow down. Driving fast uses more fuel. Every 5 mph of speed over 60 mph is like paying an extra 20 cents a gallon for gas. Try driving the speed limit and you'll need to fill up less often.
- Lighten your load. Each extra 100 pounds in your vehicle reduces your miles per gallon by 2 percent; a loaded roof rack can reduce fuel economy by 5 percent.
- Keep your car in tiptop shape. A tune-up can increase your mileage by 4 percent; replacing clogged air filters by 10 percent; keeping your tires properly inflated by 3.3 percent; and using the recommended grade of motor oil the manufacturer by 1 to 2 percent.

For more tips and info on saving gas, download the U.S. Department of Energy's free *Fuel Economy Guide* at www.fueleconomy.gov.

Each time you make a stop at the pump, fill in the odometer reading, the number of gallons you purchase, the fill-up cost, driving conditions, and the miles per gallon you're getting—that is, the numbers of gallons you've driven divided by the number of gallons it takes to fill the tank. What to do if you're not pleased with your mpg? Follow the tips in the box "Getting Better Mileage from Your Car," above, and drive less—combine errands, join a car pool, and keep the gas guzzler in the garage and instead, when possible, use public transportation or a bicycle, or walk.

Free Fuel-Tracking Tools from AAA

Before you hit the road, you may want to know how much your trip is going to set you back. The AAA Fuel Cost Calculator (www.fuelcostcalculator.com) helps you determine what you're going to spend for gas—enter the city you're leaving from, where you're going, and the make, model, and year of car you drive, and the calculator will estimate your gas expenditure down to the penny. This telltale tool is geared to intercity trips; to determine what you're going to spend if you're sticking closer to home, go to the AAA's Daily Fuel Gauge Report (www.fuelgaugereport.com), where you can see the cost per gallon in your area. Then do a little calculating on your own—divide the miles you plan to drive by your car's fuel usage (mpg), then multiply that by the cost per gallon (a handy calculator at the site www.roadtripamerica.com does this math for you). Once you see these figures, you may well think twice about making unnecessary trips.

Buying and Leasing a Car

Being Prepared Reaps Large Savings

A little knowledge can save you a lot of money when buying a car. Don't even think of stepping into a car dealership without knowing:

- **The current interest rates on car loans.** You can obtain these from your bank, the business section of your daily newspaper, and from such online sources as www.bankrate.com. When you know what the typical rates are, you'll be better equipped to negotiate a good one with the dealer's finance department.
- **Your credit rating.** Order a report from TrueCredit (www.truecredit.com) or another online service, and if your credit rating is less than stellar, do what you can to fix it. The reporting agency will provide tips, such as paying off as many outstanding credit-card balances as you can.
- **The market value of the cars and accessories in which you are interested.** You can find these in the Kelley Blue Book

Safety Matters When Buying a Car

Seat belts, electronic stability controls, and other safety features might not be as flashy as a sunroof or a surround-sound speaker system, but safety should certainly be a top priority when choosing a car. *Buying a Safer Car*, a brochure published annually and distributed for free by safercar.gov, a division of the National Highway Traffic Safety Administration, explains and rates safety features and helps you determine the vehicles in which you and your family will be the safest. Equip yourself with a copy before car shopping, and try to get the salesperson to throw in some extras, like a tire-pressure monitoring system or side-impact air bags for free or at a good price. If you'll have kids on board, also take a look at *Buying a Safer Car for Child Passengers*, which includes info on built-in child seats, interior trunk releases, and other features you might want for the family car. Download the booklets at www.safercar.gov (click under "Resources") or order copies by calling toll-free 888-327-4236.

(www.kbb.com) and at Edmunds.com (www.edmunds.com). Knowing these values will not only keep you from being overcharged but also arm you with ammunition to bargain for a lower-than-market price.

Comparison Shopping Online to Save Time and Money

You need to do a lot of comparison shopping to get the best buy on a car, but that doesn't mean you have to spend all your time on car lots fending off pushy salespeople. Instead, just click your way around www.cars.com. One of the largest websites for auto sales, cars.com rounds up cars from nearly 10,000 dealers, as well as classified ads from around the country. To see dozens of listings, select a model and make, enter the price you want to pay (for used cars only), and type in your zip code. The site also has some nifty extra features, like an auto-loan calculator you can use to determine monthly payments, and links to car reviews.

Car Buying Tips to Save You $2,000

Free advice is easy to come by when you're buying a car, but unlike words of wisdom from your next-door neighbor, the counsel of consumer advocate Jeff Ostroff is well worth heeding. Indeed, it's hard to turn a deaf ear on Ostroff's claim that his goal is to save you $2,000 when you follow the advice he offers for free on www.carbuyingtips.com. He tells you how to get the best price on new and used cars, what bargains are really scams, ways to save money on loans and insurance, and a lot more. His downloadable spreadsheets can help you determine how big a car payment your monthly budget can handle and how to come up with a good price on a new car that a dealer can't refuse. So take this piece of advice—make the site www.carbuyingtips.com your first stop when planning to buy a car.

Free Car Safety Seat Guide

If you have kids, over the years you'll probably spend quite a bit of money on infant seats, child safety seats, and booster seats—most states now require these safety measures for youngsters up to eight years of age. Before purchasing these important accessories, learn all about safety seats and compare prices of leading brands in the American Academy of Pediatrics' free online booklet *Car Safety Seats: A Guide for Families*, available at www.aap.org/family/carseatguide.htm. For more on buckling up your child safely, see page 368.

EDITOR'S CHOICE

Learn About Auto Rebate Windfalls

Manufacturers' rebates can shave thousands of dollars off the sticker price of a new car. To keep on top of what rebates manufacturers are offering, check out the "Current Rebate & Financing Offers" feature of www.cars.com and "Auto Rebates" on www.automotive.com—both list current offerings. But don't let the windfall turn your head: Continue to negotiate determinedly in order to get a lower price, one that saves you money beyond the rebate.

Refinancing Your Car Loan to Save

You may have refinanced your home to save money, but do you know that you can reap substantial savings when you do the same with your car? Say you owe $10,000 on your car loan, and currently pay 13 percent interest. That adds up to a monthly payment of $336.94 over 36 months, for a total payout of $12,129.82. Refinance that amount at 7.45 percent, and you'll pay $310.83 a month, for a total of $11,189 by the time you've paid off the car. You've just saved about $1,000. To calculate your savings, use the loan calculators at Capital One's website: www.capitaloneautofinance.com (click on "Finance Help," then "Loan Calculators," and scroll down to "Compare Another Loan"). As you'll see, you can save money by lowering your interest rate even by one percentage point.

To Lease or Not to Lease

Leasing rather than buying a car may save you money—then again, it may not. An auto lease puts you behind the wheel of a brand-new car, and your monthly payments are usually lower than they would be if you bought a new car. On the other hand, leasing deals come with some hefty fees and other hitches: You are locked into a lease, so you can't switch cars whenever you want; most leases come with a 12,000 miles-a-year mileage limit, with stiff penalties if you drive more; and you have no equity in the car, so you've accrued zilch when you hand in the keys at the end of the lease. You can determine the cost of the lease, almost down to the last penny and taking into account such factors as excess mileage penalties, with the free Lease Monthly Payment Calculator Spreadsheet in the download section of carbuyingtips.com (click on "Free spreadsheet downloads" under "Take A Break"). Use a free online loan calculator, such as the one at www.capitalautofinance.com, to compare the lease figures with the cost of buying a car with an auto loan.

Getting the Best Deal on a Used Car

To make sure you are getting the best deal on a used car, do some homework before driving off the lot with the one you like. Your first step should be to order a Carfax Vehicle History Report, which checks titles, odometers, and registrations, and can reveal if the car has been salvaged from a flood zone, used as part of a taxi fleet, been in an accident, had multiple owners, or raises some other red flags. The report costs $19.99 for one vehicle, but the better deal is $24.99 for unlimited checks, since you should get a Carfax report

TAKE CAUTION!

Before You Buy: Take a Time-Out

By the time you sit down to sign the papers on your new car, your head will probably be spinning with details and figures. Cash-back rebates, trade-in values, low-cost rust-proofing, extended warranties—who wouldn't feel overwhelmed? Before signing away your fortune in a deal that might be unnecessarily costly, shift the process into low gear. Take time to read the contract thoroughly, and question any terms you don't fully understand. If you're feeling less than certain of what you're doing, tell the dealer you want to go home and do more homework.

Q Is there an online tool I can use to calculate my fuel costs?

A Given the high cost of gasoline, fuel efficiency is an increasingly attractive feature for car buyers. To see what the most fuel-efficient vehicles are and how much money you can save by driving them, make your way to the U.S. government's website: www.fueleconomy.gov. Run some figures through the Fuel Costs Calculator (click under "Why Is Fuel Economy Important?") and be prepared for some surprises: Driving a car that gets 30 mpg costs $650 less a year than one that gets 20 mpg—that's based on the relatively modest assumptions that you pay $3 per gallon and drive 15,000 miles a year; if you drive more or gas prices go up, the savings could be even greater. For more on fuel economy and on the website, see "Guzzle Less Gas," page 53.

for every used car you consider. You can order the report on the home page at www.carfax.com. The next step is to check out the Kelley Blue Book (www.kbb.com) to see, for free, the worth of a car of the same model and year and with the same mileage and features as the car(s) you're considering.

For Long-Term Better Deals on a Used Car

Certified used-car programs offer new-car benefits at prices that are only slightly higher than those of other used cars. Certified used-car inventories usually include cars that were returned to a manufacturer at the end of a lease or that have been traded in for a new model. The cars must meet criteria for low mileage and limited previous ownership, are rigorously inspected and certified to be in good mechanical order, and come with extended warranties and such other assurances as roadside assistance. Most automakers promote "pre-owned" vehicles on their websites with features that let you choose the model and year you want and locate a nearby dealership.

Turn Your Old Car into a Tax Deduction

Does your desire to make a charitable donation coincide with a yearning to get a car out of your driveway? Whatever cause you like, from reading programs for kids to Alzheimer's care, Charitable Auto Resources, Inc., arranges pickup and sales of donated cars around the country and channels the funds to the charitable organization of your choice. The charity gets cash and you get a tax deduction, plus a no-hassle way to unload a car—and, of course, the satisfaction of doing a good deed. For more information, contact CARS toll-free at 877-537-5277, or visit www.charitableautoresources.com.

Sharing Cars and Rides

Save Big by Carpooling or Vanpooling

If you're trying to cut the cost of your commute, you've probably thought of carpooling and vanpooling. Carpoolers use a car owned by one driver, whom they reimburse for expenses, or they rotate cars and share expenses. Vanpoolers, usually a group of six or more commuters, share the expenses of operating a van to get to and from work. Here's how the savings add up.

- Using the American Automobile Association estimate that it costs an average of 52.2 cents per mile to drive a car, a 40-mile round-trip commute costs $5,250 annually, plus tolls and parking. Sharing those costs with one other person saves $2,625 a year; with two others, $3,500; with three others, $3,938.
- Some insurance companies give you reduced rates if you use your vehicle in a carpool.
- Many companies and institutions offer discounted parking to carpoolers and vanpoolers.

Share to Cut Commuting Costs

Savvy commuters save money by sharing the journey to and from work. If you find yourself looking for a ride—or riders for your car—check out such free online services as eRideShare.com (www.erideshare.com), on which you can post a notice or search through a large database. NuRide, Inc. (www.nuride.com) adds a little extra incentive to share a ride: Each time members use the service, they accrue points redeemable for gift cards at museums, car washes, sports stores, and other businesses.

Everything You Need to Start a Van Pool

Like the idea of vanpooling but don't own a van? Don't let that stop you. In some regions of the country, Enterprise Rent-A-Car offers an enterprising RideShare program that provides all you need to vanpool: a leased van, maintenance, roadside assistance, insurance, even a rider-matching service to make sure all the seats are filled. The company estimates the cost per rider ranges from $75 to $120 a month—not necessarily a steal, but probably a lot less than driving yourself to and from work. For more information, call toll-free 800-VAN-4-WORK (800-826-4967) or go to www.vanpool.com.

For the Occasional Driver, Try a Car-Sharing Group

Like it or not, we live in a car culture: No matter how avid a cyclist or walker you are, or how committed you are to using public transportation, there are times when four wheels come in handy. For those trips—a biweekly spree at the supermarket or the occasional jaunt to a faraway appointment—car-sharing might be a cost-saving option. Car-sharing puts you behind the wheel for hourly rates of about $8 that include gas, mileage, and insurance, and with most plans you also pay a one-time application fee and annual

TAKE CAUTION!

Shopping for a Used Car? Here's How to Avoid Buying a Lemon.

If you're about to purchase a used car, here are a couple things to keep in mind:

Get it checked out first: Take a used car you are considering buying for a test drive, and make a stop at the garage of a good mechanic. Ask him to listen for rattles and other unusual noises, check the alignment, and test the brakes. Have him also put the car on a lift and check for frame damage, leaks, and corrosion. You should also try the radio, lights, air-conditioning, and other components to make sure they are in good working order. The auto section of MSN network (www.autos.msn.com) provides handy tips and a thorough checklist to use when investigating a used car.

Avoid the Katrina scam: An estimated half-million cars were ruined by flooding from Katrina and other recent hurricanes, and many of these have floated into the used-car market, warns the National Automobile Dealers Association. Submersion in water, especially salt water, wreaks havoc on the sophisticated electronics in cars, corrodes metal and engine parts, and fosters mold growth. Do the same thorough checks you would when buying any used car, and also:

- Look for mentions of "salvage" or "flood damage" in the title.
- Check the car thoroughly (even the glove compartment, the underside of the dashboard, and the taillight housings) for signs of water, mud, and corrosion.
- Go to the Flood Vehicle Database on the website of the National Insurance Crime Bureau (www.nicb.org), where you can run a free check by inputting the vehicle identification number (VIN).

membership dues. Car-sharing is practical only if you need a car just occasionally and for short durations; if you're going to use a car for more than a half day, you're probably better off with a standard rental. The website www.carsharing.net, run by a nonprofit group that promotes this innovative and potentially cost-saving way to get around, provides links to firms around the country.

Take the HOV Lane to Cut Tolls, Save Time

The high-occupancy vehicle lane is a refreshingly sensible and money-saving antidote to our gas-guzzling ways. HOV lanes are out of bounds to solo drivers and geared to bus riders and carpoolers, so the drivers and riders who use them are cutting down on gas consumption. Even if you aren't a regular carpooler, you may benefit from HOVs by "slugging"—going to a so-called slug line and piling into a car with a driver and other passengers who wish to use an HOV lane to get to the same place you're going. To find HOV lanes that you can use in your comings and goings, make a stop at www.hovworld.com. You'll find a listing of HOV lanes across the country, hours they are in operation, requirements for using them, and other essential info.

More Dollarwise Reasons to Leave the Car at Home

The high cost of driving probably hits you like a ton of bricks every time you top off the tank, but also consider:

- Traffic congestion wastes huge amounts of fuel every year—varying estimates hover around 6 billion gallons.
- The fuel efficiency of a bus with just seven passengers is greater than that of a car with one occupant.

Ask About Commuter Benefits

If you're like most employees, you probably measure your compensation in terms of salary, insurance coverage, 401(k) and other pension plans, bonuses, and the occasional perk or two. Well, start thinking about commuter benefits as well. Options range from discounted bus passes and bike racks to ride-matching services. For a sampling of the benefits some commuters receive, check out:

- www.commuterchoice.com, a government-sponsored group that helps employers make the best use of alternative commuting options. You can read about creative schemes such as a parking cash-out, in which employees get an extra $100 a month in their salaries or in public transportation benefits for giving up their parking spaces.
- www.smartcommute.org, a forward-thinking transportation-management association that serves the 38,000 employees who work in Research Triangle Park, North Carolina. Click your way through the site to read about commuting alternatives discussed there; many may be available to you as well.
- www.bwc.gov, sponsored by the U.S. Environmental Protection Agency and the U.S. Department of Transportation, which recognizes employers who provide noteworthy commuter benefits. Navigate through "Success Stories" (in "Employer Profiles" under "For Employers") to see how some companies are helping their employees get to work via public transportation, car pools, and bicycles.

- On average, a car consumes more than its weight in fuel each year.
- Commuters who give up the solo drive to work for an alternative mode of transportation save on average more than $800 a year in transportation expenses.

A Free or Cheap Ride Home When You Need It

Good for you—you leave the car in the garage and walk, bike, or take the bus to work. But what happens if emergencies arise? Guaranteed Ride Home programs cover these contingencies and provide free or low-cost rides to commuters who don't drive to work but occasionally need to get home in a hurry—whether it's to take care of a broken pipe or to get some well-deserved rest after working overtime. Taxis, company vans, even rental cars often provide the transportation. In many communities, local governments and transit networks work with private companies to provide GRHs; check with any of them to see if you're entitled to a free ride and how to get it.

Walking and Biking

Free Resources for the Passionate Biker

Your bike-to-work regimen can lead to a real passion for cycling; you'll find plenty of free resources to maintain your enthusiasm at the League of American Bicyclists (www.bikeleague.org). A downloadable mileage log makes it easy to keep track of how far you pedal each day; a local resource guide steers you to bike clubs, group rides, courses, and other activities in your area; and a news roundup keeps you up to date on topics of concern to cyclists around the country.

Free Tips for Bike Commuters

If you commute to work by bike or are thinking about making the switch to two wheels, you'll get plenty of advice and words of encouragement from the Chicagoland Bicycle Federation (www.chibikefed.org). You don't have to live in the Windy City to benefit from many of the group's expertly prepared resources, including the booklet *Tricks & Tips for Commuting to Work*,

Q I want to start bicycling to work, but I don't know how safe it is to do so in my area. Any tips?

A Is your community walker- and biker-friendly? Chances are, it's not—and once you're out there on two feet or two wheels, you might be surprised by such obstacles as broken pavement and menacing dogs. The "Walkability Checklist" and "Bikeability Checklist," which you can download free from the Pedestrian and Bicycle Information Center (www.bicyclinginfo.org), are useful tools that help you assess just how walker- or biker-friendly the route to work is, and how you can address the problems you encounter. If your kids walk or bike to school, have them help you fill out the checklists—the guides pay special attention to the needs of youngsters on the road.

Tips on Getting Around Town for Less

With gas prices as high as they are, why not join other straphangers and let someone else drive you to work? Here's how to see just how much public transportation can save you.

Calculate Your Savings

It's easy to say that using public transportation is less expensive than driving, but talk is cheap, and seeing the figures in black and white is much more convincing. Handy online calculators—including one designed for residents of traffic-choked King County, Washington, but useful to commuters everywhere—help you determine how much you can save commuting by public transportation instead of driving. Go to www.transit.metrokc.gov/tops/bus/calculator.html and enter the miles you travel each day, the cost of gas and parking, and the miles per gallon you get to determine the monthly cost of driving—then what you would spend to make the same commute on public transportation. You might be surprised at just how much less expensive the public transportation alternative is.

Free Info on Your Transit Options

You probably know all the cost advantages of taking public transportation instead of driving: saving on fuel, reducing wear and tear and associated maintenance costs on your car, avoiding parking fees—the list goes on. But if you're like a lot of lifelong drivers, you may not be fully aware of the public transportation options available to you. A handy resource is the "Dump the Pump" feature on the American Public Transportation Association website (www.apta.com/gasprices). Click on an interactive map to locate public transit networks by state, with links to sites for local agencies, where you can find schedules, fares, and contact info. Another source is CommuterChoice.com (www.commuterchoice.com), where you'll find links to public transit networks in 18 U.S. cities, as well as to biking and walking resources.

Tax-Free Transport Benefits

If you ride public transit to work, you may be entitled to a tax-free transportation benefit. Federally mandated transit-commuter tax benefits give employers a break for paying their employees' transit or van pool commuting costs, up to a tax-free $105 a month, or allowing employees to take up to $105 of their monthly salaries tax-free to pay for commuting costs. (Depending on your tax bracket, these breaks could be worth an extra $30 a month.) *It Pays to Ride Public Transportation,* a brochure published by the American Public Transportation Association, explains how you and your employer can take advantage of these benefits; download the brochure at www.apta.com/research/info/online/paystoride.cfm or order a print copy by calling 202-496-4889.

downloadable for free (click on "Resources," then "Commuting") and filled with wide-ranging advice on how to use hand signals, how to pack your work clothes so they don't wrinkle, and how to keep a close eye on the road and the traffic around you. Should you be inspired to get others to join you on the ride to work, the federation's free *Bike to Work Guide* tells you everything you need to know to start a commute-by-bike program.

Free Public Bikes to Ride

Who said there's no such thing as a free ride? All you need to do is find the nearest PUB. No, we're not talking about a cozy lair where you can quaff a pint or two. This PUB is a public use bicycle, and dozens of cities around the country—including Denver, Portland, Oregon, and Minneapolis-St. Paul—offer them for free. PUBs (also called "smart bikes") are often available in busy shopping districts, near train and bus stations, and around other high-traffic areas; the idea is to hop onto a bike, ride where you need to go, and leave it for another rider. To learn more about the ins and outs of these innovative schemes, check in with the International Bicycle Fund (www.ibike.org). Go to www.ibike.org/encouragement/freebike-details.htm for information on how various communities use PUBs, how to set up a campus bike co-op, and for a free, downloadable booklet, *Smart Bikes: Public Transportation for the 21st Century*.

Free Bike Maps and Route Guides

For many cyclists, carefully choosing a route with an eye to such factors as speed, safety, scenery, level of challenge, and convenience is part of the thrill of a good ride, and planning is fun and easy with the free and low-cost bike maps available for most cities and regions. One way to find them is to go to Google or another search engine and type in "bicycle map" and the place name; clicking your way through the maps and other resources is almost as satisfying as coasting along a gradual downgrade. If you're a recreational cyclist, you can also get free help in selecting scenic rides at www.pedaling.com; to see a selection of recommended routes, click on "Search Rides" and enter a state, region, the length of ride you want, your choice of scenery, and the levels of difficulty that suit you.

Editor's Choice

Deep Discounts on Cycling Gear

So you've made a commitment to getting around in a cheaper, more eco-friendly fashion and made the switch from a car to a bike—but that doesn't mean you should be a spendthrift when you gear up. If you click your way around www.rei.com/outlet, you'll find helmets, pumps, locks, seat bags, and other essential accessories at up to 40 to 60 percent off standard retail prices. Since REI gives part of its profits to conservation and recreation efforts, you can pedal away with some added satisfaction too.

For RVers

Free Money-Saving Advice for RVers

RVers in the know check in frequently with RVers Online (www.rversonline.com), and you'd do well to follow their lead. This is where RVers share down-to-earth advice, with an emphasis on saving money—from where to find free Wi-Fi connections and inexpensive meals while on the road to the relative cost-savings of owning and renting an RV. The tips extend to cooking and storing food in a small kitchen, safe driving, buying and selling a rig, and simple, inexpensive ways to set up a satellite dish.

Free Campgrounds for RVers

Go figure. RVers spend as much as $200,000 on a rig, then go out of their way to find cheap or free places to pull in for the night. Sam's Club and Wal-Mart parking lots are among the favorite stops. You'll find many more free and inexpensive (and certainly more scenic) campsites at www.freecampgrounds.com, along with the locations of dump stations and the best-priced places to fill the tank. When you're ready to ratchet up to slightly costlier places in which to enjoy the RV lifestyle, browse through the free online listings of campgrounds and RV parks across the country at the website www.woodalls.com, the online component of one of the country's longest-established and most venerable guides to campgrounds and trailer parks.

Join the Low-Cost RV Club to Save

One million RVers must know a good thing when they see it, and that's the membership count for the Good Sam Club, the largest RV group in the world. The $19 online-only annual membership fee ($32 for two years, $45 for three) comes with quite a few perks, among them a 10 percent discount at Good Sam RV parks, a free subscription to *Highways* magazine, and discounts on RV parts and accessories. A handy trip-routing service provides info on bridge and tunnel restrictions, highway grades, and where to find dump stations and low-cost fuel. Membership also keeps you up to date with length restrictions and other laws that affect RVers. Check out the club and sign up at www.goodsamclub.com, or call toll-free 800-234-3450.

CHAPTER 10

getting gainful employment

Want to advance in your field, or change your occupation altogether? These free and low-cost resources will have you on the path to a successful career in no time.

By the
numbers

44.4

The number of employed Americans, in millions, who performed any kind of work from home in 2004. This figure includes people who telecommute full time, or worked from home as little as one day that year.

EVERY YEAR, MILLIONS OF AMERICANS look for a new job. We have all done that at some point in our life. Sometimes we've searched for new opportunities while still working or finishing school; other times we've quit our job, been fired, or taken a package. But regardless of why we're looking, we all have one thing in common: the need for timely, free, or low-cost information and services to help us take that next step. This chapter is about the information and services available to you as a job seeker, a person who has suffered workplace discrimination, or someone with pension questions or problems.

There are few sectors more important to the welfare of the economy than employment. For that reason, federal, state, and local governments expend a great deal of money and effort on helping individuals get and keep jobs. Those efforts include:

- Free training programs for youths, workers displaced by outsourcing or military base closings, and others in need of work.
- Free access to job-search boards listing hundreds of thousands of jobs around the country.
- No-cost help with résumé preparation and other job-search skills.

- Assistance for students who need jobs to survive financially.
- Apprenticeship programs, not just in the trades but also in high-demand sectors like health care.

It isn't just the government that provides information and services. Businesses, some of them Internet-based, and nonprofit groups have also stepped up to the plate to offer:

- Job training and other help for homemakers returning to the workforce as a result of divorce, domestic abuse, losing a spouse, or some other adverse circumstance.
- Tips, tips, and more tips about (and in some cases, samples of) such job-hunting staples as résumés, cover letters, the interview, and salary negotiation.
- Multiyear career internships for minority students.
- Help fighting issues of discrimination in the workplace.
- Information and assistance in getting fair pension benefits.

Finding a job—which can involve important life decisions, such as whether to go back to school, accept a salary that's offered, or change locations—is often not easy. As job seekers we need all the help we can get without spending a lot of money. The many no- and low-cost programs, services, and other tools described in this chapter can make a crucial difference in your success as you find the right job, then land it, keep it, and enjoy it.

GETTING STARTED

Free After-Graduation Job Listings

Many college students and recent grads look for internships, entry-level jobs, or other beginning opportunities. What could be better than a job bank that specializes in such positions? AfterCollege, Inc., bills itself as "the largest career network specializing in recruitment at the college level." Its website (www.aftercollege.com) alerts users to organizations that are "recent grad" friendly, and lists more than 150,000 jobs from 25,000 employers. Internships and overseas jobs are represented too. When you page through the job offerings, you can collect those you want to apply to in a "basket" and send your résumé to up to 250 employers at one time.

Free Listings of Government Jobs for Students

If you need a part-time job to ease financial pressures while you pursue a diploma or a degree, think beyond the local Old Navy. The Federal Student Temporary Employment Program promises many such jobs to students ages 16 and older all across the country. Find one that meshes with your career goals, and it will enhance your résumé. You can find free listings of federal government jobs for students at www.studentjobs.gov, a joint project of the U.S. Office of Personnel Management and the U.S. Department of Education's Student Financial Assistance office. Positions range from law clerk to laborer, and searches can be conducted by keyword, job category, or location. The website also allows students to create and store a résumé that can be used to apply for federal jobs.

No-Fee Help in Getting an Overseas Internship

If you're a student, internships are a great way to beef up your résumé and make useful contacts for future employment. If you're inclined to think outside the box, what about interning overseas? Most groups that match U.S. students with overseas jobs charge a fee, but Ireland's Dublin Internships program is free. It hooks up college juniors, seniors, and grad students with jobs matching their career interests and majors. You can intern for 15 weeks in the spring or fall semester, or 10 weeks during the summer. The work won't be paid, but you will get academic credit. For more information, go to homepage.eircom.net/~dublinternships/di_home.html, or send an e-mail to mhrieke@eircom.net.

Editor's Choice Help Getting a Paid Apprenticeship

Donald Trump isn't the only employer looking for an apprentice. Under the federal Apprenticeship Training program, you may be able to find an employer to teach you a trade and supervise you as you learn (and get paid) on the job. Typically apprentices have a high school diploma or GED and an aptitude for the trade being learned, from welding to radiology. Best of all, you don't have to come from a low-income background to take advantage of this program—all income levels are welcome. There are about 800 occupations for which you can be an apprentice, many in construction, health care, public administration, metalworking, and mechanics. To connect with employers who offer apprenticeships, contact your State Bureau of Apprenticeship and Training. You can find yours at the U.S. Department of Labor Employment & Training Administration website: go to www.doleta.gov, and click the "Advancing Your Career" link.

Where the Most Jobs Are

If you're in college or have recently graduated, you may be interested in which careers are expected to offer the most opportunities in the next decade and beyond. Details can be found here:

- www.metacrawler.com, which bundles listings from Google, Yahoo!, Msn.com, and Ask.com. Type in "hot careers" or "hot jobs" for a list of articles on the subject.
- www.careerplanner.com. Click the "Hot Jobs for the Future" link under the "Featured Articles" section. It lists nearly a hundred jobs for which the hiring trend is expected to be "up" in the next ten years (and not just in health care or information technology). It also offers an in-depth discussion of larger trends affecting industries and job categories.
- Business periodicals such as *Fortune* and *Kiplinger's Personal Finance*, available free in your local library.

Free Career Assessment Tools

Ready to graduate but not quite sure what you want to do when you grow up? There are several free quizzes on the Internet to help you pinpoint the kind of career that would mostly likely satisfy you. One place to start is the University of Missouri's website (www.career.missouri.edu); go to "Quick Links" at the lower right and find "The Career Interests Game." Choose three favorites among six fully described personality types—Realistic, Investigative, Artistic, Social, Enterprising, and Conventional—and a link will take you to further information and career suggestions for each. For each career option, there's a link to the U.S. Department of Labor's Bureau of Statistics online Occupational Outlook Handbook, which offers detailed information on the nature of the work, employment conditions, job outlook, and more.

Join the Job Corps for Free Training with Board

If you're a U.S. citizen or a legal U.S. resident between the ages of 16 and 24 and have limited financial resources, you may be eligible to participate in the U.S. government's Job Corps. Every year about 62,000 young people enter the program to learn a trade or obtain a high school diploma or GED and find a good job. Free training, career counseling, and job placement are provided at one of the nation's 122 Job Corps centers, and students receive transition support for up to a year after they graduate. There are more than 100 areas of training to choose from, including culinary arts, construction, and preparation for higher education. Most students in the

program live at the center, but some locations provide nonresidential options. Either way, you will be supplied with a bi-weekly allowance (the longer you stay, the higher the allowance gets). For more information, call toll-free 800-733-JOBS (800-733-5627).

Job Hunting

Free Listing of the Best Companies to Work For

If you're going to spend decades of your life working, you might as well spend at least some time at an employee-friendly company. When you start your search, begin with *Fortune* magazine's 100 Best Companies to Work For; you'll find a free listing of the companies, details about their finer points, and contact information for each at www.money.cnn.com/magazines/fortune/bestcompanies (the information is also broken down by subcategories). Did you know, for example, that the average salary at Yahoo is more than $117,000 or that Microsoft and Whole Foods Market both pay 100 percent of employees' health care premiums? Some of the perks are very unexpected—such as a $3,000 subsidy for Timberland employees who buy a hybrid car. For more unusual perks, see "Companies That Offer More Than Usual" (page 196).

Free Classified Ads on the Net

Classified ads are invaluable tip sheets for specific job openings, and there are plenty of opportunities to view them free on the Internet. If you're looking for a job in a specific city, try the website for the newspaper(s) covering that city. For access to a wider pool of openings, check some of these websites:

- At www.monster.com, you can search thousands of jobs across the country by keyword, job category, or location—or any combination of these elements. You can also post your résumé for potential employers to find. The site offers plenty of career and salary advice too—some of it free, some of it for a fee.
- The advantage of www.careerbuilder.com is that it partners with newspapers in 200 cities to bring you classifieds from all those areas. Like Monster, it allows you to search by job category, keyword, and location, and to post your résumé for

Q How can I find a job abroad?

A Looking for a chance to travel and immerse yourself in a foreign culture while earning a steady paycheck (typically at the prevailing rate in the city where you're working)? Go to www.jobsabroad.com and check out the free job listings, organized by country and/or field of specialty. You'll find links to jobs as exotic as harvesting fruit in Australia or as prosaic as being an au pair in Europe (and everything in between). The site is maintained by GoAbroad.com (www.goabroad.com), which promotes many different work and travel programs for students and recent graduates, including volunteer and internship opportunities. Alternatively, if you are interested in working with specific U.S. companies, check the job listings on their websites for overseas opportunities. Once you prove your mettle abroad, you may have a ready-made job waiting for you when you return to the States.

Free Government Job Help for Tough Times

The federal government has several programs to help workers who have lost jobs in adverse circumstances.

- **Dislocated workers.** The Workforce Investment Act Dislocated Workers Program gives grants to the 50 states, Puerto Rico, and the District of Columbia to provide free job placement and other assistance to those who have lost jobs because of plant closings or mass layoffs and can't get a similar one, those who were self-employed, and displaced homemakers who are no longer supported by a family member. In some cases, intensive job training and support services such as child care and transportation may also be available. Through the National Emergency Grant Program, assistance is provided to some military and defense personnel who have lost their jobs, victims of natural disasters, and those whose jobs ended because of federal government actions. For more information, go to the Catalog of Federal Domestic Assistance website (www.cfda.gov), and search for program number 17.260.
- **Trade-related layoffs.** The Trade Adjustment Assistance Program provides up to 78 weeks of weekly allowances equivalent to state unemployment benefits to workers who have lost a job because of increased imports or outsourcing. Layoffs from your place of employment must total at least three workers if there were fewer than 50 employees total; 5 percent of the workforce when employees numbered 50 to 999; and at least 50 workers in groups of 1,000 or more. Benefits are paid out only after workers have exhausted their state unemployment benefits. To find out more, go to www.cfda.gov and search for program number 17.245.
- **Health-plan tax credits.** If you're receiving Trade Adjustment Assistance or pension benefits from the Pension Benefit Guaranty Corporation (see "Lost Pensions Found," in this chapter's final section) you might be eligible for a federal tax credit covering 65 percent of your premiums in qualified health plans. The benefit is good for as long as you are eligible for TAA or PBGC pension benefits. Under the Health Coverage Tax Credit Program, you can receive the money monthly as premiums become due, or you can claim the premiums on your federal tax form. For more information, go to www.irs.gov/individuals, scroll down, and click on "HCTC: Individuals—Overview."

potential employers to find. In addition, at your request it will send you regular e-mail updates for jobs in your chosen categories and locations.

- Another good general job-search website is www.hotjobs.com, which sometimes contains jobs that are not in other databases. It, too, allows for searches by keyword, location, and job category. You can also search for job listings within specific companies in the Hotjobs database and check a smaller number of international jobs as well.

Free Job Fairs

Sometimes mailing a résumé and cover letter to prospective employers feels like sending it into the void: There's no response, and you don't know whether anyone has even looked at it. Job fairs offer face-to-face meetings with representatives from companies you might like to work for. The meetings are not as personal as an interview, but if you make enough of an impression, you may land the interview later. To find job fairs in your area, check for

Companies That Offer More Than Usual

Want to work for a business that's as interested in pleasing its employees as it is in being pleased? One good way to assess a company's employee-friendliness is by checking its willingness to go above and beyond the call of duty when it comes to perks. Companies that pay attention to employees' needs are usually satisfying places to work, and they usually have low turnover. Here's a selection of unusual perks. Beyond the value of the perks themselves, such policies demonstrate a company's positive mindset toward employees.

- Every year Brogan & Partners, a marketing company in Michigan, takes its 60 employees on free "mystery" junkets. The destinations have included Amsterdam, Iceland, and the Caribbean.
- At four hospitals in the OhioHealth network, more than 15,000 workers have access to a concierge who handles chores for them—grocery shopping, waiting for the cable guy, letting the dog out when the employee can't get home.
- At S. C. Johnson & Son in Racine, Wisconsin, retirees are given a lifetime membership at the company fitness center.
- Houston-based David Weekley Homes gives employees a 10 percent discount on the purchase of one of its homes, and it takes workers on celebratory vacations to places like Maui and Mexico.
- At steel processor Worthington Industries, near Columbus, Ohio, employees can get haircuts for $4 a pop—a small savings compared to the factory workers' profit-sharing plans, which boost earnings by 40 percent to 100 percent.
- New Belgium Brewing in Fort Collins, Colorado, gives its employees a free case of beer every week. Once workers have spent five years on the job, it sends them to Belgium to try out the beers that inspired the company in the first place.

advertisements in your local newspaper. If you'd consider other cities as well, check for national online listing sites. Careerbuilder .com sponsors fairs in various cities; for a listing, go to www.career builder.com and click on "Career Fairs" under "Job Search Tools." You can find other free listings at www.employmentguide.com (click on "Job Fairs"), or check with your state employment office.

Free Trade Show Info

Another great place to network and meet potential employers is at a trade show for the industry you're targeting. You'll find a free searchable database of trade show listings around the country (and even some in other nations) at www.tsnn.com, a comprehensive resource for the trade show, exhibition, and event world. You can conduct a search by industry, date, or locale. To get specific details on each event you'll need to be a registered user, but registration is free.

Free Listings of Government Jobs

Looking for jobs in the public sector? You can get free listings at several different websites.

- The government's official website for federal jobs is www.usajobs.com; the database contains more than 22,000 jobs across the country. You can include any or all of five elements in your search: keyword, location, job category, salary range, and pay grade (a federal government designation). Once you determine the jobs you're interested in, you can apply directly from the site—and you can post a résumé there as well.
- Search for state government job openings at www.statejobs. com, using your target state as a starting point. At the bottom of the home page, you'll find links to federal positions and municipal jobs with some of the larger U.S. cities.
- At www.govtjobs.com, listings for city, state, or county government jobs range from city manager to maintenance mechanic. Links will take you to listings of federal jobs.

For Low-Cost Networking, Use Your Alma Mater

One low-cost way to expand your job contact list is to join your college or university alumni association. Many people in a position to hire are happy to look first toward those who have graduated from the same college they have. Alumni meetings are a good place to network, and you may be able to use the alumni association's

Editor's Choice

No-Cost Targeted Classifieds

Larger job-search sites are great, but if you're seeking free listings in a specific industry or job category, try a targeted site. Journalists and editors know to check for jobs at www.journalism jobs.com or www .mediabistro.com and a host of similar sites. If you don't want to ask someone in your field, check with a search engine such as www.metacrawler .com to find job banks that meet your needs; for example, at MetaCrawler if you enter the term "engineer jobs" you'll find several different job site possibilities, including www .engineerjobs.com and www.just engineers.net.

A Temporary Solution While Job Seeking

While you are looking for a full-time job, taking temporary work in your field is a good way to research organizations while getting paid. Not only will a "temp" job help out financially; it will also give you exposure to specific companies and departments within companies that may eventually be in a position to hire you on a permanent basis. Check with your yellow pages under "Employment—Temporary" to find no-fee agencies in your area.

newsletter as a tip sheet pointing you to schoolmates who can help you get a foot in the door. If your college has its own résumé database, you can use that to alert other alumni of your availability.

Free Job Leads Through Professional Groups

If you belong to a professional association, you have a built-in source for free job leads. Many people find openings by making contacts at association conferences or seminars, or attending meetings of their local chapter. Some associations also have their own job bank, which gives you a leg up on applicants who hear of the opening through general classified ads. If you need to locate a group appropriate to your field, check the public library's copy of the *Encyclopedia of Associations*, a detailed listing of more than 100,000 nonprofit organizations around the world. You can search the book in multiple ways, including by type of association and location.

Keeping Up with Your Field—Free

Want to know where the jobs are and how to position yourself within your industry or profession? Then reading trade publications is a must. If you're in engineering, finance, IT, sales and marketing, or one of some 30 other professions and industries, you can subscribe to free magazines and white papers (anywhere from one or two to several dozen, depending on the category) for a year or more at a website that specializes in news on Internet business: www.bizreport.com; on the home page, click on "Free Magazines." (The publications are not owned by BizReport but are offered on behalf of its clients.) On the online application you'll have to answer questions that identify you as a legitimate professional in the field, but if you qualify and are, say, in human resources, you can choose from a range of titles that includes *Employee Benefit News*, *Human Resource Executive*, and *Workforce Performance Solutions*.

Free Work-at-Home Job Listings

If you're the type who's comfortable conducting business in your bathrobe, telecommuting might be a good option for you. Jobs that typically lend themselves to working from home include software programming and other computer jobs, sales, insurance underwriting, writing, copy editing and proofreading, data entry, and transcription. You might sacrifice benefits, but the tradeoff is a three-second commute. A number of websites offer telecommuting or freelance job listings, but some charge a fee to see the listings or apply for specific jobs. To get the no-cost scoop on work-at-home jobs, check Quintessential Careers at www.quintcareers.com/telecommute_jobs.html. You'll be able to take a free quiz to see whether working at home is right for you, read articles on how to make it work, and check out a long list of Internet resources, some with free telecommuting job listings.

No-Cost Federal Job-Search Help

With more than 3,300 offices nationwide, Career One-Stop Centers provide a vast network to help steer you on the right course when you are job hunting—at no cost. The U.S. Department of Labor provides funding for these centers, which are great places to connect one-on-one with an adviser who can help you sort through your career goals and the tools for finding the perfect job. Center professionals provide job-search assistance, training, and education; connect you with apprenticeship programs; help you get certifications if your industry requires them; and more. If you're about to be laid off, they can help you formulate a plan for the future and point you to programs that will help with retraining and transition. (Local Career One-Stop Centers have many different "brand" names, among them CareerLink, JobLink, and Worksource.) To locate the center closest to you, go to www.servicelocator.org. For the full range of federal resources available to job seekers, call toll-free 877-US-2JOBS (877-872-5627) or TTY 877-889-5627.

Free Online Help

If your Career One-Stop Center is too far away to visit, don't despair. Its companion website (www.careeronestop.org) is chock-full of information and services that can help you get the job or find the career you're looking for. From the home page, click on "Job Seekers/Workers." You'll be able to find sources for thousands of job listings; create a résumé; assess your employability at your desired wage level in your area; link to other resources for your occupation, such as the *Occupational Outlook Handbook* or the *Princeton Review*; and more. Lost in the sea of offerings? Career One-Stop Coach (www.onestopcoach.org) can give you interactive step-by-step instructions for making the most of the Career One-Stop site. It works by using a split-screen technique—the helpful promptings are on the right, the basic site content on the left. To get more personalized help on the Career One-Stop website, send an e-mail to info@careeronestop.org, or call toll-free 877-348-0502 or TTY 877-348-0501.

Free Networking

If you use a job site only for finding job leads and posting your résumé, you're not getting the most from the experience. About two-thirds of all jobs are found by networking, so experts recommend you join free online chats and forums, particularly at job sites that specialize in your field. By participating in chats and checking online bulletin boards, you may get a lead or make a contact that could result in an interview. At the very least, you'll get firsthand reports that alert you to emerging trends in your industry or new ventures that might produce job openings.

Free State Help in Your Job Search

Your state is interested in more than giving you an unemployment check when you lose your job. Its employment agencies are also some of the best places around to find free help in the job search—from job leads to training programs, and from tuition help to transportation and child-care assistance during your job search. As offerings vary by location, you'll need to contact your state employment agency for details. Look in the blue pages of your telephone book for the nearest office.

No-Cost Career Centers at Colleges

Don't ignore your local college or university's career center when you need help with planning your job search. Many have resources that they're only too willing to share with local residents, even if you haven't gone to school there. Community colleges in particular often receive federal Community-Based Job Training Grants to train or retrain a wide variety of workers in high-demand, high-growth occupations such as nursing and automotive repair. To learn

Q I lost my job in the aftermath of Hurricane Katrina. Can I get free help?

A If you've lost your job because of a natural disaster, you can be certain that the government or a nonprofit will fund a website dedicated to helping you find one. If you are a Hurricane Katrina or Rita survivor, for example, there's a website that connects you for free with employers eager to consider you for a new job. Employers go to the site and list positions they want to fill with hurricane survivors, or jobs cleaning up after the hurricane's mess. You can find employment in your home state or, if you prefer, a newly adopted one. At www.jobsearch.org/hurricanejobs, icons with each posting alert you to such factors as whether the job is a result of the hurricane, whether the employer is a federal contractor, and such. Any other major disaster will produce a similar site to aid survivors.

whether there's a program near you, find local colleges in the white pages of your phone book and call to see whether they have a career or job-training center.

Helpful Reports and Publications for Free

The nonprofit Conference Board is one of the premier business research and analysis organizations in the United States, and your company would have to belong for you to access much of its info. Still, there is still plenty of information available to the general public, including research about the marketplace, job trends, and more. At www.conferenceboard.org, you can download a host of free publications and reports on such topics as "Women of Color: Strategies for Leadership Success." Only members get full library services, but nonmembers needing professionals to do research can send a request for Conference Board information directly from the site at no charge.

Free One-Stop Shopping for Movers

Getting a job is one thing, but if you're relocating to take it, the worst part may be the actual moving process. Where do you find a mover? How to stay within budget? Several websites help with free advice and tips, but www.123movers.com, operated by a publisher of classified advertising publications, goes a step further. Complete a form on the site, and you can get free quotes from up to ten moving companies to learn which is the cheapest. You can also get quotes on money-saving options you might not have considered—such as self-service moving (you load the truck yourself and the movers drive, or vice versa). The site even links you to broadband providers so you can have your Internet service up and running by the time you arrive in your new home. It's free, one-stop shopping that takes the hassle out of the multitasking that moving entails.

Résumés and Cover Letters

Free Help Tailoring Résumés for Federal Jobs

There are thousands of jobs in the federal government, but applying for them can be daunting. How can you tailor your résumé to fit the needs of a federal agency, as opposed to a private employer? Edizen Corporation, a human resources consultant to government, offers free help at its website: www.edizenco.com. A detailed résumé toolkit shows you how to match your résumé to the duties and qualifications of the federal job listing. Samples help you handle such issues as requests for KSA (knowledge, skills, abilities) statements and more. A detailed list of action verbs to describe your skills and accomplishments will be helpful to any job searcher, in or out of government. Click on "Edizen Résumé Toolkit" on the site's home page.

Matching the Résumé to the Job—Free Tools

When you put together your résumé, you may find that a straightforward job history doesn't demonstrate fitness for the kind of job you really want. How do you convince a potential employer that you're marketing material if your only job has been as a server at a restaurant? That's where the concept of transferable skills comes into play. It's a way to parlay your specific experiences into more generalized skill sets—such as managing or problem solving—that match a variety of jobs. There are a number of free online tools to help you do this. At the Quintessential Careers website, for example, you'll find several free articles explaining how to use transferable skill sets in résumés and cover letters, plus a list of the skills, broken down into five categories. Go to ww.quintcareers.com/transferable_skills.html to get ideas for your résumé.

Fax Your Résumé at No Cost

Running out to Kinko's every time you want to fax a cover letter and résumé can cost you several dollars a pop. But you can send short faxes free from your home computer to potential employers in the United States or Canada from www.faxzero.com. The site lets you transmit up to two faxes a day, containing up to three pages each, by typing the desired text directly into a box provided on the site, or selecting a Microsoft Word or PDF file (such as a résumé) to upload. In lieu of charging a fee, the site attaches a cover sheet with an ad.

Free Cover Letter Samples

If you get writer's block every time you think about drafting a cover letter or thank-you note to a potential employer, it may help to look at examples of other job hunters' approaches. You can see more than 20 free samples compiled by Denver career management

EDITOR'S CHOICE

No-Cost Résumé Help from an Unexpected Source

Your County Cooperative Extension Service, part of a nationwide educational network partially funded by the federal government, is a great resource for (usually free) job-hunting help. In addition to holding career expos, the service often gives workshops or provides booklets on putting together an effective résumé. Programs vary from place to place, so it's best to check with your local office. To find your nearest Cooperative Extension office, go to www.csrees.usda.gov/extension.

College Loan Repayment Help

To recruit qualified people, several government and nonprofit organizations give assistance in paying back student loans if the loan recipient works for them for a year or two.

- AmeriCorps (www.americorps.gov), a network of local, state, and national service programs, offers more than 75,000 volunteer jobs a year through VISTA (Volunteers in Service to America, which focuses on low-income communities and individuals), Teach for America, and other organizations. Participants receive $4,725 a year to repay qualified student loans or to fund further education.
- Teachers in low-income areas or who teach subjects for which teachers are in short supply may be able to have their student loans canceled or deferred. The federal student aid website (www.studentaid.ed.gov) has more information.
- Law school students and graduates working in public service may get loan repayment financial assistance. Find out more at the Equal Justice Works website: www.equaljusticeworks.org/finance.
- Health-care workers in the National Health Service Corps (nhsc.bhpr.hrsa.gov) who work in underserved areas for two years can get up to $50,000 to pay back their educational loans.
- People serving in the Peace Corps (www.peacecorps.gov) may be eligible to have 15 percent of certain student loans (Perkins loans) canceled for each year of their first two-year service term.

consultant William S. Frank at www.careerlab.com/letters; they cover such topics as "Say Thank You with Class" and "Follow Up After a Casual Conversation." More than 50 other free examples of letters, compiled by Susan Ireland, author of *The Complete Idiot's Guide to the Perfect Résumé*, can be found at www.susanireland.com/coverletterindex.htm. Click on "Create a Résumé," and you'll also find more than 50 samples.

Free Examples of Recommendation Letters

Have you ever asked someone to send a recommendation letter, only to be asked in turn, "What do you want me to say?" Some excellent free templates can be found at www.writinghelp-central.com (click on "Recommendation Letter Writing"). The site, operated by Montreal-based business and communications consultant Shaun Fawcett, also offers free samples of résumés.

Six Free Resources That Could Help Land You a High-Paying Job

Searching for the perfect job (or any job!) is a stressful endeavor. What should you wear? How can you put your best foot forward? For answers to these and other make-or-break job-seeking quandaries, keep these resources at your fingertips.

Free Clothes for Success

Getting hired for a good job can seem like a catch-22. If you don't have a lot of money, how are you supposed to dress professionally enough to impress an interviewer? Nonprofit organizations like Dress for Success fill that gap. Thanks to cash or clothing donations from individuals and businesses, the group provides low-income women with suits to wear to job interviews, plus a week's worth of clothing once they're hired. At some locations, there's a monthly support group for the newly employed covering such topics as child care and financial planning. Check the list of 75 locations, most in larger cities and counties, at the website www.dressforsuccess.org. If your community does not have a Dress for Success affiliate, ask the social service agencies in your area whether there is a local equivalent, such as the Clothing Collaborative in Providence, Rhode Island, or Clothes That Work in Dayton and Xenia, Ohio.

No Phone? Get Free Voice Mail

If you've suffered some kind of hardship, it's more important than ever that you have a phone to stay in touch with potential employers and other contacts. Even if you don't have telephone service, you can get free voice mail that can be checked from any touch-tone phone. When potential employers call you for an interview, they get a message that sounds as if a regular answering machine has picked up. As of July 2006, Community Voice Mail is available in 19 states plus the District of Columbia, and its presence is growing. Call your nearest CVM location, which you can find at www.cvm.org, to get the names of participating agencies in your area where you can get your free voice-mail number.

Researching a Potential Employer at No Cost

Few things impress an interviewer as much as showing in-depth knowledge of the company at which you're being interviewed.

- The best resource for information (and it's free) may be people who work or have worked for the company; check with anyone you know who can give you the firsthand scoop.
- Browsing the company's website, which you can find via your favorite search engine, should

help you understand how the company views itself, what it sees as its priorities, and so on.

- You can find in-depth financial information, company profiles, and industry summaries in several business directories, particularly *Hoover's Handbook of American Business*, which costs hundreds to buy but can be found at most public libraries for free.
- Hoover's Online (www.hoovers.com) provides free abbreviated information about a company, its industry, top competitors, and key executives.
- At www.vaultreports.com, you'll find more free information, plus a taste of results in employee surveys about salary and such.

Free Salary Range Advice

When you get to the part in the negotiating process where your employer mentions a salary figure, you'll need to determine how reasonable the offer is—particularly if it's in a geographical area where you haven't worked before. At www.salary.com, you can calculate what other people are making in similar jobs in your target region. For example, if on the home page's Salary Wizard you type "bond sales manager" and choose the Worcester, Massachusetts, area, you'll find the typical median salary for that job in that area is $111,570; a chart shows that 25 percent of bond sales management jobs pay up to $94,200, and 25 percent pay $140,233 or more. There's other free information on the site too—such as what kind of job you'd need in your field to get a six-figure salary and a self-appraisal tool to help you prepare for your next performance review.

Free Calculators to Assess Salary Needs

When you search for a job, you need numbers, as in "How much salary will I need in another city to match my lifestyle in this city?" or "How much will I make if I switch to working for a nonprofit organization?" You can get free calculators for this information and more at the Economic Research Institute website: www.erieri.com. On the "Resources" page, many of the institute's salary and other calculators are offered for sale, but sprinkled throughout the offerings you'll find nearly three dozen free compensation calculators and reports (including a link to U.S. government salary data) to help you assess your situation.

Free List of Questions to Ask Your Interviewer

You've probably experienced that awkward moment when the interviewer turns to you and says, "Do you have any questions for me?" Instead of sweating bullets, have some questions prepared ahead of time. You can get a wonderful free list of dozens of suggestions from a website run by a New York-based investment research firm called Nitron Advisors: Compiled from various sources, the possibilities range from information about the company ("What do people like most about working here?") to details about the job itself ("How much freedom would I have to determine my work objectives and deadlines?").

Editor's Choice

Free Links to Diversity-Minded Employers

If you're looking for potential employers who are committed to diversity in the workplace, check out jobs.imdiversity.com (click on "Employer Profiles"). There you'll find a free list of more than 50 such employers, with links to their websites for more information. Most of the companies are high profile and range from American Express to Procter & Gamble. On the IMDiversity.com site you can also post your résumé, check diversity job boards, and read insightful articles on workplace issues in "villages" geared to African Americans, Hispanic Americans, Native Americans, Asian Americans, and women.

Women and Minorities

Free Internship Help for Minorities

For more than three decades, the nonprofit organization Inroads has placed talented minority college or college-bound students on track for success in business by helping them obtain paid internships at sponsoring companies such as Kraft, Pfizer, and GE. Participating companies provide a career plan and a mentor for the intern and promise to consider him or her for full-time employment after graduation. While students are in the program, the organization offers them intensive career development, including workshops on leadership and management skills, for free. To qualify, a student must maintain a grade average of B or better. You can find out more and submit an application at www.inroads.org.

Free Job-Training Info for Women

Job hunting can be an intimidating process, especially if you've been away from the workforce for a while caring for your family or for any other reason. The nonprofit Women Work!, The National Network for Women's Employment, is dedicated to "helping women from diverse backgrounds achieve economic self-sufficiency through job readiness, education, training, and employment." In addition to lobbying for laws that are friendly to women's employment, the organization maintains a free directory of more than 1,000 programs helping women train for and obtain jobs nationwide. The programs are typically located at universities, community colleges, YWCAs, and such. To find those in your state, call toll-free 800-235-2732 or go to www.womenwork.org (click on "Resources and Services," then on "Directory of Local Training Programs"). The site also features a job bank and job-search tips.

Free Job Board for Progressive Employment

Are you interested in working for a feminist or other progressive organization? There's a job board for you at the Feminist Majority Foundation's Feminist Career Center website, www.feminist.org—just click the "Feminist Career Center" link. Type in your search criteria, and you might find a job as a bookkeeper at the National Organization for Women (NOW), as a marketing specialist at the Nature Conservancy, or even as a police cadet in Fresno, California. You can search for full- or part-time jobs, temporary jobs, internships, or volunteer opportunities.

Free Job-Hunting and Networking Help for Women

Don't kid yourself, the glass ceiling still exists for women in business; the nonprofit women's research and advocacy group Catalyst says females hold fewer than 7 percent of the top-earning positions in U.S. companies. But Catalyst does offer free help to turn things around. At www.catalyst.org, you'll find statistics and articles about women in business, as well as hands-on help for job hunters. From the home page, click on "Services," choose "Information Center" from the scroll-down menu, then "FAQs." The last FAQ will link you to a PDF file of resources to help women with job hunting, mentoring, networking, legal issues, and more. The organization also sponsors networking events with major companies; its 2006 joint networking event with Microsoft in the San Francisco Bay Area attracted such participating companies as Nike, Johnson & Johnson, and Ernst & Young. From the home page, you can also download free publications on issues important to women in business, or sign up for a free newsletter about the latest trends.

Free Résumé Templates and Low-Cost Career Expos

Women for Hire, a group that provides recruitment services for women, charges up to $195 an hour for career coaching. But you can get some basic tools and tips for free on its website: www.womenforhire.org. For example, from the home page you can access some very good templates for chronological résumés, cover letters, and thank-you letters. You can also subscribe to a free career advice magazine and e-newsletter, and sign up to network at career expos in various cities (for a $10 registration fee). Target, Morgan Stanley, and Dell have been among the recruiters at such events.

No-Cost Job Listings for Students of Color

The online version of *The Black Collegian* magazine features free job listings for college students of color. The site's Diversity Registry links students with employers who use it to actively recruit minorities. You can search by the usual categories—location, keyword, job category, and (for a change) education level. For more information, go to jobs.blackcollegian.com and click on "Find a Job."

Help Fighting Age Bias

If you think you've suffered age discrimination, the American Association of Retired Persons may be able to help. The AARP Foundation provides legal help in situations that could lead to

important court cases. If, for example, the problem you've experienced is widespread within your company, lawyers for the foundation may represent you and your co-workers or file *amicus curiae* (friend of the court) briefs on your behalf; they can then share their own research and policy analysis to support your case. At any one time the foundation typically has about 14 attorneys handling about 70 cases on a variety of issues—including a recent one on age-based benefit packages. For more information, call toll-free 888-687-2277 or go to www.aarp.org/research/legal-advocacy.

Pensions

Free Pension-Related Counseling and Assistance

You can get free legal assistance for any question or problem related to your pension at one of six regional offices of the Pension Rights Center, funded by the U.S. Administration on Aging and other sources, including a variety of foundations. Among other services, they can help you apply for benefits, determine the amount you are due, and file an appeal if you've been wrongly denied a benefit. The Administration on Aging currently funds six regional projects offering free pension counseling to seniors; the New England project, for example, has helped more than 4,000 people recover $28 million in benefits since 1994. Contact information for each center can be found at www.pensionrights.org (click on "Pension Help"). Click on "Pension Publications" and you'll find helpful fact sheets and books to read or order.

All You Need to Know About Pensions for Free

The news is filled with stories about underfunded pensions and pension reform—but how will it all affect your retirement situation? To place your plan within the context of larger pension issues, you can download free publications and government reports on those subjects and more at www.knowyourpension.org/resource.aspx. The documents examine private pensions and other retirement issues from such diverse points of view as the government's General Accounting Office, the nonprofit Employee Benefits Research Institute, and Moody's Investors Service.

Q I've been discriminated against at work! Where can I go for free advice and legal help?

A The function of the federal Equal Employment Opportunity Commission is to enforce laws against employment discrimination based on race, color, gender, religion, age, disability, or national origin. If you believe you've suffered discrimination, it won't cost you a dime to consult with one of their customer-service representatives to see whether you might have a case. Call 800-669-4000 or TTY 800-669-6820, and you'll find a representative ready to help in one of more than 150 languages. To find the nearest district office, visit www.eeoc.gov/offices.html. If the EEOC determines that you have a basis for filing a complaint, you could end up having your case mediated for free, assuming both you and the employer agree to it.

Editor's Choice Free Information on Pension Rights

The U.S. Department of Labor's Employee Benefits Security Administration offers a variety of free publications about pension rights. At www.dol.gov/ebsa/consumer_info_pension.html, you'll find general information on such topics as "10 Common Causes of Errors in Pension Calculation," "Employer Bankruptcy: How Will It Affect Your Employee Benefits?" and "10 Warning Signs That Your 401(k) Contributions Are Being Misused." To get additional information on pension rights and ask for publications that fit your situation, call toll-free 866-444-3272.

Lost Pensions Found

If a former employer doesn't know how to contact you, you might have pension money waiting for you and not even know it! To check, go to www.pbgc.gov, the website for the Pension Benefit Guaranty Corporation, the federal agency that insures most private pensions. Click on "Workers & Retirees," and you'll find a link under "Pension Search" to check whether you're owed pension money. The list is only for people the PBGC has not been able to find, so if you're not on it, you should also check with your former employer. If you're having trouble locating the company because it's moved, merged, or gone out of business, click on "Media" on the home page, then "PBGC Publications." You'll be able to download the free PDF file "Finding a Lost Pension." This 35-page booklet by the Pension Action Center at the University of Massachusetts Gerontology Institute covers such topics as legal protections, looking for documents, places to look, and what to do if you find the pension fund.

Pension Questions Answered for Free

If you're currently employed and have questions about future pension benefits, the Pension Benefit Guaranty Corporation is still a font of free information. If you contact one of its centers, it can tell you about your current plan, estimate your benefit payment at retirement, tell you what to do if your company's plan has ended, and much more. For further information, go to www.pbgc.gov or call toll-free 800-400-7242 or TTY 800-877-8339.

big profits from your small business

Being your own boss and forging your own future are part of the American dream. Here are some fantastic finds that will help your small business save (and earn) more money.

By the numbers

99.7

Percentage of U.S. employers that are small businesses. Of the 24 million small businesses in America, 53 percent are home-based businesses.

SMALL BUSINESSES ARE TRULY THE ENGINE of the U.S. economy: They've generated 60 to 80 percent of the new jobs over the last decade and employ fully half of the nation's private workforce. A group this big and important deserves a break, and we've compiled nearly eighty of them. Small, fun things like free pen refills and business cards; and big, substantial things like tax breaks for opening new factories, six-figure grants for research and development, and low-interest loans for start-up or expansion.

You'll notice that a lot of the small-business action occurs at the state and local levels. States, serving as the testing grounds for new government initiatives, provide some of the most innovative and useful programs for small businesses. Many of these are competitive in nature; not everybody who applies for a grant, loan, tax break, or incentive will get one. That's as it should be; the nature of business is competition. So before you invest too much time and energy pursuing an offer, do your homework. Make sure a program applies to you before you apply for it.

If a program listed in this chapter is of interest to you but is located in another state, don't worry. Chances are there's a similar program in your state. All the states are eager to attract businesses and offer many of the same incentives and services, such as websites that link employers and employees, programs to promote the state's products, and even offices dedicated to helping filmmakers who work in the state. Your own state's website is the best place to learn about its small-business programs. Every state in the union has a prominent "Business" button on its home page, so start your research there.

And speaking of home pages: You'll find that just about every entry in this chapter comes with an Internet address. That's the nature of business today: Print and paper may not be entirely out, but digital communication is definitely in. Your business is likely already online, but in case yours is among the estimated 20 percent of U.S. businesses still without a website, read on for ways to set one up at no cost.

See you, and your small business, online!

Advice and Counseling

Free SBA Seminars

The U.S. Small Business Administration offers classes and seminars year-round, many of them free. Topics include Internet marketing, bookkeeping, lease negotiation, and human resources. To see what the SBA is currently offering in your state, consult its online calendar at www.sba.gov, and click the "News and Events" link.

Free or Cheap Small Business Basic Training

The Small Business Administration partners with local agencies—universities and colleges, state governments, nonprofits, chambers of commerce, and other organizations—to fund Small Business Development Centers that provide small businesses with information and assistance tailored to the geographic communities in which they operate. The range of free or low-cost services from the SBDC includes basic business training and coaching; financial, marketing, production, organization, engineering, and technical help; feasibility studies; and assistance with trade issues, technical problems, and procurement challenges. The centers reach out to minority businesspeople, persons with disabilities, veterans, women, and other members of disadvantaged groups. To find the SBDC nearest you, look in the phone book or go online to the Association of Small Business Development Centers website, at www.asbdc-us.org.

Q: I've heard a lot about the SBA. How can it help me?

A: The U.S. Small Business Administration (SBA) is the federal government's main program supporting small businesses. It provides free information about marketing, management, finance, and more to small businesses, both online and via telephone. It also offers indirect financial assistance to small business. Contrary to popular belief, the SBA doesn't give grants to start or expand businesses, and it doesn't lend money itself; instead, it sets specific rules for borrowers that, if met, enable the SBA to guarantee loans made by independent lenders. If the borrower defaults, the government pays—thus reducing the risk to the lender. To find the office nearest you and to learn more about what the SBA has to offer, visit its website at www.sba.gov, or call its Answer Desk toll-free at 800-827-5722.

Free Counseling in New Mexico

New Mexico's Small Business Development Centers offer free, confidential counseling to state small businesses in many areas, including marketing, finance, and bookkeeping. Nothing so unusual there—except, if you can't make it to one of their 19 offices around the state, they also offer a free, e-mail-based advice and assistance service. Send in your questions on a variety of small-business topics, and they'll respond, confidentially, within two business days. Learn more at www.nmsbdc.org. If you live in another state, check to see if it offers a similar program.

Enlist an MBA Student for Little or No Cost

Business schools can be great sources of free help and information. Why not work with a local professor at a nearby college or university to turn your next marketing push, expansion effort, or product rollout into a class project or case study? Or if you're just starting out, let a class help draft your business plan. You can get students to perform market research, feasibility studies, customer surveys, and much more at little or no cost, because they're getting college credit for the work. Working with a business school isn't a quick-hit money-saver; it takes some relationship-building and creative thinking. But the payoff can be huge: You get fresh ideas, youthful energy, and scientific rigor applied to your business, at big savings.

Editor's Choice No-Cost/Low-Cost Advice from Experts at SCORE

SCORE is a nonprofit organization of working and retired business owners and executives who give free, confidential advice to small businesses. SCORE (formerly the Service Corps of Retired Executives) has 10,500 volunteers who provide three main services: business advice via e-mail (available at emc.score.org); face-to-face, one-on-one business counseling for small businesses; and free or low-cost workshops on business planning, finance, insurance, real estate, and other topics via 389 chapters throughout the United States. (More than 6,700 workshops were offered in 2005; they vary by chapter, but basic introductory business classes are available on an ongoing basis at most chapters.) Remarkably, SCORE does this all with only 16 paid employees. SCORE works with the Small Business Administration but is not a part of it. To find out what's available at your local SCORE office, go online to www.score.org or call toll-free 800-634-0245.

Free Market Research from the Census Bureau

Looking at expanding your small business into a new market? Then it's time to do some market research, which you can accomplish for free with the help of the United States Census Bureau (www.census.gov). From the ongoing American Community Survey—which records statistics and tracks changes in income, homeownership, age, and more for over 800 geographic areas in the United States—to a variety of mapping products and services, many of which are free, you're bound to find the information you need. (There's so much data that finding just what you want may take some digging.) Personnel at the Census's 12 regional offices can also provide free assistance by telephone, so look up your local office (all have toll-free numbers—there's a link on the home page) and give them a call.

Small Business Services

Free Online Examples of Business Plans

Experts agree that every business—new or old, small or large—needs a business plan. But how do you create one? A good starting point is to read business plans created by others, and you can read 60 business plans for free at www.bplans.com. The plans run a gamut of businesses—from an auto parts store to a wedding planner—and include mission statements, market analysis, and financial plans. The provider of these free business plans, Palo Alto Software, wants you to buy its product so you can create your own business plans, but you don't need to purchase anything to read the sample plans.

Business Plan Competitions for Free Financing

Once you've written a great business plan, you might be able to win cash or financing in one of dozens of business plan competitions around the country. Many of these contests are sponsored by universities; three big-money examples are Rice, with more than $250,000 in prizes; the University of Texas at Austin, with more than $110,000 in prizes; and Case Western Reserve University, with $100,000 in prizes. In most university competitions, a member of your team must be a student at the sponsoring university, but that's changing: In 2006 the Iowa Business Plan Competition, with $50,000 in award money, opened its doors to any Iowan.

EDITOR'S CHOICE

Shop Around for Free Checking

Your small business shouldn't pay for a checking account. Getting a free one can easily save you hundreds of dollars a year. Community banks, credit unions, and online banks are good options. Sometimes you can get free small business checking by agreeing to keep your personal accounts at the same bank, or by opening a business line of credit. Likewise, shop around for the best interest rates for your business savings and credit accounts. You compete hard to get new business; make the banks compete for yours.

No-Cost Tax-Cost Estimates in Michigan

Ready to grow your Michigan small business, but not sure you can afford to? Among its many services, the Michigan Economic Development Corporation provides a Business Operating Cost Estimating Service, available free to all Michigan firms. By analyzing company-specific cost factors, the service estimates how expansion will affect a company's Single Business Tax, property taxes, workers' compensation insurance, and unemployment insurance. The MEDC staff provides a customized report on the estimated bottom-line impact of expansion projects. To get started, call the MEDC toll-free at 888-522-0103. Michigan also has a Small Business Advocate, appointed by the governor, who makes sure that small companies get what they need to grow and prosper. Call the advocate toll-free at 800-946-6829.

Free Real Estate Info in West Virginia

Looking for space for your small business in West Virginia? The state's Development Office maintains an up-to-date, searchable database of industrial parks, buildings, available lots, and office space on its website (www.wvdo.org/realestate/index.html). You can search by county, square footage, and other attributes, and get the addresses—and in many cases an aerial view, floor plan, and other specifications—of available buildings that meet your criteria. A search of the office-space database yields PDF documents showing photos and floor plans for the building and pertinent statistics, such as lease rates, utilities, zoning, and contact information.

Free Production Efficiency Help in Kentucky

Automation is a key to success in manufacturing, but the tools, machines, and techniques grow more complicated by the day, especially for small businesses without deep engineering benches. Fortunately, the University of Kentucky Center for Robotics and Manufacturing Systems, in Lexington, can help. They'll analyze shop layouts, solve production problems, improve production processes, educate you on new techniques and approaches, locate parts and equipment suppliers, critique product designs, and much more—without trying to sell you anything. Many of the center's services are free, and any Kentucky business, large or small, involved in manufacturing can participate. Each year the center assists some 350 Kentucky companies, entrepreneurs, and agencies. In Kentucky, call toll-free 800-227-6268, ext. 401, for more information.

Free Business News from Indiana

Small business owners in Indiana who want business news from around the state can turn to the free *Indiana Economic Digest*, online at www.indianaeconomicdigest.net. This easy-to-use, searchable website compiles business news from more than 80 Indiana newspapers, from the huge *Indianapolis Star* to the tiny *Rushville Republican*. Stories can be sorted by topic, region, county, or date.

Free Help Getting a Government Contract in Wyoming

If you have a small business in Wyoming and want it to become a supplier to federal, state, and local governments, free help is at hand. GRO-Biz is a joint state-federal program that assists Wyoming companies—especially small businesses and those owned by women, minorities, and veterans—with the paperwork it takes to land government contracts. The GRO-Biz staff then monitors more than 500 government bid services daily and matches them up with eligible businesses in the state. It also helps interpret complicated government solicitations and provides guidance on placing a successful bid—all at no cost to the companies. To participate in GRO-Biz, go online to www.gro-biz.com, call toll-free 866-253-3300 in Wyoming, or send an e-mail to grobiz@wyoming.com.

Small Business Grants

R&D Grants for High-Tech Small Businesses

Small businesses in high-technology fields can get an extra research and development boost from the government through the Small Business Innovation Research (SBIR) program and the Small Business Technology Transfer program (STTR). SBIR reserves a percentage of federal research and development funds for use in businesses with 500 employees or less—ones that typically have a harder time affording basic research projects. SBIR dollars pay for early stages of R&D, with the intention that the resulting technology will eventually be commercialized. STTR grants are geared specifically toward bridging the gap between the basic research typically done in laboratories and the product innovation typically done in small businesses; for that reason, STTR grants require participating small businesses to work with a university, nonprofit, or

> **Editor's Choice**
>
> **No-Cost Copyright Search**
>
> You're paying for the U.S. Copyright Office with your taxes, so this isn't exactly free, but at www.copyright.gov/records you can look up the copyrights of books, music, periodicals, and other documents at no cost. Although it's not perfect—only a small percentage of copyrights are registered with the Copyright Office—the search is a valuable tool if your small business produces books, movies, magazines, or even boat designs (little-known fact—the shape of ships' hulls can be copyrighted).

federally funded research organization. SBIR and STTR grants can total up to $850,000, and both are very competitive. For more information on both programs, visit www.sba.gov/sbir, or write to the U.S. Small Business Administration, Office of Technology, 409 Third Street SW, Washington, D.C. 20416.

North Carolina Small Business Fund

In 1993, North Carolina created the One North Carolina Fund, a grant fund aimed at expanding quality jobs throughout the state. In 2006, an offshoot called the One North Carolina Small Business Fund began dispensing grants to help small businesses conduct research and develop new technologies. To participate, a small business in North Carolina must be engaged in a research project funded through the federal Small Business Innovation Research or Small Business Technology Transfer program (see above); North Carolina will give additional funds of 50 percent of the federal grant, up to $50,000. Learn more at www.ncscienceandtechnology.com.

NYC Small Business Awards for Women

The New York City Commission on Women's Issues and NYC Business Solutions sponsor the annual New York City Small Business Awards, which give grants of between $10,000 and $50,000 to businesses that have created success for New York City women. In 2005, some 300 businesses competed, and $140,000 in grant awards were given out to six winners, including a restaurant, a performing arts group, and a software company. Learn more about the awards at www.nyc.gov/html/cwi/smallbiz.

Loans and Investments

Easy-Access Credit in Connecticut

Connecticut's Community Economic Development Fund provides funding for both traditional businesses (such as restaurants and stores) and nontraditional businesses (such as an ethnic-bread bakery and a provider of bounce houses for kids' parties). It issues loans of up to $250,000 at prime rate plus 1 percent to grow an existing business (banks typically charge 5 percent over prime, and even Small Business Administration loans are generally 2 to 3 percent over

Editor's Choice

Seed Money for Struggling Entrepreneurs

The Trickle Up Program, a non-profit corporation, helps people in financial need all over the world to start businesses. In the United States, Trickle Up works in 12 states where poverty is greatest; about 40 percent of its clients are in the process of moving off welfare, and 72 percent are women. Typically, Trickle Up provides a $700 grant in two parts: $500 seed money after the client completes basic (free) business training provided by Trickle Up or a partner organization, and $200 more after the business has been up and running for a few months. Contact Trickle Up online at www.trickleup.org or send an e-mail to USA@trickleup.org.

Free Stuff and Free Help from Your State

Your community wants your small business to succeed! Here are a few states that offer grants and other financial and marketing support that can get your business off the ground. Don't see your state here? Start your search online by using your state's name, plus "grant" and the industry you're in.

STATE AND PROGRAM	PROGRAM GOAL	WHAT'S ON OFFER AND HOW TO QUALIFY
ALASKA Buy Alaska Program 907-274-7232 from out of state; 800-478-7232 within Alaska; www.buyalaska.com	The program's goal is to help Alaska-based companies purchase from one another; area businesses can be listed in the "Buy Alaska Business Directory," an online registry of businesses within the state that's accessible to other businesses looking for suppliers.	Register your business for free on the buyalaska.com site. (If you are a business looking for an area supplier in your industry and don't find one, Buy Alaska will assist you.) Members get free window stickers for their businesses to acknowledge their participation.
GEORGIA Enterprise Zones in Georgia; dca.georgia.gov	To encourage private businesses to invest in underprivileged areas where poverty and unemployment are rampant.	Tax breaks and other incentives are available to business start-ups in these areas.
KANSAS Tourism Marketing Grant Program www.kansascommerce.com, then search for "TMGP"	Helps businesses, nonprofits, and communities in the state draw tourists to area attractions, hotels, and restaurants.	Reimbursement grant program pays for up to 40 percent of a marketing project; funds can be used for media advertising outside the recipient's local area.
MONTANA Made in Montana (MIM) and Grown in Montana (GIM) www.madeinmontana/usa.com	Helps more than 2,700 manufacturers, producers, and entrepreneurs in the state attract potential clients outside Montana.	MIM and GIM producers and manufacturers receive free marketing advice and can purchase stickers for their products. The Department of Commerce also publishes an online directory of Montana products.
NEVADA The Nevada MicroEnterprise Initiative; www.4microbiz.org	Supports the economic self-sufficiency of low- and moderate-income Nevada residents by helping them develop entrepreneurial skills.	Offers a 12-week course for budding entrepreneurs, and loans to help both start-up and established companies grow.
NEW HAMPSHIRE MicroCreditNH; www.microcreditnh.com	A nonprofit finance and support program for companies of five or fewer people.	Offers classes, workshops, networking opportunities, and small business support. Classes are $5 for members; membership costs $25.
NEW JERSEY Business Relocation Assistance Grant Program;609-777-0885; www.state.nj.us/njbiz/r_brag.shtml.	Gives grants to companies that relocate to New Jersey or expand in the state.	Companies need to create at least 25 new, full-time jobs to be eligible; grants can be up to $200 per job created.
OREGON Energy Trust of Oregon, Inc. www.energytrust.org	Offers programs to help businesses and homeowners reduce energy costs and encourage installation of renewable energy technologies.	Programs provide technical assistance and cash incentives, and access to tax credits. Financial incentives of up to $200,000 available.
WISCONSIN Dairy 2020 Early Planning Grant Program; website is commerce .wi.gov/MT/MT-FAX-0820.html.	To maintain Wisconsin's reputation as the premier dairy-producing state.	Grants help dairies pay for business planning or other professional services. Applicants contribute 25 percent of total project costs.

Editor's Choice

Free Tax Rate Finder

The law requires online and catalog retailers to collect sales taxes for many transactions, but there are a mind-boggling 8,000-plus different sales tax jurisdictions in North America. To make sure you're collecting the right amount and sending the money to the proper government authorities, try AvaRates Now—a free online service from sales tax–software firm Avalara, on the Internet at www.freetaxrates.com. AvaRates Now allows up to 50 tax rate lookups per month, which might be enough for a small business. If you need more lookups, Avalara will be happy to sell the service to you.

prime), as well as lines of credit and term loans. CEDF figures that your track record is more important than your writing skills: You need to have been in business longer than three years, and provide three years of tax returns, but you *don't* need to submit a business plan—just a one-page marketing/management statement. Call toll-free 800-656-4613 or go online to www.cedf.com/gyb_loans.htm.

Low-Interest Loans in Pennsylvania

Pennsylvania's Small Business First program provides low-interest loan financing for businesses of 100 or fewer employees in several industries, including manufacturing, mining, hotels, and defense. Loans of up to $200,000 can be used for real estate acquisition, the purchase or upgrade of machinery, and environmental compliance projects; working capital loans top out at $100,000. Loans are offered at below-market rates for terms that vary from 3 to 15 years based on the loan's purpose. One example of the program at work: A family-owned dairy farm with five employees got a $200,000 Small Business First loan to purchase milking equipment, allowing them to expand their operation to 770 cows. For more information on the program go to www.newpa.com/programFinder.aspx and scroll down to Small Business First.

"Woman Friendly" Credit Scores for Businesses

Count Me In, which calls itself "the first online microlender," focuses its efforts on providing small-business loans to women, who often have nowhere else to turn for business loans. It doesn't provide free money, but we include it because it provides access to needed capital for businesspeople who would otherwise have a difficult time getting it. Count Me In uses a "woman friendly" credit scoring system to make loans of $500 to $10,000 to women across the United States at rates ranging from 8 to 15 percent, based on credit history, the riskiness of the business, and the borrower's prior business experience. First loans from Count Me In must be repaid in 18 months, but subsequent loans can be for terms up to 84 months. Count Me In also provides online business training and links women with networks that expand contacts, markets, skills, and confidence. Learn more at www.count-me-in.org.

Loans for Entrepreneurs with Poor Credit

ACCION USA, a nonprofit organization (its parent organization, ACCION International, made its first loans in South America in

1973), provides small-business loans to entrepreneurs, including those who can't get bank loans due to credit problems. Clients who avail themselves of these loans work out of offices, homes, and storefronts, and include such businesses as restaurants, retail stores, computer services, beauty salons, and taxi services. Loan amounts range from $500 to $25,000, and terms run from three months to five years. Interest rates, while higher than standard bank rates, are better than most options available to people with poor credit. Many clients receive multiple loans over the years. One benefit of working with ACCION USA: It funds its loans within 20 days, and often as quickly as five days. Another benefit: You can get free legal advice from a cooperating law firm. Learn more at www.accionusa.org (presented in English or Spanish) or by phone toll-free at 866-245-0783.

Microloans and Free Help for Florida Small Businesses

The state of Florida hosts more than 20 small-business incubators, accelerators, and support organizations for emerging businesses, including units associated with Walt Disney World and NASA's Kennedy Space Center. At the Disney/SBA National Entrepreneur Center, small businesses can apply for "microloans"—short-term loans of up to $35,000 for the purchase of machinery, equipment, inventory, and working capital. The Disney NEC includes a Business Information Center, which entrepreneurs and small-business owners can use for free. It has high-speed Internet access and an extensive library of books, videos, CD-ROMs, and online resources to help you write a business plan, create an online marketing campaign, or study sample agreements and contracts. The BIC's staff can match you up with a small-business expert for free one-on-one counseling. Call 407-420-4848 or go online to www.floridanec.org.

Patient Venture Capital in Maine

One problem with venture capital is that the capitalists want their money back, often quickly. But the state of Maine runs its own "patient" venture capital fund, called the Small Enterprise Growth Fund, for its growing businesses. It's an $8 million, revolving, "evergreen" fund, seeded through state bond proceeds and funds from the Maine legislature. Its investments typically range from $150,000 to $350,000 per company, and the fund expects to realize a risk-adjusted return on its investment in five to seven years. Typical successful applicants are companies that have a distinct competitive advantage in a strong marketplace; investments from the fund usually involve purchase of preferred stock. For more information, visit www.segfmaine.com.

Tax Breaks for Arizona "Angels"

If you're looking to entice investors to your small business—and you're in Arizona—your potential angels may be eligible for a big tax break. Established in 2006, Arizona's Small Business Investment Tax Credit Program gives investors in certified small businesses an income tax credit equal to 30 percent of their investment over a three-year period. How do you get certified? Apply to the Arizona Department of Commerce. Learn more about the program online at www.azcommerce.com/finance/capinvest.asp or by calling 602-771-1124. (Be sure to ask about the program by name.)

Child-Care Facilities Grants in Tennessee

The Tennessee Child Care Facilities Corporation exists to help with the start-up, expansion, improvement, or continued operation of child-care facilities. It guarantees loans, issues loans itself, and runs a corporate/community partnership grant. The TCCFC guarantees loans of up to $250,000; its direct loan programs offer amounts up to $25,000 for existing and new centers, at the prime rate minus 1 percent. TCCFC's grant program works through local governments and school districts; through these public agencies, private child-care facilities can get funding up to $50,000. TCCFC also conducts training workshops for child-care businesses, and publishes an electronic newsletter called *Child Care & Business Exchange*. Call it toll-free at 888-413-2232.

Marketing and Publicity

Free Business Leads

Looking for leads to new business? Aren't we all? Check out zapdata.com, a service of Dun & Bradstreet, a worldwide business information provider and the people who run the D-U-N-S Number database. (D-U-N-S numbers are unique identifying numbers for businesses; a D-U-N-S number is required in order to do business with some large companies and government organizations.) Zapdata.com sells business information—contact names, fax

Editor's Choice

Your Small Business on the Internet—Free!

Every small business should have a website. Several free options are available. Dozens of free "hosts" are listed at www.free-webhosts.com. You create your own website, or hire someone to do it, and "upload" it to the host. Your Internet service provider (ISP) may also provide free hosting. If you don't want to create a website yourself, look into free template-driven services at www.tripod.com and www.geocities.com. You fill in a form online and they generate the website for you. Well worth checking out is Google Page Creator (pages.google.com), which uses simple, good-looking templates to create pages.

numbers, and other data—on more than 14 million U.S. businesses. Signing up is free. You can then generate prospect lists based on criteria such as company location, size, and industry. Answer one simple survey question when you sign up online—How did you find its website?—and zapdata.com will give you 25 free leads chosen at random from your first prospect list and two detailed company reports, also free. Check it out at www.zapdata.com.

Free Intro E-Mail Campaign

Want to dip your small-business toe into e-mail marketing? If you have a small mailing list—50 or fewer e-mail addresses—you can set up a free e-mail campaign through a company called Constant Contact (www.constantcontact.com). This online service enables you to send out messages, manage your mailing list, and track responses. Constant Contact's hope, of course, is that your business will grow and you'll need a larger e-mail campaign—one that will cost you, and that it's happy to sell you—but that seems like a fair trade-off if your initial program is successful. If your e-mail list has more than 50 names but fewer than 100, you can still get a break from the company: Your first 60 days, with unlimited messages, are free. For the free campaign to the smaller list, see www.constantcontact.com/features/affordable-pricing.jsp.

Free Online Press Releases

Is your small business making news? Tell the world, using a free, online press-release distribution service. Look into these: PR Leap (www.prleap.com), 24-7 Press Release (www.24-7pressrelease.com), I-Newswire.com (i-newswire.com), PR Web (www.prweb.com), and PR Free (www.prfree.com). All of them encourage small businesses to use them to distribute their news, and all will do it for nothing.

Free Sample Marketing Plans Online

Your small business may be catching on, but think how much more successful it could be with a little savvy marketing. At www.mplans.com, you can download and study at no cost more than 20 marketing plans for businesses as varied as a car wash, a catering company, and an accounting firm. Sample plans cover situation analysis, marketing strategy, budgeting, and more. Mplans.com, which is run by Palo Alto Software, also has dozens of free articles on marketing topics such as public relations, targeted marketing, and logo design.

Q How can I get local newspapers to give our small business some free publicity?

A It costs nothing to cultivate relationships with reporters at local newspapers and broadcasters, and the effort can pay off big in free publicity. Make yourself useful to reporters:

- Send them story ideas.
- Offer yourself as an on-the-record expert to speak about your industry.
- When you like their work, call them and tell them so (but mean it!).
- When you buy a piece of new equipment, hire a new salesperson, make a big sale, or update your menu, let them know.

Your goal is to get your news in print or on the air; many experts consider these sorts of mentions to be more valuable than advertising. When you get coverage, be sure to link to it on your website. Be honest and ethical—don't offer products or services in exchange for coverage—but don't be shy!

Finding Employees

Free Minnesota Help-Wanted Ads

Tired of paying for help-wanted ads? Companies in Minnesota can use Minnesota's Job Bank, a free service run by the Minnesota WorkForce Centers and the Minnesota Department of Employment and Economic Development. Minnesota's Job Bank is a self-service system; register your company and you can post a job opening that can be viewed by job seekers nationwide. Potential employees can also post résumés, which you (as a potential employer) may review. We found more than 23,000 jobs and 57,000 résumés when we visited the site in mid-March 2006. You can access the job bank website at www.mnworkforcecenter.org. For more information call toll-free 888-GET-JOBS (888-438-5627).

Workforce Training Grants in Massachusetts

Companies in Massachusetts can get grants to pay for employee training. And they're not just for big businesses: The commonwealth's Workforce Training Fund Express is targeted at small employers with 50 or fewer employees. Grants are up to $3,000 per employee per course and up to $15,000 per year per employer. The course or program must be chosen from a preapproved training directory, and applications can be submitted anytime. A related program, the Workforce Training Fund's General Program, is also available to small businesses: A recent applicant received $49,400 to train seven employees to operate a state-of-the-art manufacturing system. To learn more about the training grants, visit the website www.detma.org/workforcehome.htm.

Q How can I be sure that my new employees are allowed to work in the U.S. legally?

A One of the most basic laws governing businesses big and small forbids hiring illegal immigrants. To help businesses hire legal workers, the U.S. Department of Homeland Security has instituted the free Basic Pilot Program. This online service checks potential employees against Social Security Administration and Department of Homeland Security databases to remove the guesswork from the Employment Eligibility Verification (Form I-9) process; it also improves the accuracy of wage and tax reporting. To register for Basic Pilot Web-based access, go to the website https://www.visdhs.com/employerregistration and follow the instructions. You can also call the Systematic Alien Verification for Entitlements program, Basic Pilot's sponsor, toll-free at 888-464-4218.

Legal Matters

Free U.S. Poster Advisor

The U.S. Department of Labor administers several laws mandating informational posters that you must display for employees, covering topics such as the minimum wage, the Family and Medical Leave Act, and Equal Employment Opportunity. To determine which of these posters you need to post, try the DOL's online Poster Advisor at www.dol.gov/elaws/posters.htm. Through a series of simple questions, it identifies the posters and then provides you with links for downloading and printing them yourself, all for free. Note that this tool doesn't cover posters your state may require.

Free Idaho Business Red-Tape Cutter

Nobody likes red tape; we all wish we could wave a magic wand to make it go away. The Idaho Small Business Development Center has the next best thing: a free online Business Wizard that helps Idaho companies navigate the state's maze of regulatory requirements. The Wizard asks you questions about your business, and generates appropriate information about licenses, permits, taxes, and business registration. You get a customized checklist of agencies you need to contact and a plain-English explanation of why you need to talk with them. Find it online at www.idahobizhelp.org/bizwiz.htm.

Free Illinois Green-Compliance Assistance

Complex environmental regulations can be especially onerous for small businesses. In Illinois, a program run by the state's Department of Commerce and Economic Opportunity makes the load a little lighter. The Small Business Environmental Assistance Program provides free, confidential information and advice to help Illinois businesses comply with environmental regulations. Its services include a toll-free help line, easy-to-read fact sheets on environmental rules, free industry-specific workshops, and free on-site consultations about environmental issues. To find out more about the program call toll-free 800-252-3998 in Illinois or go to www.illinoisbiz.biz/dceo/bureaus/entrepreneurship+and+small+business and click on "Small Business Environmental Assistance Program."

Free No-Smoking Signs

Washington State businesses are subject to some of the strictest antismoking regulations in the nation. To help companies of all sizes comply with the rules, the state makes available a variety of nosmoking and smoking-control signs for free download—including signs in Spanish, Korean, Chinese, Vietnamese, Cambodian, and Russian. No need to go to a professional printer or buy signs; you can print out what you need from your office computer. To download the ones you need, go online to www.secondhandsmokesyou.com and click "Smoke-free businesses" and then "901 signs."

Tax Breaks for Small Businesses

Your state wants you to conduct your business affairs locally, and it'll do whatever it can to entice you to stay put. Here are a few examples of the tax help that some states will give you—if your state is not listed here, try checking with the Small Business Administration, or Googling "small business" plus the name of your state.

Good Neighbor Tax Breaks in Delaware

Small businesses in Delaware can take advantage of extra tax breaks for good works, as provided by the state's Neighborhood Assistance Act. This law encourages businesses that pay Delaware corporate tax to invest in impoverished neighborhoods and communities. The investment can be made directly (by providing services or projects to low-income individuals in an impoverished area) or indirectly (by contributing money, goods, or services to a neighborhood organization that provides services in an impoverished community). The tax credit can be up to 50 percent of the investment or donation, up to $100,000; tax credits available through the program total $500,000 per fiscal year. Contact the Delaware Economic Development Office (online at www.state.de.us/dedo/default.shtml) to learn more about the program or to get an application.

Film in Hawaii and Save

Looking for a place to film your next commercial, video game, or music video? Think Hawaii! The state is so eager for your business that it's offering a tax credit of up to 20 percent on production costs. The Motion Picture, Digital Media, and Film Production Income Tax Credit, administered by the Hawaii Film Office and the Hawaii State Department of Taxation, is available to companies that spend $200,000 or more on production costs in the state. It's also available for short films, features, documentaries, TV pilots, and even student films. Specific rules apply, so call the Hawaii Film Office at 808-586-2570 for more information, or go to the office's website www.hawaiifilmoffice.com.

Tax Credits for Nebraska Micro Businesses

Even the smallest businesses in Nebraska can get a break. The state's Advantage Microenterprise Tax Credit gives a 20 percent refundable investment tax credit to companies with five or fewer employees, including start-ups, in targeted communities. (A list of these communities—more than 125 of them—can be found online at www.revenue.state.ne.us/incentiv/microent/microent.htm.) Applicants can receive credits up to $10,000 total in their lifetime, and the credits apply to new expenditures for wages, buildings, and depreciable personal property (except vehicles). Learn more and get an application online at www.revenue.state.ne.us. Click "Businesses" and then "Nebraska Tax Incentives."

RECYCLING AND BARTERING

Free Shredding in South Carolina

This book is about getting stuff, not getting rid of stuff—but this item is an exception. The South Carolina Department of Consumer Affairs sponsors occasional Shred Days at which businesses and individuals in the state can have confidential documents, such as old bank statements or customer records, securely destroyed for free. During a Shred Day in June 2006, some 90,000 pounds of paper were shredded and hauled off for recycling. Shred Day in South Carolina even accepts floppy disks and CDs. Learn more about the program at www.scconsumer.gov or by calling toll-free 800-922-1594 in South Carolina or 803-734-4200 from out of state.

Green Grants in Ohio

In an effort to boost recycling and reduce waste, the Ohio Division of Recycling & Litter Prevention now offers Recycling Market Development Grants—financial assistance to processors of recycled materials and manufacturers who create products with recycled content. The grants also pay for research that can improve markets for recycled products. Grants are offered through solid waste management districts or authorities and local governments, but are available to private companies, including small businesses, that partner with them. If your idea is right, these grants can be very generous—up to $75,000 for R&D projects, up to $250,000 for recycling market development efforts, and up to $350,000 for manufacturing projects involving scrap tires. Those projects that affect more of Ohio and those that use the most recyclables get the highest consideration. Learn more at www.dnr.ohio.gov/recycling/grants/rmdg/default.htm.

Free California Materials Exchange

In another effort to reduce waste and the amount of stuff sent to landfills, the state of California operates CalMAX—the California Materials Exchange—a free online service that matches businesses and nonprofits that have unwanted materials with others who can use them. Sometimes the material acquired through the service is as free as the service itself—for example, in one match made through CalMAX, a horse ranch in Pleasanton, California, now uses sawdust from a wood window factory in Oakland for bedding in its stalls. The factory doesn't have to pay to have its sawdust hauled off, and the stable gets great-smelling bedding for the price of picking it up. Learn about CalMAX at www.ciwmb.ca.gov/calmax.

Savings on Supplies

Less-Than-Truckload Shipping Discounts

If your business is a member of the U.S. Chamber of Commerce, you're eligible for a 56 percent discount on less-than-truckload (LTL) shipping services from a company called Yellow Transportation. Small businesses can join the U.S. Chamber of Commerce for as little as $120 per year, and the group claims its members saved an average of $1,700 over a seven-month study period with the Yellow Transportation discount. To learn more about the program, go to www.uschamber.com/member/benefits/yellow, or call toll-free 800-638-6582.

Nearly Free Business Cards

Need business cards, but don't want to pay for them? Contact VistaPrint.com, an online printer. If you don't mind a small, unobtrusive VistaPrint advertisement on the cards' backs—trust us, it's not bad—the company will send you 250 color business cards for only the cost of shipping. VistaPrint offers dozens of colorful designs

Short on Cash? Consider Bartering

You might be able to barter for the goods and services your small business needs. When you barter, you exchange products and services directly with another business. Bartering is also a good way to bring in new customers and garner referrals. Some small businesses also join barter networks that facilitate exchanges between multiple organizations; search for a local network at the website of the National Association of Trade Exchanges (www.nate.org). Barter networks that belong to NATE agree to abide by a code of ethics and obey IRS regulations. Note that in many barter networks you pay a membership fee, a monthly fee, *and* a percentage of the value of a trade to participate; make sure your participation doesn't turn an inexpensive thing into a costly one.

to choose from (you can't do your own design or include your company logo).

Free E-Business Card in SBA Database

Business cards aren't all made of ink and paper anymore. The Small Business Administration maintains a searchable repository of business cards on the Internet. It's a free and effective way to get your business name and information in front of millions of potential customers. Get more information and add your business to the database at web.sba.gov/buscard.

Free Shipping Supplies—Delivered!

Don't pay for boxes, envelopes, labels, and other packing materials!

- The U.S. Postal Service will deliver sturdy envelopes and boxes for its Priority Mail and Express Mail services to your office for free. (The mailman stops there anyway, after all.)
- DHL provides free boxes, padded pouches, and envelopes, as well as pre-printed labels, via its website; products are usually delivered in two or three days.
- United Parcel Service lets registered shippers order free labels, "paks," and other supplies online, and will deliver them to your business.
- FedEx provides a variety of packages for its Express service, including boxes, tubes, and sleeves, also for free at FedEx stores or online.

Free Downloadable Business Documents

Need a basic business form or letter, but don't want to pay a lawyer to draft it? You may be able to find the document you need from one of several free sources. Business Nation (www.businessnation.com/library/forms/), a small-business community site, has hundreds of free forms (and many more available for a fee) ranging from acceptance of resignation to waiver of confidentiality. And in Office Depot's free online Small Business Library (access it from www.officedepot.com), you'll find downloadable documents and spreadsheets for creating a balance sheet, engaging an independent contractor, keeping track of employees' hours, and much more; you'll also find a good collection of state tax reporting forms. And we're sure you can guess how many sample letters and contracts you'll find online at www.101samplebusinessletters.com.

EDITOR'S CHOICE

Cheap Ballpoint Refills

Don't throw away that dying pen before you check www.FreeRefill.com. For some 17 different models of ballpoint, rollerball, and fountain pens—mostly freebies given out at trade shows—they provide a package of five ink refills or cartridges for a shipping fee of about $5. With refills costing anywhere from $2 to $8 apiece, this can be a great deal—if they have your pen.

Time Is Money

Free Office-Supply Deliveries

Many big-box office supply stores offer free product delivery if your order totals more than $50. (A couple of ink cartridges will usually cover that.) You can place your order online or by e-mail, phone, or fax. Free delivery means you don't pay for the gas to drive to the store, of course—but, more important, you have more time to stick to your work instead of running errands.

Tech Tools

The Free Linux Alternative

Linux is a free computer operating system, or OS. It can take the place of Microsoft Windows or the Mac OS on your computer. Many computer experts swear by Linux for several reasons: It's very reliable, it has a relatively high resistance to computer viruses, and it costs nothing. It's also more complicated to set up and run, though many versions of Linux are becoming easier and more Windows-like. To learn if Linux is right for your company's computers, check with a trusted computer expert—ideally not somebody whose job is to sell you Windows or Mac software! If you enjoy computers and want to try Linux yourself, take the free online "Getting Started with Linux" course at www.linux.org—click the "Courses" link.

Money-Saving Freeware and Shareware

Tired of paying steep prices for software? Then look for an open-source, freeware, or shareware alternative. For many basic office needs—word processing, spreadsheets, Web browsing, and e-mail—there are viable free alternatives to the big-name products. Open-source software is created and maintained by loosely organized bands of volunteers on the Internet; the best example is Open Office—a totally free Microsoft Office alternative package of programs available at openoffice.org. Freeware is usually created by one person—often for the fun of it—and given away. Shareware is also usually created by one person and given out in exchange for small, often voluntary, contributions. Check out these money-saving alternatives at www.download.com (which also hosts paid software) and www.tucows.com (which lists only freeware and shareware).

Save with Videoconferencing

With travel costs going through the roof, small businesses find that videoconferencing can be a big money-saver. The South Dakota Digital Network makes videoconferencing an even bigger bargain in that state—its nearly 300 fully interactive videoconferencing sites are available for rent at just $30 per hour. (Compare that with commercial services starting at $99 per hour and rising to triple that much.) Many of the DDN sites are at schools, technical institutes, and state universities; although the network and videoconferencing facilities are primarily meant for education, the DDN welcomes for-profit businesses as well. Learn more at www.ddnvideo.sd.gov.

Finding Free Wi-Fi

When you travel for business, don't pay for Internet access at your hotel before checking for a free wireless network. *Newsweek* reports that more than 400 U.S. cities—including Philadelphia; San Francisco; Tempe, Arizona; and Annapolis, Maryland—are rolling out "municipal wireless networks" that are free to use. In other cities, including New York, nonprofits are helping set up wireless networks. Before you hit the road, check your options online at www.jiwire.com or www.wifinder.com.

Free Photo Hosts for eBay-ers

People who sell products on eBay often want more flexible photo hosting than the online auction site provides. They want more pictures, or they want bigger pictures. For them, there's Imageshack (imageshack.us) and Photobucket (photobucket.com), two popular—and free—image hosting websites. (There are dozens of others; search the Internet for "free image hosting.")

No-Cost Web Polls

Web gurus say that interactivity—getting users to do more than simply read your site—can drive online traffic. An online poll is a fun example of interactivity—one that's easy and free to set up, using any of a handful of services, such as Sparklit (webpoll.sparklit.com), Pollhost (www.pollhost.com), and PulsePoll (www.pulsepoll.com). Two caveats: Most of these services put small advertisements in the poll area of your website; and the results of online polls aren't scientifically valid, so don't bet your next million-dollar marketing campaign on the results of one.

EDITOR'S CHOICE **Free Business Tools from Google**

A wealth of free tools for your small business is available to you simply by clicking on the word "more" on the Google home page (www.google.com): Available are anti-spyware and anti-virus software and more in the Google Pack; a photo-editing program; business and stock information; maps and directions; e-mail service; a calendar program; an instant-messaging program; foreign language translation tools; and more. In the Google Labs area, you'll find the next generation of tools they're developing. Google has a tradition of offering its tools for free, so why not take advantage of them?

Free Online Work-Coordinating Site

Want to coordinate a group of people working on a project—maybe people who aren't all in the same building, city, state, or even country? Then try Basecamp, a free online collaboration tool available at www.basecamphq.com. Basecamp lets group members post messages for all to read, set up to-do lists and calendars, and even create group-edited documents on a secure, password-protected website, all for free. If you want to attach files to your project, track users' time, or manage multiple projects, you pay a fee. Basecamp has garnered praise from *The Wall Street Journal* and *Business Week*, and boasts some 250,000 users.

Free Small Business Blogs

Need to communicate with a large group of employees, suppliers, or customers? Want to make sure everybody's getting the same message? Want to solicit their feedback? Want to do it all for free? Then you need a blog (short for Web log), a sort of online diary. Not all blogs are about politics or pop stars; many business leaders find them useful communications tools. Set up a free blog at www.blogger.com, www.livejournal.com, www.wordpress.com, Yahoo 360° (360.yahoo.com), or one of many other free blog providers.

CHAPTER 12

taking control of your money matters

From free investment advice and lower-cost insurance to bank bargains and tax breaks, here's what you need to know to keep more cash in your pocket—where it belongs.

WHO ISN'T ENTICED BY THE LURE of instant wealth, especially after hearing about people who have made it big? When the Internet company Cisco Systems went public in 1990, the share price shot up 24 percent the first day and then zoomed an astounding 60,614 percent over the next decade. Of course, you can lose big too. In less than a year, the share price of energy giant Enron plummeted 99 percent. Enron stock is now officially worthless, giving investors nothing more than a paltry tax deduction.

Over the long term, wise money management should lead to the building of wealth—but potholes pit the Yellow Brick Road to the fabled Emerald City. Misinformation, scams, and other obstacles slow the journey. This chapter helps you sidestep the traps. We point you toward free and discounted ways to build wealth and protect against losses, not only in investing but also in banking, insurance, and other money matters.

Did you know that sometimes you can buy stocks, mutual funds, and Treasury bonds without paying a commission? That on certain dates you can get free consultations with high-priced financial planners? That you may be entitled to free help in preparing your income tax returns (and free filing too)? That you may be able to get free notary public and other services from your bank? This chapter

By the numbers

678

The average American's credit score. The minimum score is 300 and the maximum, 850; 720 is considered the minimum score needed to qualify for the best interest rates and promotions.

identifies the most useful free personal finance services and resources. We'll also alert you to situations where the best things in life *aren't* free. For example, if you always carry a high balance in your checking account, opening an interest-bearing account may be better for you than one that is totally free.

To help you avoid losing your shirt, we'll tell you about free consumer protection programs. For example, you can use the National Association of Securities Dealers' BrokerCheck to check the license status and other credentials of brokers and brokerages. And if you use the National Association of Insurance Commissioners' Stop, Call, and Confirm program, you won't become one of the hundreds of thousands of people bilked by bogus insurers every year.

Money matters require thorough preparation and timely action. Waiting can be rewarding in other matters—say, when waiting for retailers' end-of-season sales—but not when it comes to saving, investing, buying insurance, and other financial issues. Every moment of delay is a lost opportunity Use this chapter to make the right decisions now.

Financial Planning at Any Age

Free Money-Management Tool Kit

The mission of the U.S. Financial Literacy and Education Commission is to provide financial education for all Americans. One way it does it is through its free *My Money Tool Kit*. Though the specific contents vary according to availability, the kit usually contains about six booklets on such topics as credit cards, debt management, and identity theft. Order it by going online to www.mymoney.gov or by calling toll-free 888-696-6639.

Federal Citizen Information Center's Free Help

Look to this government publication clearinghouse for information on all sorts of money matters (and other topics too). Among the FCIC's most useful free publications are booklets and brochures on healthy credit, certificates of deposit, identity theft, Internet investment fraud, estate planning, and private pension plans. Call toll-free 888-878-3256 to order any or all of them (you will be charged a

Editor's Choice Free One-Time Financial Planning

What kind of IRA is best for you? Are your investments well allocated, or should you move money around for safety or growth? Several times a year, personal financial advisers who may normally charge $100 an hour or more for their services will answer your questions over the phone for free. The focus is on retirement planning, but since the earlier someone starts planning, the better, people of any age can call. Sponsored by the National Association of Personal Financial Advisors and *Kiplinger's Personal Finance* magazine, Jump-Start Your Retirement Plan Days usually occur in January, February, or March and again in the fall. Call toll-free 888-919-2345 for upcoming dates and times. The consultation will be of greatest value if you pull together your financial records beforehand.

$2 service fee). Download them for free, or order printed copies without paying a service fee, from www.pueblo.gsa.gov. The website contains a full list of free or low-cost publications.

Free Financial Football Game

Play this fast-paced online game to earn yardage and score touchdowns—or sometimes even get sacked as you fight the clock. Success depends on how much you know about doubling your money, saving for retirement, and other money matters. The game, which was created by Visa, the National Football League, and Player Inc., has terrific sound. Play it at www.practicalmoneyskills.com (go to "Get Ready for Some Football," then "Click here to play").

Free Building Wealth Workbook

Published by the Federal Reserve Bank of Dallas, *Building Wealth: A Beginner's Guide to Securing Your Financial Future* is an especially useful resource for young adults and teens. Though younger people may not know it yet, every day counts in building wealth, and this free, 28-page workbook can get them started on budgeting, saving, investing, and controlling debt. The workbook also includes a glossary and worksheets to plot out financial goals, assets, and liabilities. *Building Wealth* can be downloaded from the bank's website, www.dallasfed.org/ca/wealth. To order a free printed copy, call the Federal Reserve Bank of Dallas toll-free at 800-333-4460, press 1, and provide the information requested. You can also order a free catalog of publications.

Free Financial Calculators Galore

How long will it take you to become a millionaire? How much do you need to save for your child's education? How long will it take to pay off your credit card debt? What is your net worth?

- Bankrate.com, a leading Web-based financial information source, offers dozens of free online calculators relating to investments, loans, and other topics. Using them is fun—and eye-opening too. To check out the list, go to www.bankrate.com and click "calculators."
- Choose to Save, a program of the Employee Benefit Research Institute, is another treasure trove of online calculators. If you want to know how much your employee stock options are worth, how much it will cost to raise a child, or whether you'd be better off with a credit card that offers airline mileage or a low fee, visit the website www.choosetosave.org and click the "calculators" link.

Free Financial Guide for College Jocks

What are salaries like in the real world? How can you track expenses to avoid getting into debt? What's the best way to get an investment program up and running? The NCAA and the Hartford Financial Services Group Inc. have teamed up to produce *Playbook for Life*, a free, 25-page booklet with advice, worksheets, and other resources to help young college athletes get on a solid financial footing before they go out into the cold, cruel world. Download the booklet from www.playbook.thehartford.com, or fill out the order form to have a printed copy mailed to you or to a favorite young athlete.

Money Smarts for Teens

Teenagers who need to learn money-management skills—and are there any who don't?—should check out the colorful Money Talks website run by the University of California Cooperative Extension (www.moneytalks.ucr.edu). They can watch a free video about credit, play free online games ("Gassing Up" and "What Will an Accident Cost You?" are favorites), e-mail questions to "Ask $am," and discover other cleverly packaged information to get them on the road to financial independence.

Free Money-Learning Program for Preschoolers

Whether parents teach them about it or not, preschoolers develop a sense of what money is all about. But are they learning what you

want them to learn? Teach them about saving, making good choices, and other basic money-management skills with the free Thrive by Five program developed by the Credit Union National Association. The program consists of activities that parent and child can do together and other instructional resources and tips. To download the activity worksheets and see what else Thrive by Five has to offer, go to www.creditunion.coop and click on the colorful program logo.

Home, Auto, and Life Insurance

Free Insurance Information

The industry-sponsored Insurance Information Institute is the central insurance resource for consumers. Its website (www.iii.org) offers a video on home insurance, an auto insurance quiz, and all sorts of other information on all types of insurance. The institute publishes more than a dozen free brochures on fire safety, hurricane awareness, and other topics. A full list is available from www.iii.org/individuals/brochures. You can download them there, or request a free printed copy by sending a self-addressed, stamped envelope to Insurance Information Institute, Publications Department, 110 William Street, 24th Floor, New York, New York 10038. The institute also provides free home-inventory software. Download it from the website www.knowyourstuff.org, and use it to list your possessions in case you experience flood or fire damage or a burglary.

Learn for Free What Insurance You Need

Are you an empty nester? A young single? The head of a young family—or an established one? A young single? Different life stages have different insurance needs. Find out what auto, home, health, and life insurance *you* need at this stage of your life by "enrolling" in InsureU at www.insureuonline.org. Once you've completed the short, free course, which was developed by the National Association of Insurance Commissioners, take a quiz to see what you've learned.

Free Insurance Info from Your State

State insurance commissions are charged with protecting the interests of consumers, which makes them a top source of information,

Take Caution!

Slow Down, or Your Insurance Will Go Way Up

A speeding ticket can cost more than you think. Not only will you have to pay the fine (which can be up to an unbelievable $2,000 in a construction zone in Georgia), you may also have to pay more in car insurance for a minimum of three years. In North Carolina, speeding in excess of 55 mph, but less than 76 mph, can cause rates to go up 45 percent; reckless driving can mean a 90 percent increase. If you get a ticket, it is usually worth your while to show up in court, especially if your driving record is good. Depending on regulations in your state, your fine may be reduced, the ticket may not be put on your record, and your premiums may not be increased.

advice, and assistance in resolving insurance disputes. If you live in Washington State, for example, the Consumer Advocacy Group will help you with insurance issues and investigate formal complaints—for free; call its hotline toll-free at 800-562-6900, or send an e-mail to cad@oic.wa.gov. Washington also offers dozens of free publications on auto, health, and other types of insurance, which can be downloaded from www.insurance.wa.gov (click on "Publications") or ordered in printed form. To see how your state insurance commission can help you, check its website, which the National Association of Insurance Commissioners has made blissfully easy to find. Go to the NAIC website (www.naic.org), click on your state, and you'll be taken there right away.

Free Guidance on Flood Insurance

Many people mistakenly believe that homeowners insurance covers flood damage. It doesn't. To decide whether you need separate insurance to cover damages from flooding, visit the National Flood Insurance Program's home page: www.floodsmart.gov. There you can assess the risk in your area and estimate premium costs. Rates, set by the government, average about $400 a year. You can also receive a free flood information packet by mail. Request it through the same website (click on "NFIP Resources" at the top and then on the "Order now" link on the right). You can also use the website to find an authorized agent in your area. The National Flood Insurance Program maintains a toll-free call center at 888-379-9531; personnel can answer questions, help you assess your flood risk, send out the information packet, and find you an agent.

Raise Your Deductible to Cut Premiums

Drive premiums down with higher deductibles. Increasing your auto insurance deductible from $200 to $1,000 can slash the cost for collision and comprehensive coverage by up to 40 percent or more. Raising the deductible on a homeowners policy from $250 to $2,500 can cut premiums by 30 percent. Higher deductibles have another benefit: People submit fewer claims, so their insurance is less likely to be canceled.

Don't Pay for Collision Coverage Again on Car Rentals

Most car-rental agreements include liability coverage, which means that drivers are covered if they damage property or injure someone. But the rental agreement doesn't cover damage to the rented vehicle.

If you hit a deer or back into a tree, you are out of luck unless you have paid for a collision-damage waiver. CDWs come at a high cost—up to $20 a day. The good news is that you may already have paid for collision coverage through your auto insurance or receive it as part of your agreement with your credit card issuer. Check with them before you rent. Make sure that you find out about any limitations, such as the maximum number of days for which the rental car will be covered.

Free Info on Renters Insurance

If you rent, don't make the mistake of assuming you are covered by your landlord's insurance—you aren't. Tenants need renters insurance to compensate them for water damage, theft, and other losses.

Free Help Avoiding Identity Theft

More than 500,000 Americans have their identities stolen every year by criminals who illicitly obtain their Social Security numbers or other personal information and use it to open credit card accounts, obtain loans, or rob their victims in other ways. Repercussions can be severe—identity theft has even caused some victims to be arrested for crimes they didn't commit.

- Fight back: The Federal Trade Commission is the lead agency charged with helping protect consumers against ID theft. Call it toll-free at 877-438-4338 to request free information, or go to www.consumer.gov and follow the "ID theft: what it's all about" link. People who have had their identities stolen may find the ID Theft Affidavit particularly helpful.
- Don't buy ID theft insurance. The Ohio-based State Auto Insurance Companies and some other insurers offer ID theft insurance as part of their homeowners policies. If the insurance comes "free" (that is, as part of the overall package), great. If you have to buy it on your own—don't. For one thing, it isn't really insurance. It doesn't protect you from having your identity stolen or reimburse you for money that you lose as a result. It covers only out-of-pocket expenses associated with fixing the problem, such as notarized copies of documents, and sometimes lost wages and/or legal fees. But such expenses generally don't amount to much. According to a 2005 survey, they average only $587, *including* lost wages and legal fees.
- Be diligent and vigilant. The best identity theft insurance comes from what you can do yourself for free. Guard your Social Security number and other personal information, shred financial documents, check credit card and other statements carefully, and get your free credit reports annually (see "Free Credit Reports," page 251).

Annual Property Insurance Checkup

Nearly everyone knows the importance of having an annual health checkup, but the idea of having an annual *insurance* checkup may come as a surprise. If you're a homeowner, you should discuss coverage with your insurance agent every year—in person if at all possible, rather than by phone. If your car insurance is with the same group, put it on the agenda too. If you need to make changes to the policy, you can take care of the paperwork then and there. Unlike a medical exam, an insurance checkup is free, and it can reap financial rewards. Your agent may alert you to discounts that you haven't taken advantage of, such as for smoke or car alarms or a new home security system. You may decide that you need additional coverage in certain areas. Even if you don't end up with a big reduction in annual premiums, chances are that your coverage will give you greater protection because it will better reflect your needs.

The Insurance Information Network of California has published a free brochure, *Renters Insurance*, that helps tenants determine how much insurance they need and answers many other insurance-related questions. Request a free printed copy by writing to Renters Insurance, c/o IINC, 3530 Wilshire Boulevard, Suite 1610, Los Angeles, California 90010. You can also send a request for an e-mailed digital brochure to consumer@iinc.org.

Health Insurance Savings

Free Info on Getting Health Insurance

Does your state have a high-risk pool for people who have difficulty getting coverage? Is there an external review process if an appeal to the insurance company is denied? Thanks to the Georgetown University Health Policy Institute, you can find out about state programs that help residents obtain, keep, and make the most of their health insurance. The *Consumer Guide for Getting and Keeping Health Coverage* for all 50 states and the District of Columbia is available free at the website www.healthinsuranceinfo.net. It includes summaries of special state programs that help residents pay for health care.

Halve Your Health Premiums with a High Deductible

Choosing health insurance with a high deductible can slash premium costs by 50 percent or more—and cut taxes too. What qualifies as a high-deductible plan is federally mandated and adjusted annually for inflation. For 2006 the minimum deductible was at least $1,050 for an individual and $2,100 for a family. (Some plans have no deductibles for preventive care.) Once you have a high-deductible health plan, you can open a Health Savings Account at a bank, insurance company, or other institution to help pay for expenses the plan doesn't cover. An amount of money no greater than your deductible can be deducted from your salary before taxes, deposited in the HSA, and withdrawn as needed to pay medical expenses. Any money not spent remains in your account and is rolled over every year. More information is available at www.treasury.gov. Just follow the "Health Savings Account" link under the "Taxpayers" heading.

Stop Smoking to Cut Premiums in Half

Smokers are often stunned to discover how much their life insurance costs drop after they have kicked the habit. Their premiums may be reduced by 50 percent. Health and homeowners insurance premiums may also drop, though not as significantly. For information on how to stop smoking, see "Free Help for Quitting Smoking," page 106.

Reducing Long-Term-Care Premiums

Insurance to cover lengthy nursing home stays or at-home custodial care costs thousands of dollars a year. How much you'll pay in annual premiums depends on the age at which you sign up and the benefits that you choose. To slash premiums by up to 50 percent or more, choose a policy that covers care for a maximum of five years or less—not for a lifetime. Studies show that fewer than 10 percent of claimants use nursing home or other long-term-care benefits for a longer period of time.

Avoiding "Too Good to Be True" Insurance

Bogus insurance companies rip off thousands of people each year. To avoid becoming a victim, carefully check out any plan that costs significantly less than its competitors or promises to cover anyone regardless of risk. If a policy seems too good to be true or if you've never heard of a company that wants your business, call the National Association of Insurance Commissioners hotline toll-free at 866-470-6242. The NAIC's free "Stop, Call, and Confirm" phone

Q My health insurer has just denied a claim. How can I dispute it?

A Health plans are required to follow federal and state rules for handling complaints and appeals through internal reviews. Most states also have a second level of review, one that uses independent sources. To teach people how to work the system, Consumers Union and the Kaiser Family Foundation have published *A Consumer Guide to Handling Disputes with Your Employer or Private Health Plan.* Although it doesn't cover Medicare or Medicaid, anyone belonging to another health plan should find the guide enlightening. To obtain a free printed copy, request Publication #7350 from the Kaiser Family Foundation (Attn: Publications), 2400 Sand Hill Road, Menlo Park, California 94025. It can also be read or downloaded online at www.kff.org. Click the "Costs/Insurance" link, then "Consumer Protections."

Check Your Medical Information Report

Big Brother may be watching you. If you apply for individual health or life insurance, the insurer will report any information that it considers significant—say, that you smoke or have high blood pressure—to the Medical Information Bureau, Inc., which may then pass along the information to other insurers. The MIB database contains coded information on millions of Americans. Technically, the MIB is a consumer-reporting agency and must provide a free annual copy of any information that it has on you upon request. Call toll-free 866-692-6901 to see whether you are listed in the database and, if so, to request a copy of the report. If the report has errors, you have the right to have them corrected, which may help you get better or cheaper insurance down the road.

service will tell you whether a company is legitimate. Even if it is, you might do well to check the company's complaint history at the NAIC website: www.naic.org/cis.

Investments: First Steps

More Free Online Classes for Investors

Learn all about stocks, bonds, funds, and investment portfolios from Morningstar, Inc. (www.morningstar.com), a leading independent investment research provider. Most of Morningstar's free online courses offer lessons and quizzes at five different levels (the bond course has two). The classes are aimed at both novice and experienced investors, so you can start at any level you choose. Level 1 in the funds course focuses on Net Asset Value. Level 2 looks at risk and helps students choose their first funds. Levels 3 and 4 explore the different kinds of mutual funds. Level 5 includes signals to sell and cost-basis calculations. You can take classes without registering. But if you do register—for free at www.morningstar.com/cover/classroom.html—you can accumulate points for the work you do and then redeem them for Morningstar newsletters, books, and other products.

Free Program on How to Invest

Though "online seminar" may sound deadly, anything from the Motley Fool, the playfully named financial information firm, is certain to be lively as well as informative. The free, eight-step program teaches the basics and more—what to buy first (an index fund), investments to avoid (penny stocks are on the list), coping with paper losses (the headline is "How to Not Freak Out When the Market Is Feeling Frisky." Tables show the power of saving and compounding, and links take you to in-depth resources elsewhere on the Web. The Motley Fool gives out homework assignments too—no pain, no gain. Enter the classroom through the website www.fool.com/shop/howto and click on "How to Start Investing" (you'll find it under "How-To Guides"). The same Web page has a link to another free online seminar, "How to Get Out of Debt."

Valuable Investment Info for Free

Weiss Ratings' Guide to Bond and Money Market Mutual Funds costs $499 a year, plus shipping and handling fees. A subscription to the monthly *Standard & Poor's Bond Guide* is $375 for the first year. A year's worth of *Value Line Investment Surveys—Small and*

Vanguard's Free Investment Guides

The Vanguard Group, a highly regarded investment-management company, offers more than 20 free, informative brochures to people with or without Vanguard accounts. Both printed and electronic versions are available. The Plain Talk Library includes *Investment Basics*, *Create an Investment Plan*, *Be a Tax-Savvy Investor*, and a brochure on the increasingly popular exchange-traded funds. Fund Essentials has brochures on index investing, international investing, investing for income, investing for tax-exempt income, and other topics. To request brochures, call Vanguard Client Services toll-free at 800-662-2739, and press 0 to reach an operator. You can also read, download, or order the guides online, but getting to the right websites isn't easy—at least not in mid-2006. Go to www.vanguard.com, click on "Personal Investors" and then on "Planning & Education" at the top. Clicking on "Plain Talk library" in the right column will take you to the Plain Talk publications. Once you are there, click on the link at the left for the Fund Essentials investment guides.

Mid-Cap Edition costs $249. Timely investment information costs big bucks, but chances are that the most important publications are available free at your local library. Thanks to computerized databases, you may even be able to log in from home and look up data at any hour of the day or night. Check with the reference librarian to see what is available for use in print and online.

Learn About Stocks Free by Game-Playing

Here's a way to jump into investing without spending or risking a dime. The Virtual Stock Exchange is a free online trading simulation game in which you build and manage a portfolio and compete to increase the size of your "investment" against whomever you choose—yourself, friends or other people you know, or hundreds or even thousands of total strangers. Playing the game can be an entertaining way to learn about investing. You'll see how you would have fared if you had put real money into a portfolio and how you're doing against others who are involved in the same game. The game comes from MarketWatch, Inc., a subsidiary of Dow Jones & Company, Inc. Register for free at www.vse.marketwatch.com/game.

Check Out a Broker for Free

Before you open a brokerage account or change brokers, check out the broker's professional background and registration and licensing status, as well as the conduct of the firm and the individual broker. BrokerCheck is a free service of the National Association of Securities Dealers, which regulates the broker/dealer profession. It has more than 6,000 firms—and more than 850,000 individuals—on its list. Although you won't find everything about possible misdealings on BrokerCheck (and you may find some unsubstantiated complaints), it is still a helpful investment tool. To use the service, call toll-free 800-289-9999, or request information online at www.nasdbrokercheck.com.

Commission-Free Treasury Securities

You can now buy any sort of Treasury security—short-term bills, medium-term notes, long-term bonds, Treasury Inflation-Protected Securities, and savings bonds—directly from the government online. No commission is charged, as it often is if you purchase Treasury securities through a bank or brokerage. You will not receive any paper securities. Instead, the securities are listed in your online

Q How can I get detailed information on publicly held companies?

A An extremely important tool for investors, corporate annual reports contain information on current assets and liabilities, net income, and other aspects of a business, plus a carefully crafted, must-be-read message from the CEO. Anyone can call a company and order an annual report or get it from the corporate website. Even easier—have *The Wall Street Journal*'s annual report service send it to you for free. Request reports for companies of interest by calling toll-free 888-301-0506, or order them online at wsjie.ar .wilink.com (you'll be asked to fill out a brief customer information form).

account, where you can track their value, transfer or sell them, or redeem them anytime after the minimum holding period. Use the Treasury Direct website (www.treasurydirect.gov) to set up an account or find out more. Another U.S. Treasury website, https://www.treasurydirect.gov/indiv/help/tdhelp/default.htm, answers commonly asked questions about setting up an account, purchasing securities, and other topics.

MUTUAL FUNDS AND 401(K)S

Commission-Free Mutual Funds

One way of reducing investment risk is diversification—that is, having shares in many different investments rather than just a few. Mutual funds, which own shares in a number of different stocks and/or bonds, are an easy, well-established way to develop a diversified portfolio. There are two types—load funds, which charge an up-front commission (the "load"), and no-load funds, which have no up-front fees. Every dollar that you put into a no-load fund is invested in the fund. In contrast, paying a load immediately cuts the size of your investment. The assumption behind paying a load is that you'll get better advice and better performance, but many studies show that loads don't outperform no-loads. Be sure to ask about loads and other fund costs when requesting information from a mutual fund.

Analyze Mutual Fund Costs Free

No-load or not, all mutual funds have management fees and other expenses. If two funds perform equally well before expenses, the one with lower costs will have the better overall rate of return. To see the impact of fees and expenses on your mutual fund investments, use the free online Mutual Fund Expense Analyzer from the National Association of Securities Dealers, a self-regulatory securities industry organization. The analyzer calculates total fees and expenses for various holding periods (say, five years) and indicates the projected value after the deduction of all fees and expenses. You can also analyze exchange-traded funds, which are similar to mutual funds but trade more like stocks. This valuable tool is available at www.nasd.com (click on the link under "Investor Information").

EDITOR'S CHOICE

Getting a Bulk Discount on Mutual Fund Fees

In the past, some "load" mutual funds (see "Commission-Free Mutual Funds," page 243) offered discounts on up-front charges to large investors, but the fact that they did so wasn't well known. A new regulation requires disclosure of the breakpoints—the levels at which the load is reduced. The National Association of Securities Dealers has a breakpoint search tool at www.nasd.com (click on the link under "Investor Information"). Use the data on breakpoints to avoid investing an amount just below where you would be charged a reduced load.

Free Mutual Fund Performance Check

Experts suggest that investors keep their holdings over the long haul—but sometimes a mutual fund performs so poorly that you should consider selling it and putting your money elsewhere. FundAlarm, an online resource maintained as a free public service by Roy Weitz, CPA, alerts you to mutual funds that have consistently underperformed their benchmarks (the indexes against which they are compared). You can also see which funds are on the honor roll because they have outperformed their benchmarks. Check your holdings at www.fundalarm.com.

Rolling 401(k)s Over Without Incurring Penalties

With luck and good planning, you'll have a hefty chunk of change in your retirement plan when you retire or switch jobs. Though a cash payout may sound tempting, it can have dire tax consequences: When a 401(k) is cashed in early, the average person loses as much as 46 percent of the money to taxes and penalties. Rolling over the funds into an individual retirement account is often the smarter choice. The *T. Rowe Price Rollover Planner* is a free, interactive CD-ROM that details the various options and explains how to roll over your account. Call toll-free 800-401-1802 to order the rollover planner. You do not have to be a T. Rowe Price customer to receive the CD.

MORE FREE INVESTMENT TOOLS

Free Database on Insider Trading

Many insider stock trades are perfectly legal, but company directors and other high-placed insiders must now report them within two business days. A result of the Enron scandal, the requirement for near-instantaneous reporting has helped level the playing field for ordinary folks. Although insiders buy and sell shares for any number of reasons—not just because they expect the share price to rise or fall—savvy investors use the transactions as yet another way of trying to gauge a company's future. One of the best free insider-trading databases is at Yahoo! Finance. Go to finance.yahoo.com, get a stock quote for the appropriate company, then click on "Insider Transactions" under "Ownership."

Learn About Online Investing Free

Though online investing is a great way to cut trading costs, those new to it may find the process riddled with problems and perils. To speed the learning curve, use the free tools at the Investing Online Resource Center (www.investingonline.org). There you'll learn the eight rules for success, find out which online brokers have the best reputations, and walk through the process of opening an account. Try the exciting Investing Simulator Center to discover what it's really like to trade online. More experienced online investors can look at the section "Already Investing Online?" for tips on placing orders in fast-moving markets. The Investing Online Resource Center is a project of the North American Securities Administrators Association, an investor-protection group.

No-Fee Stock Buys with Dividend Reinvestment

More than a thousand companies offer dividend reinvestment plans, popularly known as DRIPs or DRPs. Through these programs, shareholders can use their dividends to buy additional shares directly through the company or its agent, without paying a commission. Usually owning one share is all you need to enroll in a plan. DRIPs allow you to buy small numbers of shares over time—that is, to "drip" money into your account rather than pouring it in. Since you buy at the current share price, you don't run the risk of investing a large amount of money when the market is at its peak. Another bonus: Some DRIPs allow investors to purchase stock at discounts of up to 10 percent. Moneypaper Inc., a publisher of investment literature and online investment services that specializes in DRIPs, maintains a free online list of companies that offer DRIPs at www.directinvesting.com/moneypaper/companies/mp.cfm. The ones that are shown in boldface and/or underlined are completely fee-free. For a separate list of fee-free DRIPs, go to the Web page www.directinvesting.com/moneypaper/companies/nofeeco.cfm.

Learn About Options and Futures Free

As you gain experience as an investor, you may become intrigued by some of the chancier types of trading, such as options and futures. Both options and futures involve purchasing the right to buy or sell a commodity or a security at an agreed-upon price on a specific date or within a specific time frame. (The difference is that investors can choose whether or not to exercise an option. With futures, they are *obligated* to do so.) The Chicago Board of Trade,

No-Cost Help for Tax Preparation

Is there anything more confusing and frustrating than filing your tax returns? It's hard to keep track of which forms you need, what you can claim (and can't), and how the laws have changed. Fortunately, there are a number of sources—most available online—that are here to help you navigate your way to an easier, cheaper tax filing!

Guide to Free IRS Services

The Internal Revenue Service offers so much free material to help taxpayers navigate the system that it has published *The IRS Guide to Free Services* (Publication 910). To order this free publication, or other publications and current tax forms, call toll-free 800-829-3676. You will automatically receive two copies of any form that you order, plus applicable instructions. Printed copies can also be ordered from www.irs.gov/formspubs (on the home page, under "Order," click on "Forms and publications by U.S. mail"). Delivery takes up to 15 days. To download forms and publications, go to the site and click on the appropriate category. Both current and previous years' forms are available online. After downloading a form, you can simply print it out and fill it in as usual.

Free Tax Preparation Checklist

One of the most onerous tax chores is getting the information together as the deadline approaches. H&R Block's handy online checklist tells you which documents people in different situations—IRA account holders, those who are self-employed, and so on—will need. Print it out from www.hrblock.com/taxes/doing_my_taxes/tax_preparation.html. Other free H&R Block tools include a self employment tax estimator, an alternative minimum tax estimator, and a withholding calculator. Find them all at www.hrblock.com/taxes/tools.

Free Help from the IRS

Call the toll-free IRS tax help line—800-829-1040—to get answers to your federal tax questions. Normal hours are from 7 a.m. to 10 p.m. local time, Monday through Friday, although they may be extended during the tax season. Keep a record of your conversation. Sometimes it may be useful to call back after you have assimilated the information and ask another representative the same questions or follow-up ones. If you receive incorrect information from the IRS, you are still responsible for paying your tax in full, but you will not be charged any penalty for filing a return that was incorrect because of an IRS error.

Free Tax Return Preparation

The IRS runs the Volunteer Income Tax Assistance program for people with moderate to low incomes—currently (in 2006), $38,000 or below. Trained volunteers at about 14,000 locations, such as libraries, schools, and malls, help prepare tax returns, making sure that their clients get all the deductions and credits they are entitled to. Most locations offer free electronic filing. To find a VITA site near you, call the toll-free IRS help line: 800-829-1040. VITA also runs tax-counseling programs for military personnel (see page 329) and for people ages 60 and older (see page 312).

Free Online Tax Returns

The IRS has arranged for a number of companies to offer free tax preparation and free Internet filing. Eligibility for the Free File program varies from year to year. To see whether you qualify this year, check the criteria at the IRS website: www.irs.gov/efile. For tax returns filed in 2006, most free offers were restricted to taxpayers with adjusted gross incomes of $50,000 or less, but anyone could use the free proprietary software at www.taxact.com to prepare and electronically file a federal return. If you use a company's free software, you may be bombarded with solicitations for other products and services, but you are under no obligation to buy anything.

Free Taxpayer Advocate Service

If you have a problem with the IRS that has not been solved through normal processes, you can request free, confidential help in resolving the problem. The Taxpayer Advocate Service—an independent office within the IRS—is for people who are facing significant cost (including fees for professional representation), have experienced a delay of more than 30 days in resolving the issue, or did not receive a response from the IRS by the date that it was promised. You can contact the Taxpayer Advocate Service by phone—toll-free at 877-777-4778—or fill out the form available through the website www.irs.gov/advocate (click on "Contact Your Advocate!"). Many states have set up similar systems to help with problems at the state level.

Free Filing for State Tax Returns

More than 40 states, including California, Colorado, Illinois, and Pennsylvania, offer free electronic filing to some or all of their residents. To see if this service is available in your state, visit the Federation of Tax Administrators website (www.taxadmin.org/fta/link/internet.html); if it is, click on your state to jump to its e-filing website. To obtain state tax forms, go to the tax form page of the website, www.taxadmin.org, and click on your state. The Federation of Tax Administrators also provides a list of state tax holidays—days when certain items are exempt from state sales taxes.

Find Your Refund Status

Instead of simply waiting and hoping, you can look online to find out whether the IRS has received your return and processed your refund. Click on "Where's My Refund?" at www.irs.gov/individuals. If the IRS mailed out your refund more than 28 days ago and you have not yet received it, you can initiate an online tracing process.

a major exchange that deals with options and futures, has published several dozen free print and/or electronic publications for prospective investors. Topics include gold and silver futures, how the e-cbot (electronic Chicago Board of Trade) market works, and a Treasury futures reference guide. To order these or other CBOT publications, go to its website (www.cbot.com) and enter "publications" in the search field.

Don't Fall Victim to Investment Scams

Investment frauds are so lucrative for the perpetrators that new ones are popping up all the time. Have you heard about the "misdialed" phone calls? The victim comes home and finds that a message for someone else has been left on his or her answering machine—a message that goes on and on about a super-duper stock that is about to take off. Naïve people might rush out and buy the stock, driving up its price and enriching the coffers of the fraudster who left the message. Don't fall victim to the latest scams. Learn about them at the National Association of Securities Dealers website: www.nasd.com/investorinformation/investoralerts. The NASD also publishes *Investor News*, a free e-mail newsletter that alerts you to the latest swindles, their new publications, and other items of interest to individual investors. To sign up, go to www.nasd.com/contactus/emailsubscriptionservice/index.htm and click on "Email lists for Individual Investors."

Banking for Less

Free Money Transfers

Certain banks enable customers with online accounts to transfer money for free or at a very low cost compared with Western Union or other well-known money transfer services. For example, Wells Fargo customers can transfer money to other Wells Fargo customers at no charge. You need to know only the other person's account number and the name exactly as it appears on his or her account statement. Specific information is available on the Web page www.wellsfargo.com/wf/help/faqs/transfers_faqs, or call toll-free 800-869-3557. Citibank provides free incoming transfers and charges $5 to transfer money to other Citi customers in the United States or Mexico and $10 to customers elsewhere—except India, where the transfer is free. Enter "global transfer" in the search field at www.citibank.com, or call toll-free 800-374-9700. Check with your bank about its money-transfer policy and fees. Note that banks may set maximum or minimum limits on transfers.

Check Out a Bank Free

Bank Find, a free service of the Federal Deposit Insurance Corporation, allows you to look up branch locations, website addresses, insurance coverage, and other information on banks around the country. Enter the bank's name, zip code, or city at www2.fdic.gov/idasp/main_bankfind.asp to get the information you need.

Fun Free Publications About Banking

Accumulating money can be thrilling, but learning about banks and banking just doesn't have the same pizzazz. The Federal Reserve—the central bank of the United States—has livened up the learning with snazzy online Flash presentations on the life of a check and the life of a dollar bill. Click on the titles at www.federalreserveeducation.org/pfed. You can also obtain free Federal Reserve comic-style booklets on checks, banking, and other topics (see "Free Comics About How Money Works," page 387).

Get Your Bank Freebies

When's the last time you paid a friendly visit to your banker? Competition for customers is so hot among banks these days that they're giving away services they used to charge for.

- Free checking should be easy to find—but ask about fees for bounced checks, stopped checks, and other privileges before you sign up. If you tend to keep a large balance in your checking account, consider an account that offers a high interest rate, regardless of whether or not it is free. Bankrate.com maintains a free, regularly updated database on accounts at various banks. From its home page (www.bankrate.com) click on "Compare rates" and then on "Checking & Savings."
- If you need a safe place to keep jewelry, documents, or other items that are valuable to you, ask your bank whether it provides free safe-deposit boxes. Sometimes only the smaller boxes

Q How can I avoid the fee that machines charge to count my change?

A Now and then you scrape all of the pocket change off your dresser into a coffee can and take it to a machine to be counted and transformed into usable bills. When you do this, avoid change-counting machines in supermarkets that take 5 percent or more of your money as a fee. Instead look for a friendly financial institution (the Commerce Bank in the Midwest, for instance) that allows customers and noncustomers alike to walk in and have coins counted for free. The website www.theunderstory.com lists some locations that have offered free or low-cost coin-counting services in the past. Or ask around at your local banks.

are free, or free offers are good only for a limited amount of time or for certain types of bank accounts. Another word of warning: Don't lose your key. If you do, the bank may have to break open the safe-deposit box—and guess who gets charged for that!

- If you need to have a document notarized, your bank may offer the service for free to some or all customers. Other places that may have free notary public services include libraries, local government offices, large or benevolent employers, and colleges and universities (only for students, faculty, or staff).

Credit Cards

Discounts with Store Credit Cards

Stores love it when customers charge purchases to their store cards instead of bank-issued credit cards—it costs them less in processing fees. So retailers offer incentives to encourage customers to open charge accounts. For example:

- People who sign up for Macy's credit cards may get a 10 percent discount on their first purchases.
- Talbots gives $25 "appreciation dividends" for every $500 in net purchases charged to the store card and a 10 percent birthday discount on one day during the customer's birthday month.
- Kohl's charge customers receive special discounts 12 times a year.

But beware—any discounts may be more than wiped out if you don't pay on time because retail credit cards can have very high interest rates. Also, applying for several credit cards within a year can hurt your credit rating.

Credit Card Freebies

Don't miss out on limited-time offers from your credit card company. In mid-2006, MasterCard offered a free sunglass care kit and visor clip with a $15 purchase at Sunglass Hut, a free JC Penney portrait package valued at $19.98, and discounts at various hotel chains and other businesses. Look for these offers with your credit card statement, check the credit card company's website regularly, or phone the company to find out about the current offers for which you qualify. Note that restrictions may apply, and not all cards are eligible for a particular promotion.

Free Purchase Protection

Buying merchandise with a credit card can come in handy if the item is stolen or damaged, or stops working, within a certain amount of time. Many credit card issuers will refund the purchase price (up to a specified limit) for an item that is stolen or damaged within 90 days. They may also double the warranty period on products bought with the card. Purchase protection comes as a standard feature of many cards, and you don't have to do anything special to enroll. But there are time limits on filing a claim—so if you intend to put one through, call the credit card company's customer service department promptly to find out what to do and by when.

Free Credit Reports

Thanks to a recent amendment to the Fair Credit Reporting Act, everyone can now obtain one free credit report a year from each of the three major credit-reporting agencies (Equifax, Experian, and TransUnion). It's a service not to be missed. The reports may contain errors that could hurt your credit rating—or show that someone else has opened accounts in your name. Free credit reports can be obtained through the individual agencies, but the easiest way to get them is through www.annualcreditreport.com, the authorized central source.

- To get a report on the spot, request it online by visiting www.annualcreditreport.com and selecting your state. Make sure you go to the right website. There have been problems with websites that have similar URLs. These websites may give you your free credit reports, but they are not authorized by the government, may not be secure, and may not give you your "free" credit report unless you purchase something else.
- If you don't need a report right away, you can request one by calling toll-free 877-322-8228, or by printing the request form off the website and mailing it to the address indicated. Phone and mail requests are processed within 15 days.

Stagger your requests throughout the year—that is, use Annualcreditreport.com to order a report from a different agency every four months—so that any problems become apparent early on.

Opt Out of Credit Card Solicitations for Free

Signing up for too many credit cards can hurt your credit score as well as encourage you to pile on debt. To avoid being tempted by promotional offers, take advantage of the credit reporting agencies' free Opt-Out service. Answer the questions at the toll-free number 888-567-8688 to opt out permanently or for a five-year period. You can also use the same toll-free number to opt back in.

Free Help for Compulsive Overspenders

Modeled after Alcoholics Anonymous, Debtors Anonymous has a 12-step program to help compulsive spenders and others who have problems with debt. The emphasis is not on dealing with creditors or paying bills but on overcoming the propensity to rack up bills. More than 400 U.S. chapters run free in-person meetings or regularly scheduled telephone or online sessions. Check online at www.debtorsanonymous.org for information about meetings and other services, or call the organization's headquarters at 781-453-2743.

CHAPTER 13

seeking and securing unclaimed assets

You could be rich and not even know it. Be a finder—and a keeper—by following these easy tips for recovering missing money, locating lost items, and more.

YOU MAY BE RICHER THAN YOU THINK, and in this chapter we'll tell you how to locate "unclaimed" funds that may belong to you, as well as pension or Social Security money you may not have received. You'll also learn how to take advantage of some of the best deals around on all kinds of items that have been lost or stolen or otherwise gone astray—and that can be yours for the bidding at auctions or in foreclosure deals.

At any given time billions of dollars from investment accounts, inheritances, paychecks, utility deposits, and other sources languish in state unclaimed assets or unclaimed funds offices, waiting to be reunited with their rightful owners. California has more than $4.8 billion in its coffers. New York has an astounding $7.2 billion, including more than $1.7 million in a single account. Could it be yours?

Although many businesses—some legitimate, some not—want you to pay them to search for money that is properly yours, you can do it yourself for free. This chapter gives you the tools you need to locate missing or unclaimed assets (including pensions that may be due you) through state, federal, and other channels. Check out the websites and other sources that we've listed. The hours you spend searching for your money may turn out to be among the most lucrative in your life.

By the **numbers**

1.7

Number of Americans, in millions, who were owed tax refunds in 2002 and, as of 2006, had not claimed them.

The government is in no hurry to dispose of missing financial assets. Generally, these are held until the right person claims them—which can be years or even decades later. Unclaimed physical property is a different story. Police departments, storage facilities, and other places that end up with vast quantities of lost, stolen, or forfeited items eventually sell or auction them off. Many go for bargain prices—$2 bicycles, new inkjet cartridges for 25 cents each, designer clothing at 95 percent off. We'll tell you how to find the best buys, and where you should watch your step.

You can also get terrific bargains on pricier items—if you know where and how to shop. Are you searching for a well-maintained fleet vehicle? Check out the U.S. General Services Administration sales. In the market for a used boat? Salvage auctions may be the place to go (as long as you bring a marine surveyor on board). Do you want a good buy on real estate for investment purposes or personal use? Foreclosed or confiscated property may be the answer—as long as you proceed with caution. Whether you're looking for a two-bedroom home or a 200-head sheep farm, you don't want to get fleeced. Exploring unconventional sources for bargains requires a careful eye, but it is a truly exhilarating experience that no bargain hunter should miss.

Missing Money

Searching State Unclaimed Property Offices

If a business owes you money and can't locate you, the money goes to the state's unclaimed asset fund after a certain amount of time (it varies by state). Billions of dollars from uncashed payroll and dividend checks, dormant savings accounts, utility bill deposits, and other sources await their rightful owners. The best way to find out whether you have unclaimed assets is through the website of the National Association of Unclaimed Property Administrators (www.unclaimed.org), a nonprofit organization affiliated with the National Association of State Treasurers. The NAUPA website has contact information for—and Internet links to—unclaimed property departments in every state. You can look up anyone on www.unclaimed.org—friends, neighbors, even celebrities and businesses—but you can't claim the money unless it is rightfully yours.

Keeping What Is Rightfully Yours

Here are some steps you can take to make sure your money doesn't end up in state coffers:

- Cash all checks right away. If you don't receive a dividend check or other regular payment that's due you, call to find out why.
- Don't let accounts go dormant. If you haven't initiated any activity in a year or so—if, for example, you let bank certificates of deposit roll over automatically—write to the institution and confirm your current address.
- When you move, notify all institutions and government agencies with which you do business. Communicate your new address in writing, preferably in typed form to avoid misinterpreted handwriting. Don't delay. Bear in mind that the U.S. Postal Service will forward mail for free—but not forever. First-class mail is forwarded for 12 months (six months for a temporary change of address) unless the sender has put a "Do not forward" notice on it. During the next six months, it is returned to the sender, labeled with the recipient's new address. After that, all address information is purged from Postal Service computers, and mail is returned to the sender labeled "Forwarding order expired."

Usually you won't know how much money awaits you until you have filled out the forms and received the official check, which may happen within several months or take more than a year. Though the typical unclaimed asset amounts to less than $100, some claimants have received checks for thousands of dollars or more.

Using Asset Recovery Services vs. Doing It Yourself

If you receive a notice in the mail indicating that unclaimed assets have been found in your name, most likely the information came from your state's unclaimed property listings. The company that sent you the notice would like to help you recover your assets—for a fee, of course. The cost ranges from a flat fee of $10 or more (in cases where the amount of money to be claimed is likely to be small) to as much as 35 percent of recovered assets. Before you sign a contract, check with the Better Business Bureau (search.bbb.org) or your state attorney general's office to make sure the company is legitimate. Some solicitations are outright scams. Even if an asset-recovery service checks out, you will still have to process a fair amount of paperwork. Instead, consider doing it all yourself—for free as described in the preceding entry.

Q **I never got my tax refund! Who can I call to get it?**

A In 2005, some $73 million in refunds—averaging $871 apiece—failed to reach their destinations because recipients had moved or had addresses that were incomplete. If you think you may be owed a refund from a past tax year, call the IRS toll-free at 800-829-1040.

Life Insurance Payouts from Deceased Relatives

If you suspect that a deceased individual had a life insurance policy for which you are the beneficiary, but you can't find it, you'll have to play detective to learn where to file a claim. There are all sorts of clues. The National Association of Insurance Commissioners suggests looking through the deceased's personal papers to see whether there are records of other types of insurance (the life insurance policy may be from the same company). Address books may contain the names of insurance companies or agents. Canceled checks may show payments for premiums. If you can't find the policy right away, wait. In the coming months, a premium notice may arrive in the mail.

Mortgage Insurance Refunds

People who have paid back certain mortgages insured by the Federal Housing Administration may be due a refund on their mortgage insurance premiums. Eligible loans must have originated between September 2, 1983, and December 8, 2004, and borrowers must have paid an upfront mortgage insurance premium at the closing and not have defaulted on their mortgage payments. Check with your mortgage company to see whether you are owed a refund. You can also obtain information by phoning the U.S. Department of Housing and Urban Development toll-free at 800-697-6967; or by writing to the department at P.O. Box 23699, Washington, D.C. 20026. Inquiries should include your name, FHA case number, the date when the mortgage was paid in full, the property address, and your daytime phone number. More than a billion dollars have already been paid out in refunds, which average just under $1,000 apiece.

Bonds and Banks

Uncollected Savings Bonds

Each year, more than 15,000 savings bonds—and 25,000 interest payments on them—are returned to the U.S. Department of the Treasury because they couldn't be delivered. To find out whether this has happened to you, go to www.treasurydirect.gov and click the "Search for Your Securities in Treasury Hunt" link. The database can also identify savings bonds that are no longer earning interest. About $13 billion worth of bonds fall into this category. Why not cash them in and put the money where it will continue to grow?

Missing U.S. Savings Bonds

People throw out bonds by mistake, or file them in some mysterious place where they're never to be seen again. Sometimes bonds are stolen or destroyed in a fire or flood. If you have misplaced one, don't despair. If you submit the proper paperwork, the government will replace it for free. To begin the replacement process, download form PDF 1048 at www.publicdebt.treas.gov/sav/savlost.htm, or request a printed copy on the same website. You can also write to the Bureau of the Public Debt, Division of Customer Assistance, Parkersburg, West Virginia 26106.

Unpaid FDIC-Insured Deposits from Failed Banks

When a financial institution fails, the Federal Deposit Insurance Corporation becomes responsible for the payout of insured deposits and dividends. The FDIC database contains information on FDIC checks that have been returned or never cashed. See whether your name is on the unclaimed funds list by searching at the site www2.fdic.gov/funds/index.asp. You can also obtain information from the FDIC's consumer call center—call toll-free 877-275-3342; press "2" for information about closed institutions.

Insured Accounts from Liquidated Credit Unions

The National Credit Union Administration—the government organization that insures most U.S. credit unions—makes payouts to members of failed credit unions. If a payout can't be delivered, the money stays with the NCUA for a period of time, after which it reverts to the states. If you believe that the NCUA may be holding funds in your name, call it at 512-231-7900; or send an e-mail to amacmail@ncua.gov. You can also write to the NCUA's Asset Management and Assistance Center, 4807 Spicewood Springs Road, Suite 5100, Austin, Texas 78759.

Funds from Inactive Canadian Bank Accounts

If an account in a Canadian bank or trust company has had no activity for 10 years and the owner cannot be contacted, the balance is turned over to the Bank of Canada. People who think they may have long-lost funds in a Canadian bank should search the database at www.bank-banque-canada.ca/en/ucb/index.html. You can also ask

EDITOR'S CHOICE

No-Fee, Paperless Savings Bonds

To prevent future loss, hold your savings bonds electronically, not in paper form. You can now buy Treasury securities online free of commissions and keep them online without paying any maintenance fees. All transactions can be done electronically through www.treasurydirect.gov. You can even trade in your current paper bonds for electronic bonds, using the SmartExchange program. Details are available on the treasurydirect.gov website.

If You Are Owed Pension Money

Pensions may go missing under a variety of circumstances (three scenarios are discussed below). *Finding a Lost Pension* is a free, 34-page publication from the Pension Benefit Guaranty Corporation, an independent agency of the U.S. government. The publication includes tips on how to search, sources of free help, and other information. Order a printed copy from the Communications and Public Affairs Department, Pension Benefit Guaranty Corporation, 1200 K Street NW, Suite 240, Washington, D.C. 20005. You can also download it at www.pbgc.gov. Click "Workers & Retirees," then "PBGC Publications."

Scenario #1

Your Company Goes Out of Business

If your company is no longer in business, turn to the Pension Benefit Guaranty Corporation for help. The PBGC is the federal agency that guarantees pension payment for people enrolled in private, defined benefit plans (such plans pay a specific monthly amount to retirees).

The agency holds millions of dollars in unclaimed pensions and maintains a "missing participants" list. Search your name—or a deceased relative's, if you are the beneficiary—at the website www.pbgc.gov/search.

For information, you can also call the PBGC toll-free at 800-326-5678; or write to the Customer Contact Center, Pension Search Program, 1200 K Street NW, Suite 710, Washington, D.C. 20005.

Scenario #2

Your Employer Hasn't Paid You Yet

If your former employer is still in business and you believe you are entitled to a pension that you haven't received, send a certified letter to the company's employee benefits department, requesting your most recent statement and the summary description of the plan that was in effect when you left.

The company must provide that information within 30 days. If there is a problem, call the U.S. Department of Labor's Employee Benefits Security Administration toll-free at 866-444-3272.

Scenario #3

You Worked for the Government

If you worked for the U.S. government in any of dozens of agencies or served in the armed forces, the folks at the Thrift Savings Plan may be looking for you. The TSP has a list of some 14,000 people whose retirement accounts are considered abandoned. Check it out at the site www.tsp.gov/lostpar/index.html.

You can also call the TSP toll-free at 877-968-3778; or write to the TSP Service Office (Attention: Lost Participant), P.O. Box 385021, Birmingham, Alabama 35238.

for help by calling toll-free 888-891-6398; by sending an e-mail to ucbalances@bankofcanada.ca; or by writing to Unclaimed Balances Services, Bank of Canada. 234 Wellington, Ottawa, Ontario, K1A 0G9.

Holocaust Claims for Lost Assets

The Holocaust Claims Processing Office assists World War II Holocaust victims and their heirs in recovering financial assets and artwork that was lost to the Nazis between 1933 and 1945. Although the free service is under the auspices of the New York State Banking Department, you can use it even if you don't live in New York. For more information, go to www.claims.state.ny.us, or call 800-695-3318.

Unclaimed Residuals for Performers

Residuals are payments made to actors, dancers, and other performers when a movie or television program is shown after its initial use—say, when it is released on video or DVD. Residuals are spelled out in performers' contracts. The Screen Actors Guild maintains an Unclaimed Residuals database on its website: www.sag.org. Check it out if you are, or were, a performer and think that you may have unclaimed residuals. A deceased performer's heirs are entitled to his or her unclaimed residuals. Surprisingly, some famous people are listed in the database—including Christopher Reeve, Natalie Wood, and Tallulah Bankhead.

Stolen or Seized Goods

Nationwide Online Police Auction Site for Bargains

Hundreds of police departments use the website Property Room (www.propertyroom.com) to dispose of seized, stolen, and unclaimed items. Founded and managed by former police officers, Property Room auctions off an eclectic mix of new and used merchandise, ranging from GPS navigation systems to camping equipment to a 2003 Honda all-terrain vehicle. In mid-2006, the bargains included designer clothing with a retail value of $513 that sold for $20 and two porcelain lamps in good condition that sold for $15 and $34 apiece (value when new: $1,200 each). The auction

Editor's Choice

Lost Social Security Checks

Some $500 million in Social Security checks go uncashed every year because they are undeliverable or misplaced, or have been destroyed accidentally. If your check is more than three days late in the mail—or if you have lost a check—call the Social Security Administration at 800-772-1213. Social Security checks can be deposited until a year after issue. Then they become void, but you can have them replaced by calling the same number. For safer, quicker payment, Social Security encourages beneficiaries to enroll in its direct-deposit program. Call the same number, or sign up at your bank.

site also has listings from carefully selected liquidators and other merchants. Be sure to check shipping/handling estimates before you buy. Sometimes the estimates are not available until after you begin the bidding process and have input your zip code. You can bow out at that point simply by not finalizing your bid.

Free "Steal It Back" Property Recovery Service

Property Room, which auctions off items from police property rooms across the country (see preceding item), also runs a retrieval service for lost and stolen goods. Here's how StealItBack works: If an iPod or other item has been lost or stolen, the owner files a police report and sends the information to Property Room. StealItBack searches the Property Room database to see whether the item is in inventory. If and when it shows up, the item is sent to the police department where the loss or theft was reported and then returned to the owner. The entire process is free, but people who want to use it must register—also for free—at www.propertyroom.com. Then follow the "Register Your Stuff" link at the lower right on the Property Room home page.

Local Police Auctions for Real Deals

Some police departments, such as those in San Diego, California, and Columbus, Ohio, continue to run local, in-person auctions for unclaimed and seized property. Local auctions are likely to have fewer bidders than online auctions, so you may get an even better deal. At a recent police auction in Wheeling, West Virginia, dozens of bicycles went for about $2 apiece. Keep an eye out for announcements in newspapers, or call police departments nearby to find out whether they dispose of property in this way.

Auction of Property Seized by Feds

Every year, the U.S. Department of the Treasury sells off the personal property of drug smugglers, money launderers, and other convicted criminals at about 100 auctions nationwide. Vehicles, electronics, and jewelry—a dramatic example in mid-2006: several thousand Tahitian pearls smuggled into the United States by airline passengers who had taped them to their bodies—are among the most popular items. In a 2006 auction, two vehicles—a 2001 Jaguar XK8 convertible and a 2001 Honda Odyssey EX minivan—whose owner had bilked victims out of more than $20 million in health insurance claims, sold for $38,000 and $14,500, respectively. Bids

Auction Fever—and How to Prevent It

Most of the items sold at auction are secondhand, and their value is determined simply by what people are willing to pay for them. Yes, there are price guides to used cars, antiques, and other expensive items—and people who have registered at eBay (registration is free) can see how high the bidding went on comparable items sold in the past 15 days. But how much of a bargain you get always depends on the auction environment—the number of people who want the merchandise and how desperately they want it.

Auction fever is a well-known, often costly condition. Bidding goes so fast—and bidders get so embroiled in winning—that people may end up paying more than an item is worth. To prevent auction fever, carefully inspect the merchandise and determine your maximum bid before bidding starts. Your best bet is to attend smaller or out-of-the-way auctions, where you may not be competing with many dealers. In fact, at some auctions you may be the only bidder. Unless a high minimum bid has been set or the item will not be sold unless a "reserve" price is met, you'll get what you want at a rock-bottom price.

Be aware that many auctions levy a buyer's premium, a certain percentage of the "hammer price" that is paid by the buyer on top of the final bid. Buyer's premiums range from 10 percent to 20 percent and are sometimes staggered—that is, the percentage is reduced on the amount that exceeds, say, $100,000. Chances are that you will also pay sales tax, which is calculated after the buyer's premium is added in. Always check the terms before you bid. Federal government auctions do not charge buyer's premiums.

can be made in person or submitted by mail (some Treasury auctions also allow live Internet bidding). The competition may be fierce, or you may be the only bidder. Look up current listings at www.cwsmarketing.com/current/index.cfm. You can sign up to be notified about future auctions through a link on the same page.

U.S. Marshals Online Auction of Forfeited Assets

Best known for serving court papers and protecting witnesses, the U.S. Marshals Service also manages the Department of Justice's asset-forfeiture program. Forfeited assets come from convicted racketeers, child pornographers, and other criminals. Every year the USMS auctions off more than 14,000 items in such categories as real estate, cars and other vehicles, jewelry, sports equipment, and consumer electronics. Proceeds are used to further the nation's

law-enforcement efforts. Check out the current listings at www.bid4assets.com (click on "U.S. Marshals Service"). Bid4assets also auctions off property for other government agencies, including real estate from county tax sales and used office equipment from the Department of Energy.

Canadian Auctions of Seized and Surplus

If you live near Canada, it may be worth your while to attend auctions of seized and surplus goods in Montreal, Ottawa, and other Canadian cities. A recent auction included a 1999 electric Ford Ranger pickup truck (it sold for about US$5,700), three electric scooters (the lot went for roughly US$770), office furniture, clothing lots, and a satellite dish antenna. More details are available at the website: crownassets.pwgsc.gc.ca/text/index-e.cfm; click on the "auctions" link. The province of British Columbia runs a separate, ongoing Internet auction at www.bcauction.ca/open.dll/welcome. Items listed recently included new digital video cameras, print cartridges, commercial crab traps, used mountain bikes, a used, handheld GPS unit, wristwatches, and a gold-plated Irish Claddagh bracelet.

Lost and Found

Bargains at the Unclaimed Baggage Center

U.S. airlines lose thousands of checked bags every day. Though eventually most are returned to their owners, many end up at the Unclaimed Baggage Center, a bargain hunters' paradise in Scottsboro, Alabama. Nearly a million customers a year visit the huge store, shopping for clothing, cameras, jewelry, books, and other unclaimed baggage items that are usually priced at 50 percent to 80 percent off retail. New cargo items go for 20 percent to 50 percent off. You don't have to travel to Alabama to take advantage of some of these deals—a wide variety is for sale at www.unclaimedbaggage.com (click on "Let's Shop"). The online store is full of gems. Merchandise available in mid-2006 included a new pair of Dolce & Gabbana jeans, a German-made violin bow in good condition, camcorders, cameras, and even a stethoscope. Most items can be returned if they are not what you want (sometimes a restocking fee is charged). If you see an

Q **I've lost a valued treasure. What's the best way to get the word out to residents of my city?**

A The Internet provides new hope for people who lose pets, keys, cell phones, watches, backpacks, or other property in any of the more than 300 locations around the world (as of mid-2006) that are craigslist sites. A kind soul who finds your property just might post a free notice about it on www.craigslist.org. To check whether your lost property has been listed, go to the craigslist home page, follow the links to your area, and click on the "lost & found" section under "community." If your property isn't there, try again in a day or two. An even better way to speed return of a lost item is to post your own notice describing what you lost and where. It's easy to do.

item that is clearly yours at the Unclaimed Baggage Center and want it back, you must buy it, unfortunately.

Great Bargains at Post Office Auctions

If a package is undeliverable and has no return address, the U.S. Postal Service may auction off the contents at mail-recovery centers in Atlanta, Georgia, or St. Paul, Minnesota. Every year tens of thousands of items, including jewelry, books, television sets, clothing, sports equipment, and musical instruments, are sold at bargain

How Not to Lose Your Luggage

Take these steps to reduce the risk of your bags going astray and ending up at the Unclaimed Baggage Center:

- Choose a nonstop flight. Next best are flights that involve an intermediate stop but no change of planes. The worst option? Itineraries that involve changing from one airline to another.
- Luggage should be distinctive. Buy colorful pieces, or attach sturdy, bright-colored tags, and/or paint stripes or other markings on the outside of the bag.
- Remove all old labels.
- Put your itinerary and contact information in a conspicuous place *inside* each bag.
- Don't pack bags to near-bursting. Over-stuffing makes the latches more likely to spring open.
- Don't check in at the last minute.
- Try to get a look at the airline tag placed on each piece of checked baggage to make sure that it shows the correct flight number and three-letter destination code—EWR for Newark Liberty International Airport, for example, or LHR for London's Heathrow Airport or OAK for Oakland, California. If you don't know the right code, ask.
- Keep your baggage-claim tickets in a safe place.
- If your luggage doesn't come off the baggage-claim carousel with others on the same flight, have an airline representative fill out a report and give you a copy before you leave the airport. Get the agent's name and the appropriate telephone number to call for following up.

If the airline declares your luggage to be irretrievably lost, you will be compensated for up to $2,800 (less on international flights). Most airlines will not cover loss of computer or photographic equipment, jewelry, and certain other valuable items. If you can show that the bag and its contents were worth more, you can claim the difference on your homeowners or renters insurance policy. The difference may also be covered by your credit card company (if you charged your ticket) or your travel agency (if you obtained the ticket through the agency).

prices. Items are often sold in lots—which means that winning bidders may end up with some items that they want and others that they can resell online or at a garage sale. Learn about upcoming auctions by writing to the Atlanta Mail Recovery Center, 5345 Fulton Industrial Boulevard SW, Atlanta, Georgia 30378, or the St. Paul Mail Recovery Center, 443 Fillmore Avenue, St. Paul, Minnesota 55107. The Atlanta schedule is also available online at www.usps.com/auctions. Occasionally some local postal facilities run their own auctions. For more information, write to the U.S. Postal Service Consumer Advocate, 475 L'Enfant Plaza SW, Room 5911, Washington, D.C. 20260.

Self-Storage Locker Auctions for Surprise Bargains

Everyone loves bargains. If you also like surprises, self-storage auctions will be right up your alley. But note: It's a *dark* alley. Storage facilities auction off stored items when people renting space fall behind on their payments. Prospective bidders can look into the units from the doorway (veteran shoppers suggest bringing a flashlight), but they cannot touch anything or go inside. Furniture, bicycles, and other large items may be visible, or you may see just a mishmash of boxes with who-knows-what inside. Bids are for the entire contents of a unit, not single items, and everything may go for only a couple of bucks. Though many people attend the auctions to find merchandise to resell, you may pick up kitchen items, toys, and other items that anyone can use. Check newspapers for auction announcements, or call nearby facilities. The Self Storage Association maintains an online list at www.selfstorage.org; enter your zip code to get contact information on facilities in your area.

Real Estate Deals

Government Sale of Seized and Surplus Property

Many federal agencies sell off confiscated and surplus real estate—including residential homes, commercial property, vacant land, and even historic lighthouses—by auction or sealed bid. Check the website www.propertydisposal.gsa.gov/property to find out what's available in each state, Puerto Rico, Guam, and the Virgin Islands. For the full inventory, click on the "Real Estate Sales List" on the same Web page. Listings have contact information, a property description, and, in many cases, a photograph. To obtain a free printed copy of the list, write to the Federal Citizen Information Center, Pueblo, Colorado 81009; or call it toll-free at 888-878-3256. How much of a bargain you get depends on location, condition, type of property, and just plain luck. Unfortunately, ordinary folks can't bid on historic lighthouses—only individuals who represent government or nonprofit organizations can do this.

Foreclosed HUD Homes for Bargain Prices

When homeowners default on their mortgages, the lenders take back the property to resell. Single-family homes with defaulted Federal Housing Authority loans are sold by the U.S. Department of Housing and Urban Development at prices that average about two-thirds of the appraised value. Prospective buyers can search for local listings at the HUD website (www.hud.gov/homes/index.cfm). Bids are placed through authorized real estate brokers. Most property is sold "as is"—so be sure to have the home inspected thoroughly before you close the deal. HUD offers special deals to teachers, police officers, firefighters, and emergency medical technicians, who can buy single-family homes in designated "revitalization areas" at even lower prices. Check out the Good Neighbor program at www.hud.gov/offices/hsg/sfh/reo/goodn/main.cfm (see "Half-Price Homes for Teachers, Police, Firefighters, and EMTs," on page 392).

Discounted Foreclosed Homes from Freddie Mac

Freddie Mac—officially, the Federal Home Loan Mortgage Corporation—is a publicly traded business that buys mortgages from lenders, packages the mortgages into securities, and sells the securities to investors. If a homeowner fails to pay back the loan, Freddie Mac may sell the property at auction or through a local Realtor. At any one time, Freddie Mac's HomeSteps program (www.homesteps.com) has from 10,000 to 15,000 listings. Occasionally homes sell at hefty discounts. One foreclosed South Carolina home carrying a loan balance of $100,470 was bought for $60,000 by an investor who resold it three months later for $125,000.

Freddie Mac's twin "sister"—the Federal National Mortgage Association, or Fannie Mae—also sells foreclosed homes. To find out about available Fannie Mae property, click "Resources" at www.fanniemae.com, then go to "Fannie Mae-owned Property Search."

TAKE CAUTION!

Be Wary of "Government Property" Ads

Ads touting stupendous deals on government-owned real estate (and autos, too) are bait to lure you into buying auction information. The Federal Trade Commission says that the information the guides provide is the same as—or even less detailed than—what you can get for free from official government websites, such as www.propertydisposal.gsa.gov and www.autoauctions.gsa.gov. Sometimes outright fraud is involved.

Bargain Bank Foreclosures

The safest way to buy a foreclosed home is through a bank. There are no unpaid taxes, liens, or tenants to worry about—and you may get extra financial breaks, such as free title insurance and reduced mortgage rates, down payments, or closing costs. The best bargains are homes in poor condition, which can be bought for as much as 30 percent or 40 percent below market value. Location is key to getting good value, especially in fixer-uppers. You can obtain listings of bank-foreclosed homes from courthouses and lending institutions, or look for default notices in local newspapers.

Pre-Foreclosure Deals

Many investors who once swooned over tech stocks have shifted their focus to foreclosed homes, and some savvy bargain hunters now even seek out homes in the "pre-foreclosure" stage. Pre-foreclosure means that a mortgage is in arrears and a foreclosure lawsuit or notice of default has been filed. Homeowners in pre-foreclosure may decide to sell privately to avoid going through the foreclosure process and the resulting blots on their credit ratings. The time during which a home stays in the pre-foreclosure stage varies by state and averages between three and ten months. Buying pre-foreclosures involves solid detective work—that is, searching county records to find out which properties are in this stage—and topnotch negotiating skills (potential buyers must deal directly with a homeowner who is facing foreclosure). The first step: Find out more about the process at *The Wall Street Journal* website homes.wsj.com/indinvestor/20050203-lucier.html. Sample letters to initiate contact with pre-foreclosure homeowners are available at www.foreclosure.com/edocs.html.

DOA-Foreclosed Rural Homes for Sale

Rural Development—a unit of the U.S. Department of Agriculture—acquires property on which loans are in arrears and sells it through local USDA servicing centers. How good a deal you get depends on such factors as condition and location. Some 400 to 500 properties are available at any one time (Texas has the most). To find out about single-family housing available in your area—including listing price, property details, taxes, and a photo—click on your state at www.resales.usda.gov.

VEHICLE, BOAT, AND OTHER AUCTIONS

Used Fleet Car Bargains from Uncle Sam

Every year the General Services Administration, the agency that provides services to other federal agencies, auctions off tens of thousands of fleet vehicles. Cars, trucks, and vans—all American-made and some with engines that use ethanol or other alternative fuels—often go for prices that are substantially below retail. Auctions are held throughout the year at dozens of locations nationwide. You can search the GSA website (www.autoauctions.gsa.gov) by location, date, and vehicle make and model. It's even easier to sign up for the free Vehicle Search Agent: Click on the link at the bottom of the page www.autoauctions.gsa.gov/vehiclesearch.cfm; the service will notify you by e-mail when the vehicle you want becomes available. Do your homework before bidding (see "Getting the Best Deal on a Used Car," page 181).

Rock-Bottom Prices for Salvaged Boats

Watercraft damaged in hurricanes and other disasters may need a fair amount of work, but insurance companies and other parties may sell them off through salvaged-boat liquidators at rock-bottom prices. BoatUS (Boat Owners Association of the United States) lists liquidators at www.boatus.com/hurricanes/liquidators. Though bids can be placed long distance—online or by fax—would-be bidders should hire a marine surveyor to inspect the boat first.

Bargain Prices for Mustangs—Real Ones!

No, not cars—horses. *Live* horses. Every year the Bureau of Land Management sells 5,000 to 7,000 wild horses (and some burros) to people who have enough space and meet other stringent criteria. The animals are rounded up from BLM lands, taken to permanent adoption centers in Arizona, California, Colorado, Illinois, Kansas, Nebraska, Nevada, Oklahoma, Oregon, Utah, and Wyoming (as well as temporary facilities across the United States), and sold to buyers in person or over the Internet. The usual minimum price—$125—represents a true bargain, but the BLM notes that it takes time for buyers to find the right horse for them, transport it home, and then train it. For more information, call the National Wild Horse and Burro Program toll-free at 866-468-7826; or check the website www.wildhorseandburro.blm.gov.

CHAPTER 14

getting help for community nonprofits

Are you trying to make your community a better place, but you need a helping hand? With these tips, money and gifts are yours for the asking.

By the numbers

3.2

Percentage of income (before taxes) that the average American gives to charity. The average household donates about $1,620 a year.

WE AMERICANS LOVE TO DO GOOD. This irrepressible urge shows up in the hundreds of thousands of nonprofit organizations we have created in the United States—groups dedicated to everything from building neighborhood vest-pocket parks to, literally, saving the world. People and organizations involved in philanthropy deserve a break—a discount, a freebie, a grant—and breaks and deals for nonprofits are what this chapter is all about.

Many of the programs described here are sponsored by businesses. Corporate philanthropy is growing—up 14 percent from 2004 to 2005, according to the Committee to Encourage Corporate Philanthropy. Many company-based programs look to their employees for guidance—they match employee cash contributions, give grants to programs in which their employees volunteer, and help employees buy the company's products for use by nonprofits. The biggest challenge to tapping employee-driven corporate programs may be bringing your nonprofit to the attention of the employees of a particular company and getting them to sponsor projects or volunteer for you. Look to your current volunteer base and see what assistance their employers have to offer.

There are also many gifts-in-kind offers—gifts of products instead of cash. Companies donate products for a number of reasons: to do good, to encourage use of their products, to reduce their inventories, to get tax deductions. While the reasons vary, the results are the same: Your nonprofit gets things it needs for little or no money. Programs described here are mostly national or broad in geographic scope, but don't forget about smaller, local companies when you look for in-kind donations; they may actually be a better bet.

We've also included federal and state grant programs (note that some federal programs are operated on the state level). We give examples of grants for specific states, but there are likely to be similar programs in other states as well. Government grants change with the political winds, so always make sure you're working with current information before applying.

Virtually all cash grant programs from private foundations have a tight focus—either they're directed toward nonprofits in a particular geographic area or they give only to nonprofits with specific goals. If a program described here appeals to you but is out of your nonprofit's sphere of concern, don't fret. This chapter represents just a tiny fraction of the grant money and gifts that are out there.

If you aren't yet involved in a nonprofit, take heart: The chapter finishes up with a number of free or inexpensive resources to help you start, fund, operate, staff, and grow your nonprofit.

EDITOR'S CHOICE

Target's Grants Program

Target Store Grants support nonprofits in the arts, family violence prevention, and reading with awards of up to $3,000. In fiscal year 2005, for example, the Connecticut Children's Medical Center in Hartford received funds for children's books, and the Homer Township Public Library in Illinois got money to offer family quilting classes. Target's grants program is locally administered by individual stores. Applications are available at stores, or online at www.target.com (click on the "Community" link).

CORPORATE PHILANTHROPY

Wells Fargo Funds for Low-Income Housing

Does your nonprofit help to renovate or build homes for low-income families? Do you count Wells Fargo employees among your volunteers? If the answer is yes to both questions, you may be eligible for grants ranging from $2,500 to $25,000 per home through the Wells Fargo Housing Foundation (the average grant is $10,000). The Wells Fargo employee volunteer must make the application, but the company encourages nonprofits to contact local Wells Fargo branches and invite employees to volunteer. To learn more about the program, go to https://www.wellsfargo.com and search for "housing foundation."

EDITOR'S CHOICE A Jolt of Cash for Nonprofits from Starbucks

Through its regional marketing offices, Starbucks donates money or products to support local organizations and events in the areas of arts and culture, literacy, diversity, education, the environment, and AIDS awareness. Past grant recipients have included youth leadership programs in Denver, a child-designed playground in Kirkland, Washington, and children's libraries in the New York metro area. Successful grant recipients have often begun by developing a relationship with employees at their neighborhood Starbucks; if you're such a regular at a Starbucks that the barista knows you as "tall double soy latte," it can't hurt to enlist him or her in your quest for a grant. A list of regional marketing offices can be found online on the Web page www.starbucks.com/customer/cs_regions.asp.

Ace Hardware's Gifts for Little League Parks Upkeep

If your Little League ballpark needs sprucing up, look into Ace Hardware's Fields for the Future program. Directed at "in need" fields, the program selects five leagues each year (one in each Little League division) for $2,500 worth of Ace products and a full day's labor from a skilled team of Ace workers. Each winning league also gets $2,500 worth of Ace Gift Cards. Contact your local Ace Hardware store for more information.

Help for Running Track Renovation from Nike

The Nike-sponsored Bowerman Track Renovation Program, named after company co-founder Bill Bowerman, gives community-based, youth-oriented organizations, including nonprofit athletic booster clubs, up to $50,000 in matching cash grants to refurbish or construct running tracks. The program has $2 million in funds and will give away about $200,000 per year through May 2009. Nike encourages, but doesn't require, recipients to use Nike Grind material (made of recycled, ground-up sneakers) as a track surface. To learn more or to get an application, call Nike at 503-671-6453 and ask for the Bowerman Track Renovation Program.

Cash Cards and Merchandise from Costco

Costco Warehouse stores provide both product donations, such as food and beverages, and Costco Cash Cards to select nonprofits in their communities for events and fund-raisers. (The company notes that the number of requests typically far outstrips the number of items available for donation.) Provide the manager of your local

Costco Warehouse with a copy of your nonprofit's IRS tax documentation and a written request, on organization letterhead, at least four weeks before you want a donation.

Kroger's Discount Gift Certificate Program

The Kroger Company, parent company of grocery chains including Kroger, Ralphs, Dillons, Fry's, and Fred Meyer, provided more than $28 million to more than 25,000 schools and nonprofit organizations in 2005, through discounted gift certificate and rebate programs. (This is in addition to the chain's in-kind donations to food banks.) It works like this: Your organization buys gift cards at 95 percent of face value and sells them at 100 percent, keeping the difference. The Animal Control & Welfare Project in Hinton, West Virginia, for example, has earned several thousand dollars through the program. To see if your organization is eligible to participate (along with nonprofits, clubs and religious organizations are welcome), contact the manager of your local store; to search for stores go to www.thekrogerco.com, then click the logo of the Kroger chain in your area.

Free Franchises and Grants from Ben & Jerry's

Though Ben & Jerry's, the famed Vermont ice cream maker, is now owned by a large international company, it still maintains much of its small-town, do-gooder impulse. It operates two programs that might interest nonprofits:

- PartnerShops are Ben & Jerry's scoop shops owned by community-based nonprofits. The organization must be dedicated to providing job training and life skills development programs for people ages 15 to 21; the shop becomes a tool in that mission. Ben & Jerry's waives the $30,000 franchise fee for PartnerShops and provides additional support. Thirteen exist now; the company is currently looking for community partners in Miami, Boston, Los Angeles, and Atlanta.
- The Ben & Jerry's Foundation gives grants of up to $15,000 to nonprofit grassroots organizations that are dedicated to progressive social change and that address societal and environmental problems. Early 2006 grantees include the Cascadia Wildlands Project in Eugene, Oregon, which got $7,500 to protect old-growth forests; the Citizens Coal Council in Washington, Pennsylvania, which received $12,000 to help

EDITOR'S CHOICE

Cash Grants from Your Local Wal-Mart

If you're near a Wal-Mart or Sam's Club store or distribution center, put it on your target list, because these companies fund nonprofit organizations that "improve the quality of life in the local community." Examples: a $500 grant to an organization in Ashland, Kentucky, that helps persons with disabilities train and land jobs, and a $1,000 grant to CrimeStoppers in Greenville, North Carolina. Grants are made at the local level, so contact your store's manager or its community-involvement manager. More information is available online at www.walmartfoundation.org.

hold regulatory agencies and mining firms accountable for their actions; and ECO-Action in Atlanta, Georgia, which received $10,000 to support its work with Georgia communities confronting environmental health threats. Learn about both programs at the company website, www.benjerry.com.

Volunteer Programs

Employee Volunteers from Cisco

Cisco Systems, a leader in Internet-based networking technologies, makes it easy for nonprofits to solicit volunteers from its workforce. The company's Volunteer Connection Tool (which you can find at cisco.cybergrants.com/sgrquiz) lets a nonprofit specify a need (such as one-time or ongoing help, special skills, and so on); if a Cisco employee in your area finds that your needs match his or her interests, you'll be contacted. The company also maintains a Product Grant Program that donates networking equipment to nonprofits that meet its eligibility criteria. Learn more online at www.cisco.com/go/pgp.

Prudential CARES About Volunteering

Employees and retirees of Prudential Financial can earn cash grants for the nonprofits with which they volunteer through Prudential CARES Volunteer Grants. Those who volunteer at least 40 hours in a year for a single nonprofit can apply for grants that range from $250 to $5,000 for that organization. And the company's Personal Volunteer Day Program gives Prudential employees one paid day off annually to volunteer at a charitable organization.

Volunteers from ExxonMobil Bear Cash

Every nonprofit loves volunteers, but—dare we say it?—some volunteers are better than others. Case in point: ExxonMobil employees and retirees. The company maintains a Volunteer Involvement Program to support employees and retirees who volunteer on a regular basis. When an ExxonMobil employee or retiree gives at least 20 hours of volunteer time to a charitable nonprofit organization in a calendar year, that organization is eligible for a $500 grant from the company's Individual Volunteer Grants fund. A single organization can receive up to $5,000 per year this way.

Q Our nonprofit needs volunteers. How can we get the word out?

A Most nonprofits need more than money and stuff to do their work; they need people, ideally volunteers, who are willing to help. VolunteerMatch, a free online service, links nonprofits in all 50 states with people who are willing to work for them; some 40,000 groups use the service, including MenzFit of Silver Spring, Maryland, which provides interview-appropriate clothing for low-income men looking for work; various regional chapters of the National Multiple Sclerosis Society; and San Francisco's nonprofit Exploratorium science museum. Nearly a half-million people have used the site to volunteer; what's more, some companies use Volunteer Match to help their employees find opportunities to serve. Learn more and sign up your organization at www.volunteer match.org.

GuideStar: A Crucial Website for Nonprofits

Every nonprofit that hopes to receive money or products from foundation or corporate sources should update its listing on the GuideStar website. GuideStar starts with basic IRS-provided data but lets you add information about your nonprofit's goals, accomplishments, and leadership; the Guide Star database is used by more than two dozen philanthropy websites. Registering with GuideStar—it's free—also lets your nonprofit solicit donations online through two giving websites, JustGive and Network for Good, at no registration cost (those sites charge 3 percent of whatever you raise through them, as a processing fee for handling credit cards). Go online to www.guidestar.org, send an e-mail to customerservice@guidestar.org, or call toll-free 800-784-9378.

AIG Employees Paid to Volunteer

Your youth-related nonprofit can look to volunteer help from employees of American International Group, a large nationwide insurance company. Through the company's StepUp program, AIG employees can take up to two paid hours per month from work to volunteer with approved organizations, including Boy Scouts, Girl Scouts, 4-H Clubs, and youth athletic programs. To find a local AIG office, go to www.aig.com and click on the "Office Locations" link.

GIFTS IN KIND

Central Source for In-Kind Donations

Gifts In Kind International serves 200,000 charities around the world (two-thirds of them are in the United States), linking companies that want to donate nonperishable non-pharmaceutical products with nonprofit groups that can use them. For the donor companies to get a tax write-off for donated products, nonprofits must serve the elderly, the sick, the poor, children, or Title I schools. In 2005, Gifts in Kind International handled $850 million worth of products—and CEO Richard Wong assures nonprofits that these aren't stale or unwanted items. The most popular are personal care

Q Are there any software companies that give nonprofits discounts?

A Microsoft donates software to nonprofit organizations in the United States and Canada through a group called TechSoup (www.techsoup.org, or 800-659-3579 ext. 700). Eligible organizations can make one request per year, and can receive up to six software titles and 50 licenses per title in a two-year period. TechSoup charges a small administrative fee—for example, $20 for Microsoft Office 2003 Professional. You'll need to create an account with TechSoup and submit proof of nonprofit status. Organizations that don't meet Microsoft's eligibility criteria, or that want more titles, should look into the Microsoft Open License Charity program to purchase software at reduced prices. Go to www.microsoft.com and type "open license charity" in the search box. Also see "Free Technology Products and Advice," opposite.

and hygiene products destined for homeless shelters and other human-services organizations; other offerings include clothing, books, and electronics. Contact Gifts in Kind International at 703-836-2121, look at its online catalog at www.giftsinkind.org, or send an e-mail to registration@giftsinkind.org.

Free Paint for Nonprofits

Is your nonprofit's building looking a little shabby? Would some free paint help? Go to www.paintrecycling.org and register for free paint from the National Council on Paint Disposition. NCPD can connect you with a local paint retailer who has excess inventory—usually the result of discontinued products or mis-tinting of custom paint. All donations are full containers (quarts, gallon cans, or five-gallon cans) of first-quality paint. Several containers of different paint colors can be mixed together to get a usable quantity of one color—such mixed paint is usually a pleasing medium beige.

Surplus Goods for Nonprofits

The National Association for the Exchange of Industrial Resources solicits new, overstock inventory from U.S. corporations and gives it to member nonprofit groups and schools for the cost of shipping and handling. The merchandise itself is free; the annual membership fee is $595, but the average member receives $19,000 worth of new supplies each year. NAEIR publishes a catalog of products five times a year and sends out a semi-monthly flyer. Nonprofit members located near NAEIR's warehouse in Galesburg, Illinois, can visit, for $40, and take as much as they can carry. Learn more at www.naeir.org.

HP Computer and Printer Discounts

Employees of Hewlett Packard can help nonprofits get computers, printers, and other HP gear through the company's Product Gift Matching Program. In this program, an employee contributes 25 percent of the list price of a product and the company pays the rest. Equipment gifts can be up to $20,000 per employee per calendar year. HP has another program, the HP Technology for Community Grant Initiative, that in 2006 awarded 104 mobile and wireless technology packages worth $17,000 each to nonprofits in human services, workforce development, the environment, arts and technology, and community and economic development. (More than 2,000 organizations applied.) Learn more about both programs and get questions answered at www.hp.com/hpinfo/grants/us/index.html.

Editor's Choice Playgrounds from Home Depot and KaBOOM!

Children's playgrounds are often sorely absent in underprivileged neighborhoods. The Home Depot and KaBOOM!, a national non-profit organization, are trying to change that and have undertaken a program to build or refurbish 1,000 play spaces in 1,000 days throughout North America. To learn more and to get on KaBOOM!'s list of communities that want play spaces, go to www.kaboom.org. KaBOOM!, which also works with other corporate and foundation donors, has a free Getting Started Kit available to communities that want to build a play space. And each Home Depot store also has funds to support local community projects through product donations; contact the manager at your local store.

Free Seeds to Beautify and Feed Communities

Want to add some beauty to your neighborhood, or plant vegetables to feed hungry people in your community? Contact the America the Beautiful Fund, which for decades has distributed tons of free seeds and bulbs to 20,000 communities in the United States. The seeds and bulbs are a year old—they're leftovers provided by seed companies—but they boast a 90 to 95 percent germination rate. You'll be asked to fill out a simple form, write a letter about your project, and pay a small shipping fee. Go to www.america-the-beautiful.org to read about the program and get an application form.

More Donated Computers

The National Cristina Foundation helps nonprofits to get donated computer equipment. Nonprofits must use the equipment for training, job development, educational programs, and other projects that improve the lives of people with disabilities, students at risk, and economically disadvantaged people. (The computer can't be used in your nonprofit's front office for administrative work, or go to an individual in need.) Read more about the program at www.cristina.org, or call 203-863-9100 for more information.

Free Technology Products and Advice

If your nonprofit is in need of computer technology and IT advice, look up TechSoup (online at www.techsoup.com). The website connects nonprofits with donated and discounted technology products and software from 25 different vendors (as part of those companies' gifts-in-kind programs) and offers free technical support and information to nonprofits. On its website, TechSoup also provides free or low-cost ways for nonprofits to use the Internet to improve their operations, such as a matchmaking service between nonprofits and technology consultants called Consultant Commons and a suite of tools and advice for using the Internet for outreach and fund-raising called NetSquared. TechSoup is headquartered in San Francisco and runs "local editions" in New York and Los Angeles, but most of its power is accessible anywhere there's an Internet connection.

Federal and State Grants

Federal Community Food Projects

To promote self-sufficiency and food security in low-income communities, the U.S. Department of Agriculture provides grants to help eligible nonprofit organizations carry out community food projects. The USDA's Community Food Projects Competitive Grant Program seeks to increase the access of low-income people to fresher, more nutritious food supplies and to promote the self-reliance of poorer communities in providing for their own food needs. The one-time grants come in the form of matching funds (the nonprofit organizer must raise at least 50 percent of the budget) and range from $10,000 to $300,000. Recent grantees include the group called Community Involved in Sustaining Agriculture of South Deerfield, Massachusetts, which got $125,000 to develop stronger farmers' markets; and the Dixon Cooperative Market in Dixon, New Mexico, which received $34,681 to start a food market supplied by 50 local farmers. Learn more about these community food programs at www.csrees.usda.gov/fo/communityfoodprojects.html.

Federal Dollars for Housing Counseling

Nonprofits involved in helping homeless or low-income people find housing can apply for money from the federal department of Housing and Urban Development under the Housing Counseling Program. Funds must be used to provide information, advice, and assistance in housing matters, and the nonprofit must provide matching funds from another source. In fiscal year 2005, some 349 local agencies got Housing Counseling Program grants, including the Citizens for Affordable Housing in Nashville, Tennessee ($19,215), the Bishop Sheen Ecumenical Housing Foundation in Rochester,

Q How can nonprofit groups get discounts on postage?

A Doing good often requires getting the word out by mail, and fortunately the United States Postal Service provides discounted services to nonprofit groups. Nonprofit Standard Mail costs about 40 percent less than regular mail; to get started, ask for Publication 417, "Nonprofit Standard Mail Eligibility," at your local post office, or download it for free at pe.usps.com (click on "Nonprofit Standard Mailing Eligibility"). To take advantage of the reduced rates, file Form 3624, "Application to Mail at Nonprofit Standard Mail Rates," at the post office where your organization will do its mailing. There's no cost to apply, but there may be annual fees, depending on the mailing services you use. The rules for nonprofit mailing are complicated, and the Postal Service's documents can be confusing; for a simpler summary, check out www.nonprofitmailers.org.

Get to Know Grants.Gov

If you're interested in federal grants, you need to learn about Grants.gov, the government's secure website for grant applications and information. On it, you can search through some $400 billion in federal grants, see recently posted grants, apply online, track your application through the approval process, and more. The government's goal is to have 100 percent of grant applications handled electronically, and it's well on its way to that goal: All federal grant opportunities are now posted on Grants.gov; some 75 percent of federal grant application packages are there; and in the first three-quarters of fiscal year 2006, Grants.gov handled 45,000 grant applications. Learn more and sign up—it's free—at the website www.grants.gov.

New York ($32,190), and the Open Door Counseling Center in Hillsboro, Oregon ($21,680). To receive a grant, an organization must be approved by HUD; other rules apply. To begin the process, contact your local HUD office; they're listed online at www.hud.gov/localoffices.cfm.

Aid for Historic Buildings in Texas

The Texas Preservation Trust Fund gives grants to preserve historic buildings in the state. The Abilene Preservation League got $15,000 from the fund to preserve its dilapidated 1913 Elks Lodge, historically the site of many community events. It's being transformed into a Center for the Arts for the town. To qualify for a grant, a building does not have to be public; archeological sites, commercial structures, and even water towers are eligible as long as they have played a documentable role in the culture or history of Texas. Learn more at www.thc.state.tx.us; click on "Grants and Economic Incentives."

Funds for Delaware Arts Groups

In Delaware, nonprofit arts groups (as well as individuals and schools) can apply for grants from the Delaware Division of the Arts. Grants, which can be for general operating support as well as for specific projects, range from a few hundred dollars to tens of thousands; most are in the low four figures. Funds for the grants come from the state and the National Endowment for the Arts. Examples of 2006 grant winners: the Delaware Dance Company, which received $3,400; the Delaware Choral Society, which received

Great Free Reading for Grant-Seekers

There are dozens and dozens of books about how to apply for grants. Before you spend serious money on one, visit www.cnmsocal.org/grantseekers/intro.html and read *The Grant-Seeker's Handbook*, published by the Center for Nonprofit Management in Los Angeles. It explains much of what you need to know in clear, straightforward language. Another wonderful set of free online resources is collected and published by Authenticity Consulting (www.managementhelp.org).

$1,735; and the Dover Art League, which received $6,407; all of these grants were for general operating support. Visit the website www.artsdel.org to learn more.

Grants for Tree Planting and Care in North Carolina

North Carolina's Urban and Community Forestry Grants, funded by the federal government and administered by the state's Division of Forest Resources, encourage community-oriented programs run by nonprofit groups (in addition to projects by the state's towns and cities) with matching grants. Funded programs include volunteer-run tree nurseries, temporary volunteer-maintained "pocket parks" on undeveloped land, and support of nonprofit tree-planting groups. Among fiscal year 2007 grantees are the Frisco Native American Museum in Dare County and the Tree Adoption Program for the Youth in Deaverview. For more information about the program go to www.dfr.state.nc.us/urban/urban_grantprogram.htm.

Nationwide Foundation Grants

Cash Boost for Interactive Public Art

If the crown jewel of your budding neighborhood park or youth program is to be an interactive art piece—one that prompts people to interact with each other, that responds to its environment, or otherwise challenges artistic conventions—look to the Black Rock Arts Foundation for money to help pay for its creation. Among the artworks created with the help of 2005 BRAF grants are *The Clachan*, a grove of steel trees in Arizona; a sound installation called *Quiet City* in New York; and an award-winning "art car" called *ArtCarTraz* created by juveniles in correctional facilities in three Southern states working with a BRAF grant recipient artist. Grants typically range from $2,500 to $5,000. Information and application instructions are available online at www.blackrockarts.org, or call 415-626-1248 to learn more.

Grants to Digitize Historic Recordings

In an age when everybody seems to have a digital camcorder, it's hard to believe that some of America's musical heritage is slowly slipping away. But it's true. To counter that problem, the Grammy Foundation, funded by the people who present the Grammy Awards, gives grants to organizations and individuals involved in archiving and preserving the music and recorded sound heritage of the Americas. Recent grantees—including the Northshore Concert Band in Evanston, Illinois; The Kitchen, in New York City; and Other Minds, in San Francisco—used Grammy Foundation Grants to digitize their sound archives. The Grammy Foundation awards grants as small as $1,000 and as large as $50,000. Learn more at the website www.grammy.com/grammy_foundation/grants.

Aid for Nonprofits Preserving Wildlands

Nonprofits that work for the long-term protection of forests, wildlands, rivers, nearshore marine ecosystems, and estuaries should contact the Harder Foundation of Tacoma, Washington. The

Recognition for Community Bands

The John Philip Sousa Foundation, named in honor of the great American band conductor, annually presents the Sudler Silver Scroll to community concert bands that maintain musical excellence for several years and that play a positive role in their communities' cultural life. There's no cash associated with the prestigious award, but winning bands receive an engraved plaque, musicians in the band receive certificates, and the band's director gets a diploma denoting the Sudler Order of Merit. The award is named in memory of Louis Sudler, a Chicago businessman, musician, and patron of the arts. For more on the award and the nomination process, visit www.loyno.edu and search for "Sudler Silver Scroll."

foundation's 60 grants in 2005 ranged from $3,500 to $120,000, with most grants in the $10,000 to $30,000 range; grantees include the High Country Citizens' Alliance, which protects natural areas near Crested Butte, Colorado ($5,000), and the Southern Utah Wilderness Alliance, which protects desert lands ($20,000). Funds are not available to government organizations. For information, contact the Harder Foundation at 253-593-2121, or send an e-mail to grants@theharderfoundation.org.

Let Tony Hawk Help Build Your Skateboard Park

The Tony Hawk Foundation, founded by the famed skateboarder, annually awards more than $100,000 to charities or local governments that want to build skateboard parks in low-income communities. Grants range from $1,000 to $25,000, with many in the $5,000 range. For an application, write to the Tony Hawk Foundation, 1611-A South Melrose Drive #360, Vista, California 92081, or send an e-mail to contact@tonyhawkfoundation.org. More information and printable applications can be found online at www.tonyhawkfoundation.org. The website also has advice for communities that want to organize, plan, fund-raise for, and design a skateboard park.

Baseball and Softball Teams: Try "The Ripken Way"

The Cal Ripken Sr. Foundation provides equipment grants and matching funds for field renovations to nonprofit youth baseball and softball programs throughout the United States. (Other foundation grants are given to youth baseball and softball programs run by schools and local governments.) All programs support the four fundamentals of "The Ripken Way": Keep it simple, explain the why, make it fun, and celebrate the individual. Get more information at www.ripkenfoundation.org; by e-mail at info@ripkenfoundation.org; or by calling toll-free 877-RIPKEN1 (877-747-5361).

Regional Foundation Grants

Boost for Environmental Projects in the Twin Cities

Nonprofits involved in protecting the environment in the Minneapolis-St. Paul area can apply to the Marbrook Foundation

Editor's Choice

Help for Youth Music

Remember the movie *Mr. Holland's Opus*, about a music teacher and his students? Inspired by the story, Michael Kamen, who composed music for the film, founded the Mr. Holland's Opus Foundation. The foundation's Special Projects Program gives grants to community after-school music programs and youth orchestras; its Melody Program targets qualified K-12 programs. As of mid-2006, the foundation as a whole, which also benefits school music programs, has helped more than 100,000 students and provided new and refurbished instruments worth $4 million. Learn more at www.mhopus.org, or call 818-784-6787.

(www.marbrookfoundation.org) for assistance with their goals. Recipients in 2005 included Friends of the Mississippi River; the Parks and Trails Council of Minnesota, which purchases land and supports the region's parks; and the Thomas Irvine Dodge Nature Center, an environmental education center. Each received a grant of $5,000. Marbrook Foundation grants have been as small as $3,000 and as large as $71,000; other areas the foundation supports are education, mind and spirit, the arts, social empowerment, health, basic human needs, and Native American families. Contact the foundation at 1450 U.S. Trust Building, 730 Second Avenue South, Minneapolis, Minnesota 55402, or read more online.

Small Grants for Neighborhood Improvements in New York

Citizens for NYC provides small grants, education, and assistance to New York City neighborhoods that want to improve themselves. In 2006, it gave 90 grants of $500 each to support neighborhood projects and organizations; a smaller number of Flagship Awards of $1,000 support pioneering projects that can be reproduced in other neighborhoods. Past examples of grant-winning projects: graffiti removal programs, murals, open-space preservation, litter pickups, and membership drives for neighborhood groups. Get an application and learn more at www.citizensnyc.org.

Aid for Health Projects in Cleveland

The Cleveland Foundation, the city's community foundation, gave more than $17 million to health-related organizations in 2005. These grants ranged from the huge ($1.1 million in operating support to the Cleveland Clinic) to the small ($3,000 to American Legion Post 540 for recreational programs at a veterans hospital). The Cleveland Foundation also gives grants in other areas, including arts, the environment, youth, and economic development; its total

Turned Down? Ask Why

If you don't get funded by a grant-maker, contact them and ask why. Don't be defensive. Thank them for considering your application, express genuine disappointment, and then ask for constructive feedback on your proposal. Your goal should be to create a relationship with the grant-maker's staff. Taking their advice can help. If you think you've been unfairly turned down for a federal grant, enlist the aid of your elected representatives.

Help from Professional Sports Teams

Many professional sports teams have foundations or community relations departments that support charities in their local communities through player appearances, donations of merchandise, and other help. Some examples:

Baseball

The San Francisco Giants

The San Francisco Giants provide in-kind donations to thousands of Bay Area nonprofits each year. The team asks organizations to submit a written request on letterhead at least a month prior to the event. More info is online at www.giants.mlb.com; click on the "Community" button.

Basketball

The Chicago Bulls

The Chicago Bulls' program, CharitaBulls, donates autographed sports items and tickets to local charity groups, helping them to raise more than $125,000 annually. The team also provides in-kind donations to teachers, sports groups, after-school programs, and community organizations to use as incentives and prizes. For more information, see www.nba.com/bulls/community/outreach.html.

Football

The Pittsburgh Steelers

The Pittsburgh Steelers provide team items and memorabilia (but not game tickets) for charity auctions in western Pennsylvania. Detailed rules are at www.steelers.com (click on the "Community" tab), or write to the team's Community Relations department, 3400 South Water Street, Pittsburgh, Pennsylvania 15203.

Hockey

The Carolina Hurricanes

The Stanley Cup-winning Carolina Hurricanes' Kids 'N Community Foundation funds scholarship programs, youth hockey, education, children's health programs, the arts, and other causes throughout the Raleigh, North Carolina, area to the tune of more than $450,000 per year. Contact executive director Emma Bennett, at 1400 Edwards Mill Road, Raleigh, North Carolina 27607, for a grant application, or go online to www.carolinahurricanes.com/custom/radC6453.asp, where you can also read about other community programs sponsored by the Hurricanes.

Check Out Local Community Foundations

You'll notice that some of the grants listed here come from local community foundations. These organizations, designated to focus philanthropy in a geographic area, are among the fastest-growing sectors of philanthropy in the United States today, according to the Columbus Foundation; in 2004 (the last year surveyed), 636 U.S. community foundations received $4.2 billion in gifts from donors, held $39.4 billion in assets, and made $3 billion in grants to nonprofit organizations. Some community foundations also host training events and social gatherings for area nonprofits. A community foundation in your area is a great place to turn for grants, advice, and connections to the local philanthropic community; check your yellow pages under "Foundations–Educational, Philanthropic, Research" to see if there's a community foundation in your area.

giving in 2005 was more than $85 million. Learn more about the Cleveland Foundation and apply for a grant online at its website www.clevelandfoundation.org.

Grants for Nonprofits in Rhode Island

Rhode Island may be our smallest state, but it has a large and active philanthropic community, much of which works through the Rhode Island Foundation. The foundation supports nonprofit programs in many areas, including basic human needs (food, shelter, clothing, and health programs), leadership development, the arts, and more. The human needs grants are awarded every month (many grant programs at other foundations are quarterly or even annual) and can be as high as $5,000; recent recipients include Blackstone Valley Community Action in Pawtucket, which received $5,000 for food, rent, and utilities assistance; the East Bay Mental Health Center in Barrington, which received $2,500 for basic needs; and the Rhode Island Family Shelter in Warwick, which got $2,500 to purchase food for the families residing in the shelter. Contact the foundation online at www.rifoundation.org, or call 401-274-4564.

Editor's Choice Grants to Support Youth and Help Families

Nonprofit organizations in Illinois, Indiana, and New York that strive to support youth and strengthen families are invited to contact the Barker Welfare Foundation. (Nonprofits in other geographic areas are sometimes considered.) Founded by Catherine B. Hickox in 1934, the foundation carries on her charitable philosophy to this day. Recent recipients of Barker Welfare Foundation grants include Children's International Summer Villages, Inc., which received $2,000 to support its summer camp program; Citizens Concerned for the Homeless, Inc., of Michigan City, Illinois, which received $5,000 for general operating support; and El Rancho de las Golondrinas in Santa Fe, New Mexico, which received $10,000 over three years for its education center. Interested nonprofits are encouraged to call the foundation at 516-759-5592 to see if they fall within its general policy on giving grants.

More Help for Nonprofits

Proposal Writing 101

Nonprofits need to learn the basics of proposal writing to apply for foundation money, corporate grants, and government funds. A free online proposal-writing course (available in English, Spanish, French, Russian, Portuguese, and Mandarin) can be found at the website of the Foundation Center, the leading U.S. authority on grant-makers and grants (www.foundationcenter.org). Many other free resources await on the site, including contact information and schedules for the center's offices in New York, Atlanta, Cleveland, San Francisco, and Washington, D.C.; lists of the classes (many of them free) offered at each office; a catalog of publications in their libraries; and more.

Free Legal Assistance for Nonprofits

Does your nonprofit need help with paperwork, resolving disputes, or addressing other legal issues? Look for a lawyer who is willing to work *pro bono publico*—the Latin phrase means "for the public good." Look online at www.findlegalhelp.org (run by the American Bar Association) or contact your state Bar Association to locate a pro bono lawyer. Bar Associations generally won't refer you directly to a free lawyer but can usually point you toward local resources, such as legal aid societies or local organizations of attorneys. Another online clearinghouse is www.probono.net, which boasts more than 25,000 registered users, 60 percent of them volunteer lawyers from private firms. Nonprofits in the arts are especially fortunate: Volunteer nonprofit "lawyers for the arts" programs in many states match arts organizations with lawyers who want to help. In any Internet search engine, type "lawyers for the arts" (in quotes) and the name of your state or city to locate an organization that can help you.

Volunteer Accountants

Bookkeeping can be one of the more onerous tasks in running a nonprofit. The good news is that an easy-to-use website can connect your organization with an accountant willing to volunteer his or her services. The Clearinghouse for Volunteer Accounting Services (online at www.cvas-ca.org) has matched hundreds of small nonprofits with volunteer accountants since 1985; on its website, you can post your nonprofit's need or search through a database of accountants who might be willing to help.

Cash from Customer Loyalty Cards

Customer loyalty cards, used by merchants to reward regular customers with discounts and rebates, can also reward nonprofit groups through a company called eScrip. When a customer uses his or her loyalty cards at Safeway, Eddie Bauer, Linens 'n Things, Macy's, OfficeMax, and any of dozens of regional merchants, a nonprofit selected by the customer gets a donation through eScrip, which takes a 15 percent cut for its trouble. It costs nothing to register your nonprofit with eScrip; learn more at www.escrip.com.

Books to Help You Start a Nonprofit

If you're just at the start of your nonprofit journey, look into the helpful and relatively inexpensive books from Nolo Press, a publisher of self-help legal books.

- The book *How to Form a Nonprofit Corporation*, by Anthony Mancuso ($49.99), helps you navigate the complicated legal paperwork involved in becoming a federal 501(c)(3) nonprofit corporation.
- *Starting & Building a Nonprofit: A Practical Guide*, by Peri H. Pakroo ($29.99), takes you through the nuts and bolts of creating an organization.
- For more fund-raising advice, turn to *Effective Fund-Raising for Nonprofits: Real-World Strategies That Work*, by Ilona Bray ($24.99).

EDITOR'S CHOICE

Money from eBay Auctions

MissionFish helps nonprofits raise money through eBay auctions. In cooperation with eBay's Giving Works program, Mission Fish lets eBay sellers designate your nonprofit as a beneficiary of a portion of their sales. Nonprofits can also use MissionFish to convert in-kind donations to cash (within legal limits, of course) and to put special-event auctions online to reach new audiences. Learn more and register—it's free—at www.missionfish.org.

Free Help Finding Nonprofit Board Members

For many nonprofits, the key to successful fund-raising is having a diverse, involved, well-connected board of directors. But recruiting board members, especially outside your usual circles, can be difficult. Enter boardnetUSA, a free online service that matches individuals who are interested in serving on nonprofit boards with the organizations who need their service. BoardnetUSA has more than 10,000 candidates—people who've expressed interest in serving on a nonprofit board—in 47 states, and has placed thousands of individuals on boards. Learn more and sign up at www.boardnetusa.org.

Learn Nonprofit Management Skills from Verizon

If your nonprofit organization is spending too much time and energy on the business side of its operation—and not as much as you'd like on helping people—check out the suite of free online tools provided by the Verizon Foundation at foundation.verizon.com/resourcecenter. These tools can help with planning, prioritizing needs, and decision-making; technology use; communicating your organization's message to the community; fund-raising, including online fund-raising; recruitment of board members, staff, and volunteers; and evaluation of the success of critical projects. Through the Verizon Foundation Resources Center, nonprofits gain access to national training partners and other business resources to enhance their management capabilities and thus their ability to achieve sustainable goals.

Get Your Nonprofit on TV—for Free

Local cable companies often provide television channels, studio space, and training for community groups, including nonprofits, that want to get their message out. These "community access" channels are created by the agreements that cable providers sign with local communities, so offerings vary from place to place. In the Chicago area, Comcast operates 15 studios and a regular slate of training classes; many churches use the public access channels to broadcast their services. If you're interested in seeing your nonprofit on the air, check with your local cable operator or municipality to see what community access facilities are available.

No-Cost Website for Your Neighborhood or Group

Neighborhood Link provides neighborhood and community organizations with free, interactive websites that allow communication within organizations and with local governments. Tens of thousands

One-Time Project? Find an Established Nonprofit Sponsor

Many donors and foundations don't want to give money to a project that's not run by a nonprofit organization. And some organizations doing pilot or one-shot projects don't want to spend the time or money required to get official nonprofit status. If this is your situation, look for a like-minded nonprofit organization to become your fiscal sponsor. It works like this: Your donors and grant-makers give their contributions to the nonprofit, which takes a small percentage (usually between 2 and 10 percent) and writes the checks for your project. Your costs and income appear on the nonprofit's books and tax return. The process is complicated—but it's simpler than becoming a nonprofit yourself. To avoid problems, look for a nonprofit that's experienced at fiscal sponsorship.

of U.S. neighborhoods and groups have sites that include school information, a community calendar, discussion boards, links to local government officials, and more. Clubs and nonprofits can also use Neighborhood Link to coordinate projects like graffiti removal and park or trail restoration. Learn more at www.neighborhoodlink.com. For more free website providers, see page 220.

Free Online Services by and for Nonprofits

Grassroots.org, a nonprofit organization itself, provides many free services online to nonreligious nonprofit organizations involved in education, the environment, health, homelessness, government reform, and other causes. Among its services: free Internet domain registration (that is, acquiring an Internet name for your organization, such as www.YourNonprofitName.org) for one year (it's $10.99 per year after that); free website hosting (free sites carry a small Grassroots.org advertisement); information, assistance, and advice on incorporation; and an e-book, *Make Millions and Make Change*, on "social entrepreneurialism"—that is, earning a healthy living by running a valuable nonprofit. Among Grassroots.org's clients you'll find the Central Delta Depot Museum in Brinkley, Arkansas, and the Quilter's Guild of Arlington, Texas. Take advantage of its free services at www.grassroots.org.

Getting Meeting Space Donations

Need to host a meeting or event for your nonprofit? Before you take out the checkbook to rent a hall, ask local companies if they can

Free Strategies for Getting Your Message Out

All of these strategies will cost you little more than your time and effort but can provide big payback in terms of free publicity, help with fund-raising, and awareness of your cause.

- **Write a radio public service announcement (PSA).** A 30- or 60-second script, submitted to local radio stations to announce an upcoming event, project, or fundraiser, provides an inexpensive way to spread the word. The hard part is finding out who at a radio station should get your PSA; the best way to find out is to call the station.
- **Submit an op-ed article or a letter to the editor.** The opinion page of the local paper reaches a lively, engaged, audience. Make sure your letter or article has a strong opinion, is well-written (get objective feedback on your writing), and timely. Strive to inform the reader, rather than simply invite him to an event, sell him on your cause, or complain about a perceived injustice. Look on the opinion page of your local paper to find the address to which you should submit your article or letter.
- **Send a press release.** Announce your news to the media with a written press release. All the important information—who, what, when, where, and why—should be in the first paragraph. (Elaborate on these subjects in subsequent paragraphs.) Include contact information so editors can find you to ask questions. Distribute your press release using a free press release service (you'll find several on page 221) but don't neglect sending personal copies to your local media—especially low-budget weekly newspapers that are often hungry for content.
- **Establish a speaker's bureau.** Offer yourself and the key personnel in your organization as experts to the media and as speakers for public events and service-group meetings. Prepare stock presentations with your organization's mission and goals, beneficiaries, supporters, and other basic information. The purpose of a speaker's bureau is to raise awareness of your cause generally and of your organization specifically.

With all of these strategies—especially PSAs and press releases—don't wait until the last minute. Eight weeks is an appropriate lead time for sending event-related announcements.

provide meeting space. Many such donations of space are done informally—you won't find a link on the company website inviting you to "Use our meeting rooms for free!"—so you'll need to be creative. Start by asking your own board members if their companies can let you use a room. Then do some networking to learn about other companies and their relationships with nonprofits; if they are involved in other ways, they may be open to your request for space.

Part Three

SUPER SPECIAL BARGAINS FOR SUPER SPECIAL PEOPLE

Senior Citizens • Active-Duty Personnel and Veterans

People with Disabilities • New Mothers

Community Service Employees and Teachers

Chapter 15

rewards for senior citizens

Once upon a time you hated having to show your ID to buy beer and be admitted to nightclubs. But now that you're "of a certain age," flashing your ID can yield tons of freebies and bargains.

ONE OF THE GREAT ADVANTAGES of becoming a senior citizen is that you are suddenly eligible for all kinds of special discounts, services, and programs from both the government and businesses. These benefits touch almost every area of your life—health, finances, travel and transportation, entertainment, leisure activities, shopping, to name the most notable. These bargains and freebies are too numerous to be contained in a single book, much less a single chapter, but we have made every effort to bring you the best of them and to give you an ample sampling of the enormous variety of perks available to you just because you've reached that "certain age."

Speaking of which, the age at which you qualify for a senior discount or program varies from business to business and program to program. It can be anywhere from 50 to as high as 70 in a few cases (see "Defining 'Senior,'" page 294). In this chapter, we've included freebies, discounts, and benefits available to people as young as 50 as well as ones available only at a later age. It's also important to remember that when we've listed deals available to residents of one state or locality, similar bargains or discounts are frequently available in other locations. You have to ask.

Some discounts for seniors are advertised, but many are not. Get in the habit of asking whether a business or service offers such deals.

By the numbers

84.9

Life expectancy of Asian Americans, according to a Harvard School of Public Health study. The life expectancy of high-risk urban blacks? Just 71.1 years.

If you are reluctant to do this in person, call ahead and ask. Even if the discount turns out to be small, it's still extra cash in your pocket. Always carry a driver's license or other proof of age with you. (And be sure to ask whether the senior discount or rate is the best one available. Sometimes there might be a special sale, promotion, or midweek or off-season rate that's a better deal.)

Many retail stores, supermarkets, and malls have Senior Days when discounts are in effect. Some fast-food restaurants offer half-off beverages or free morning coffee, and many restaurants feature special senior discounts or deals on meals. Movie theaters, museums, theme parks, golf courses ... there are too many senior-citizen prices for anyone to remember! So keep a record for yourself. Although the discounts tend to be small, they add up over time to big savings.

Where do you find other sources of seniors-only specials and deals? Start with your local senior center, church, and chamber of commerce. For government programs, contact your mayor's office, local area agency on aging (see "The National Aging Network," page 293) or state or municipal department of aging. And then of course, there's the Internet, which is a gold mine of products, programs, services, and information that can help put money in your pocket at any age.

Everyday Bargains and Benefits

Free Call-Up Rides

Cities and towns across the United States have government-sponsored Senior Ride or Dial-A-Ride Programs that provide seniors, usually age 60 and over, free transportation to and from medical appointments, shopping, hair stylists, and so on. In Alhambra, California, for example, the program provides free curb-to-curb transport anywhere within the city for any purpose, and up to two miles outside city borders for medical appointments. Seniors can reserve in advance for single trips, or schedule a ride on a daily or weekly basis. In addition to its Dial-A-Ride program, Randolph Township, New Jersey, also provides a free van service that takes seniors to a different shopping center four days a week. Other places, like Clark County, Nevada (includes Las Vegas), offer half-fare taxi coupons. To find out what's available in your community,

EDITOR'S CHOICE

Half-Price Mass-Transit Deals

If you're 65 or older, you can ride on public transit for half price in most U.S. cities, including Las Vegas, Atlanta, New York, and Miami. In San Francisco, you ride for just one-third of the price. In Washington State, seniors pay half-fare for ferry rides. In Puerto Rico, seniors 60 and older pay half-fare on mass transit buses and on San Juan's Tren Urbano; those 75 and older ride for free. In many places, the deals are available to residents only and you need to get a special senior pass. But in some places—including San Francisco—the discount is available to all seniors; so no matter where you are, always ask about senior fares.

contact your local Area Agency on Aging (see "The National Aging Network," opposite); the Eldercare Locator (visit www.eldercare.gov/eldercare/public/home.asp or call toll-free 800-677-1116); or the toll-free National Transit Hotline: 800-527-8279.

Extra Discounts on Tuesdays at the Mall

It's great getting 25 to 65 percent off retail prices at the nation's outlet malls. But if you're a senior and shop on Tuesdays at certain stores in many of these malls, you can add another 10 percent to your savings. At most Premium Outlet Malls, shoppers age 50 and over get an extra 10 percent discount when they present a photo ID with proof of age to the cashier at participating stores. To see if the senior discount is available at a particular mall, go to www.premiumoutlets.com, click on "Sales & Events," select a mall, and look for "50-Plus Shopper Club," where you'll find a link to a list of stores. Prime Outlets has a similar program, called "Prime Timer Tuesdays" or "Prime Time Shoppers," for people 55 and older. To check the availability of the program at one of these malls, go to www.primeoutlets.com, click on "Outlet Locations," select a mall, and look under "What's New."

Free Guide to Senior Deals in Texas

Austin, Dallas, and San Antonio each has its own *Seniors Guide*—a free, annual book that directs residents to senior-friendly businesses and services and includes discount coupons, consumer tips, a medical diary, and more. To access the guides' roster of businesses and services online, go to www.seniorsguide.net, click on "Senior-Friendly Businesses," and select the type of business (they're listed alphabetically, from accountant to wheelchair lifts). To sign up to receive your city's book in the mail, call 512-257-7607; or send an e-mail to texas@seniorsguide.net.

Special Discounts for Seniors in Seattle

All Greater Seattle residents ages 60 and older can get a Gold Card that provides access to a wide range of services as well as a host of discounts from participating restaurants, theaters, retailers, and other businesses listed in the annual *Special Discounts Directory* for seniors published by the Mayor's Office for Senior Citizens. Cardholders are also entitled to free admission to the Seattle zoo and aquarium and 50 percent off a dog or cat license. Throughout the year, the Mayor's Office for Senior Citizens distributes free tickets to recreational, cultural, and sports events on a first-come,

The National Aging Network

Established by the Older Americans Act of 1965, the National Aging Network is the primary federal vehicle for delivering community-based assistance and services to Americans ages 60 and older and their families. Consisting of agencies at the federal, state, and local levels, the national network was set up to provide services that enable older people to live in their own homes for as long as possible. Any American is eligible to receive network services, although priority is given to those in greatest need.

Heading the network is the federal Administration on Aging; it oversees network programs and grants money to State Units on Aging, which work with state agencies and other public and private groups that provide programs, services, and support for seniors. State Units grant money to Area Agencies on Aging that work on the local level. An Area Agency on Aging (AAA) can be a public or private nonprofit organization; its area might encompass a city, a single county, or several counties. If you or a family member needs support services (say, transportation to a medical appointment), it is your local AAA that you should contact. AAA services include:

Access services: information, referrals, escorts, and transportation.

In-home services: health, delivered meals, chores, rehabilitation, and home repair.

Community-based services: legal help, employment counseling and referral, fitness programs, alternative community-based living facilities, senior centers, and more.

Caregiver services: respite, counseling, and education programs.

Institutional services: preadmission screening programs, rehabilitation, skilled nursing facilities, and continuing-care retirement communities.

To find the nearest AAA, go to the Administration on Aging's online Eldercare Locator at www.eldercare.gov/eldercare/public/home.asp; or call toll-free 800-677-1116. For fuller descriptions of AAA services, visit the main "Elders & Families" section of the Administration on Aging's website (www.aoa.gov/eldfam/eldfam.asp; click on "Services for Seniors"); you can also write to the Administration on Aging, Washington, D.C. 20201; or call 202-619-0724.

first-served basis. For more information about senior programs in Seattle, go to www.seattle.gov/humanservices/mosc/default.htm.

State Discount Cards for 60-Plus

On their 60th birthdays, Ohio and West Virginia residents receive a free discount card from their state governments that gives them access to discounts and savings from thousands of participating businesses. If you live in Ohio and don't receive a Golden Buckeye card in the mail when you turn 60, call toll-free 866-301-6446, ask at your local senior center or library, or visit the website www.goldenbuckeye.com. West Virginians who don't receive their Golden Mountaineer Discount Card should call toll-free 877-987-3646, or go to www.state.wv.us/seniorservices and scroll down to the card application form link.

Improve Your Driving and Lower Your Insurance Costs

If you are 55 and older and complete a Driver Improvement Course with your local AAA (Automobile Association of America) Club or an AARP Driver Safety Program, you could qualify for a reduced premium on your auto insurance. Many states, including California, Colorado, and New York, mandate such a discount. (To see if a discount is mandated in your state, check with your insurance company.) AAA's course is $25 for members 55 and older. AARP offers a classroom course for $10 (as of mid-2006) and an online course for $15.95 for members ($19.95 for nonmembers). For more on these courses, go to www.aaa.com and input your zip code; or log on to www.aarp.org (click on "Family, Home, and Legal").

Free Advice from Sage Seniors

Got a problem Emily Post can't solve? Or a sticky situation with an in-law, friend, or co-worker? Write about your problem to the Elder Wisdom Circle, a nonprofit organization of volunteer seniors age 60

Defining "Senior"

When you become a senior citizen, a whole new world of opportunities and money-saving benefits opens up for you. But when are you officially a senior? For the American Association of Retired Persons, the magic age is 50. Several popular restaurant chains offer less-expensive senior menus to customers 55 and older. The federal Older Americans Act defines "older" as 60 and up. Many public transit systems across the United States cut fares in half for riders who've turned 65, while the Social Security Administration sets full retirement age from 65 to 67 years old, depending on your year and month of birth. The truth is, with people living longer, healthier, and active lives, turning 50—or even 60 or 70—is far from over the hill. Have you heard? Sixty is the new forty.

and over. You will get a personal, confidential response from an experienced elder within just a few days. You can even request a second opinion, if you like. (No medical, legal, tax, or investment advice will be offered.) Based in the San Francisco Bay area but with members around the United States, the Elder Wisdom Circle is dedicated to sharing the wisdom learned from a lifetime of living. Learn more and read sample letters at www.elderwisdomcircle.org; if you're interested in becoming an EWC Elder, click on "Offer Advice." You can also write to the Elder Wisdom Circle, 506 Tampico, Walnut Creek, California 94598; or call 925-945-8814.

EDITOR'S CHOICE

Making Dreams Come True

Know someone living in an elder-care facility who wants a dream fulfilled but lacks the means to make it happen? The nonprofit group Second Wind Dreams makes dreams come true for elderly persons, from arranging a visit to a family farm or an amusement park to buying watercolor supplies. The experience brings joy to the dreamer and creates bonds between people. For more information, visit www.secondwind.org; call 678-624-0500; or write to Second Wind Dreams, 1031 Cambridge Square, Suite G, Alpharetta, Georgia 30004.

Especially for Grandparents

Tax Credits for Grandparenting

If you are raising a grandchild, you deserve credit for doing so, and the Internal Revenue Service agrees—to the tune of three kinds of tax credits. In 2006, the tax credits were as follows:

- If you or your spouse is employed and your income is below $34,000, you could be eligible for the Earned Income Tax Credit if your dependent grandchild is under age 19 (under 24 if a full-time student).
- If you have to pay for child care so you can work or look for work, you might qualify for the Child and Dependent Care Credit, which could mean up to $3,000 per year in tax relief.
- The Child Tax Credit is worth up to $1,000 in saved taxes if your grandchild is under 17 and your family income is less than $110,000 (less than $75,000 if you are a single grandparent responsible for parenting).

If you qualify, you can take advantage of all three credits. For more information, call the IRS toll-free at 800-829-1040; or go to www.irs.gov/pub/irs-pdf/p972.pdf.

Government Breaks for Grandparents and Grandkids

It's tough enough living on a fixed income and often nearly impossible to manage financially if you are also trying to raise your grandkids. The government has several programs that could help.

- Your grandchildren may be eligible to receive Medicaid benefits, even if you don't qualify for or receive Medicaid yourself. In such cases, Medicaid eligibility is determined by the child's income, not yours.
- Similarly, the Temporary Assistance for Needy Families program won't count your income if you apply on behalf of your grandchild (your income would be considered if you were applying for family benefits). TANF's benefits include food stamps, money, and day care.
- The Children's Health Insurance Program offers medical and dental care to children who qualify.

Call your local social services (or human services) office or Area Agency on Aging (see "The National Aging Network," page 293) for more information on these and similar programs.

Free Information on Grandparenting

Whether you're among the growing number of Americans raising their grandchildren or just want to develop a closer relationship with your grandkids, the "Grandparenting" section of the AARP website is a terrific source of free information, advice, and assistance. Go to www.aarp.org, click on "Family, Home and Legal," then select "Grandparenting." You'll find links to the AARP Foundation Grandparent Information Center (GIC) and its local support database; fact sheets for grandparents raising children; and advice on visitation rights, healthy living for grandparents raising grandkids, and how to manage the stress of caring for children later in life. You can also order free booklets in English or Spanish and sign up for a free newsletter, *The GIC Voice*, that gives tips and advice on the challenges of raising grandchildren. For a list of links to other websites of interest to grandparents, click on "Internet Resources on Aging" on the GIC page, select "Family, Personal Relationships, and Online Community," and click on "Grandparenting." You can also request grandparenting information by calling toll-free 888-OUR-AARP (888-687-2277) or writing to the AARP Grandparent Information Center, 601 E Street NW, Washington, D.C. 20049.

Free Helpful Newsletter for Grandparents

The *Grandparent Connection* is a free, monthly, online newsletter for grandparents that was started and edited by Lauren Teegarden, a teenage granddaughter in Oregon, to improve communication and

Q I've heard there's a program that lets seniors make free phone calls at Christmas. Is this true?

A For more than 25 years, Merrill Lynch has opened its arms at Christmas to senior citizens, inviting them into more than 50 corporate offices nationwide to make free phone calls to family or friends anywhere in the world. In December 2005, more than 10,000 seniors ages 60 and older took part. Ask about the Christmas Calls Program at your senior center, church, or local Department of Aging; or e-mail Merrill Lynch—on www.ml.com, click on "Contact Us," then on "Corporate Citizenship (Philanthropy)" to access the Global Philanthropy e-mail link.

AARP

You don't need to be retired to join the American Association of Retired Persons, which now goes entirely by the abbreviated moniker AARP. In fact, many members are not retired. The only requirements are that you be age 50 or over and pay annual dues of $12.50 (less if you pay two or three years at once), which also covers membership for your spouse or partner. AARP members are automatically eligible for a host of discounts and deals on hotels and motels, car rentals, vacations, insurance, legal assistance, and more. (AARP benefits are featured throughout this chapter.) Membership includes a free monthly magazine and news bulletin. With its millions of members, AARP is a powerful advocate with federal and state governments on issues such as Medicare, Social Security, consumer safety, and pension rights.

In addition, AARP's website (www.aarp.org) is a treasure trove of free, clearly written information, resources, and advice on health, travel, employment, retirement, money management, exercise, computer learning, caregiving, grandparenting, driver-safety training, prescription drugs, games, and much more. On the site's home page, you can sign up for free e-mail newsletters, check out job openings (click on "National Employer Team"), and access "AARP in Your State" to find news, special events, and community-service opportunities in your area. The website includes a large and excellent list of links to other sites and a state-by-state guide to transportation for seniors. You can also contact AARP by calling toll-free 888-OUR-AARP (888-687-2277); or by writing to AARP, 601 E Street NW, Washington, D.C. 20049.

understanding between grandparents and their grandchildren. Thoughtful and well written, the newsletter contains insightful articles and advice from the grandchildren's perspective, a question-and-answer section, and activities and crafts to do together. Sign up to have the newsletter e-mailed to you, or read it online at meridian-skydesign.com/grandparentconnection.

Read *Grandparents Magazine* Free Online

This is a delightful—and free—interactive, online magazine for grandparents and their grandkids. Go to www.grandparents-magazine.net to check out its array of articles, book and toy reviews, word games, activities, gift ideas, lyrics to nursery rhymes and kid's songs, and printable pages for coloring that feature children's favorite fictional characters. Don't miss the website's growing guide to children's tourist attractions in various cities. Become a member for free (just fill out the form on the website) and you'll receive periodic e-newsletters and be automatically entered in contests and sweepstakes.

Don't Overlook Kids-Eat-Free Nights

You may be attracted to the discount offered to senior citizens by the chain eatery in your neighborhood—perhaps a modest 10 percent off when you dine on Sunday evenings. But take a closer look at that restaurant's offerings. The same restaurant may allow children to eat totally free on another night—say, Tuesdays. If you like to take your grandkids out for a good time, you'll save a bundle by paying full price for your own meal but getting a free ride for the youngsters.

Learning for Seniors

Free College Tuition for Seniors

Parents of teenagers often struggle to pay exorbitant college tuition fees. But the picture is much different at the opposite end of the age spectrum. Senior citizens can often get free or very low cost college tuition. For instance, at Arkansas State University, state residents ages 60 and up get free tuition and credit for their coursework. At Idaho's Boise State University, they pay only $5 per credit. In Massachusetts, state law waives tuition at public colleges and universities for seniors 60 and older; admission is dependent on available space. There may be other fees involved (for labs, parking, books), but if you're thinking of getting a degree, perhaps for a second career, it's worth asking about special breaks for older students at the admissions office of your local college or university; or contact your state's Department of Higher Education (see Appendix, page 396). In addition, many colleges and universities let seniors audit classes without charge or for a nominal fee, usually depending on space available in the course or with the instructor's permission.

Free or Low-Cost Classes from OASIS

OASIS is a nonprofit organization that provides "lifelong learning and service opportunities" to adults ages 50 and over. Sponsored nationally by Federated Department Stores and BJC HealthCare, OASIS operates in 26 cities across the United States—including

St. Louis, Albuquerque, and Los Angeles. It offers classes that are free or low cost ($10 or less per session in many cases) on an enormously varied range of subjects such as painting with watercolors, ballroom dancing, yoga, everyday Spanish, computers, digital photography, politics, history, and fiction writing. Class sessions generally last an hour and are held in local department stores or other community spaces. For more information, go to www.oasisnet.org, where you can see whether there's an OASIS city near you and browse the online catalog for that location. Join OASIS for free by filling out the brief online questionnaire; or call 314-862-2933. Members receive a class catalog in the mail three times a year.

Finding a Job

Free Job-Search Advice for 50-Plus

An excellent resource for senior job seekers is the career-development website Quintessential Careers (www.quintcareers.com). It's loaded with advice, tools, and resources for job seekers of all ages, but if you're over 50 and in the job market, don't miss Katherine Hansen's article "Résumé, Cover Letter, and Interview Strategies for Older Workers" at www.quintcareers.com/older_worker_strategies.html; it clearly spells out specific do's and don'ts and smart techniques for successfully handling the challenges of a job search when you're older. At the bottom of the page is a link to "Job and Career Resources for Mature and Older Job Seekers," where you'll find links to an array of career resources and job sites.

Job Assistance for Low-Income Seniors

The U.S. Department of Labor's Senior Community Service Employment Program gives grants to nonprofit organizations and state and territorial governments to provide work-based training for low-income people ages 55 and older. Participants are placed in part-time (about 20 hours a week), government-subsidized, community-service jobs in such facilities as day-care and senior centers, government agencies, schools, hospitals, and landscaping centers. SCSEP participants can also receive classroom and computer training, individual counseling, and other services to support their

Q How can I find low-cost computer training courses?

A One way to get started is to ask whether your local library, senior center, church, high school, or community college gives computer instruction. Classes are often given free or at very lost cost. And you can use a free computer at a library to practice on your own. Another place to learn is with SeniorNet, a nonprofit organization that sets up seniors to teach people 50 and older to use computers at Learning Centers throughout the United States. A $40 annual membership fee provides access to low-cost courses, free or low-cost computer labs, a free newsletter, and discounts on computers and software. Call toll-free 800-747-6848; or visit www.seniornet.org. Once you know how to access the Internet, visit www.cyberseniors.org, which has terrific computer tips for beginners and lots more that will interest you.

For Seniors Surfing the Net

The Internet is a window onto a world of information, fun, shopping, learning, and communications—all right at your fingertips. Many, many websites are exclusively devoted to the interests of seniors.

To speed your search for a specific topic or category, or just to see what's out there for you, check out these websites, which round up Internet resources for seniors:

- Internet Sites for Seniors, from the public library in Fort Smith, Arkansas: www.fspl.lib.ar.us/irseniors.html
- AARP's Internet Sources on Aging: www.aarp.org/internet resources
- Sites for seniors in the Yahoo Directory: dir.yahoo.com/Society_and_Culture/Cultures_and_Groups/Seniors
- Seniors Online at Refdesk.com: refdesk.com/seniors.html

Comprehensive government websites provide links to government programs, services, and other resources for seniors:

- The "Elders and Families" page from the website of the Administration on Aging (see "The National Aging Network," page 293): www.aoa.gov/eldfam/eldfam.asp
- Senior Citizens' Resources: www.firstgov.gov/topics/seniors.shtml
- From the Department of Health and Human Services, a roundup of federal resources: www.eldercare.gov/eldercare/public/resources/federal.asp.

transition to unsubsidized jobs. And they have access to the invaluable job-search services of the Career One-Stop Centers sponsored by the U.S. Department of Labor (see "No-Cost Federal Job-Search Help," page 000). For more on SCSEP, go to www.doleta.gov/seniors; or call toll-free 877-US-2JOBS (877-872-5627).

Free Help for Older Job Seekers

Experience Works is a nonprofit organization with offices in 38 states and Puerto Rico devoted to helping low-income people ages 55 or older get job training and employment. Often working closely with the federal government's Senior Community Service Employment Program (described above), Experience Works provides older workers with job skills and placement assistance for such occupations as teacher's aide, home health aide, and computer operator. To learn about eligibility requirements and training programs in your state, call Experience Works toll-free at 866-EXP-WRKS

(866-397-9757); or go to www.experienceworks.org (select "Get Training for a Job," then search by your state and county).

No-Cost Senior-Friendly Job Finder

Job seekers ages 50 and up can register for free at www.seniors4hire .org and access the site's database of jobs at companies that value—and actively recruit—mature employees. You can also join Seniors4Hire's job notification e-mail list and forward a confidential résumé directly to employers. Other senior-friendly job sites to check are www.seniorjobbank.org and www.dinosaur-exchange.com (the latter has an international focus). The "National Employer Team" page of the AARP website (www.aarp; click on "Money and Work," then "Careers" and "Finding a Job") provides links to companies actively looking to hire older workers. While you're at it, also check out the community resources, interviewing strategies, and résumé-writing guides on the "Finding a Job" page.

Retirement Resources

Free Info on Where to Retire

Thinking about where you would like to live when you retire? The website for *Where to Retire* magazine offers free brochures to nearly 150 (as of mid-2006) retirement communities across the United States. Go to www.wheretoretire.com and click on "Free Retirement Info" to request the brochures that most appeal to you. You can also subscribe to the magazine either online, where it is offered at 55 percent off the newsstand price, or by calling 713-974-6903.

Inexpensive Gateway to Retirement Resources

The Retirement Living Information Center (www.retirementliving .com) is a wide-ranging resource for anyone considering retirement and relocation. You can consult a state-by-state guide to different types of retirement communities and senior housing; read the free monthly online newsletter *Retirement Living News;* check updates to the section describing new retirement communities; compare the tax burden you'd have to shoulder in each state (a complex subject, clearly explained); link to online publications; and more. To use the various resources in the Great Places to Retire section, including a "Decision Guide for Planning Your Retirement Destination," you'll need to become a member for a one-time fee of $19.95.

Free Retirement Planning Tool from AARP

The free Retirement Planning Calculator on the AARP website helps you figure out how much money you need to save and invest today to enjoy your retirement in the future. A handy option at the end of your personalized financial report is the "Recalculate" button, which lets you alter key figures for a revised estimate of your retirement income. To access the calculator, go to the AARP Web page www.aarp.org/money/financial_planning (click on "Retirement Planning Calculator" under "Session 7: Retirement Planning"). While you're at it, check out the other helpful links in "Session 7," as well as the U.S. Department of Labor's article "Top 10 Ways to Prepare for Retirement" under "Additional Resources."

Senior Travel Deals

Lifetime Free Entry to National Parks for $10

The Golden Age Passport is a whopper of a deal for people ages 62 and older who visit U.S. national parks and other federal recreational areas. The passport costs a mere $10 and provides free lifetime admission to lands operated by the National Park Service, the Bureau of Land Management, the Forest Service, the U.S. Army

More Protection for Your Retirement Accounts

In April 2006, the U.S. government increased the amount of free insurance coverage it provides for certain types of retirement accounts at banks and credit unions from $100,000 to $250,000. The accounts include self-directed individual retirement accounts, self-directed Keogh accounts, "457" Plan accounts, and self-directed 401(k) accounts. To qualify for insurance, the accounts must be in banks and savings associations insured by the Federal Deposit Insurance Corporation and credit unions insured by the National Credit Union Administration. The insurance protects your money if the financial institution fails. For more details, call toll-free 877-ASK-FDIC (877-275-3342).

Corps of Engineers, and more! Your spouse and children will also be admitted free, and, in many cases, so will other passengers in your car. The passport also reduces by half some of the fees you'll encounter in those parks—for parking, camping, swimming, and launching a boat, for instance. You must purchase the pass at a national park, wildlife refuge, or other federal recreational area where there's an entrance fee. For more information on this and other National Parks passes go to www.nps.gov/fees_passes.htm.

Inexpensive Learning Adventures with Elderhostel

If you're the type of traveler who is always curious and likes to learn something new, then a low-cost Elderhostel trip is perfect for you! The world's largest educational travel organization for older adults, Elderhostel caters to folks ages 55 and up and, as a nonprofit group, keeps its prices low. Some trip programs cost less than $600 (a five-night natural history adventure on Georgia's barrier islands is one example), and a few scholarships are available to defray program fees. Accommodations range from inns and hotels (and ships) to university apartments and dormitories. Elderhostel provides learning adventures, led by experts in their fields, in some 90 countries and all 50 states, with activities that include hiking, biking, rafting, lectures, field trips, social events, and free time. To learn more about Elderhostel programs and sign up for free catalogs and informational e-mails, go to www.elderhostel.org; or call toll-free 800-454-5768.

Super Senior Deals at State Parks

Seniors get great deals at state parks and forests too—ranging from significant reductions in admissions fees to free lifetime admission passes. The minimum age requirement varies widely from state to state but is usually 60 or older. Some states offer seniors a free or reduced-cost license to hunt and fish. Sometimes the discounts are limited to nonpeak times. New York State, for example, gives free vehicle admission to 62-plus seniors (show a driver's license) on non-holiday weekdays, and Washington State offers 62-pluses deeply discounted camping and moorage October through March and on some weekdays in April as well as free passes to seniors with a household income below $35,000. As you can see, the rules can be complex; so contact your state's parks department (often called the Department of Natural Resources) to learn about available senior discounts and passes.

Q **Which carrier has the best airfare deals for seniors?**

A You can save more than 50 percent off regular fares on Southwest Airlines if you are age 65 or older. As of mid-2006, the coast-to-coast fare for seniors was discounted more than 60 percent; the precise amount will vary according to your itinerary. Reservations are changeable, refundable, and don't need to be made in advance. Southwest also offers great family vacation packages to such places as Disney World and Universal Studios, as well as discount tickets for major theme parks around the United States. Check out Southwest Airlines' special offers at www.southwest.com; or call toll-free 800-435-9792.

Free and Low-Cost Hospitality-Exchange Programs

Hospitality exchange programs enable member-travelers to tap into a network of essentially free lodging in many countries around the world. The concept is simple: When you travel, you stay in the spare bedroom of other members. In return, you occasionally host member-travelers in your home. ElderTravelers is one such program for people ages 50 and up. Its more than 2,300 members are located in every U.S. state, four Canadian provinces, and 41 other countries (as of mid-2006). You pay nothing except an annual $40 membership fee. For full details, go to www.eldertravelers.org. In the similar Evergreen Club (www.evergreenclub.com), also for people 50 and older, and the Affordable Travel Club (www.affordabletravelclub.net), for people over 40, members pay a small nightly gratuity in addition to annual membership fees.

Senior Home Swaps for a Small Fee

Rather than forking over cash for hotels at your vacation destination in the United States or abroad, wouldn't it be nice if you could just swap homes with someone who wanted to visit your town on the same dates? You could strike a deal without any money changing hands! That's exactly the idea behind home-exchange programs. One such group is Seniors Home Exchange, geared exclusively to people ages 50 and up. The registration fee (as of mid-2006) is $79 for three years or $100 for lifetime membership—relatively little money compared to the potential savings with a single exchange. For more information, visit www.seniorshomeexchange.com.

Cruise Cheap as a Gentleman Host

Guys, how would you like to take exotic cruises for less than $30 a day? You get a nice passenger cabin, food, discounts on clothes, and a laundry and beverage allowance, plus round-trip airfare to the ship and home again. If you're age 40 to 70, a fair dancer, presentable, and refined, you stand a good chance of being hired as a "gentleman host" in the cruise industry. Your primary duties: dance with the single ladies who are flocking to cruises, and serve as a good representative of the cruise line. If you don't like to dance, consider other jobs, such as exercise trainer, doctor, photographer, and member of the casino staff. The Working Vacation Inc. is one of the industry's primary recruiters of gentlemen hosts; check out details at www.theworkingvacation.com.

Editor's Choice Luxury Hotels for Half Price

AARP members save up to 50 percent off regular rates at the Sheraton, Four Points by Sheraton, St. Regis, Le Meridien, Luxury Collection, W Hotels, and Westin—all fabulous hotels in the Starwood chain. However, you must make a 21-day nonrefundable advance purchase and arrive on Thursday, Friday, or Saturday. For more impromptu getaways, members can still save up to 25 percent on everyday reservations. Sign up for Starwood's free Preferred Guest Program for even more good deals, including points for dollars spent, upgrades, late checkouts, and e-mail alerts about special promotions. For more on Starwood offers exclusive to AARP members, go to www.starwoodhotels.com/aarp.

Assemble a Tour Group and Travel Free

Many travel companies arrange tours specifically for people ages 50 and over. One of the oldest, Grand Circle Travel, offers escorted international tours and cruises as well as adventure trips and extended vacations. If you refer a friend who signs up with GCT, you'll earn $100, while your friend gets a $50 credit. Put together a group of 10 people to travel with you, and you'll travel completely free! Find out more about Grand Circle Travel's offerings and deals online at www.gct.com, or call toll-free 800-959-0405. On the site, you can sign up to receive a free catalog, a free e-newsletter, and e-mail alerts about last-minute deals. You can order Grand Circle Travel's excellent free booklet, *101 Tips Plus for Mature Travelers,* by calling its toll-free number.

Senior Fun and Games

Cheap Senior Seats at MLB Games

Root, root, root for your home team with tickets priced specially for seniors!

- In Los Angeles, senior Dodger fans ages 55 and over can buy tickets at the stadium for specified seats, 1 1/2 hours before game time, for only $4.
- The Cincinnati Reds sell seniors 60 and up half-price tickets for nonpremium seats for certain games before game day.

- In New York City, the Yankees offer fans 60 and over a limited number of $5 tickets to select games (marked SC on the schedule). Tickets are sold at Yankee Stadium two hours prior to the game at the Advance Ticket Window.
- On Senior Fan Days, New York Mets fans ages 60 and over (and their guests) can purchase half-price tickets for seats in various locations at Shea Stadium. Order tickets online at www.nymets.com (select "Special Ticket Orders" under "Tickets"), by phone at 718-507-TIXX (718-507-8499), or in person at the Advanced Ticket Window at Shea.

Only some Major League Baseball teams offer seniors specials, so check with your city's team(s) for the discounts they offer.

Half-Price Symphony Seats for Seniors

Many symphony orchestras offer substantial savings on regular ticket prices for seniors.

- The Pittsburgh Symphony Orchestra and the Grand Rapids Symphony offer half-price tickets to people ages 62 and older.
- The New York Philharmonic sells a limited number of same-day tickets to select concerts for only $12.
- You need be only age 60 to get half-price tickets for Thursday, Friday, or Saturday concerts by the Cincinnati Symphony Orchestra; if you organize a group of 10 or more senior music-lovers for a Friday morning CSO concert, you'll all get 50-percent-off tickets, plus a free backstage tour, free pre-concert lecture, free bus parking—and your group name will be printed in the program!

If you love music, learn the score about your own local orchestra's discount programs.

Half-Price Tickets at D.C.'s JFK Arts Center

In Washington, D.C., both the John F. Kennedy Center for the Performing Arts and the National Theatre give seniors ages 65 and older a 50 percent discount for designated performances. At the National Theatre, half-price Special Patron Tickets are offered for sale to seniors at the box office and only for performances on Tuesday or Wednesday evenings or Sunday matinees. The offer is subject to availability and certain restrictions; go to the Web page www.nationaltheatre.org/tickets/halfprice.htm for details. For some

Kennedy Center attractions, a limited number of specially priced (half-off) tickets are available at the box office on the day of performance (advance tickets can be purchased only for the first performance of a designated attraction). Another Kennedy Center perk: Parking is free while buying your tickets (you must arrive before 6 p.m. and stay no longer than one hour). For more information, go to www.kennedy-center.org/tickets/spts.html.

Museum Discounts for Seniors

Museum-going is a terrific pastime no matter what your age, but seniors have an extra incentive in the form of hefty admission discounts.

- In New York City, the Metropolitan Museum of Art's suggested admission price of $20 for adults is cut in half for seniors 65 and older, while at the Museum of Modern Art seniors 65 and over with ID save $4 off the regular $20 adult admission fee.
- At the Art Institute of Chicago, the senior discount is more than 40 percent.
- Seniors get 55 percent off at Seattle's Science Fiction Museum.
- Even better are the deals offered by the Smithsonian Institution's museums in Washington, D.C., and the J. Paul Getty Museum in Los Angeles—admission is free to all (at the Getty, though, there is a $7 parking fee).

Wherever you are, in the United States or abroad, make sure to ask for the senior discount at museums and other cultural institutions. Odds are you'll be pleasantly surprised.

Discount and Free Skiing for Seniors

It's never too late to ski! The 70+ Ski Club has more than 15,000 members, with 5,000 over age 80 and hundreds over age 90. Club membership gives you access to discounted or free skiing as well as the benefits of schussing with like-minded skiers and good companionship après ski. To join you must be at least 70 years old and a downhill skier. Annual dues are $10 for singles, $15 for couples (both spouses must be eligible). You can download an application at www.altitude800.com/70+skiclub; or call for more information at 518-346-5505 (East Coast) or 949-951-3005 (West Coast). The Over the Hill Gang International offers skiing discounts and organizes ski trips for seniors; membership is open to skiers ages 50 and over. For more information, go to www.othgi.com; or call 719-389-0022.

Editor's Choice

Cheap Thrills at Theme Parks

For those ages 62 and older, the savings are even more thrilling at some big theme parks than at the nation's museums. Here's a sampling of senior discounts at theme parks across the United States:

- 62 percent off at California's Knott's Berry Farm
- 73 percent reduction at Worlds of Fun in Missouri
- 75 percent off at Cedar Point Amusement Park in Ohio
- 43 percent discount for seniors ages 55-69 at Pennsylvania's Hershey Park; for those 70 and over, the discount is nearly 60 percent.

Health Care Savings for Older Americans

Medicare is not the only source of reduced cost or free health care assistance available to seniors. For those who meet the eligibility requirements, there are a number of other organizations and agencies that provide help. Here is a sampling.

Free Eye Care for Seniors

The Seniors EyeCare Program, under the auspices of the American Academy of Ophthalmology, offers free medical eye care for people ages 65 and older who have not seen an eye doctor for at least three years and who are not covered by an HMO or the Department of Veterans Affairs. Eligible seniors receive a comprehensive medical eye exam and up to one year of treatment at no cost for any eye disease diagnosed during the initial exam. If you have Medicare Part B coverage or other health insurance, you can still access the program; the doctors will accept reimbursement and not charge you a penny. Eyeglasses and prescription drugs are not covered. For details, call toll-free 800-222-EYES (800-222-3937); or go to www.eyecareamerica.org.

Save on Eyeglasses and Eye Tests

AARP members can save 30 percent on glasses at LensCrafters, Target Optical, or participating Sears Optical and Pearle Vision stores. You'll also save on the cost of an eye exam. Some of these stores offer a free glaucoma pressure test and a personalized Eye Health Exam Report that explains the results of your exam. Be prepared to show your AARP membership card. To find a provider in or near your zip code as well as how much you'll save on the eye exam, go to www.aarp.org (select "Member Discounts and Services" and then "Vision Discounts"); or call AARP Vision Discounts toll-free at 888-352-3924. Many independent eyeglass providers also offer this discount, so be sure to ask! For more eyewear savings, see "Designer Frames for 60% Off," and "Try On Half-Price Frames Online," both on page 74.

Free Alzheimer's Helpline

The Alzheimer's Association operates a 24/7 toll-free Helpline for people who need information or support for dealing with individuals who have this disease. The staff answers questions about memory loss, dementia, Alzheimer's medications and other treatments, living-arrangement decisions, legal and financial issues, and how to find the best care. In addition, the Helpline can guide you during a crisis and refer you to community programs for continuing support. The Helpline number is 800-272-3900; or learn more at www.alz.org.

Another reliable source of assistance is the Alzheimer's Disease Education & Referral Center (ADEAR), a government-funded service of the National Institute on Aging. ADEAR can answer questions, send you free publications, and direct you to clinical trials and services in your area. Call 800-438-4380; or go online at www.nia.nih.gov/alzheimers/alzheimersinformation.

Free Medical Facts at Your Fingertips

For medical information on issues of particular interest to seniors that's up-to-date, authoritative (it's from the National Institutes of Health), and easy to understand, go to nihseniorhealth.gov. A click away are a free quarterly magazine, directories of resources and providers, access to a database of millions of medical articles (many summarized), information about drugs and herbal supplements, and free subscriptions to e-mail alerts on topics of your choice. Developed especially for seniors by the National Institute on Aging and the National Library of Medicine, the site features large print that can be made even larger. The "Speech On/Off" option at the top of each page enables you to have the copy on the page read aloud. (Bring a set of headphones if you plan to do this at a public library computer.)

Elder-Care Benefits from Employers

More and more companies are offering benefits to employees who are helping their elderly relatives. These benefits range from referral services for finding caregivers and legal help to adding an elder to an employee's health insurance plan to free emergency elder-care services, such as placing an in-home aide with the senior after an operation. Some companies offer emergency elder care for free; others charge a small copayment. Find out what your company offers. State governments are also beginning to help employees with elder-care problems. While the federal government allows up to twelve weeks of time off each year under the Family and Medical Leave Act, that time is unpaid and thus not viable for many people. California's answer to this situation is a program that pays 55 percent of an employee's wages (up to a maximum of $728 per week) for up to six weeks' leave to care for an ill parent or relative. Other states may follow California's lead.

Free Prescription Medicines

If you have a limited income and need help paying for medications, even if you have Medicare Part D drug coverage, you may qualify for free or nearly free prescription medicines from a patient assistance program. The Partnership for Prescription Assistance will match you with the programs best suited to your needs. The PPA can also direct you to a free health clinic in your area. Call toll-free 888-4PPA-NOW (888-477-2669) to talk with a specialist; or visit www.pparx.org, where you can find programs for which you could be eligible. RxAssist is another program that can help you find free or affordable medications; go to www.rxassist.org.

Free Health Booklets for Seniors

No matter what your age, the National Institute on Aging has many free publications about topics of interest to folks 50 and older, such as healthy aging, exercise, safety, care-giving, illnesses, medicines, doctors, planning for the future, and more. You can read some publications online (in English or Spanish) at www.nia.nih.gov; or order those and others by calling toll-free 800-222-2225 or by writing to the National Institute on Aging, Building 31, Room 5C27, 31 Center Drive, MSC 2292, Bethesda, Maryland 20892.

Q **How old do I have to be to start collecting Social Security?**

A The age at which people can retire with full Social Security benefits has crept up—it now ranges from 66 to 66 and 10 months for those born from 1943 to 1959, to 67 for those born in 1960 and later. You can collect benefits as early as age 62, but the amount per month will be less because it's extended over more years. Wait until your full retirement age and you'll receive your full monthly benefits. If you delay collecting until you reach age 70, you'll pocket even more per month because the payout is over fewer years, based on average life expectancy. To find out what your Social Security benefit would be at different retirement dates and levels of future earnings, use the Social Security Administration's free online calculators at www.ssa.gov/planners/calculators.htm.

Medicare and Social Security

Free Medicare Information

A treasure trove of free services and resources, in both English and Spanish, www.medicare.gov is the official U.S. government website for people with Medicare. Among its many features are:

- *Medicare and You,* a summary of Medicare benefits, rights, and protections and answers to frequently asked questions. The 104-page handbook is available in PDF format in both English and Spanish.
- MyMedicare.gov: a free, secure Web portal that lets registered beneficiaries access personalized information about benefits and services. Users can view claim status and eligibility and enrollment information, view or modify prescription drug lists, replace a Medicare card, access online forms, and more.

The site also enables beneficiaries to compare Medicare Part D Prescription Drug Plans, Medigap policies in their areas, and local hospitals and nursing homes. There's a Long-Term Care Planning Tool, a directory of participating physicians, and a directory of helpful websites and phone numbers, including Medicare's toll-free main information line: 800-633-4227. If you're on Medicare, this is one website you'll definitely want to bookmark.

Free Counseling on Medicare Rights

The Medicare Rights Center is the largest independent source of help and information for people with Medicare. It offers free counseling, operates several hotlines, publishes a terrific free weekly e-newsletter called *Dear Marci,* lets you compare Medicare plan options, gives you a resource list of discount drug programs, and more. Visit www.medicarerights.org; or call the toll-free consumer hotline at 800-333-4114 between 9 a.m. and 5 p.m., Eastern time, Monday through Friday.

"Extra Help" from Medicare to Cut Drug Costs

Low-income people 65 and older may qualify for free or low-cost prescription drugs under special Medicare programs known as "Extra Help." Find out more at www.medicare.gov, at www.medicarerights.org, or at www.aarp.org/medicarerx. At the AARP site, you can also view, download, or order two free guides:

The New Medicare Prescription Drug Coverage: What You Need to Know and *Extra Help for People with Limited Incomes.*

Free State Help on Medicare from SHIP

The State Health Insurance Assistance Program (SHIP) is a national program that offers free help and individual counseling to people insured by Medicare and their families. The program is funded by federal grants directed to the states. SHIP's trained counselors are prepared to advise beneficiaries, by phone, e-mail, or in person, on such topics as Medicaid and Medicare Advantage eligibility, enrollment, claims, fraud and abuse, Medicare Supplemental Insurance, and more. To contact the SHIP in your state or to find a counselor near you, go to www.shiptalk.org and click on the appropriate link; or call toll-free 800-MEDICARE (800-633-2273) and ask for health-insurance counseling.

Free Social Security Publications

The Social Security Administration issues a wide variety of free informational booklets and brochures for its various programs. Three especially useful ones are *Understanding the Benefits* (#05-10024), *What Every Woman Should Know* (#05-10127), and *Retirement Benefits* (#05-10035). To read these and other SSA publications online or download them in PDF format, go to www.ssa.gov/pubs/englist.html. Another great source of free information on retirement planning and money matters in general is the website www.mymoney.gov; click on "Retirement Planning" or any other topic of interest listed.

More Help for Seniors

Property Tax Relief for Senior Homeowners

If you own your own home and are over 65, you could be eligible to pay reduced property taxes, depending on your state's current tax rules. New York's School Tax Relief Program allows qualifying senior homeowners to exempt $50,000 of their primary home's value from school property taxes. A home can be a house, condo, co-op, mobile home, or farm home. To qualify in 2006, annual income had to be under $66,050. In Texas, qualifying seniors can exempt

Time Is Money

Are You Eligible for More Benefits

You may be entitled to receive benefits from government and private programs—and not know it! Since this is true for many Americans age 55 and older, the National Council on Aging has devised a very easy-to-use online service to identify programs a senior might be entitled to. More than 1,300 programs exist, covering health care and medicines, supplemental income, transportation, meals, rent, property taxes, heating bills, legal advice, and more. Benefits are in the form of financial help or low-cost services. Just log on to www.benefitscheckup.org and fill out the confidential comprehensive Benefits CheckUp questionnaire to get a list of the programs for which you may be eligible, along with a description and contact info.

Avoid Higher Medicare Premiums

If you are 65 or older and a U.S. citizen and have worked for at least 10 years in Medicare-covered jobs, you are entitled to free coverage under Medicare Part A, which helps cover costs at hospitals, skilled nursing facilities, and hospices, and for some home health care. Part B, for which most people pay a monthly fee, helps cover doctor and outpatient fees, lab work and x-rays, and other things Part A doesn't cover. Part D is Medicare's prescription drug benefit, for which you need to choose a plan and pay fees.

If you are already receiving Social Security benefits when you turn 65, you will automatically receive a Medicare card. If a card doesn't arrive, call the Social Security Administration toll-free at 800-772-1213; or contact your local Social Security office. You can sign up for Part A at any time. But if you don't sign up for Part B during your initial enrollment period—three months before and after you turn 65—and decide to enroll later, the premiums will be higher for as long as you have the coverage. Worse still, it will cost more for every year you delayed taking it. (There's also a penalty for not enrolling in a Part D prescription drug plan when you first become eligible; for a basic overview of Medicare Part D eligibility and enrollment rules, go to www.medicare.gov/pdphome.asp and www.aarp.org/health/medicare/drug_coverage). If you or your spouse is working and has health insurance and/or drug coverage, you can postpone signing up for Parts B or D without penalty. If you are retired and have health insurance through your former employer, you should still enroll in Medicare because your retiree insurance will kick in only after Medicare does.

$25,000 of their home's value from school taxes. To get these types of savings, seniors must file an application with the local town tax assessor's office. It's worth the trouble to file—more than two million senior New Yorkers saved nearly $700 apiece in 2005-2006 and more than 600,000 saved more than $1,000 apiece. For more information, inquire at your local tax assessor's office or with your state Department of Taxation and Finance.

Free Assistance with Tax Forms from IRS and AARP

People ages 60 and older can get free tax guidance and help with filling out forms from IRS-trained volunteers under the Internal Revenue Service's Tax Counseling for the Elderly program. Call the IRS toll-free at 800-TAX-1040 (800-829-1040); or check online at www.irs.gov or www.cfda.gov to find the IRS office closest to you. Also from the IRS is Tax-Aide, an AARP–administered program that places trained tax volunteers at thousands of convenient sites like libraries, senior centers, and malls during tax season to help low- and middle-income people, especially those 50 and older, fill out their tax forms. Tax counselors are also available to answer phone queries. To find the nearest Tax-Aide site, call toll-free 888-AARP-NOW (888-227-7669); log on to www.aarp.org/money/taxaide; or use the IRS contact information given above.

Free Tax Deduction Summary from the U.S. Senate

If you want to see all the deductions seniors are entitled to, get a copy of the free U.S. Senate Special Committee on Aging report "Protecting Older Americans Against Overpayment of Income Taxes." To download the four-page publication, go to www.aging.senate.gov and do a Quick Search for "Protecting Older Americans"; or request a copy by calling 202-224-5364.

Free Legal Hotlines for Seniors

More than half the states have free legal hotlines just for people ages 60 and up. The hotlines are staffed by attorneys who can give you advice over the phone. Some may also review a document for you, prepare a letter, or provide you with a legal form—but there might be a small fee for such services. Some hotlines are limited to specific areas of the law. If you need additional legal help, the hotline can refer you to a legal services program or a lawyer who won't charge an arm and a leg. To find out if you live in a senior-hotline state, go to www.aoa.gov/eldfam/elder_rights/legal_assistance/legal_hotline.asp or to AARP's www.legalhotlines.org; or call your local Area Agency on Aging (see "The National Aging Network," page 293).

Free Legal Consultation

If you're an AARP member, you (and a spouse or partner) can get a free 30-minute consultation with a lawyer in your area to answer a question or learn how to solve a legal problem. If you hire a lawyer from AARP's Legal Services Network, you'll get a 20 percent discount on services and be entitled to a lower fixed fee for a will or a power of attorney. It's a good idea to prepare carefully for any meeting with a lawyer, and AARP has some useful tips for you to follow on its website. Go to www.aarp.org/lsn to find a lawyer near you and get other helpful legal information. If there is no lawyer in your area, call toll-free 888-687-2277; or write to AARP Legal Services Network, 601 E Street NW, Washington, D.C. 20049.

EDITOR'S CHOICE

Finding Elder-Law Attorneys

You can be connected with an elder-law specialist—many certified by the National Elder Law Foundation—in your area at www.elderlawanswers.com. You can also learn about various legal topics of interest to seniors (including retirement, estate planning, and long-term-care insurance), get advice on working with an attorney, and sign up for a free newsletter.

The website of the National Academy of Elder Law Attorneys, Inc. (www.naela.com) has a database of member lawyers that is searchable by zip code so you can find those nearest you. You'll find a list of questions to ask an elder-law attorney.

CHAPTER 16

active-duty personnel and veterans

Active and retired military servicemembers are entitled to a host of grants, benefits, and resources not available to civilians. Read here to see how your service can yield big savings.

By the **numbers**

1,178

Monthly pay, in dollars, that a new U.S. military enlistee made in the 2006 fiscal year. This does not include allowances for clothing, food, housing, and other special bonuses.

WHEN YOU SIGNED UP FOR A TOUR of duty in the armed forces, you put yourself in line to receive a lifetime's worth of great benefits. We honor our active-duty servicemembers and our veterans with financial aid for education, low-cost health care, low-interest home loans, discounts on travel and shopping, help finding a job, and much, much more. The benefits to which servicepeople, their families, and veterans are entitled range from a free day at an amusement park to a helping hand with child care to a loan guaranty to buy a home or a college education via the GI Bill.

You can start taking advantage of your military privileges the minute you sign on the dotted line, and the Servicemembers Civil Relief Act (SCRA) goes into effect. When you're in the armed forces, you get used to programs with long names and snappy acronyms like this—they're everywhere in military life. Many lead you to big savings. SCRA does so by limiting the amount of interest you pay on your credit card debts to 6 percent and allowing you to defer life insurance payments while you're in the service.

There are a lot of similar money-saving schemes around, and if you're a member of the armed forces or a veteran you'll do well to keep an eye out for everything to which you and your family are entitled. Because there is so much out there, it's important to:

- Keep informed. Check in with the Family Services Office on your base; research health plans and other services available from the Department of Veterans Affairs (VA); and see how AMVETS, the American Legion, and dozens of other organizations can serve you. Throughout this chapter, you'll find dozens of resources that help you keep up to date with the many benefits you've earned.
- Take full advantage of what you deserve. In this chapter, you'll find many ways to save money that are sometimes overlooked, like re-using your VA loan guaranty to purchase a retirement home, or making sure that you and your college-bound kids check out all the many scholarship opportunities available through your military connections. And don't overlook the education benefits you're entitled to even if you don't want to go to college—the GI Bill also applies to trade-school and on-the-job training programs. Sometimes all you need to do is ask.

One last word of advice—and consider this an order. Enjoy the many benefits earned by serving your country. You deserve them.

Know Your Benefits

A Go-To Website for Free Info

Whether you've just signed up for service or are reminiscing about your World War II experiences, you'll do yourself a big favor by making sure you know about the many benefits and bargains available to members of the armed forces, veterans, and their dependents. Military.com is a Web-based military and veteran organization with eight million members that does a first-rate job of rounding up the array of benefits to which members of the military and veterans are entitled. You can join the group for free, and even nonmembers can access detailed explanations of the GI Bill, Veterans Affairs health care, and other benefits. Membership brings such advantages as the chance to peruse job listings, hook up with military buddies, and take advantage of discounts on shopping and other services.

Editor's Choice

Service Sites for Active-Duty Benefits Listings

Members of the armed services should make frequent visits to the websites of their branches, where updated listings of financial-assistance resources, family services, vacation and recreation opportunities, and other benefits are posted:

- For the Army: www.army.mil/wellbeing
- For the Navy and the Marine Corps: www.lifelines.navy.mil
- For the Air Force: www.af.mil (click on the AirForce OneSource link in the right column)
- For the U.S. Coast Guard: www.uscg.mil/hq/g-w/hrhome.htm

Essential Resources for Veterans

Your first step to reaping the financial rewards that are part of your veterans benefits is determining whom to contact for information and to order forms, determine eligibility, and ask detailed questions.

In general:

- For overall information about benefits: Call toll-free 800-827-1000 or visit www.va.gov.
- To find your nearest VA health centers, offices, and other facilities: Check with www.va.gov/directory/guide/home.asp.
- To order forms: Go to www.va.gov/vaforms.

For specific benefits:

- Education benefits: Call toll-free 888-442-4551 or visit www.gibill.va.gov.
- Burial and memorial benefits: See www.cem.va.gov.
- Home Loan Guaranty: Go to www.homeloans.va.gov.
- Survivor benefits: Check www.vba.va.gov/survivors.
- VA health care: Call toll-free 877-222-8387 or visit www.va.gov/health.

Basic Site for Free Vet Benefits Info

The U.S. Department of Veterans Affairs—established as a Cabinet-level department in 1989, succeeding the Veterans Administration—should be your first stop when looking into veterans benefits. Links from the home page on the VA website (www.va.gov) will lead you to detailed explanations of such benefits as health care, home loans, education opportunities, and burial services. Especially useful is the booklet *Federal Benefits for Veterans and Dependents,* available for reading online as a series of Web pages or in a downloadable PDF format; the link is on the VA's Public and Intergovernmental Affairs home page at (www.va.gov/opa). You'll also find lists of VA offices and medical facilities, with e-mail addresses, mailing addresses, and phone numbers.

Benefits and Bargains for Vets

Get Hefty Discounts with a Veterans Advantage Card

One of the great advantages of being a veteran is your eligibility for the Veterans Advantage card, a private-sector benefits program founded by veterans that offers vets and active servicemembers hefty discounts on a tempting menu of goods and services. Savings include a 15 percent discount on Amtrak tickets, 10 percent off Dell computers, special rates on long-term-care insurance, discounts at many car rental agencies, and much more. Browse an updated list of offerings and read about the program at www.veteransadvantage.com. A so-called "free" one-month trial membership actually carries a $4.95 processing fee; a regular one-year membership is $59.95, an amount that you will recover pretty quickly if you make use of the extensive discounts that come with membership. You can enroll online; however, on the website the fees and some other details you might care about are buried in hard-to-find fine print, so it's best to call customer service at 203-422-2526 to review fees and terms before investing in a membership.

Cost-Saving Benefits from Faith-Based Veterans Groups

Veterans of Jewish heritage can enjoy the benefits of membership in the Jewish War Veterans of America, while Catholic veterans can join the Catholic War Veterans of the U.S.A. In addition to providing a strong voice that helps lobby for veterans issues, these groups offer such cost-saving benefits as membership in low-cost group insurance plans, access to credit unions that offer low-cost loans, discounts on car rentals and long-distance calling plans, eligibility for scholarships, and more, including referral to useful resources for veterans. To learn more about these groups and their benefits, contact:

- Jewish War Veterans, 1811 R Street NW, Washington, D.C. 20009; call 202-265-6280, or visit www.jwv.org.
- Catholic War Veterans of the U.S.A, 441 North Lee Street, Alexandria, Virginia 22314; call 703-549-3622, or go to www.cwvorg.

Discounts on Amtrak for Actives and Vets

Your military service, past or present, entitles you to a discount on Amtrak. Active-duty servicemembers and their families receive 15 percent off most routes, including the popular Auto Train service to and from Florida (the discount applies to the rail fare only, not to the vehicle transport). Veterans holding a Veterans Advantage card (see "Get Hefty Discounts with a Veterans Advantage Card," opposite) save 15 percent on coach-class fares. To learn more, go to www.amtrak.com; or call toll-free 800-USA-RAIL (800-872-7245).

Q How can I find out which veterans benefits I qualify for?

A Free help is just a phone call away, at the National Association of County Veteran Service Officers (NACVSO), a network of trained professionals who work for state veterans-affairs departments, and at AMVETS, a veterans-service organization. Counselors at both are well briefed in the many benefits available to veterans and dependents, and advise veterans on what national and state benefits are available to them, help them complete and submit claims applications with the necessary documentation, and assist with follow-up. To locate one of these resourceful counselors, go to:

- NACVSO: Go to www.nacvso.org and click on the "Member States & Benefits" link.
- AMVETS: Visit www.amvets.org (click on "What We Do," then on "Veterans Services"); or call toll-free 877-7AMVETS (877-726-8387).

Housing Grants for Disabled Vets

Veterans with certain service-related disabilities may be eligible for some substantial housing-related benefits. For instance, those with permanent disabilities may be entitled to a $50,000 Specially Adapted Housing Grant to outfit a house they are purchasing or building to fit their needs, with a goal to ensuring an independent lifestyle. To learn the details, go to www.homeloans.va.gov/sah.htm. Veterans with disabilities may also be exempt from funding fees and some other costs associated with the loan; for more information, check with your Regional Loan Center (locate it at www.homeloans.va.gov/rlcweb.htm), or call toll-free 800-827-1000.

Adapt-a-Car Assistance for Service-Disabled

A service-connected disability needn't keep you off the road. Veterans and active servicemembers with disabilities that limit their ability to drive a conventional car—they may have lost a limb or have limited mobility in a joint—can receive up to $11,000 toward purchasing or adapting a car or other vehicle. For more information, contact your VA regional office toll-free at 800-827-1000.

Priority Farm Loans and Aid for Vets

If you find yourself humming "Green Acres is the place for me," then talk to the like-minded folks at the U.S. Department of Agriculture. The agency gives preference to veterans when allocating funds through its Farm Agency and Rural Development programs. Both administer a bumper crop of loans and guaranties for buying, improving, or operating farms, as well as housing in rural towns with populations of 20,000 or less. For more information, contact the Farm Service Agency at www.fsa.usda.gov or the Rural Development office near you (find a list at www.rurdev.usda.gov).

The GI Bill

Uncle Sam Wants You to Get a Free Education

The GI Bill has put a lot of Americans through college, and you'd be wise to take advantage of the enormous financial rewards of this package. In a nutshell, this benefit provides as much as $37,000, tax

The VA Home Loan Guaranty Program

You might not live like a king or queen while you're in the service, but the VA Home Loan Guaranty Program gives veterans a lot of help financing their castles once they reenter civilian life. The Department of Veterans Affairs is not the lender; the VA guarantees the loan that you obtain from a bank, mortgage company, or other lender.

VA-guaranteed loans are available to veterans who have served:

- 181 active-duty days during peacetime.
- 90 or more days in World War II or the Korean or Vietnam wars.
- 24 months of active duty since August 2, 1990.
- At least six years in the Selected Reserves or National Guard.

Eligibility extends to:

- Widows and widowers of veterans and active servicemembers who died as a result of service-connected disabilities, provided they have not remarried. Eligible, too, are surviving spouses who remarry after age 57, and spouses of servicemembers listed as missing in action or prisoner of war for more than 90 days.
- Veterans who want to use the loan a second time—provided they've paid off the original loan. The same loan guaranty that helped you buy your first house when you came out of the service could help finance your retirement home.

Loan benefits include no down payment (the VA guaranty covers the amount lenders would otherwise require to be paid up front); in many cases, lower interest rates than those on conventional loans; no prepayment penalties; and a mandatory one-year warranty that ensures a home built with VA-guaranteed financing meets VA standards and specifications.

Remember: VA home loans apply when you are buying a home, condominium, or manufactured home, and when you are renovating your home, buying a lot for a manufactured home, installing solar heating and other energy-efficient systems, or refinancing a home loan.

For general information, rules of eligibility, online videos and pamphlets, and frequently asked questions about the VA Home Loan Program, visit www.homeloans.va.gov. For phone numbers and other information for Regional Loan Centers where you can speak with a representative, go to www.homeloans.va.gov/rlcweb.htm.

For more information, contact your VA regional office, call 800-827-1000; or go to www.homeloans.va.gov/veteran.htm.

free, for higher education. The servicemember's contribution is only $1,200 (a $100 per month deduction in pay for 12 months while you're in the service). Eligible recipients include servicemembers who have put in at least two years of active duty, veterans with two or three years of service (depending on the amount of time for which you signed up), some activated National Guard and Reserve members, and others. Some points to keep in mind:

- Veterans can receive payments for 36 months of full-time study, and for the equivalent amount of part-time study.
- Payments can be applied to courses at colleges, universities, and at business, technical, or vocational schools; apprenticeship or on-the-job training; flight training; teacher-certification programs; preparatory courses necessary for admission to a college or graduate school; and other programs.
- Eligibility expires ten years after discharge from service, with some exceptions.

For more information, contact your local VA office; go to www.gibill.va.gov; or call toll-free 888-GI-BILL-1 (888-442-4551).

Get Paid for On-the-Job Training

You don't have to go school to take advantage of your GI Bill benefits. The On-the-Job Training Program allows you to receive up to $878 a month, for a total of $14,000 over two years, if you participate in an on-the-job or apprenticeship training program. The OJTP is open to men and women who have been out of the service for no more than ten years; are full-time, paid employees; are supervised 50 percent of the time; and meet other criteria. To learn more, contact your local VA office; go to www.gibill.va.gov; or call toll-free 888-GI-BILL-1 (888-442-4551).

GI Bill Education Benefits for Family Survivors

Dependents of veterans can benefit from the GI Bill, too. The Survivors and Dependents' Educational Assistance Program benefit picks up the tab, up to $827 a month, for spouses and children between the ages of 18 and 26 of veterans who died in action or from a service-connected disability. Benefits apply to colleges and vocational and business schools; they also cover correspondence courses for spouses. For more information and details on applying, contact your local VA office; go to www.gibill.va.gov; or call toll-free 888-GI-BILL-1 (888-442-4551).

Use Buy-Ups to Increase Your GI Bill Benefit

Talk about a good return on your investment. Buy-ups allow active service personnel to make an additional contribution of $600 to the standard $1,200 GI Bill contribution. Here's the payoff: For each $100 extra you contribute, you get $25 a month more in benefits. So, for the additional $600 contribution, you get an extra $150 a month, up to $5,400 over the three-year life of the GI Bill.

Beyond the GI Bill: AMVETS Scholarships

You might think that you and your college-age kids don't have much in common, but here's something you share. Vets as well as their children are eligible for an AMVETS National Scholarship to help cover the cost of college, junior or community college, or a trade or technical school. The veterans service organization awards $1,000 to $4,000 scholarships on the basis of scholastic achievement and demonstration of financial need. Only vets who have exhausted the GI Bill and other education benefits are eligible. To learn more, contact AMVETS at 877-7AMVETS (877-726-8387); or visit www.amvets.org.

Free Tuition Assistance for Actives

Active servicemembers can start getting their money's worth out of the military's great education benefits even before the GI Bill kicks in. The Armed Forces Tuition Assistance program pays up to 100 percent of tuition for members of the Army, Navy, Air Force, Coast Guard, and Marine Corps, as well as some Reservists and members of the National Guard. Each branch administers its own tuition-assistance program, so guidelines vary, but most branches pay as much as $4,500 a year for course work at accredited schools. To learn more, check with the Education Service Office of your military branch.

Health Benefits

VA Treatment for Service-Tied Health Problems

Vets who have suffered disabilities and in other ways sacrificed their good health in service to their country are entitled to extra health benefits that in many cases can help make life as a civilian easier. The VA provides special programs for:

DOD and VA Health Care Networks

Whether you are an active servicemember, a retiree, or a veteran, you have access to two of the world's largest—and least expensive—health care networks. The more you know about the health care benefits provided by the Department of Defense and the Department of Veterans Affairs, the more you'll save on services that range from checkups to hospitalization to prescriptions to dental care. The two networks are:

- *TRICARE,* the military health care program for active servicemembers, retirees, and their families. Some Reservists and National Guard members are also eligible. The amount of coverage and costs vary among the three TRICARE levels: Prime, Standard, and Extra.
- *The VA Medical Benefits Package,* for any former member of the armed forces who received an honorable discharge. Participants are assigned to Priority Groups that deliver different levels of care at varying costs.

The first steps in taking advantage of these health benefits are to familiarize yourself with the networks and to determine the plans for which you are eligible and that work best for you. You'll find a thorough overview of TRICARE programs, eligibility, and benefits at www.mytricare.com; or you can call toll-free 877-363-6337. You can learn more about your veterans health benefits at the Veterans Health Administration home page (www.va.gov/health) or by calling toll-free 877-222-8387.

- Blind veterans, who may be entitled to rehabilitation programs and special equipment and visual aids.
- Veterans of the Gulf War, who are entitled to a free medical examination and treatment for Gulf War syndrome and other ailments related to service in the Persian Gulf.
- Veterans who were exposed to the defoliant Agent Orange in Vietnam.
- Veterans who were exposed to radiation at Hiroshima and Nagasaki, Japan, at the end of World War II.

For more information on services and eligibility, contact your nearest VA medical facility; or call the VA's toll-free number for special health issues: 800-749-8387.

Free Help for Returning Injured Vets

The Heroes to Hometowns program helps communities across the country honor injured veterans with a much-needed network of support. The Department of Defense and the American Legion work

EDITOR'S CHOICE Greyhound Discount for Trip to VA Facility

Heading to a Veterans Affairs hospital or clinic for treatment? If the trip involves travel, consider going by Greyhound bus. The company gives patients of VA facilities a 25 percent discount, but to take advantage of the savings, you have to utilize some of that paperwork of which the military is so fond—in this case, a Request for Reduced Rate Transportation form (VA 3068; see your VA hospital representative). There's no need, though, to schedule a doctor's visit to take advantage of other Greyhound savings for veterans. Any passenger holding a Veterans Advantage card (see "Get Hefty Discounts with a Veterans Advantage Card," page 316) gets a 15 percent discount.

with community groups, state and local governments, and other entities to provide services that help the vet and his or her family settle into civilian life—finding housing and equipping it for the disabled, creating a car pool for hospital visits, arranging child care, and much more. For more information from the Department of Defense, call toll-free 703-692-2054, or go to www.militaryhomefront.dod.mil (click on "Troops and Families," then "Military Severely Injured Support"). Or check the American Legion website (legion.org; click on "Veterans Get Help" under "Military Support").

Free Airfare to VA Hospitals for Injured Servicemembers

Money shouldn't keep servicemembers who have been injured in the line of duty from spending time with their loved ones, and that's why Operation Hero Miles provides free airfare to servicepeople who are undergoing treatment at Veterans Affairs medical centers as a result of their service in Afghanistan and Iraq, as well as to their families. Servicemen and -women able to travel may use the tickets to visit family during the course of treatment, or family members can use the tickets to visit servicemembers who are recovering at VA medical centers. Many U.S. airlines supply the tickets, using frequent-flier miles that civilian travelers donate. For more information on how to take advantage of Operation Hero Miles—or how to donate miles to the program—go to www.heromiles.org.

Low-Cost Accommodations for Family Visitors

Families visiting injured servicemembers who are receiving care at VA and military medical centers can find homelike and extremely low-cost accommodation at a Fisher House—one of 34 residences (four more are in design or under construction as of mid-2006) funded by the philanthropic Fisher House Foundation. Usually located within walking distance of medical facilities, the houses provide lodging for an average cost of less than $10 a day. They accommodate 16 to 42 guests, who share kitchens, living rooms, and laundry facilities during stays that average 12 to 14 days. Since the first Fisher House began welcoming visitors in 1990, the program has served more than 70,000 families and saved them an estimated $60 million. For more information, go to www.fisherhouse.org; or call toll-free 888-294-8560.

Editor's Choice

Special VA Benefits for Women

Some 1.2 million of the 26 million U.S. veterans are women, and the numbers are growing. If you're one of them, you're entitled to the services of 130 women's clinics in the Veterans Affairs system and eight Women Veterans Comprehensive Health Centers around the country. Special services include osteoporosis screening, menopausal care, infertility treatment, maternal health, and counseling for domestic violence. For more information, see the Women Veterans Coordinator at your local VA hospital; or visit the VA Center for Women Veterans website: www.va.gov/womenvet.

R & R Benefits for Actives

See Disney World at Reduced Prices

Folks in central Florida are sprinkling a little magic dust to make a visit to DisneyWorld and other area attractions affordable for visiting military servicemembers and their families. Bargains include:

- Reduced-price tickets to such Disney attractions as the Magic Kingdom, Epcot, Disney MGM Studios, Animal Kingdom, and Typhoon Lagoon and other water parks.
- Reduced rates at Disney's Swan and Dolphin Resort in Lake Buena Vista and at Radisson Resort Orlando.

You'll find an overview of discounts and links that help you take advantage of them at an unofficial online guide to Walt Disney World called Dis; just go to www.wdwinfo.com and click on "Military Discounts."

Free Admission to Busch Parks

As part of the Budweiser Here's to the Heroes program, Anheuser Busch offers active members of the military, Reserves, or National Guard and up to three dependents complimentary one-day, once-a-year admission to its Adventure Parks: SeaWorlds in Orlando, San Diego, and San Antonio; Busch Gardens in Tampa, Florida, and Williamsburg, Virginia; Sesame Place in Bucks County, Pennsylvania; Water Country USA in Williamsburg; and Adventure Island in Tampa. To take advantage of your free day's outing, go to the website herosalute.com, fill out the brief registration form, submit it electronically, and then print out a copy. After that, all you have to present it at the park you choose to visit along with your valid active-duty service ID.

Cheap Campgrounds Across America

Seems like some soldiers never get tired of sleeping in a tent. The armed services operate campgrounds and RV parks across the country, many of them located on military installations and available to traveling servicepeople for free and at very low cost. You can find these facilities together with a description of what they offer, at the "Paths Across America" page of the Army's MWR website (www.armymwr.com; click on "Travel," then scroll down and click on "Paths Across America"); you'll also find listings of private campgrounds and RV parks that offer favorable rates to traveling servicemembers.

Uncle Sam's Top-Notch, Low-Cost Resorts

You knew when you signed up that serving in the armed services wasn't going to be a vacation. But when you're actually going on vacation, you can save a lot of money at hotels and resorts around the world operated by the Armed Forces Recreation Group and other not-for-profit military groups. Raising the standards of military housing to new heights, these properties include Shades of Green, a hotel and resort complex at Walt Disney World in Florida (www.shadesofgreen.org); the Marines Memorial Club & Hotel, in downtown San Francisco (www.marineclub.com); Hale Koa, a resort on Waikiki Beach in Honolulu (www.halekoa.com); and Edelweiss Lodge and Resort, a retreat in the Bavarian Alps of Germany (www.edelweisslodgeandresort.com). These and other hostelries provide low-cost lodging to active servicemembers and their families, disabled veterans, and some other guests. For a good overview of what's available, go to www.armymwr.com/portal/travel/recreationcenters or to www.military.com/travel.

Low-Cost Vacation Deals

Airline employees looking for low-cost vacations have long booked with Interliner, a travel agency whose sole mission has been to provide the industry with low-cost cruises and resort packages. Now Interliner is extending the same deals to military personnel, offering

EDITOR'S CHOICE

Off-Duty Travel Bargains

When it's time for some off-duty relaxation, head for offdutytravel.com, a website where the U.S. Army's MWR (Morale, Welfare, and Recreation) service rounds up great travel deals. You don't have to be in the Army to participate—active-duty and retired members of any branch of the armed forces, Reserves, and National Guard, as well as family members and civilians employed by the Defense Department, can take advantage of low-cost airfares, cruises, and hotel packages. Offerings range from $244-a-week resort condo rentals to a $1 per month membership in the Good Sam Club, the world's largest group of "Good Samaritan" RV owners.

Help for Military Families

If you're part of a military family, you will want to pay regular visits to two websites: www.militaryonesource.com and www.militaryhomefront.dod.mil. Military HomeFront is the official Department of Defense website for troops and their families and is a clearinghouse for resources offered by government agencies and the private sector; it's loaded with info about military housing, pay, insurance, and other matters. Military OneSource is a roundup of services and benefits that help make military life more livable.

Here are some more helpful sources for military families:

Free Family Support from the American Legion

Members of the American Legion take an "I've been in your shoes" approach and offer free support to families of active service personnel deployed overseas. Knowing full well what the stress of separation during war is like, these volunteers help out military spouses with grocery shopping, child care, lawn care, fixing the family car, and other chores. To request assistance, call toll-free 800-504-4098; or send an e-mail to familysupport@legion.org.

Discounted Relocation Assistance

Many private-sector companies offer military families hefty discounts to help lighten the financial load of relocation. These discounts include (as of mid-2006) 50 percent off the cost of shipping pets on American Airlines; a month of free service from Extra Space, one of the largest self-storage outfits in the United States; and savings on home closing costs from Military Relocation Services. You'll find these and other savings at www.military.com/discounts, under "Relocation."

Free Car Care for Air Force Families

When Air Force servicemembers fly off for deployments, the Car Care Because We Care program of the private, not-for-profit Air Force Aid Society takes care of the land-based vehicle you care about most: the family car. Stateside spouses can get free oil and filter changes, lube jobs, and safety checks. And a major problem needn't ground you—you may be entitled to an interest-free loan for repairs. For information on the many ways the society lends a helping hand to Air Force families, go to www.afas.org; or check with the Family Support Centers on most Air Force bases.

For Expectant and New Parents

There are any number of free services for military parents-to-be. Members of the Navy and Marine Corps anticipating the blessed event or adjusting to parenthood are entitled to a free layette (also known as a Junior Seabag) that includes bedding and clothing for the little one, and comes with free lessons in budgeting for baby. Air Force parents can expect a delivery of Bundles for Babies that includes blankets and diapers. To learn about programs for expecting and new parents, check with the Family Services Office of your branch of service.

Help Finding Subsidized Child Care

Minding the kids when duty calls is easier and cheaper with Operation: Military Child Care, a program coordinated by the Department of Defense and the National Association of Child Care Resource and Referral Agencies. Families of active-duty servicemembers and members of the National Guard and Reserves are eligible for assistance in locating licensed child-care centers in their communities and receive a subsidy to help defray the costs. Eligibility extends through the first 60 days after return from active duty, as well as for 60 days while a nonmilitary spouse looks for a job. For terms of eligibility and to find a participating child-care provider, contact Child Care Aware, a program of the National Association of Child Care Resource and Referral Agencies (NACCRRA) toll-free at 800-424-2246; or log on to www.childcareaware.org.

Free Advice for Military Teens

Army brats, unite! If your mom or dad is in the military and you move around a lot, think of yourself as being part of an elite club. Military Teens on the Move is a cool website designed just for you, loaded with free advice on adjusting to a new place, links to free online dictionaries and study aids, info about sponsorship programs that match you up with kids your age when you get to the new base, and a lot more. Check it out at www.dod.mil/mtom.

Commissary Scholarships for Military Children

You can pick up more than low-cost groceries at the commissary on your base. If you have college-age kids, grab an application for the Scholarships for Military Children program. Every year, the $1,500 award is presented to at least one student associated with each of the 265 commissaries around the world. The scholarships are intended to help take the sting out of tuition, fees, and room and board for full-time students with a parent on active duty or who are Reservists, members of the National Guard, or retired from the military. Survivors of deceased members of the military who have military dependent ID cards can also apply. To find a commissary near you, check www.commissaries.com.

Service Branch Scholarships for Family Members

Many parents worry about the cost of educating their children. Those in the military can get a little extra help with scholarships awarded exclusively to the children of active, retired, and deceased servicemembers. Scholarships vary considerably, depending on the service branch; awards include $2,000 for an academic year to dependent children of servicemembers who are serving or have served aboard the USS *Tennessee*, and many annual grants of $1,000 given to vets by the not-for-profit Image America Foundation. Other family members can benefit too: The Army's Stateside Spouse Education Assistance Program helps defray educational costs for spouses of active-duty Army soldiers, as well as widows and widowers of Army soldiers who have died while on active duty. To learn more about the many scholarships available, contact the Family Services Office of your service branch. To see what scholarship funds might be available to your family, use the handy Scholarship Finder at aid.military.com/scholarship.

Servicemembers Civil Relief Act

Joining the service is one way to avoid the high interest on your credit card debts. The Servicemembers Civil Relief Act (SCRA) is a federal law that provides active servicemembers with a great deal of financial and legal protection, so they can "devote their full energy to the defense needs of the nation." What this means is that SCRA can save you a lot of money, by:

- Placing a limit of 6 percent interest on debts incurred before active duty began.
- Allowing you to terminate leases and other contracts.
- Allowing you to defer life insurance payments for two years during service and up to two years after leaving the armed forces.
- Protecting against foreclosure on mortgages and other installment loans if you cannot meet payments.

To learn more about the protection to which SCRA entitles you, contact the Legal Assistance Office of your service branch.

some of the best buys around on Caribbean cruises, room-and-meal packages in Mexico, and other good-value R & R opportunities. Interliner's low rates are valid for currently employed and retired airline employees and military servicepeople, reservists, and their parents; veterans qualify for many of the special rates. You can browse through the offerings at www.interliner.com, and call toll-free 800-421-2261 to discuss rates and other details.

Financial Matters

Capital Gains Tax Break on Home Sales

Military personnel stand to benefit from a provision of the capital gains regulations. By law, all taxpayers are excluded from paying capital gains tax on up to $250,000 for an individual and $500,000 for a married couple in profits earned from the sale of a home that has been a principal residence for at least two years during a five-year period. Military personnel can extend the residency requirement to two years during a ten-year period, provided they have been assigned to an active-duty post 50 miles or more from their primary residence. To learn more, contact the Legal Assistance Office of your service branch.

Free or Discount Help Filing Taxes

The bad news is that if you're in the military, you still have to pay taxes. The good news is that military personnel can often have their taxes prepared by professionals for free or at discounted rates. Many bases have tax centers that help you file, for free. Jackson Hewitt, the national tax-service giant, takes $20 off the cost of tax preparation for military personnel and vets through such membership sites as military.com, militaryconnections.com, and VALoans.com. TurboTax offers free and reduced-price tax preparation and e-filing services for some military personnel. Check www.statetaxfreedom.com for more information and to find out if you are eligible to use the online service without charge.

Emergency Help for the Financially Squeezed

Soldiers, sailors, and other servicepeople—often including vets—who find themselves in a financial squeeze may be able to find some help at the relief and assistance societies associated with the various branches of the military. Army Emergency Relief (www.aerhq.org), Coast Guard Mutual Assistance (www.cgmahq.org), the Air Force Aid Society (www.afas.org), and the Navy-Marine Corps Relief Society (www.nmcrs.org) provide emergency financial assistance to active and retired servicepeople and their dependents for food, rent, medical expenses, and essential personal needs.

Bereavement Benefits

Extensive Free Assistance for Survivors

If your spouse died in active service, you and your dependents are entitled to the many free services and benefits that the Department of Veterans Affairs and other organizations provide. Benefits range from bereavement counseling to financial compensation to education and job-training opportunities. The first stop when looking for the benefits to which you may be entitled is the VA's Survivor Benefits Home Page (www.vba.va.gov/survivors), where you'll find an extensive, user-friendly overview of benefits and links to government agencies, armed services relief societies, and many other resources.

Q Do servicemembers qualify for free legal advice?

A Yes. One of the unsung benefits of military service is the free legal advice that Department of Defense Legal Assistance Offices provide to, among others, members of the armed forces on active duty, retirees, and members of the Reserves and National Guard on active duty and recently released from active duty. The offices are handy for such everyday tasks as notarizing documents, and can also draft wills, provide advice on leases and other landlord matters, answer questions on tax matters, and in some cases prepare and file forms, as well as handle such complex matters as divorce cases and immigration issues. To find Legal Assistance Offices, click on the link at www.military.com/benefits/legal-matters/legal-assistance.

Free Peer Support and Help for Survivors

There's no quick fix for the pain of losing a loved one, but the Tragedy Assistance Program for Survivors is on hand to help. This not-for-profit group is devoted solely to the survivors of service-members and veterans, offering free peer support, crisis intervention, assistance with paperwork associated with death and burial benefits, and a Good Grief Camp for youngsters. For more information, call the toll-free TAPS hotline at 800-959-TAPS (800-959-8277).

Free Help for Visiting Gravesites

Paying homage to a fallen relative can bring a great deal of emotional comfort. When doing so, you may be able to receive some financial assistance and free help from the American Battle Monuments Commission.

- Immediate family visiting the overseas graves and memorial sites of servicemembers who lost their lives in the two world wars may be eligible for a no-fee passport—a savings of $97.
- Visitors to graves and memorial sites can receive information on routes, transportation, and accommodations.
- The commission also helps locate gravesites, supplies photos of headstones and tablets of the missing, and provides other services.

Arranging a Military Burial

Servicemembers who die while on active duty and all veterans who have been discharged under any condition other than dishonorable are entitled to free burial in any of the 120 U.S. national cemeteries. In many cases, spouses and other dependents are also eligible. Other benefits include:

- A headstone, to be placed on a grave anywhere in the world, whether or not it's a national cemetery or a private facility.
- A burial flag.
- Perpetual care of the gravesite.
- An honor detail to perform a ceremony that includes the presentation of the flag and the playing of taps.

The same benefits apply to veterans interred in the veterans cemeteries that are maintained by many states. For a full description of burial benefits, call a Veterans Benefits counselor toll-free at 800-827-1000 or visit www.cem.va.gov/cem, where you'll also find a listing of national and state cemeteries. For questions about headstones and markers, call the VA's toll-free number: 800-697-6947.

For more information on these and other services, visit the American Battle Monuments Commission's website (www.abmc.gov), call 703-696-6900, or write to the American Battle Monuments Commission, Courthouse Plaza II, Suite 500, 2300 Clarendon Boulevard, Arlington, Virginia 22201.

Free Gold Star Lapel Buttons

Honor a family member who's been killed in action by wearing a Gold Star Lapel Button. You are entitled to a free pin if you are a parent, widow or widower, or child of a member of the U.S. armed forces who died in one of the world wars or a conflict since then. To apply for a button, go to www.military.com/benefits/survivor-benefits, click on "Gold Star Lapel Button," and download the form.

Back to Civilian Life

Free Storage of Belongings for Retirees

Retiring from the military and starting a new life as an ordinary civilian? Take your time to look around for a house, because you are entitled to store your belongings for free for up to one year at the last base where you were stationed. Should you need a little longer to settle down, you can request an extension. Free storage for household items is also available for up to 90 days for active military personnel who are relocating. To learn more, check with the Family Services Office of your service branch.

Free Mentoring from Former Military Members

You probably know all about the benefits of networking when it comes to looking for a job and advancing in your civilian career—learning about job openings, getting advice, meeting like-minded men and women who can help you climb the organizational ladder. Well, when you joined the military, you connected with one of the largest networks in the world, with thousands of veterans on hand to help you succeed in civilian life. Many offer their advice and a chance to talk about the job path of your choice through the Veteran Career Network on military.com. Just go to military.com/mentor and type in the field that interests you, along with location and

Editor's Choice

No-Cost Military Skills Translator

Most folks find it difficult to write a winning résumé. If you're a vet, you can get some free help creating and polishing that important document. HireVetsFirst.gov is a website sponsored by the Department of Labor to help veterans find jobs. Included are several handy, free résumé-writing tutorials, geared especially to translating military experience to the civilian sector, as well as a Military Skills Translator, an easy-to-use tool that helps you match your military training and education to specific jobs.

Free Resources for Entrepreneurial Vets

Veterans who want to start their own business should make a stop at VetBiz.gov, a website maintained by the Small Business Administration that steers entrepreneurial vets to free business help.

Resources include:

- Veterans Business Outreach Centers that provide business training, counseling, referrals, workshops, and other services for eligible veterans who own or are considering starting a small business.
- VetFran, a federally run program that informs veterans about franchise opportunities and helps them acquire franchises at a discount.

other optional criteria, and you'll find contact details for nearby vets who can help you find work in your chosen field.

Free Job Search Assistance

Servicemembers about to leave the military can get free job-search assistance, including help fine-tuning their résumés, from the Department of Labor's Transition Assistance Program. Three-day seminars, offered at many bases, help soon-to-be-civilian servicemembers assess their skills, set career objectives, and brush up on interview techniques. The Department of Labor reports that participants land jobs three weeks sooner that those who don't enlist in TAP. For more information, go to www.dol.gov/vets/programs/tap.

Free Job Counseling

Veterans get a little extra push into the job market at Career One-Stop Centers. These government-funded programs match employers and job seekers across the country. Many are staffed with specialists who provide vets with free interview coaching, career counseling, job placement, and other services that help make the skills they acquired in the military a plus when entering the civilian job market. To find a center near you, call toll-free 877-US2-JOBS (877-872-5627); or go to www.servicelocator.org. (For more on Career One-Stop Centers, see "No-Cost Federal Job-Search Help" and "Free Online Help," both on page 199).

Free Resource Advisor

Career counseling, federal and state benefits, training programs—it's easy to be overwhelmed by all the resources available to veterans making the transition from the armed services to the civilian job market. You can click your way through the many offerings and opportunities on the e-Vets Resource Advisor, on the Internet at www.dol.gov/elaws/vets/evets/evets.asp. The site does a lot of the search work for you; just click on the "General Services" button, then check out "Transition Assistance," "Opportunities with the Federal Government," and other categories of interest. The e-Vets Resource Advisor will bring up links to relevant websites.

CHAPTER 17

deals for people with disabilities

Having a disability is hard enough—never mind the effort and expense involved in purchasing items like hearing aids and prosthetics. Get what you need for less with these grants, giveaways, rebates, and deals.

By the numbers

35,000

Amount, in dollars, it costs to modify a home to make it quadriplegic accessible.

LIVING WITH A DISABILITY HAS NEVER BEEN EASY. The good news is that today a wealth of services and assistance is available for those who need it. Little things, like discounts on Broadway theater tickets and free hearing aid batteries. And big things, like free guide dogs, grants to purchase assistive devices, vocational training, and money from automakers to adapt a new car to your needs. Some of these offerings are provided by private associations and charities with long histories of doing good work; others stem from the Americans with Disabilities Act, which in 1990 provided recognition of and legislated support for persons with disabilities (see “The Americans with Disabilities Act,” page 337).

This chapter opens with descriptions of some of the government programs that serve persons with disabilities, such as those administered through the Social Security Administration and the various state departments of rehabilitation. Among these are some of the most basic and important programs, including ones that focus on sustenance and employment. We’ve also provided information about scholarships and cash grants available from public, private, and nonprofit groups, targeted specifically to disabled persons.

Is it your dream to study library science or nursing? Need funds in an emergency? You'll find help here. You'll learn about free and discounted assistive technologies, communication tools, and mobility aids that can help you do the things you want to do. You'll also learn about free or inexpensive programs—provided by both volunteers and government programs—to make your home safe, accessible, affordable, and comfortable.

Several items focus specifically on free or inexpensive aid for children with disabilities—programs, funds, and services that can help them learn, participate, and thrive. Again, the offerings range from the substantial (free medical care from the Shriners) to the small but important (free braille books for blind kids). You'll also find information about free or discounted recreational opportunities, both indoor and outdoor, from simple pleasures like reading and Web surfing to camping, skiing, fishing, and sailing.

Comprehensive as it is, this chapter is not all-encompassing; indeed, dozens and dozens of books, articles, and websites have been dedicated specifically to services, products, and funds available for disabled persons. One reason we can't cover every program or offering is that many services for persons with disabilities operate on a local level. To make the most of what's available in your community, see "Consulting a Social Worker," page 350, about the person who is often the gateway to local programs and services, and "For More Information," page 357, which lists organizations that are rich resources for further research.

Government Programs

Free State Rehabilitation Resources

Every state in the nation has a department of rehabilitation, funded in part by the federal government. These offices can provide money for education and training, assistive devices, help with health insurance, referrals to public, private, and nonprofit agencies, and many other services intended to help people with disabilities lead safe, productive, fulfilling lives. (Specific programs vary from state to state.) State department of rehabilitation services are free and are used by some 1.2 million Americans, more than 80 percent of whom are significantly disabled. Look in your phone book's state government pages under "rehabilitation" or "vocational rehabilitation," or consult your state government's website.

Vocational Rehabilitation Help in Florida

Florida's Able Trust (also known as the Florida Governor's Alliance for the Employment of Citizens with Disabilities) helps disabled Florida residents, and the organizations and schools that serve them, with vocational rehabilitation needs. For individuals, grants may cover equipment needed for employment, money for education, and assistance with small business start-up costs. Grants for employment-related accommodations average $2,000 to $3,000. In Florida, call toll-free 888-838-ABLE (888-838-2253); outside Florida, and for users of a teletypewriter (TTY) phone, call 850-224-4493. More information is available online at www.abletrust.org.

Free Federal Job Counseling

The U.S. Department of Labor's Job Accommodation Network is a free consulting service available to disabled job seekers and employers who want to hire, retain, and promote applicants with disabilities. Consultants, who work by telephone, answer questions and provide comprehensive, up-to-date information about accommodations (ranging from wheelchair ramps to flexible schedules), devices, and strategies for the disabled. Follow-up is by phone, e-mail, fax, or regular mail; information—including idea sheets for accommodating specific disabilities, product information on assistive technologies, and fact sheets about certain disabilities—are available in English and Spanish, in braille and large-print formats, and as audiotapes and CDs. To contact the network, call toll-free 800-526-7234 or visit its website at www.jan.wvu.edu.

Low-Interest Adaptive Equipment Loans

Many states offer low-interest loans for the purchase of adaptive or assistive equipment or services for persons with disabilities. One example is Credit-Able in Georgia (www.credit-able.org), which provides loan guarantees for Georgians and their employers to purchase hearing aids, vehicle modifications, computers, software, and other necessary tools. Other examples of similar loans in other states include Show Me Loans in Missouri (www.at.mo.gov/loans.shtm) and the TechConnect Low Interest Loan Program in Illinois (www.techconnect.iltech.org/home.aspx). The best way to find these programs is to visit your local independent living center (see "For

EDITOR'S CHOICE

Social Security Disability Program

If you're unable to work for a year or more due to a physical or mental impairment, the federal Social Security Disability program can replace part of your lost earnings. Benefits continue until you're able to work again, or until you reach Social Security's retirement age (at which time regular Social Security payments kick in). The main requirement is that you must have paid into Social Security for a certain period of time (the rules change from year to year). To begin the application process, which can be lengthy, contact your nearest Social Security office, call 800-772-1213 or TTY 800-325-0778, or apply online at www.ssa.gov.

The Americans with Disabilities Act

The landmark Americans with Disabilities Act, signed into law in 1990, was a culmination of decades of work by persons with disabilities and their advocates. It recognized persons with disabilities as full citizens, entitled to an active, meaningful life; gainful employment; education; and access to public spaces such as government buildings, stores, and restaurants. The ADA, among many of its benefits, opened the eyes of businesses nationwide to the fact that persons with disabilities are a substantial market to be served, rather than a group to be marginalized or pitied.

Prior to the ADA, many programs for persons with disabilities operated through private charities, especially ones associated with a particular type of illness (such as muscular dystrophy) or a specific disability (such as blindness or hearing loss) or injury. Many of these organizations still thrive and do excellent work for their communities—providing financial and in-kind assistance, delivering information, organizing social events and support groups, and advocating to various government groups. The legislative actions of the ADA and related government programs dovetail nicely with the operations of private and nonprofit groups.

More Information," page 357) or search your state website using the term "assistive loan program."

Telecommuting Loan Programs for Working at Home

Will your employer allow you to work at home? This kind of work, known as telecommuting or telework, appeals to some disabled people. Several states have low-interest loan programs to help individuals with disabilities acquire adaptive or assistive technologies designed specifically for telework, such as home office modifications or videoconferencing equipment. Notable programs include:

- The Iowa Telework Program (www.iowaable.org), which offers loans at 2 percent interest for amounts up to $10,000.
- The Utah Assistive Technology Foundation (www.uatf.org).
- The KATCO (Kansas Assistive Technology Cooperative) Telework Loan program (www.katco.net).

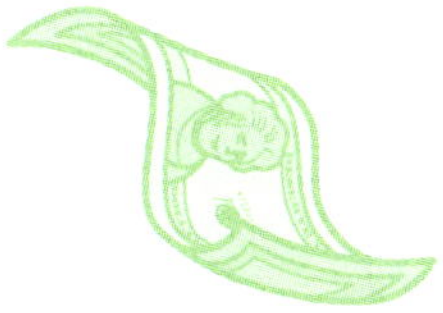

Federal Income Assistance

In addition to Social Security Disability, Supplemental Security Income can help blind and disabled people (and others) who have

What kind of financial assistance is available for disabled veterans?

Veterans who have served 90 days or more in wartime, who are permanently and totally disabled, and who are in financial need are eligible for an annual pension of $10,162 or more through the Department of Veterans Affairs—regardless of whether their disability is service-related. To apply, request VA Form 21-526 from your local or regional VA office.

little or no income. SSI is a federal program funded by general tax revenues, not Social Security taxes, and is intended for such basic needs as food, clothing, and shelter. To apply, contact your local Social Security Office or call toll-free 800-772-1213. For people who don't speak English, the Social Security Administration will provide an interpreter at no cost.

Federal Tax Credits

If you're retired on permanent and total disability, you may be eligible for the Credit for the Elderly or the Disabled when you pay your federal taxes. Even if you haven't retired formally, you're considered retired on disability when you stop working because of your disability. Use Schedule R for Form 1040 or Schedule 3 for Form 1040A to compute the credit. (You can't take the credit if you file Form 1040EZ.) The maximum amount of this credit is $1,125.

Property Tax Deductions

Property or income taxes got you down? Make sure you look into deductions, postponements, and exemptions to your state property taxes, as well as deductions or credits on your state income tax. For example, Florida residents who are blind or disabled may qualify for a $500 annual property tax exemption—and for veterans with a service-related disability, the amount climbs to $5,000. In Arizona, a property tax exemption for persons with disabilities reduces the assessed value of real property by up to $3,000 (and reduces property taxes accordingly). Since tax relief programs for persons with disabilities vary by state, a reliable tax adviser can help determine what's right for you.

Federal Hiring Incentives

An estimated 70 percent of blind or severely disabled Americans are unemployed. To help improve this bleak statistic, the federal government encourages the employment of the blind or severely disabled through the Javits-Wagner-O'Day (JWOD) Program. Run by the Committee for Purchase from People Who Are Blind or Severely Disabled (a federal agency), the program orchestrates government purchases of products and services from nonprofit organizations employing the blind or severely disabled. If you're interested in a job with such an organization, check the National Industries for the Blind website at www.nib.org, or visit the NISH (formerly National Industries for the Severely Handicapped) website at www.nish.org.

Scholarships and Grants

Specialty Scholarships

Plenty of scholarships are available in specific academic programs for individuals with disabilities. For example:

- Nursing students should check the pulse of scholarships offered through Exceptional Nurse (www.exceptionalnurse.com).
- Students of entomology—that's insects—should cast their net to include the Stan Beck Fellowship, sponsored by the Entomological Foundation (www.entfdn.org).
- If you're a graduate student studying communication sciences and disorders, read about scholarships that are available from the American Speech-Language-Hearing Foundation (www.ashfoundation.org).

Ask the counseling service at your school about scholarships that are right for you; or use the resources available through the Foundation Center (see "For More Information," page 357).

Scholarships for Women with Disabilities

Are you a woman with a physical disability attending graduate school? Look into an Ethel Louise Armstrong Foundation, Inc., scholarship, which provides between $500 and $2,000 per year for women with physical disabilities in master's and higher degree programs. Visit its website (www.ela.org) or call 626-398-8840.

Library Science Grants

Interested in advanced study in library science? Look up the Century Scholarship, offered by the American Library Association. This $2,500 grant funds services or accommodations at an ALA-accredited university offering a master's degree or doctorate in library science. (Funds can be used only for accommodations that aren't required by law, such as a large-screen text reader for a student's personal use.) ALA Century Scholars who work in a Texas library for two years can get an extra $2,000 through the Texas Library Association. For more information, visit the ALA site (www.ala.org/), or call toll-free 800-545-2433 or TTY 888-814-7692.

Federal Scholarship Info on Cassette

If you'd like to apply for a federal scholarship but have difficulty reading due to your disability, you can request a free cassette

EDITOR'S CHOICE Free Software for Legally Blind Students

Freedom Scientific, a producer of technology-based products for the blind and visually impaired, awards up to $20,000 worth of its software each year (20 individual titles costing $1,000 each) to students who are legally blind and attending college or graduate school in the United States or Canada. Among the products offered by the Freedom Scientific Technology Scholarship Award Program are the company's three software products: JAWS, a screen-reading program for Windows; MAGic, a screen-magnification program; and Open Book, a document-scanning and document-reading program. Learn more at the website www.freedomscientific.com.

recording of financial aid information. Call the Federal Student Aid Information Center toll-free at 800-4-FED-AID (800-433-3243) to request one. Their hours are 8 a.m. to midnight (Eastern time) Monday through Friday, and 9 a.m. to 6 p.m. on Saturday; services are available in English and Spanish.

Free Federal Grant-Finder Software

Two computer programs for searching federal and foundation/nonprofit grants are available for free download from their publisher, IDLOGIC. The programs—Grant Gate, which can also help you complete application forms for foundation and nonprofit grants, and Federal Money Retriever—can be used only for personal and home use, and not by organizations or companies. Go to www.grantgate.com/free.htm to get these valuable programs.

Local Aid for Persons with Disabilities

If you're disabled and need financial assistance, help may be right around the corner. Many small regional organizations provide assistance to persons with disabilities in their communities:

- In Howard County, Indiana, there's the Adams Rotary Memorial Fund.
- San Franciscans can contact the Avery Fuller Welch Children's Foundation or the Chronicle Season of Sharing fund.
- Connecticut options include the Bridgeport Ladies Charitable Society and Charitable Society in Hartford.
- Meridian, Mississippi, has the Care Consistency Foundation.
- In Cloud County, Kansas try contacting the Cloud County Children's Trust.

- Residents of Philadelphia can look up the Elizabeth Roe Dunning Club.

Similar groups exist in many communities around the nation; it may take some digging to locate them, but the resources in "For More Information," page 357, can help.

Cash Grants for Oregonians with Disabilities

The Blanche Fischer Foundation has assisted Oregonians with physical disabilities since 1981. The foundation gives direct cash grants to physically disabled residents of Oregon who demonstrate financial need. (It does not provide assistance for those with mental disabilities.) Recent grants have included $200 for van lift repairs for an individual in Gresham and $425 to a person in Grants Pass who needed hand controls for a vehicle. To request an application, call 503-819-8205 or send an e-mail to bff@bff.org. More information is available online at www.bff.org.

Assistance for Artists with Disabilities

The Artists' Fellowship Inc., a private charitable foundation headquartered in New York City, gives grants to professional fine artists who become disabled. Grants are available to painters, graphic artists, and sculptors (but not to commercial photographers, filmmakers, performance artists, and artists in other media). In 2004, the last year records were available, the fellowship gave 44 grants ranging from $300 to $11,100. Learn more and obtain an application at www.artistsfellowship.com or by calling 646-230-9833.

Financial Aid for Persons with Spine Injuries

Travis Roy was a promising hockey player at Boston University in 1995 when an accident in a game cracked his fourth vertebra,

Access Newspapers by Phone Free

The NFB Newsline, run by the National Federation of the Blind, makes some 200 newspapers nationwide available via telephone, including *The New York Times*, *The Washington Post*, *USA Today*, and *The Wall Street Journal*. Users can select newspaper, section, and articles by pushing buttons on a touch-tone phone. For a list of the newspapers available, visit www.nfb.org/nfb/Newspapers_by_Phone.asp. For information or to sign up, call toll-free 866-504-7300.

leaving him paralyzed from the neck down. Optimistic and ambitious in spite of his injury, he established the Travis Roy Foundation, dedicated to research and one-on-one assistance for individuals with spine injuries. The foundation has paid for upgrade and maintenance of wheelchairs, vehicle modifications such as hand controls and lifts, home modifications such as ramp and elevator installation, and other adaptive equipment. Grant recipients must reside in the United States and demonstrate financial need; grants typically range from $4,000 to $7,500 and are paid directly to equipment suppliers. Download a grant application from www.travisroyfoundation.org.

Assistive Technologies

Free Hearing Aids

Need a hearing aid but can't afford one? At least three charities—one for adults, two for children—provide hearing aids free of charge.

- Hear Now is a national nonprofit program for adult residents of the United States that collects and recycles used hearing aids from donors. Call toll-free 800-648-4237, go online to www.sotheworldmayhear.org/forms/hearnow.php, or write to Hear Now, 6700 Washington Avenue South, Eden Prairie, Minnesota 55344.
- The Miracle Ear Children's Foundation provides free hearing aids and services to children 16 years of age or younger in low-income families; to learn more, call toll-free 800-234-5422 or visit www.miracle-ear.com/resources/children_request.asp.
- The HIKE (Hearing Impaired Kids Endowment) Fund, a philanthropic project of Job's Daughters International, provides about 100 children (up to 20 years old) with hearing aids each year; learn more at www.thehikefund.org.

Lions Clubs Vision Programs

In 1925, Helen Keller addressed the Lions Clubs International convention and challenged members to be "knights of the blind in this crusade against darkness." The Lions took on the challenge and since then have provided many services for preventing blindness and mitigating its effects. Programs, which vary by community, include cornea banks, scholarships for the blind and visually impaired, assistive technology centers, transportation, and much more. In addition, Lions clubs offer vision screenings, eyeglasses, and sports goggles to Special Olympics athletes and provide quality eye care, eyeglasses, braille-writers, large-print texts, white canes, and guide dogs at no cost for thousands of people each year. To learn what's available in your area, send an e-mail to programs@lionsclubs.org.

Free Voice-Generation Software

Jouke Visser, a Dutch programmer with a disabled child, has created pVoice—a computer program for Augmentative and Alternative Communication. People with disabilities who cannot speak or type select photos or symbols in pVoice to generate speech output—the user can click on a picture of a glass to request a drink, or create words and phrases by clicking letters and word combinations. The program is available to anyone who wants it at www.pvoice.org. Visser and a team of volunteers have translated pVoice into 15 languages, from English to Chinese (additional software is required for some languages—see the website for details). Visser offers pVoice free of charge because, as he says, "Why should anyone be charged for such a basic need as communication?" We couldn't agree more.

No-Cost Computers in Indiana

Computers serve as a lifeline for many disabled people, especially those who have trouble with mobility and transportation. Disabled residents of Indiana can receive a free computer through Assistive Technology Through Action in Indiana (ATTAIN, Inc.), a public-nonprofit partnership. Its Attain-a-Computer program acquires donated computers from individuals, organizations, and companies; repairs them; installs legal, licensed software; and distributes them to disabled Indianans who lack the financial means to buy a computer on their own. For more information about the program and to obtain an application form, contact Attain-a-Computer at 317-486-8808, toll-free at 800-528-8246, or visit the group's website: www.attaininc.org. Similar computer-assistance programs exist in many other states and communities, and each has its own eligibility criteria. A listing of many such programs can be found online at www.resna.org/taproject/at/statecontacts.html.

EDITOR'S CHOICE

Free Hearing Aid Batteries

Got a hearing aid, but need new batteries? Sonus, a national hearing-care company, will provide one free card of hearing aid batteries if you will fill out a form on its website (www.sonus.com/freebatteries.asp).

Free Adaptive Phone Devices

Residents of some states can receive free or discounted telephone devices, including amplified phones, teletypewriter (TTY) phones, or alerting devices that flash or vibrate when the phone rings. Participating states include (but aren't limited to) Alaska, Arizona, California, Colorado, Illinois, South Carolina, and South Dakota. Go to your state website and search for TEDP, which stands for Telephone Equipment Distribution Program. In addition to traditional TTYs, most states have now rolled out the Captioned Telephone (CapTel) program, which uses automated speech recognition and a trained operator to put a caller's spoken words on a small screen on the phone. In most participating states, CapTel phones are free or deeply discounted. Visit www.captionedtelephone.com for information.

Phone Service for the Hearing Impaired

Hearing-impaired persons can use the 711 Relay service, a free program administered by the states, to talk with hearing people on the telephone. The hearing-impaired person types on a teletypewriter (TTY) phone, and the words are read to the hearing person by an operator, known as a communication assistant. When the hearing person responds, the communication assistant types the words, which appear on the TTY of the hearing-impaired person. Strict federal rules on confidentiality govern the behavior of communication assistants and ensure that no record is kept of the calls. To access the system, simply dial 711 from any phone.

Free Directory Assistance

If you have a disability that makes it difficult to operate a telephone, you may be able to get free directory assistance from your phone company. Contact your phone company's business office and ask how to apply. Typically, you'll be asked to have your doctor fill out

Making the Internet Accessible

Do you run a website for persons with disabilities or know of a site that needs to improve its accessibility? If so, check out the Web Accessibility Initiative at www.w3.org/WAI. It offers tips and advice for making a site useful for everyone. Some of its pages can be highly technical; you'll find clear, basic guidance by clicking on the "Evaluating Accessibility" link.

a form that you will submit. Note that the free service may cover only local, not national, directory assistance.

Staying Mobile

Half-Price Public Transportation

Many, many public transportation agencies around the country—from the largest (New York City's Metropolitan Transportation Authority, with more subway cars and buses than any other agency in North America) to the tiny (Middletown, Ohio, with just six buses)—offer discounts of 50 percent or more to persons with disabilities. While there's usually some paperwork and medical documentation involved, it's worth it—especially with the high price of gasoline. Contact your local transit agency for an application.

Low-Cost Paratransit Services

The Americans with Disabilities Act requires that most public transportation systems provide paratransit services—that is, curb-to-curb, shared-ride transportation—to individuals who can't use regular buses or trains. Paratransit is almost as good as a taxi, but at a small fraction of a taxi's cost; indeed, by law a ride on paratransit can cost no more than twice the cost of a regular bus or train ride. There are restrictions: You have to have a documented disability, and the trip must begin and end within three-quarters of a mile of a bus route or rail station. Many systems require you to book their services well in advance of your trip. Contact your local transit agency to apply. Locate your transit agency at ww.apta.com/links/state_local.

Greyhound Discount for Companion

Persons with disabilities who travel on Greyhound buses may bring a personal care attendant (PCA) with them for half of the regular fare. The attendant must ride with the passenger for the entire trip and be at least 12 years old. Request a PCA ticket at least 24 hours before departure, or 48 hours if you require a wheelchair lift-equipped bus.

Free Wheelchairs at Airports and Museums

Every major airport, many museums, and even some parks offer the use of a wheelchair at no cost. At airports, this service also includes someone to push the chair—an airport employee or contractor who knows how to find the proper luggage carousel, a bathroom, and the taxi stand (a lifesaver when you're in an unfamiliar airport). This service is free, though a tip of a few dollars is usually expected. When you check in for a flight, ask the ticketing agent, who can arrange for a wheelchair to take you to the gate and for one to be waiting for you at the end of your flight.

Free Guide Dogs for the Blind

Guide dogs provide many blind people with independence and mobility. Several organizations provide guide dogs free of charge, including these:

- Southeastern Guide Dogs, Inc., in Florida, Georgia, and North Carolina (www.guidedogs.org).
- Pilot Dogs in Ohio (www.pilotdogs.org).
- Guide Dogs for the Blind in California and Oregon (www.guidedogs.com).
- Guide Dogs of America (www.guidedogsofamerica.org) in California.

The Guide Horse Foundation (www.guidehorse.org) in North Carolina provides free miniature horses as guide animals for the blind. Most guide dog centers provide free transportation and room and board to individuals who are training to use a guide dog. For a list of 16 guide dog schools in the United States and contact information, visit www.gdui.org/schools.html.

No-Cost Hearing and Service Dogs

Guide dogs have worked with the blind for more than 70 years; much more recently, two other working dogs have come on the scene: Hearing dogs for the deaf and hard of hearing respond to doorbells, ringing telephones, and other audible cues; and service dogs for the disabled can turn on light switches, open doors, and provide a steady shoulder to lean on as a person moves from place to place. Like guide dogs, these animals are often available at no cost. To learn about hearing dogs, contact International Hearing Dog, Inc. (www.ihdi.org). For service dogs, contact Canine Companions for Independence at www.caninecompanions.org. Other organizations also help to provide these animals; for example, some SPCAs and humane societies train working dogs for persons with disabilities.

Reduced-Cost Prosthetic Limbs

You have to love an organization whose motto is "We're not asking for much … just an arm and a leg!" The Limbs for Life Foundation helps amputees in financial distress acquire advanced prosthetic limbs. The foundation helps about 700 amputees per year. A below-the-knee prosthesis normally priced at around $7,000 (in 2006) costs just $1,500 through Limbs for Life, while an above-the-knee prosthesis that would cost around $16,500 is available for just $2,000 through the foundation. Learn more online at the site www.limbsforlife.org or by calling toll-free 888-235-5462. Another organization that helps low-income amputees to get prostheses is the Barr Foundation Amputee Assistance Fund; visit it online at www.oandp.com/barr.

Equipment Loans for Coping with Disabilities

If you have trouble affording walkers, wheelchairs, hoists, or other equipment you need in order to live with your disability, look for an equipment closet or lending library run by a local charity or nonprofit. Examples include the RACORSE (short for Recycling, Allocation & Conservation of Operating Room Supplies & Equipment) Network in the San Francisco Bay Area (call 415-478-5405 or 510-251-2273), KC-HELP (for the Knights Community Hospital Equipment Lend Program) in Washington State (www.rc.net/knights/kc3307/help/help.htm), and the Kansas Equipment Exchange (www.equipmentexchange.ku.edu).

Wheelchair Giveaways

Wheelchairs are essential to mobility for some people with disabilities, but they can be expensive. If you can't afford a wheelchair, contact a nationwide program called Orphaned Wheelchairs, which matches used wheelchairs with people who need them, at 503-375-9523. In Wisconsin, look into the Wheelchair Recycling Program, with offices in Milwaukee and Madison or visit it online at www.wrp.org. The Easter Seals program in your area may also have wheelchair giveaway or recycling programs; enter your zip code at www.easterseals.com to contact your local Easter Seals office.

Free Visor Cards for the Hearing Impaired

Deaf or hard-of-hearing people can download and print a free visor card for use on their car. The card identifies you as being unable to hear, so that during a routine traffic stop a police officer won't

Q I'm an amputee. How can I put my odd shoes to good use?

A Some amputees need only one shoe, and hate to let the extra one go to waste. People with foot deformities—and those with different-size feet—often have trouble getting pairs of shoes that fit well. If you're in any of these situations, several organizations will try to match you with folks who have complementary needs. Write NOSE—the National Odd Shoe Exchange—at P.O. Box 1120, Chandler, Arizona 85244. For a free online shoe-swapping registry, visit bioped.com/sole mates.html. And the Minus One Club, online at www.rcjone.com, facilitates exchanges of shoes and gloves for amputees.

misinterpret a failure to respond as hostile. Download your card at www.hearinglosshelp.com/articles/visorcards.htm. Some states, including Kansas and Maine, issue similar official identification. Connecticut offers hearing-impaired drivers a free, bright-green envelope to hold their driver's license, registration, and insurance card. The envelope, printed with tips for communicating with the hearing-impaired, is available from any Department of Motor Vehicles office in the state.

Muscular Dystrophy Association Equipment Loans

Many local offices of the Muscular Dystrophy Association have equipment loan closets that provide used wheelchairs, walkers, bathing equipment, van lifts, and more, all in good condition, to persons with muscular dystrophy. MDA also offers financial assistance for the purchase of wheelchairs or leg braces—up to $2,000 every five years toward one new device if you're over 18 years of age, and up to $2,000 every three years if you're 18 or younger. What's more, the association will pay up to $500 per year for repairs or modifications to a wheelchair, scooter, or leg braces, even if they weren't acquired with help from the association. Restrictions apply, of course. To find your local MDA office, enter your zip code at www.mdausa.org/locate.

Help with Adaptive Car Devices

Major automakers, including Chrysler, Ford, GM, Honda, Toyota, and Volvo, provide up to $1,000 worth of assistance for adapting one of their vehicles for a disabled driver or passenger. Adaptive devices include ramps, lifts, hand controls, and power assists that work with the driver's range of motion. Up to $200 is available from some automakers for "alert hearing" devices that help deaf motorists drive safely. Programs are geared toward new-vehicle buyers, so ask about them when you're shopping for a car.

House and Home

Low-Cost Home Meal Deliveries

Meals on Wheels, best known for providing home-delivered meals to seniors in need, also serves many younger persons with

Editor's Choice

Disabled Parking Benefits

Most people know that disabled parking placards or license plates, issued by the states, are must-have items for qualified drivers, but they can also be big money-savers. In all states, placards give you preferential parking privileges and allow you to have your gasoline pumped, and in some states, placards let you park in metered spaces for longer than the designated time. A disabled placard can also get you free parking at some hospitals and public attractions and facilities, such as the San Francisco Zoo; San Antonio International Airport, in Texas; and on city streets in Madison, Wisconsin. It never hurts to ask.

disabilities who find themselves homebound. Specifics vary from community to community, but many programs provide at least one hot meal every day, around lunchtime, delivered to the home. The service is usually free, although there's often a suggested contribution. To find the Meals on Wheels program in your area, go online to www.mowaa.org and enter your zip code, or call the government-run Eldercare Locator toll-free at 800-677-1116.

Aid for Disabled Vets

Disabled veterans in financial need and whose disabilities are due to their military service have many programs and services available through the Department of Veterans Affairs. Here are just two:

- Qualified disabled veterans can receive funds for the purchase or modification of a vehicle or for adaptive equipment for a vehicle. Active-duty personnel also qualify for this program under the same criteria as veterans.
- Certain disabled veterans can receive a Specially Adapted Housing grant of up to $50,000 to modify a home for greater accessibility. In addition, loans of up to $33,000 are available to supplement SAH grants.

For more information on VA programs for the disabled, call your nearest VA offices and ask for the free VA Pamphlet 26-69-1.

Low-Interest State Home Loan Programs

Several states have home ownership programs designed to help persons with disabilities finance the purchase of a home. In Connecticut, look into the Home of Your Own (HOYO) low-interest mortgage program through the Connecticut Housing Finance Authority (www.chfa.org); in Washington State, check out HomeChoice, a down payment assistance program through the Washington State Housing Finance Commission (www.wshfc.org); and Texas offers both HOYO and HomeChoice programs through a public-nonprofit partnership, with information at www.texashoyo.org. Look for a similar program in your state.

Help with Barrier-Free Living

Disabled residents do best when they stay in their own homes, so many communities sponsor accessibility, safety, and barrier removal programs. Three examples:

- In Pierce County, Washington, the ADA Loan Program provides seven-year, zero percent loans of up to $7,500 to help low-income residents make their homes accessible. Better yet, the loans are forgivable, meaning that if you sell the house before the loan term is up, you need to pay the balance but no interest; if you stay in the house the full seven years, the loan is forgiven entirely. For more information, call 253-798-7038.
- In Austin, Texas, the Architectural Barrier Removal program builds wheelchair ramps, installs handrails and grab bars, and modifies bathrooms for elderly and severely disabled homeowners and renters; call 512-974-3863.
- In Arlington County, Virginia, the Barrier Removal Program helps individuals with disabilities remodel their homes for independent living; for information, contact AHC, Inc., at 703-486-0626 or send an e-mail to ahc@ahcinc.org.

Consulting a Social Worker

Many programs and services for persons with disabilities operate at the local or community level. A social worker is often the best person to help you learn about and access them.

Social workers work with a client one-on-one and take a comprehensive, personalized view of an individual's situation. Their expertise is in focusing on the issues, support systems, resources, and programs that best suit a person's needs and financial situation.

Some social workers are employed in institutional settings, such as hospitals, nursing homes, and rehabilitation centers. Others work for state or county medical agencies. Persons with disabilities can also look to organizations that deal with their specific disabilities, such as Easter Seals, the Muscular Dystrophy Association, the National Multiple Sclerosis Society, or groups that aid the visually or hearing-impaired. Private social workers can cost as much as $100 to engage, but those working for institutions, government, or nonprofits can often be utilized at no cost.

Ask questions of a social worker before you engage his or her services. Inquire about education and accreditation (they must be licensed by the state; many also belong to the National Association of Social Workers, which enforces a code of ethics). You can find a social worker locator online at www.helpstartshere.org, or ask other persons with disabilities for recommendations.

Free Wheelchair Ramp Programs

Will it play in Peoria? It will if it's a free wheelchair ramp, provided by the city's Adopt-a-Ramp Program. Peoria pays to build wheelchair-accessible ramps for the houses of low- to moderate-income homeowners with physical disabilities. The program has built 15 to 20 ramps a year for nearly ten years. For more information, contact the City of Peoria, Neighborhood Division, 456 Fulton, Suite 402, Peoria, Illinois 61602, or call 309-494-8651. Other communities, including Shreveport, Louisiana, and Hampton County, Virginia, have similar programs. Carpenters unions in some communities also perform this service.

Help with Utility Bills

Home energy costs seem to climb higher every day; if your disability or associated medical device causes you to use a lot of electricity or other fuel, you may qualify for assistance under the Low-Income Home Energy Assistance Program (LIHEAP). This program is coordinated by your local utility, so contact it for information. For information about LIHEAP funds for your area and charities that can help with utility bills, go online to www.liheap.ncat.org/sp.htm and click on your state.

Kids with Disabilities

Free Guide to Toys for the Differently Abled

Toys "R" Us offers a terrific resource for parents of children with disabilities. Go to the mega toy store's website at www.toysrus.com to use the free "Toy Guide for Differently Abled Kids." In it you'll find toys with just the right mix of skill-building and play values, as well as helpful tips on how to choose the right toy for that special child in your life. For example, the guide sorts toys by the type of skills they promote—including language or cognitive skills and fine or gross motor skills. It was produced with the support of the National Lekotek Center—which offers a toy resource helpline toll-free at 800-366-PLAY and special needs toy lending libraries at its sites in Florida, Georgia, Illinois, Michigan, New Jersey, Pennsylvania, and Virginia—and the United Parents' Syndicate on Disabilities.

Free Care at Shriners Hospitals and Rehab Centers

The Shriners Hospitals for Children provide free medical care for children who need orthopedic care, treatment for spinal cord injury, and burn care. The Shriners, a fraternal organization, operate 18 orthopedic hospitals in the United States, three burn hospitals, and one hospital that provides orthopedic, burn, and spinal cord injury care. To receive free care, a child must be under 18 years of age and, in the opinion of the hospital's chief of staff, able to benefit from the hospital's care. To apply, contact any Shrine Temple or Shrine Club (look in the phone book for one near you), or call toll-free 800-237-5505. Learn more about the services that Shriners offer online at www.shrinershq.org.

No-Cost Books for Kids with Spinal Injuries

A child dealing with a spinal cord injury has many questions and worries. The National Spinal Cord Injury Association can help address them with three age-appropriate books: *Rebecca Finds a New Way*, for ages 4-8; *Follow Your Dreams*, for ages 9-12; and *Tell It Like It Is*, for ages 13-18. These books, written by Connie Panzarino, the late author, activist, artist, and director of the Boston Self Help Center, are available free to children with spinal injuries; call the NSCIA Resource Center toll-free at 800-962-9629. Information booklets, a magazine, and other information for adults and families dealing with spinal cord injury are also available, at no cost, by calling that number.

California "Camperships"

Children with disabilities in California (up to age 18) can receive grants and "camperships" through the Native Daughters of the Golden West Children's Foundation, which serves families of average income who aren't eligible for other aid. Grants have covered braces, wheelchairs, speech therapy, hospitalization, medications, therapy, and more. Jewell McSweeny Memorial Camperships and Hazel B. Hansen Memorial Grants help send children to special camps for the blind and deaf. Get an application at www.ndgw.org or from any Native Daughters member.

Help for Disabled Children of Vietnam Vets

Qualified children of Vietnam veterans who suffer from spina bifida are eligible for monthly financial assistance and vocational training and rehabilitation from the Department of Veterans Affairs. Children must be natural (not adopted) children who were born after the veteran's Vietnam service; children with spina bifida occulta are not eligible. Nearly $18 million in direct financial benefits were paid under this program in fiscal year 2006. Contact your local or regional Department of Veterans Affairs office to request an application, VA Form 21-0304, and send it to VA Regional Office, Veterans Service Center (339/21), Box 25126, Denver, Colorado 80225

Free Braille Book of the Month

Children love to read their favorite books over and over again, and blind kids are no exception. With this in mind, the American Action Fund for Blind Children and Adults offers blind children a free braille book every month to keep. Featured titles are current and appropriate for the reader's age. The program is available to blind children, blind parents, teachers of the blind, schools, and libraries serving the blind. Download and print out an application at www.actionfund.org/application.htm and submit it by mail to AAF Free Braille Books Program, 1800 Johnson Street, Baltimore, Maryland 21230.

No-Cost Library for Visually Impaired Kids

The Kenneth Jernigan Library in Tarzana, California, is a free lending library containing some 40,000 braille and "Twin Vision" (a combination of braille and printed word) books for children. This unique library is run by Jean Dyon Norris, inventor of Twin Vision books, and staffed mostly by volunteers. To apply for the program, parents just need to fill out a simple form; books are sent by mail, and no postage is required to return them. Visit its online site www.actionfund.org/kjlibaps.htm to submit an application online, or call the library at 818-343-2022 to request a free information packet.

Recreation and Entertainment

Free Golden Age of Radio Classics

Nothing sparks the imagination (and tickles the funny bone) quite like an old-time radio show, especially those from the golden era of radio. Blind, visually impaired, and disabled people can listen to more than 10,000 of these wonderful old radio programs—for free—at www.fearyoucanhear.com. The name comes from the large number of suspense shows the website makes available, but the collection also includes dramas, comedies, children's programs, westerns, detective stories, soap operas, and more. Created by Troy Thayne of Sandy, Utah—a legally blind programmer—the website, fully accessible to the visually impaired, features famous shows like *Terry and the Pirates*, *The Lone Ranger*, *The Jack Benny Show*, and even historic baseball broadcasts. People who aren't blind, visually impaired, or disabled can listen, too, but are asked to donate $5 per month to help to keep the site free for the blind.

Free Home Deliveries from Libraries

If your disability keeps you homebound, you can probably still take advantage of the offerings at your local library. Many library systems, including those in Alexandria, Virginia; Charlotte County, Florida; Marin County, California; and Seattle, deliver books, usually for free, to disabled people who can't leave their houses or apartments. (Many also put their catalogs online, so you can use your computer to select materials to borrow.) Contact your local library to see if it has such a program. Libraries also often loan other helpful products and services for disabled people, such as books on tape, large-print books, braille books, and closed-captioning decoders for VCRs.

Free National Library Service for the Disabled

The Library of Congress operates the free National Library Service for the Blind and Physically Handicapped (NLS), which gives blind or disabled people access to braille, large-print, and recorded periodicals, books, and music. The NLS will lend you the materials and the equipment you need to enjoy them, and pay the postage fees involved, too. To find out more, go online to www.loc.gov/nls (accessible for the visually impaired) to look up your local provider (they're organized by state), or call 202-707-5100 or toll-free 800-424-8567.

Low-Cost Book Files for the Visually Impaired

Bookshare.org is an online community serving visually impaired and otherwise print-disabled people (such as those with dyslexia). Taking advantage of an exemption in U.S. copyright law that permits publications to be reproduced in special formats for the disabled,

Bookshare.org coordinates the efforts of thousands of individuals who regularly scan books, and facilitates sharing of those files in the NISO/DAISY XML-based format for talking books and the BRF format for braille devices and printers. Joining Bookshare.org costs $25, and membership is $50 per year, which covers as much as you can read. The organization has more than 27,000 books in its library, including all of the titles on *The New York Times* bestseller lists. Find out more at www.bookshare.org.

Free Braille-Conversion Software

Braille documents can wear out after repeated readings. As a result, many blind persons are interested in copying or converting them to computer-readable text files. Free software for scanning and converting braille documents, called LaBraDoR, can be downloaded from labrador.software.free.fr. LaBraDoR, written by Denis Nouais of France, runs on the free Linux operating system. To learn more about Linux, see "The Free Linux Alternative," page 228.

Free New York Travel and Accessibility Info

Visiting New York City? The Mayor's Office for People with Disabilities will send you a free copy of *Access New York*—just call 212-788-2830. This 100-page, large-print book provides accessibility information for New York's cultural institutions, theaters, nightlife, sports venues, and tours.

NYC's Theatre Access Project Offers Half-Price Tickets

Among the programs of New York City's Theatre Development Fund (TDF) is the Theatre Access Project, described as "an invitation to the best of New York City's Broadway, Off-Broadway, and dance for theatergoers with physical disabilities." TAP provides special discount tickets (usually 50 percent off full price) in the orchestra section. These are set aside for people who are hard of hearing or deaf; who are partially sighted or blind; who require aisle seating for medical reasons; or who use wheelchairs or cannot climb stars. For theatergoers with mild to profound hearing loss, TAP presents both open-captioned and sign-interpreted performances each month, scheduled for specific dates. Tickets must be purchased well in advance through TAP, and all seats are on a first-come, first-served basis. To join TAP, a free service, go to www.tdf.org/tap, or send a self-addressed, stamped envelope to TDF/TAP, 1501 Broadway, 21st Floor, New York, New York 10036.

EDITOR'S CHOICE

Get the Best Braille Calendar—Free

For adults, the AAF each year publishes a free braille calendar that it rightfully describes as "the best in the world." Requests for the calendar must be submitted in writing to the American Action Fund for Blind Children and Adults, 18440 Oxnard Street, Tarzana, California 91356.

Low-Cost and Free Fishing Licenses

Fishing is a wonderfully relaxing pastime, but it can be expensive. The state of Montana, which has some of the best fishing in the United States, offers its blind residents a lifetime fishing license for just $10—a whopper of a discount over the usual $26 annual fee. (Medical certification is required to get the license, and out-of-state residents need not apply.) You can get an application at any local office of the Montana Department of Fish, Wildlife, and Parks, or write to the department at 1420 East Sixth Avenue, P.O. Box 200701, Helena, Montana 59620-0701. For more information, call 406-444-2535. An even bigger catch: Some states, including Oklahoma, Mississippi, Connecticut, Illinois, and New Jersey, offer free fishing licenses to people who are legally blind, and there are also some states that don't require a license.

More Free Fishing Options

Disabled veterans in the state of Pennsylvania can get a free fishing license, as well as a "combo" stamp that covers trout and salmon fishing and fishing on Lake Erie. Check with your county treasurer's office, the Fish and Boat Commission's office in Harrisburg, or any of the six regional law enforcement offices. In Iowa, disabled veterans can get a lifetime hunting/fishing combined license for $31. Persons with disabilities do not need a fishing or hunting license in Connecticut, Illinois, Mississippi, New Jersey, South Carolina, Texas, and Wisconsin.

State Park Discounts

If you are a permanently disabled California resident, you can purchase a state parks discount pass for just $3.50, which will give you a year-round 50 percent discount on facilities fees—including parking and camping fees—in all state-operated parks except Hearst San Simeon. The discount doesn't apply to small or supplementary fees, and it can't be used with any other discount program. For more information, and to download the application and eligibility requirements, go to www.parks.ca.gov and click on Park Passes & Applications. You can also apply in person at any state parks district office, or at the Park Pass Sales Office, 3930 Seaport Boulevard, West Sacramento, California. Colorado, Oregon, Indiana, Florida, and other states also offer persons with disabilities substantial discounts on state-park fees, though rules vary from state to state.

Deals for Skiers with Disabilities

The Whistler Blackcomb ski resort in Whistler, British Columbia, Canada, doesn't offer discounts for skiers with disabilities, but it does offer free lift tickets to the "ski buddy" who accompanies a disabled skier. This amounts to a 50 percent net discount for a disabled skier and companion. With daily lift tickets at Whistler averaging $70 Canadian ($62 U.S.) in 2006, it's a cool deal and a substantial savings overall. Of course, some restrictions apply. For more information, call toll-free 800-766-0449 or 604-932-3434, or see www.whistlerblackcomb.com/about/plan/disabled.htm. U.S. ski resorts such as Alpine Meadows, Crested Butte, Squaw Valley,

For More Information

The services and benefits described in this chapter are just the tip of the iceberg. For more about what's out there to make your life better at little or no cost, check out the following resources:

- Centers for Independent Living are for people with disabilities, run by people with disabilities. And because they're locally run, they are a wonderful resource for learning about the products and services (such as transportation, benefits counseling, housing information) that are available to you close to home and free or at reduced cost. Look in your local phone book, or search online at either www.virtualcil.net/cil or www.ilusa.com.
- AbleData, online at www.abledata.com, provides information on assistive technology and rehabilitation equipment, searchable by state, type of equipment, and other criteria. It's sponsored by the National Institute on Disability and Rehabilitation Research.
- Reference Service Press has published a remarkable book, *Financial Aid for the Disabled and Their Families, 2006-2008*, by Gail Ann Schlacter and R. David Weber. It describes nearly 1,300 funding programs for persons with disabilities and gives contact and application information for each. Order it online ($40 plus shipping) at www.rspfunding.com.
- The Foundation Center, the nation's leading authority on philanthropy, has created a searchable Internet database of information about more than 6,000 foundation and public charities that give grants to individuals. You can access this database for one month at a cost of $9.95 at gtionline.fdncenter.org.
- The National Assistive Technology Technical Assistance Partnership maintains a list of assistive technology programs organized by state at www.resna.org/taproject/at/statecontacts.html.

Telluride, and Vail have offered substantial discounts for disabled skiers in the past; check before you go.

Low-Cost Adaptive Sailing Programs

Sailors with disabilities can join the Bay Area Association of Disabled Sailors (BAADS) in San Francisco for just $36 per year, and then sail on the bay on Sunday afternoons for free with the club. Learn more online at www.baads.org. Similar "adaptive sailing" programs exist in other cities with active sailing communities, including Rumson, New Jersey; Jacksonville, Florida; and Madison, Wisconsin.

CHAPTER 18

bargains and freebies for new mothers

There's no more exciting life change than the birth of your first child, but little did you know how quickly child-care expenses can rack up. Follow these tips and watch the free formula, diapers, food, and advice roll in.

IN THIS DAY AND AGE THE MIRACLE of birth does not come cheap. Delivery and associated medical services can tally upward of $2,000 in out-of-pocket spending beyond what the typical insurance plan covers. And the cash register really starts ringing when you get your bundle of joy home.

Fortunately, many organizations, government agencies, and companies offer assistance to offset the expenses of prenatal classes, formula and baby food, diapers, car seats, bottles, and more. Advice and specific information on everything from prenatal nutritional requirements and breast-feeding techniques to the basics of caring for a newborn are yours, at no cost, in many pamphlets, books, and downloadable PDFs available from national organizations. And nurses staff 24-hour hotlines operated by companies and hospitals—wise parents record these numbers in case they need answers in the middle of the night.

Check manufacturers' websites for coupons and free samples—some companies will mail them to you at each stage of your baby's development. Sometimes a phone call will net you a one-time gift from a company, even if its website lists no offers, and if you call back regularly, some will send additional coupons.

You'll also find coupons and free samples from online clubs, which in addition offer sweepstakes, calendars and planners, informational

By the numbers

4.1

Number, in millions, of babies born in the U.S. in 2004. Of that number, 29.1% of those babies came into the world by cesarean delivery.

e-mail newsletters, special deals, and other neat stuff for expectant and new parents. Be sure to contact local organizations—even your hospital and doctor's office—for complimentary samples and services.

Did you hit the parental jackpot? Parents of twins, triplets, and other multiples may be eligible to receive unadvertised benefits from certain manufacturers, including extra coupons and multiple-item discounts. In most cases, you'll have to provide proof of birth, such as copies of birth certificates, to receive the goods.

No time to clip coupons and watch for discounts? Check eBay. People auction off lots of coupons and samples for brand-name baby food, formula, diapers, and wipes; go to ebay.com/baby-coupons. You are effectively paying for the person's time and effort in locating, clipping, sorting, listing, and shipping the coupons; the coupons themselves are, of course, free.

Happy hunting, and congratulations on your new arrival!

While You're Expecting

Free Prenatal Fitness and Nutrition Advice

Eating right and staying active are especially important when you're pregnant—for your own and your baby's sake. BabyFit.com offers all kinds of advice to help mothers-to-be stay in shape. Register at www.babyfit.com and get free guidance and support: a personalized pregnancy exercise and nutrition plan, a pregnancy nutrient tracker, a daily fitness plan with exercise demos, and e-mailed pregnancy, nutrition, and fitness tips for each week of your pregnancy.

No-Cost Hospital Prenatal Classes

Many hospitals offer free classes to their expectant and new mother patients. The classes are usually taught by nurses, with the participation of physicians, and cover pregnancy, labor and delivery, newborn care and CPR, breast-feeding, postpartum care, and preparing siblings, among other topics. For example:

- New York Hospital in New York City (212-746-3215) offers patients who give birth there a free walk-in consultation on breast-feeding problems.
- Parents of babies who will be born at the University of Chicago Hospitals (www.uchospitals.edu) can attend a free four-week

class in labor preparation and infant care led by a pediatrician and registered nurse.

- The Institute for Health Education at St. Luke's Hospital in Chesterfield, Missouri, in suburban St. Louis (www.stlukes-stl .com, 314-205-6069) holds free courses in the natural approach to labor as well as a class for grandparents.

Most hospitals will give you a free preview tour of the birthing center so you'll know what to expect when the big day comes. Call your hospital to check on its offerings.

Federal Nutrition Support

If you are nutritionally at risk or know someone who is, help is available from the Special Supplemental Nutrition Program for Women, Infants, and Children. The WIC Program, as it is better known, is a Federal Food and Nutrition Service program that aims to safeguard the health of low-income, at-risk women, infants, and children up to age five by supplementing their diets with nutritious foods. WIC clinics offer education and counseling about nutrition, and provide screening and referrals to other health, welfare, and social services. An eligible child or a pregnant, postpartum, or breast-feeding mom usually receives WIC benefits for six months to a year, at which time the mother or the child's guardian must reapply. To apply to participate in the WIC Program, contact your state or local agency to set up an appointment; you'll find the phone numbers on the WIC site at www.fns.usda.gov/wic.

Free Pregnancy Calendar

Expecting parents typically count the weeks until the baby is due. Babyzone.com offers a free planner, a calendar, and week-by-week e-mail updates that help you chronicle your baby's growth. Check out the interactive Baby Names Basket, which keeps track of the names you are considering for your little one. When you become a member, fill out a short survey form about acid reflux disease and you'll be sent a free trial certificate and kit from Prevacid, as well as other companies' free offers and magazine subscriptions. You can also earn rewards and a free bib by answering additional surveys.

Ask the March of Dimes for Free

Do you know the signs of preterm labor? What foods should pregnant women avoid? Can exercise be harmful to your unborn baby?

The Pregnancy and Newborn Health Education Center at the March of Dimes Foundation can give you the information you need about prematurity, preconception, pregnancy, childbirth, genetics, and birth defects. The center answers questions in both English and Spanish via e-mail or real-time chat during weekday business hours. Information specialists with master's degrees in various health fields have access to a staffed medical library, online database subscriptions, and current medical journals to obtain up-to-date information. The information and referral services are free and confidential. You can also sign up for a monthly e-mail newsletter that contains foundation news, personal stories, and tips for a healthy pregnancy. For all of this, visit the March of Dimes website at www.marchofdimes.com.

No-Cost Classes for Dad, Too

With all the attention showered on moms-to-be, dads and grandparents can feel left out. If that's the case in your family, Babies "R" Us has a solution. Its free in-store educational seminars offer expectant and new moms, dads, and grandparents baby-care information, product demos, question-and-answer sessions, and refreshments, all designed to make everyone feel a part of the process. The Dads in Training event, for example, includes a special seminar on how fathers can take an active role in feeding their newborns. Check www.babiesrus.com for the store nearest you, then call or visit a store's guest services desk for the dates and times of specific events.

Free Samples from Your Doctor

Don't be shy about asking your doctor for samples. Depending on what drug reps visit their office, your OB-GYN and pediatrician may have free samples of prenatal vitamins, formula, baby shampoo, allergy and asthma medications, topical antibiotics, antacids, pain relievers and fever reducers like Tylenol, Motrin, and Advil, and, for later down the road, birth control pills. Ask for samples every time you go in for an appointment.

Free e-Newsletters Outlining Your Baby's Development

Free e-mail newsletters are a great way to follow your baby's development in utero and after. To get on the mailing list of BabyCenter, an online resource for expectant and new parents, go to babycenter .com and punch in your due date and e-mail and mailing addresses. The first newsletters are weekly, when things are really changing;

later they'll become monthly or less frequent. The site offers BabyCenter members a free subscription to stage-based *BabyCenter* magazine, packed with health, beauty, fitness, and fashion information. It also rounds up lots of special free offerings (samples and coupons) and lets you plug into hundreds of bulletin boards, where you can read comments and chime in on such topics as feeding choices, TV watching, and money and shopping.

Interactive Pregnancy Nutrition Tracker for Free

For stage-specific pregnancy or baby information tailored to your baby's birth or due date, register on Nestlé Infant Nutrition's Very Best Baby Collection site. You'll also have access to an interactive pregnancy weight tracking chart and nutrition tracker, a baby growth chart, and an immunization calendar. Other benefits include complimentary issues of *Very Best Baby Collection* magazine, again pegged to your stage of pregnancy or to your baby's age, and savings "checks" for infant nutrition products. If you are interested in signing up for the Very Best Baby Collection, call toll-free 800-284-9488 or visit www.verybestbaby.com.

Free Advice from the Pampers Parenting Institute

Join the Pampers.com club, and you'll receive e-newsletters from the Pampers Parenting Institute containing expert advice tailored to your pregnancy week or your child's stage of development, along with special offers and samples. As a Pampers.com club member, you can opt in to receive special offers from Pampers' parent company, Procter & Gamble, receive weekly parenting advice in Pampers' *Parents Pages*, and receive a free month of the "What to Expect" online pregnancy guide.

Newborns and Infants

Hospital Freebies

Hospitals can be a wealth of free services for new parents. Here are three examples:

- Mothers who give birth at Mary Lanning Memorial Hospital in Hastings, Nebraska, can receive a free-of-charge visit from a home health nurse skilled in nursery or postpartum care; the

Editor's Choice

Freeware Baby Album

Virtualsoft's Baby Album is freeware (free software) that allows you to record, keep, and share memories from this special time. Use it to closely follow your pregnancy or make a record of the high points in your baby's life. You can also create a multimedia album by adding pictures, drawings, and video and audio clips directly into your pages, then publish the album to the Internet or a CD-ROM. Available in English, French, German, Dutch, and Portuguese, the basic edition of this software is downloadable—free—from www.virtualsoft.biz.

nurse, who comes to the home 24 to 48 hours after the mother is discharged, spends up to an hour checking that mother and baby are recovering well, and answering parents' questions.

- At St. Luke's Hospital in Houston, the Women's Services Department's "warmline" at 832-355-3064 is a 24-hour-a-day free telephone support service for new parents; a nurse who specializes in caring for newborns is on hand to answer questions on baby care at 832-355-4254.
- Mothers who deliver at Greenwich Hospital (www.greenhosp.org) in Greenwich, Connecticut, may return for a mother/baby assessment with a consultant 48 to 72 hours after discharge. Greenwich Hospital also offers a neonatal intensive-care unit mentor either during or after the baby's stay in the unit.

Many hospitals and clinics around the country provide similar no-cost services. Even if home visits are not free, some insurance companies will cover them fully.

Q **How can I send out birth announcements without spending a lot of money?**

A Instead of ordering expensive printed birth announcements, you can send out free "e-announcements" by joining Similac's Welcome Addition Club. Go to the site at www.welcomeaddition.com, fill out the short online form, plus your friends' and family's e-mail addresses, and your blessed event will be announced instantaneously. In addition, the club offers a Mom's Planner to help you keep track of important dates before and after the baby's arrival. Drop-down menus and the month-at-a-glance view make this calendar a great solution for busy moms and their babies.

Greetings from the President

Your new bundle of joy will cherish for years to come a welcome-to-the-world greeting from the President of the United States. Send a postcard with your baby's name, address, and birth date to the White House Greetings Office, 1600 Pennsylvania Avenue NW, Washington, D.C. 20502-0339, or fax the information to 202-395-1232.

Coupons and Other Offers from Huggies

The average infant requires 10 to 12 changes per day for the first three months. That's a lot of diapers. Kimberly-Clark, the makers of Huggies diapers, encourages parents of children who are 26 months of age or younger to join its mailing list. Members receive periodic postal-mail deliveries of coupons and product information for diapers, pull-ups, and wipes. To sign up, call toll-free 800-544-1847, then press 1 to register for the automated mailing list. Visit www.huggiesbabynetwork.com to find information from baby-care experts on teething, assessing your baby's hearing, language development, and more. Two fun interactive features on the site: the virtual nursery decorator and a keepsake book for your baby.

Playtex Diaper Genie Rebate for Twins

Another bonus for parental jackpot winners: Playtex offers parents of twins or other multiples a $7 rebate for its Diaper Genie diaper

Meet Your Uncle Sam

Does your baby have a Social Security number yet? The number and the card are free and can be obtained as soon as you give birth. When you give information for your baby's birth certificate in a hospital setting, you'll also be asked whether you want to apply for a Social Security number for your newborn. Or you can apply later at a Social Security office. If you are adopting a child, the Social Security office can assign him or her a number even before the adoption is complete. For more information, go to www.socialsecurity.gov or call toll-free 800-772-1213 or TTY 800-325-0778. There's a very practical reason for getting your baby a Social Security number as early as possible: You'll need to list the number on your tax return when you claim your little one as a dependent in the first full tax year after birth. For more information on the tax implications of childbirth, call your local Internal Revenue Service office, toll-free at 800-829-1040, or visit www.irs.gov.

disposal system. Call toll-free 800-843-6430 before the babies are three months old. Leave your name and address via the automated system, and the rebate form will be mailed to you. Be prepared to provide proof of multiple births (such as copies of birth certificates) when you return the form. For more information on the Diaper Genie, go to www.playtexbaby.com.

Pampers "Gifts to Grow" Rewards Program

Members of Pampers.com (see "Free Advice from the Pampers Parenting Institute," page 363) can convert those countless diapers into gifts by participating in the Pampers Gifts to Grow Rewards Program. Inside each package of Pampers diapers, training pants, and wipes is a rewards program code. Enter the code online at Pampers.com to accrue rewards points. When you've accumulated enough points, you can redeem them for items from the Gifts to Grow catalog, such as a Dora the Explorer backpack, a free month of movies from Blockbuster.com, a $5 coupon toward the purchase of Earth's Best organic infant food, a Bob the Builder DVD, and other gifts from featured Pampers partners.

Free Baby Bags and Totes

Many hospitals give out diaper bags provided by formula companies to new parents. Enfamil's and Similac's mini totes each contain samples of formula and coupons, support materials for new parents, and

Build a Child-Care Library—Free

The federal government's Consumer Information Center, located in Pueblo, Colorado, is a gold mine of free information for parents.

- The three-page *Got a Sick Kid?* brochure (#506M) offers tips for giving medication and using the recommended vaccine schedule to protect against the major childhood diseases (also available in Spanish).
- The 11-page *Ear Infections and Language Development* booklet (#323K, $0.50) explains the signs and symptoms of hearing damage, and treatments for it, and includes a language development worksheet for keeping track of your child's progress.
- The 65-page *Handbook on Child Support Enforcement* (#505N) is a guide for getting payments owed to you and your children, and lists state and federal offices to contact for more information.

The quarterly Consumer Information Center Catalog lists more than 200 helpful publications on many topics. For your free copy, write to the Consumer Information Catalog, Pueblo, Colorado 81009, call toll-free 888-8-PUEBLO (888-878-3256), or go to www.pueblo.gsa.gov. Many CIC publications are also downloadable as PDFs.

plenty of room for diapers. The Nestlé Very Best Baby Backpack includes a removable changing pad, bottle holders, an ice pack, a music CD, a photo album, a bottle, and samples of formula. (If you're nursing and don't plan to supplement, consider donating the samples to a women's shelter.)

SAFETY FIRST

Tracking Baby Product Recalls for Free

You can also check with manufacturers to see if any of their products have been the subject of a safety campaign, which calls attention to products that need to be repaired, modified, or replaced. Many times all that's needed is a simple replacement part to improve the product's performance. Other times you may need to return the item for a refund. For example, Evenflo's online system (at www.evenflo.com) lets you track products that have been recalled. If you have questions about a particular Evenflo safety campaign, call the Evenflo ParentLink Department toll-free at 800-233-5921.

Free Kit for Childproofing Window Blinds

From 1991 to 2000, the U.S. Consumer Product Safety Commission received reports of 160 child strangulations involving cords on window blinds. If you have window blinds with loops bought before November 2000, visit the Window Covering Safety Council website at www.windowcoverings.org, or call toll-free 800-506-4636, to receive a free repair kit for each set of blinds. The kit includes small plastic attachments to prevent inner cords from being pulled loose. Instructions for cord stop installation are easy to follow, and the repair can be done in minutes without removing the blinds.

Other Aids for Childproofing Window Blinds

Another way to protect your child from window blind mishaps is by equipping your blinds with a pair of safety break-away tassels or safety cleats, available free except for the cost of postage from No Brainer Blinds and Shades. Replace your blinds' current tassels with the new break-away ones, or for a quicker, easier solution, tightly wrap the cords around cleats (hooks) so they are out of reach of children or pets. Mail a self-addressed stamped envelope with a minimum of $0.43 postage for shipment within the United States to Free Safety Offer, Three Brainer Tower, 4660 Beechnut, Houston, Texas 77096. Write the word "tassel" or "cleat" on the return envelope. For more information, visit www.nobrainerblinds.com/info/9901_safe.php, or call toll-free 888-466-2724.

Free Info on Protecting Your Baby from Lead

Your baby deserves to live in a lead-free home. The Office of Healthy Homes and Lead Hazard Control's Community Information and Outreach site offers a wide assortment of free materials, from informational brochures to large, full-color posters. Among the publications are:

- *Runs Better Unleaded (How to Protect Your Children from Lead Poisoning)*
- *Ten Tips to Protect Children from Pesticide and Lead Poisonings Around the Home*
- *Healthy Beginnings: Lead Safe Families,* which is also available in Chinese, Haitian-Creole, Khmer, Polish, Portuguese, Russian, Spanish, and Vietnamese.

To acquire these and other publications and products, contact the U.S. Department of Housing and Urban Development at 451 7th

Take Caution!

Is your home childproof?

The U.S. Consumer Product Safety Commission is charged with protecting the public from unreasonable risks of serious injury or death from the more than 15,000 types of consumer products that are under the agency's jurisdiction—including cribs, car seats, high chairs, and other baby products. The CPSC has published a number of free booklets in both English and Spanish, and provides information about product recalls. To order the publications, call the CPSC hotline toll-free at 800-638-2772 or TTY 800-638-8270, download the documents from the site at www.cpsc.gov, or write the CPSC at 4330 East West Highway, Bethesda, Maryland 20814.

Street SW, Washington, D.C. 20410, call 202-708-1112 or TTY 202-708-1455, or visit this page on HUD's official website: www.hud.gov/offices/lead/outreach/communityoutreach.cfm.

Free Child Safety Publications

The National Center for Missing & Exploited Children offers a large selection of free publications in English and Spanish for par-

Buckling Up Baby

Nothing is more important than keeping your precious newborn cargo safe and secure at all times. Here are a few suggestions:

- Is your child's car seat up to standards? Check with the manufacturer or call the U.S. Department of Transportation's Vehicle Safety Hotline toll-free at 888-DASH-2-DOT (888-327-4236). This information is also available online at the National Highway Traffic Safety Administration website at www.nhtsa.dot.gov. If the seat has been recalled, follow the instructions to have it fixed or replaced. To be notified of future recall notices, you can download and send in a registration card.
- Are you sure you've installed your child's car seat correctly? Why not attend a car-seat safety check? Many local fire departments, police stations, health care facilities, and Babies "R" Us stores periodically hold these events, and they will examine your car-seat installation at no charge. Find an inspection location in your area at www.seatcheck.org, which is a national safety program launched by DaimlerChrysler, the NHTSA, Graco, and others to disseminate information about car-seat inspections and safety regulations.
- If you can't afford a car seat, there are organizations that will help you, either by giving you a seat or subsidizing one. First call your local police station, county family services department, or hospital. If they have nothing available, then contact the NHTSA, the National SAFE KIDS Campaign (www.safekids.org), or SafetyBeltSafe U.S.A. (www.carseat.org).
- If you'll be renting a car, either near home or at a distant destination, or if you have guests with small children, ask your local automobile club or one at your destination if they have loaner car seats available. The Automobile Club of New York, for example, has a car-seat loan program that makes a limited number of infant, convertible, and booster seats available to American Automobile Association members for up to two weeks; advance reservations are required (for the holidays they should be made as far in advance as possible). Check the club's site at www.aaany.com for more information.

ents and caregivers. *Just in Case You Need a Babysitter* (English item #12, Spanish #14) provides information on hiring a babysitter as well as safety tips to keep in mind when employing one. *Just in Case You Need Daycare* (English item #07, Spanish #35) can help you find a reliable daycare provider. To view the list of publications, visit the organization's website at www.missingkids.com. You can order booklets using the online form, by mailing in a downloadable order form, or by calling toll-free 800-THE-LOST (800-843-5678).

> **EDITOR'S CHOICE**
>
> **No-Cost Child ID Kit**
>
> A missing child is every parent's nightmare. Sign up for the ChildSafe Network at www.childsafenetwork.org for a free child identification kit. This kit can be an invaluable tool for law enforcement officials trying to identify and rescue a missing or abducted child. Membership in the ChildSafe Network also entitles you to instant online access to the most current database of registered sex offenders from the participating states.

Caring for Your Baby

Free Pediatrics Manual for State Farm Customers

What's the best nutrition for your infant? When should you see a doctor? How do you handle your toddler's temper tantrums? Is your child developing normally? These are among the many questions about child care, including special situations, that are answered in the American Academy of Pediatrics' book *Caring for Your Baby and Young Child: Birth to Age 5*. If you're a new or expecting parent and a State Farm Insurance customer, you are eligible to receive a complimentary copy of this 752-page comprehensive parenting manual—a $20 value. Contact your local State Farm agent, call toll-free 888-733-8368, or order the book online at the State Farm site www.statefarm.com/lifevents/baby.htm.

Free CDC Vaccination Hotline

Hepatitis B, diphtheria, polio, measles, mumps, rubella—your baby needs to be immunized against these and other potentially deadly diseases soon after birth, but childhood vaccination schedules can be confusing. The CDC Info hotline, a service of the Centers for Disease Control and Prevention, provides answers to common questions about baby shots, diseases, and other health issues. Call the hotline toll-free at 800-232-2522 twenty-four hours a day, seven days a week. Or check out the website at www.cdc.gov, from which you can order *Parents' Guide to Childhood Immunizations*, a free 68-page booklet introducing parents to 13 childhood diseases and the vaccines that protect children from them. Also available are no-cost publications on autism, fetal alcohol syndrome, and early hearing-loss detection.

Feeding Your Baby: Help Is Here

No new mother should ever feel concerned about whether she is giving her child the best possible nourishment. Whether you breast-feed or bottle-feed your new baby, there's a wealth of free guidance and samples out there. Here are some of the best. Remember, your hospital may also offer classes on feeding and caring for newborns.

Free Breast-feeding Guide

The National Women's Health Information Center, part of the U.S. Department of Health and Human Services Office on Women's Health, publishes *An Easy Guide to Breastfeeding,* a booklet that explains the benefits of breastfeeding for babies and mothers, and provides answers to frequently asked questions. It's available free of charge in Spanish, Chinese, and three English-language editions (one geared to all women, another to African American women, and a third to American Indian and Alaska Native women). To order the booklet, call toll-free 800-994-9662 or TTY 888-220-5446), or write to the center at 8270 Willow Oaks Corporate Drive, Fairfax, Virginia 22031. For more information and other resources, visit www.4women.gov.

Free Breast-feeding Support

As natural as breastfeeding is, it doesn't always come easy. For a regular dose of encouragement and support as well as plenty of useful information for nursing mothers, sign up for Nurture Note e-mails from Lansinoh, a breastfeeding support and products company. All you have to do is fill in your name and e-mail address and your baby's due date or birth date at www.lansinoh.com. You'll start receiving Nurture Notes once a week for the first 12 weeks of breastfeeding and then once a month until your baby is one year old.

Free Breast-feeding Info

Clothing retailer Motherwear's free, downloadable *Essential Breastfeeding Guide* contains 34 pages of answers, insight, and detailed information on breastfeeding and related topics. Motherwear's e-newsletters with stage-based breastfeeding information are geared to your specific month of pregnancy or motherhood. The company's catalog also includes tips from nursing moms. To receive a free copy, fill out the form on the site at www.motherwear.com, call toll-free 800-950-2500, or write to P.O. Box 927CBI, Northampton, Massachusetts 01061.

Free Formula Samples

Become an Ultra Bright Beginnings Customer Club member, and you'll receive a day's supply of baby formula—a 4.2-ounce sample, enough for four feedings—along with a $4 coupon. As a member, you'll qualify for giveaways and contests and have the opportunity to receive more coupons simply by participating in surveys. Sign up at www.brightbeginnings.com. For nutritional information on the company's baby formulas, call toll-free 800-410-9629 or e-mail info@brightbeginnings.com. Parents of multiples can call the manufacturer, PBM Products, toll-free at 800-538-8254 to receive a one-time gift of store-brand formula and coupons redeemable at Target, Wal-Mart, Kroger, or Albertsons. Send proof of births to PBM Products LLC, 204 North Main Street, Gordonsville, Virginia 22942, Attn: Debbie Burdyck. Then call toll-free 800-485-9918 every 30 days thereafter for additional coupons.

Toll-Free Baby Feeding Hotline

Nestlé's Very Best Baby toll-free hotline at 800-242-5200 offers recorded answers to feeding questions and explains how to prepare formula. You can also sign up with a representative to receive booklets on nutrition and recipes as well as product coupons.

Free Organic Baby Formula Samples

It's never too early to go organic. Sign up at www.parentschoiceformula.com to receive a full day's supply of USDA-certified Parent's Choice Organic baby formula. Also available on the site are coupon packs, the Parent's Choice newsletter, and occasional e-mail offers and promotions.

Gifts and Offers from Enfamil

Enroll in the Enfamil Family Beginnings Program and receive up to $250 in gifts, including pre- and postnatal information, up to $60 in formula "checks," a diaper bag, samples, and special offers for a Fisher-Price toy and J. C. Penney portraits. Your membership entitles you to receive e-mails containing timely information and activity ideas for you and your baby. Register at www.enfamil.com or call toll-free 800-222-9123 for more information. If you are a parent of multiples, ask your doctor to contact his or her Enfamil rep for a complimentary gift and other special offers for your new brood.

24/7 Toll-Free Advice from Gerber

Have a question about caring for or feeding your baby? Specialists at the Gerber Parents Resource Center are available to help around the clock. Call toll-free 800-4-GERBER (800-443-7237) or go to https://www.gerber.com/contactus, type in your phone number, and someone will call you back. In addition to getting answers to your questions, you can request a prenatal package of samples and coupons for Gerber Baby Care items and breast pumps, plus the booklet *Start Healthy Stay Healthy: What Parents Should Know About Teaching Good Eating Habits.* You'll continue to periodically receive coupons appropriate to your baby's age. Parents of twins and other multiples can request additional coupons. The Growing Up Gerber club also offers a personalized website, parenting tips, special offers, and about $45 in coupons.

No-Cost Resources from Evenflo

The parenting resources department at Evenflo, maker of car seats, strollers, breast pumps, bottles, and more, publishes free brochures that can be sent to you by mail. The *Breastfeeding Guide* includes information on the basics of pumping and storing your milk, *Safe Passage* explains the proper selection and use of car seats, and *Put Big Kids in Boosters* offers advice about choosing and using the proper car seats as your child grows. Order the booklets at www.evenflo.com. You can also view the brochures online and download and print them out as PDFs.

Editor's Choice

Coupons from Beech-Nut

If you send in 48 proofs of purchase from any Beech-Nut Naturals, First Advantage, or Table Time products, you'll get four coupons for $1 off any 10 Beech-Nut items. Print out the offer form from www.beechnut.com and mail it to Beech-Nut EB 711, P.O. Box 2610, St. Louis, Missouri 63116. The company also offers e-mail newsletters with information customized to your baby's age; helpful articles on subjects such as picky eaters, first teeth, and diet; and monthly coupons. The offers are available at the Beech-Nut site or by calling toll-free 800-BEECH-NUT (800-233-2468). Check the site for a free downloadable solid food feeding guide.

No-Cost Children's Vaccinations

Your child may be eligible for free vaccinations through the federal Vaccines for Children Program. To qualify, the recipient must be 18 years old or younger and meet at least one of the following criteria: be eligible for Medicaid, have no health insurance, be a Native American or Alaskan Native, or have health insurance that does not cover vaccinations. VFC vaccinations can be obtained at your doctor's office, at private or public-health clinics and hospitals, and at participating schools in certain states; more than 50,000 providers are enrolled in the program nationwide. For more information, visit www.cdc.gov/nip/vfc/default.htm, call the CDC Information Contact Center toll-free at 800-232-4636, e-mail nipinfo@cdc.gov, or write CDC National Immunization Program, NIP Public Inquiries, Mailstop E-05, 1600 Clifton Road NE, Atlanta, Georgia 30333.

Free Johnson & Johnson New Parent Pack

Generations of American babies have been bathed, shampooed, powdered, and oiled with Johnson & Johnson baby products. To get a free Johnson & Johnson New Parent Pack, consisting of a one-time gift of coupons and samples, call toll-free 800-526-3967 and press 1 for baby products. Since this is an automated system, it will only send the pack to the registered address of the phone number you punch in. For printable step-by-step guides and streaming how-to videos on caring for your baby, from bathing to breast-feeding, go to the company's baby products site at www.johnsonsbaby.com.

Free Baby Sunproofing Brochure

Just one blistering sunburn in childhood can double the risk of developing melanoma later in life—so says the Skin Cancer Foundation. Learn how to protect your infant or toddler against too much exposure to the sun by reading the foundation's full-color brochure *Sunproofing Your Baby*, which gives advice on sunburn treatments, skin cancer warning signs, protective clothing, and sunscreen. Also available is *For Every Child Under the Sun: A Guide to Sensible Sun Protection;* this booklet features a 10-step guide to sun protection for the whole family; dispels common myths about sun, skin, and aging; and offers tips on selecting and using sunscreens. These and other informational brochures are part of the Skin Cancer Foundation's Children's Sun Protection Program. Order them online for just $0.60 each at www.skincancer.org, or write to the foundation at 245 Fifth Avenue, Suite 1403, New York, New York 10016.

"I'm Ready for My Close-Up"

Your baby ought to be in pictures! These photo studios make it easy.

- Visit the Sears Portrait Studio site (www.searsportrait.com) or call toll-free 866-292-4949 for special offers, such as a free 8x10 print for new moms. To receive the Military Family Portrait Special of 20 percent off in-studio and online portrait purchases, show your military ID at the time of your photo session.
- To celebrate your child's birthday, join the Olan Mills Birthday Club at www.olanmills.com and receive a free photo package of one 8x10 portrait, one 5x7 portrait, and wallet-size photos, plus a 20 percent discount on additional purchases.
- J. C. Penney Portraits has specials for parents of multiples who join the Birthday Club at www.jcpenneyportraits.com/multiples.
- Join the Wal-Mart Portrait Smiles Club at www.goportraits.com to receive discounts, special offers, bonus greeting cards, and a complimentary 8x10 portrait.

Orajel Coupons and Rebates

With each tiny tooth, your baby is that much closer to a full set of pearly whites. Fill out a short survey at www.orajel.com, and Orajel will send you coupons for its products, such as teething pain medicine and baby tooth and gum cleanser. You also can download a $1.50 manufacturer's mail-in rebate on the purchase of any Orajel, Orajel Toddler, or Baby Orajel product. And the site answers questions about caring for your baby's teeth and suggests ways to make brushing fun.

Free Teething Tips from Anbesol

When your baby is teething, everyone knows it. And it can take up to three weeks for him to cut a single tooth! Anbesol offers coupons for its pain relief gel for babies and tips for parents on how to ease the discomfort of teething. At Anbesol's website (www.anbesol.com) you'll find a printable tooth chart, starting at six months of age and continuing to six years, so you can keep track of your baby's teeth as they come in.

Baby's First Circus Ticket Is Free

After the birth of your baby, you may think your home has become a three-ring circus. Why not take your child to see real lions, tigers, bears, and clowns at a Ringling Bros. and Barnum & Bailey performance? Every child under 12 months and living in the continental United States is entitled to receive his or her first ticket to the circus free (the ticket voucher can be exchanged for a free ticket to a performance anytime, anywhere—there's no expiration date). Fill out the online form at www.ringling.com/offers. For multiple births of three or more, or for recently adopted children older than 12 months, submit the form online, then print out a copy of the completed form for each baby, attach a copy of each birth certificate or proof of adoption, and mail to Baby's First Circus Program, Feld Entertainment, 8607 Westwood Center Drive, Vienna, Virginia 22182. On with the show!

Free Gymboree Preview Class

Think your newborn is too young for school? Think again. Gymboree Play and Music has classes for the birth-to-six-months set and all the way up to three- to five-year-old big kids. Classes for the littlest ones include Baby Signs, parent and baby fitness, and music. To attend a free preview class, go to www.gymboree.com, print out a free class coupon, and call your local Gymboree to schedule a time. Check the site to find locations where you can schedule your preview online, or call toll-free 877-4-GYMWEB (877-449-6932).

TODDLERS

Low-Cost Coping Information

Dealing with a child's behavioral problems can be one of a parent's toughest challenges. How do you put a stop to grocery-store tantrums? What discipline strategies help rather than hurt? How do you keep your cool when your baby just won't stop crying? Prevent Child Abuse America offers a series of colorful, pocket-size guides to help you cope with the inevitable stresses of parenting. Each 10-page booklet provides parents and caregivers with quick tips on parenting with love, even when time is short and tempers flare. There's also a 24-page guide written especially for teen parents. You can order these publications online at www.pcaamerica.channing-bete.com for between $0.59 and $1.75 each. Prevent Child Abuse America also offers fact sheets—on topics such as discipline techniques, preventing and recognizing child abuse, and helping your child be successful in

Q **Where can I score some free baby gear?**

A With more than 300 sites in all 50 U.S. states and more than 50 countries (as of mid-2006), the ubiquitous Craigslist is a virtual garage sale put on by neighbors you didn't even know you had. To find free baby stuff, log on to www.craigslist.org, click on your city, then look under the "for sale" heading for the "free" link. Now type "baby" into the keywords field. If you're lucky, you'll find cribs, swings, bouncers, strollers, and other items in varying states of use that are free for the taking. Remember to act fast—the good stuff never languishes.

Editor's Choice Save for College as You Buy

Every time you buy diapers, toys, or even something special for yourself, you could at the same time be contributing to your child's college fund. The Upromise College Fund is a 529 Plan, which is similar to a 401(k) plan, except it offers tax advantages for saving for college rather than retirement and can be transferred between family members. There's no fee to join: Just go to www.upromise.com. As a Upromise member, you'll get a percentage of your spending deposited back into your Upromise account when you make eligible purchases of certain products and services from participating companies such as ExxonMobil, Citi, Eddie Bauer, McDonald's, Coca-Cola, and Procter & Gamble—or when you use your own credit, debit, and grocery and drugstore cards to shop online. You can also invite other family members to contribute to your child's Upromise college account. For more information on 529 plans (also called qualified tuition programs), consult your tax adviser or the IRS at www.irs.gov.

school—that you can download from the organization's website at www.preventchildabuse.org.

Free Shoe Measuring System

Want to order shoes for your kids online but not sure of their current sizes? Here's a simple solution: Log on to www.kidsnshoes.com/kidsnfeet.htm for KidsNshoes' easy-to-use shoe measuring system. Follow the directions for printing the measuring system on any standard printer, and you'll be ready to measure your children's feet at home anytime.

No-Cost 24/7 Cold and Allergy Hotline from Triaminic

According to the San Diego Children's Hospital and Health Center, toddlers catch colds between five and ten times a year. That's a lot of sniffles. Triaminic, the makers of cold and allergy medication, provides a 24/7 resource for information and tips about your child's cold and allergy needs. Call the Triaminic Clinic toll-free at 800-KIDS-987 (800-543-7987). To receive a personalized newsletter and special offers from Triaminic via e-mail, sign up at the website www.triaminic.com.

Free Child-Care Info

If you're looking for quality child care in your community, call Child Care Aware toll-free at 800-424-2246 or log on to www.childcareaware.org. This nonprofit initiative connects parents with local

Free Magazines for New Parents

Did you know you can get glossy publications about being a parent delivered right to your door at no cost?

- Receive a free full-color quarterly magazine based on your baby's age when you join Growing Up Gerber at www.gerber.com.
- Answer a short survey at www.americanbaby.com and you'll receive *American Baby* magazine free of charge. Every issue is loaded with parenting information from the experts, such as what to eat when you're eating for two, pre- and postnatal exercises for you and your baby, and tips for keeping your newborn healthy.
- Get a complimentary subscription to *Babytalk* magazine, from the publishers of *Parenting* magazine, at www.babytalk.com. This publication for new moms includes articles on pregnancy, health and fitness, relationships, baby development and activities, and buying guides.
- If you're expecting or already have twins or other multiples, call toll-free 800-328-3211 to request a sample issue of *Twins Magazine*.
- *Parenting* magazine will send you a free trial issue if you subscribe; visit the site at www.parenting.com. If you find you're not interested in the publication, you can cancel and keep the initial issue.

child-care resources and referral agencies nationwide. In addition to a no-cost parent newsletter, Child Care Aware offers several free publications, including *Matching Your Infant's or Toddler's Style to the Right Child Care Setting; Five Steps to Choosing Safe and Healthy Child Care;* and *A Guide for Dads: Give Your Child an Early Lead in Life … Quality Child Care.*

Lowered-Fee Child-Care Services for Veterans

While you are serving your country, you can get a break on the high cost of child care. National Guard and Reserve Service members activated or deployed in support of the global war on terrorism are eligible to receive a fee reduction in child-care expenses through the National Association of Child Care Resource and Referral Agencies (www.naccrra.org/militaryprograms). This national network of more than 850 child-care resource and referral centers helps families, child-care providers, and communities find, provide, and plan for affordable, quality child care. Once you've found an appropriate provider, the subsidies will be paid directly to them. To apply for reduced-fee child care from Operation: Military Child Care, the military member, spouse, or legal guardian should contact Child Care Aware (a program of NACCRRA) toll-free at 800-424-2246 or log on to www.childcareaware.org.

Free Reading Readiness Kit from Target

Reading might seem a long way off for your little tyke in diapers, but this is the time to get started. Reading to your child early on instills a lifelong love of books. And Target's "Ready. Sit. Read!" program gives parents of babies, toddlers, and school-age kids a host of ideas for encouraging the reading habit. Register online at target.com/readysitread to receive a free starter kit backpack. The kit includes an overview on how to host a book club, a fun story to read with your children, and ready-to-go invitations to send to friends. You'll also receive a "read-o-meter," which is both a bookmark and a timer to keep track of each reading session, a door hanger with reading tips, and a book club flag. Check the site for suggested book lists, coupons, and promotions, such as discounts on books sold at Target.

Free Potty Training Kit from Charmin

When your child is ready to ditch the diapers, Charmin, the toilet tissue company, offers a free Potty Training Kit. Sign up at www.charmin.com to receive by mail fun and easy-to-use training materials that include a poster, reward stickers, an interactive storybook, and a picture frame magnet. When your child has successfully completed potty training, you can print out the diploma from "Charmin University."

CHAPTER 19

community service employees and teachers

Those who educate and those who protect and serve can save big with these money-saving finds and freebies.

By the numbers

458

Average amount of their own money, in dollars, that American teachers spent on school supplies for their classroom in 2004, according to the National School Supply and Equipment Association.

IF YOU'RE THE KIND OF PERSON who lives to serve others, you may well be a teacher or other community service provider. The deep personal satisfaction many people get from teaching or serving the public often outweighs the drawbacks, such as relatively low pay and a stressful work environment.

Today teachers face a monumental task, with pressure to improve standardized test scores and competition for students' attention from a seemingly endless stream of distractions outside the classroom. Time-pressed teachers are looking for ready-made lesson plans and activities that energize the learning process without costing an arm and a leg at the bookstore or online. Luckily, the proliferation of free or low-cost resources on the Web has made the job of accessing affordable teaching aids a lot faster and easier. There are hundreds of sites where teachers can find materials like lesson plans, supplies, and activity sheets to enhance the classroom experience. In this chapter you'll find some of the best. The federal government and the National Education Association are also gold mines of information and resources for teachers, as you'll see in the following pages.

There are also bargains aimed specially at educators, first responders—police officers, firefighters, and emergency medical technicians

(EMTs)—and sometimes other civil servants. While they can obviously take advantage of the offers described throughout this book, the search for freebies and discounts geared specifically to community service employees may involve research and a certain amount of determination. There are discounts available on a host of items—from cruises to hotel rooms, rental cars, and housing—but you often have to ask for them. Many businesses offer reduced prices to first responders to acknowledge and thank them for putting their lives on the line every day, but such deals aren't always widely publicized. This chapter helps you figure out where to ask.

And last but not least, we point you in the direction of a terrific benefit available only to teachers and community service employees—a pair of federal programs that can take a huge chunk off the mortgage bills of teachers, law enforcement officers, firefighters, and EMTs by offering them government-owned homes in revitalization areas at half price. It's a way of saying thank you by helping to stretch limited budgets, but it's also a way to make communities stronger. With teachers and police officers living nearby, parents and schools form deeper bonds and the neighborhood becomes safer. And from that, we all benefit.

Resources for Teaching English

Free Fun with a Favorite Author

Children's book author and illustrator Jan Brett has sold more than 30 million books, and the rich style she brings to her illustrations of animals and fairy tales makes her books popular among the younger set. To the benefit of teachers everywhere, Brett has created a website (www.janbrett.com) to enrich the classroom experience. Surf the site to find, among other fun projects, alphabet book-jacket covers to print out for free; an African lion safari coloring mural that can be enlarged to cover a classroom wall; classroom helper job charts; instructions for drawing one of her armadillo characters, beginning with a simple circle; and flash cards for letters, colors, and numbers. One of the coolest pages features a drawing of a Jan Brett gingerbread house; students drag and drop the elements of trim wherever they like on the house, then print out the finished product as a greeting card.

Editor's Choice

Deductions for School Supplies

Many teachers pay for supplementary materials out of their own pockets to help students learn more effectively. Public or private school teachers who teach in elementary or secondary schools for at least 900 hours in a school year can take a federal tax deduction of up to $250 for books, software, computer equipment, or other classroom supplies they've provided. Principals, counselors, instructors, and aides are also eligible. Some restrictions apply. For more information, call toll-free 800-TAX-FORM (800-829-3676) or order IRS Publication 17 from the website www.irs.gov.

EDITOR'S CHOICE

Getting Kids to Read the Book

The easiest time to get kids to read books may be when the film version is in local theaters. Walden Media, a film production company, helps teachers capitalize on that moment. For example, when the movie version of *Charlotte's Web*, opened, the company offered teachers a free *Charlotte's Web* wall planning calendar on its website (www.waldenmedia.com), along with five reproducible lessons based on the book. Walden has also formed partnerships with teachers, museums, and businesses to provide teaching tools, such as activity guides, discussion topics, and enhanced DVDs.

No-Cost Storytimes with Pro Storytellers

It's time for a story, and you want to treat kids to a professional reading. At www.storylineonline.net, you'll be able to play streaming video of dozens of famous actors reading children's books for free. Kids will be thrilled to hear stories read by folks who know how to bring the written word to life, such as Lou Diamond Phillips reading *The Polar Express* or Elijah Wood delivering *Me and My Cat*. (For adults, the most fun may be listening to Al Gore read *Brave Irene*.) The site, sponsored by the Screen Actors Guild, offers accompanying activities and lesson ideas for each book.

Free Reading Info and Fun Activities

For a free online guide to the best in children's literature, go to the Reading Planet website (www.rifreadingplanet.org/rif), sponsored by Reading Is Fundamental, Inc., the nation's largest nonprofit children's literacy organization. The site helps teachers, students, and parents search an annotated list of 1,000 children's books organized by age group, author, and category. Children can post reviews of their favorite books, write their own endings to stories, and create word puzzles. Games let them navigate a spaceship to collect words, or color and print fun pages.

Audiotapes at a Bargain Cost

Every teacher has grappled with the problem of children who have difficulty learning to read. When students have visual problems or another disability such as dyslexia, you can help them get free CDs of their textbooks by joining a national nonprofit group called Recording for the Blind & Dyslexic. An annual fee of $35, plus a $65 registration fee, puts an individual in line for hundreds of dollars' worth of CD textbooks. Schools can get a membership for between four and twelve students for $350 a year (more for more students). Members can even request that the group record a book not yet in its catalog of more than 109,000 titles. To learn more about the program, visit the RFB&D website (www.rfbd.org).

Free Ideas for Kids Making Books

Children love to make their own books, but they can get bored with the standard page-turning format. Enter Susan Kapuscinski Gaylord, who has written about bookmaking and conducted workshops with more than 10,000 students and 2,000 teachers. On her website (www.makingbooks.com), Gaylord provides step-by-step instructions

Book Discounts for Teachers

Some bookstores, both the larger chains and the smaller independents, will give educators a discount.

- At Borders bookstores (www.bordersstores.com), you'll get a 20 percent Classroom Discount Card for books, music, and videos purchased for classroom use when you show proof that you're a teacher or librarian in preschool through twelfth grade.
- Barnes & Noble bookstores (www.bn.com) offers a 20 percent discount on hardcovers and 15 percent on paperbacks.
- Book Warehouse, The Book Market, and Foozles (www.book-warehouse.com) run a Teachers of America program that gives teachers, librarians, and homeschoolers a 15 percent discount on the already discounted books that the company distributes.

Your best bet is to go into your bookstore of choice and inquire about educator discounts in person. In all likelihood, you'll be able to get savings on the spot.

for making a variety of interesting books with little more than paper, scissors, and glue. In the case of the "Who Am I" book, she shows how to make a series of simple folds and cuts in a 12x18-inch piece of paper to fashion four folded pages holding clues to an identity—an animal, historical figure, number, anything you want—that is revealed at the book's center when all the pages are opened. Gaylord's tips, resources, and sample projects are well worth a look.

For Math, Science, and Health Teachers

82 Free Science Experiments for Grades 4-8

Well-designed science experiments are worth their weight in gold, and the Charles Edison Fund website provides 82 of them for free; go to www.charlesedisonfund.org/Experiments/experiments.html. So far the fund has distributed some 60,000 copies of its teaching kit for grades 4-8. Experiments concentrate heavily on energy, including electricity and nuclear. Each hands-on project offers simple directions, is inexpensive to conduct, and can be downloaded directly from the website. (The kit itself can be ordered for the cost

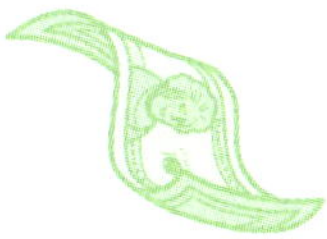

of mailing.) The fund even has an awards program that provides engraved certificates for students who complete an experiment, and a matching T-shirt and cap for the student the teacher identifies as the best. You'll have to register and provide feedback on the experiments you use, but the investment of time is worth it.

Free Lessons in Building a Home

Looking for an interesting way to "bring home" concepts in math, science, social studies, English, or technology? The National Association of Home Builders offers teachers in schools with 100 students or more a free copy of its CD-ROM game "Building Homes of Our Own." Students gather information, deal with problems, and make decisions to get a home built and sold. They do math as they measure materials and calculate costs. They communicate with business contacts using language arts skills, and use social science or hard science skills as well. The product features 2-D and 3-D graphics, animation, and audio clips. It also comes with a teacher's guide specifying lesson plans in a variety of subjects, plus additional activities. An index ties each lesson to a specific national standard. To find out more about it, go to www.homesofourown.org and click on "In the Classroom" to view sample lessons in your field.

Free Space-Related Programs from NASA

Kids are fascinated by outer space—and that's a good thing, because it's a nifty way to teach a variety of concepts in science, math, and technology. The National Aeronautics and Space Administration maintains a website, NASAexplores (www.nasaexplores.com), that delivers articles, lessons, and learning activities on 30 different space topics. Materials are customized to grades K-4, 5-8, and 9-12. For example, an article on the use of NASA technology in football helmets, uniforms, and stadiums leads to an activity in which students in grades 9-12 design a helmet to protect eggs in a fall or one in which younger kids (K-4) identify types of helmets and their benefits.

Free Health and Fitness Curriculum

As childhood obesity becomes a national concern, health and fitness teachers are trying to educate kids on the benefits of exercise and healthy eating. To help educators integrate these topics into their classroom teaching, the American Council on Exercise (ACE) has developed an Operation FitKids Youth Fitness Curriculum, which teachers can download for free at www.acefitness.org. Designed for

Q How can I make learning math more fun for my students?

A The next time your math students ask, "But when will I ever *use* this?" consider signing up for the free "We All Use Math Every Day" math initiative that ties in with the CBS television series *Numb3rs*. In the popular series, a genius mathematician helps his FBI agent brother solve and even predict crimes by using math concepts and equations. Developed by Texas Instruments and the National Council of Teachers of Mathematics in partnership with CBS, the initiative offers educational math activities for grades 7-12. Teachers who register on the site get a free kit and poster and can check the website a week before each episode airs for activities geared to that week's story. For more information, go to www.cbs.com/primetime/numb3rs and click on the "We All Use Math Every Day" icon.

third, fourth, and fifth graders, the seven-lesson module covers such topics as deciphering food labels, identifying healthful snacks, and the importance of strength exercises. To download the curriculum, go to the ACE home page and click on "Youth Fitness."

For Social Studies Teachers

No-Cost Help Bringing History Alive

There's plenty of free help for social studies teachers on the History Channel website (www.historychannel.com). For one thing, very early every morning the History Channel airs *History Channel Classroom*, an hour-long block of commercial-free, copyright-cleared educational programming that can be taped for showing in the classroom; a website calendar, accessed from www.historychannel.com/classroom, alerts teachers to which programs air when. The shows offer an in-depth look at such subjects as an archeological dig at Jamestown and the history of Independence Day. Each program listing contains relevant vocabulary words, with links to definitions, and questions to spark classroom discussions. The rest of the classroom area of the site features ever-changing lesson plans and teacher's manuals.

Free Online Resources for Women's History

March is Women's History Month, and what better way to celebrate it with your students than to familiarize them with some of the women who have made the world a better place? You can download one-minute MP3 audio recordings about 25 such women from the National Women's History Museum at www.nwhm.org. On the home page, click on the icon that takes you to the recordings, which include commentary on such well-known high achievers as Clara Barton and Nellie Bly as well as newer role models like Nobel Prize-winning geneticist Barbara McClintock. Then check out the site's Educational Resources section for lesson plans, quizzes, quotes, and biographies of distinguished women, from abolitionists to writers.

Freebies for Religion Classes at Catholic Schools

Thousands of educators teach religion classes at Catholic schools, and it isn't always easy for them to find free classroom materials. A

Editor's Choice

Free Environmental Studies Resources

The environment is a huge topic in school curricula these days. The U.S. Environmental Protection Agency provides a wealth of free lesson plans, activities, and Web resources. At the EPA website (www.epa.gov/teachers), you can access information by clicking on "Teaching Resources" or "Order EPA Publications." Publications on global warming, wetlands, and many other issues are usually downloadable and offer lists of programs, resources, contacts, and other information. Those that aren't downloadable can be ordered online. There are even free coloring books for younger students.

group called Resources for Catholic Educators has recognized the need and developed a website that offers at no cost thousands of items of clip art (symbols, images of Jesus and characters and stories from the Bible, even graphics highlighting concepts like "glory," "love," and "peace"); lesson plans (for example, on the Beatitudes); coloring pages; crossword puzzles; and educational features, such as "Saint of the Day" and "Daily Wisdom." There is also a calendar with links to Mass readings for each day in the month. Go to www.silk.net/reled to explore the site's wealth of offerings.

Free Hotlist of Virtual Field Trips

Field trips present a great opportunity for hands-on learning, yet often sites that would benefit your class are too far away to visit. That's when it helps to have a master list of online exhibits with links from museums and other educational institutions throughout the world. Want your students to take a virtual tour of the Tower of London, do a virtual frog dissection, or cruise through a dinosaur safari? You'll find links to such exhibits on the Online Exhibits Hotlist provided by Philadelphia's Franklin Institute. Visit the site sln.fi.edu/tfi/jump.html to browse the offerings.

No-Cost Resources for Globalization 101

If you teach social studies to high school students, you can find free resources for teaching "one world" topics at globalization101.org, a website sponsored by the Carnegie Endowment for International Peace and the Stavros S. Niarchos Foundation. Click on "For Teachers" and you'll find comprehensive information and lesson plans for units on international trade, women and globalization, and technological change, among other subjects. For instance, a lesson plan in the Culture & Globalization unit contains activities that explore the spread of U.S. culture across the globe, including a role-playing exercise on a dispute between the United States and Canada. Along with lesson plans, the site features a dozen in-depth issue briefs, news analyses, downloadable videos of "Ask the Experts" interviews, and an array of useful links.

Free Geography Aids from *National Geographic*

If you're looking for resources to help teach kids the difficult subject of geography, it's hard to beat the lesson plans, maps, and other materials that are available free at the *National Geographic* website (www.nationalgeographic.com/xpeditions/lessons). Not only are they classroom-tested, but they cover all national geography standards, the five geography skills, and the latest perspectives on the subject. Lessons are organized by grade and by the standard being taught, so they're easy to access. There's one, for example, on how to determine the latitude and longitude of several different American cities and another on the differences between Earth and Mars. An interactive "museum" called Xpedition Hall, which comes with a free teacher's guide, takes your students on geography journeys across different terrains, countries, continents, even into outer space. An interactive atlas lets you customize a map of any country in the world, at two different levels of detail. Altogether, this is a site teachers of geography won't want to live without.

The UN Explained in Free Teacher's Kits

The United Nations is often in the news, and it's a complex topic to explain. The world organization lays out its inner workings in free kits, some for teachers and others for the general public. The teacher's kits are geared for either the elementary or middle/high school level and tell you how to get other educational materials on world issues. Publications included in the kits take readers on a pictorial tour of UN headquarters, provide information on what the organization does and how the public can help, and detail the functions of the UN's many agencies. To request either the elementary or middle/high school kit, write to United Nations Public Inquiries Unit, Department of Public Information, Room GA-57, United Nations, New York, New York 10017. You can also e-mail your request to inquiries@un.org. For more information, go to www.un.org/geninfo/faq/teacherskit/teacherkit.htm and click on the link to the kit you're interested in.

Free Help Explaining the Role of Juries

Civics and government classes sometimes grapple with the issue of the jury's place in the U.S. system of justice. "The American Jury: Bulwark of Democracy" (www.crfc.org/americanjury) is an online resource guide that explains the jury's role in our legal, social, and political life. It features lessons, information, and resources developed by the Constitutional Rights Foundation Chicago with high school teachers and scholars from around the country. For example, lessons give kids a chance to conduct their own mock jury deliberations and to research historic jury trials like those of the Chicago 7 and Sacco and Vanzetti.

EDITOR'S CHOICE

Free Animal Protection Info

Kids often feel protective toward animals, and they can learn a lot about teamwork by organizing to keep animals safe. At the National Association for Humane and Environmental Education website (www.nahee.org), clicking on "For Teens" takes you to free step-by-step instructions to help older students start a teen advocacy group. If you teach elementary school, you can get the group's monthly classroom newspaper, *KIND (Kids in Nature's Defense) News,* for free with the support of a sponsor—a business, individual, or organization that NAHEE has identified as willing to foot the bill. Click on "Adopt-a-Classroom" to find potential sponsors.

Our Favorite Free Classroom Materials

Of all the tons of teaching materials that are available to teachers, here are some that we think merit special recognition. They rise above the ordinary by being imaginative and by appealing to kids' curiosity—and sometimes by being fun to use. And all are readily available on the Internet.

Free Word Worksheets and Games

Buying books with word worksheets can be costly—and the sheets can be hard to customize to your needs. Put together your own flash cards, word scrambles, matching columns, and bingo boards for free at the Personal Education Press website (www.educationalpress.org). The worksheets are printed directly from your browser, ready to copy for class. Just pick the selection of words you want to include and the style you prefer. You can print out your word game in a variety of shapes—for example, word searches come in squares, Christmas trees, Cheshire cats, and other designs. The site features words best suited to the lower grades, including word families like "ought" and "ow" and vocabulary from such books as Dr. Seuss's *Hop on Pop* and Betsy Byars's *My Brother, Ant*.

Free Reading Skills Books

Stephen Schutz had so much trouble learning to read that at age nine he was still struggling to master the skill—but master it he did. He went on to earn a Ph.D. in physics and to co-found the Blue Mountain Arts publishing company with his wife, poet Susan Polis Schutz. To help children who are struggling to read, Schutz created www.starfall.com, an innovative website where learning-to-read books and writing journals for grades K-2 can be downloaded and copied for free (or bought in bulk for a low price). The books teach reading and other skills with an eye to fun; click on *Gingerbread Man*, for example, and you'll be prompted to choose shapes and colors for eyes, nose, buttons, and other features before the gingerbread man starts running. The teachers' section suggests imaginative exercises for compiling journals. Books emphasize a phonemic approach to reading (*Zac the Rat* for the short "a" sound and *Peg the Hen* for short "e"), and free lesson plans are provided.

Free Algebra-Teaching Software

Some kinds of math can be hard to teach from a dry-erase board. If you're teaching algebra, calculus, or differential equations in middle or high school, the University of Arizona invites you to download and copy its commercial-quality math software for free. The review programs help you identify students' weaknesses and take appropriate action before class gets into full swing. Slide shows provide graphical screen images that would be tough to duplicate on a board, enlivened with animations and zoom functions. Interactive demos, logic games, and simulations add a bit of playfulness to the learning experience. To find out more and download the programs, go to www.math.arizona.edu/software.

Free Science Posters from Tufts

For a series of striking wall posters designed to get kids interested in science, check out the collection offered to teachers for free by the Wright Center for Science Education at Tufts University. Beautifully rendered graphics illustrate such topics as the electromagnetic spectrum, scale and size, and cosmic evolution. The center will send you its current collection, along with a teacher's guide, if you write a letter on your school's stationery to Wright Center, Department P, Room 267c, 4 Colby Street, Medford, Massachusetts 02155. To view the posters, go to www.tufts.edu/as/wright_center/svl/posters/posts.html.

Free Educational Software

Sheppard Software, a company that designs educational software and online games, will give about a dozen of its registered software programs—they usually cost about $15 apiece—to teachers, schools, and home schools for free. The offerings range from World Geography Games, distributed as freeware, to Brain Builder math puzzles shareware for ages 4 to 12. Just download the software and install it on your computer. Other programs help with preparing kids for the SAT; still others quiz them on presidential trivia (which chief executive had 15 children?) or facts about the states. On the main site, you can print out vocabulary flash cards and point your students to quizzes. Go to the Web page www.sheppardsoftware.com/teachers.htm for your free software, and navigate back to the home page for additional goodies.

Free Human Genome Poster

If you're a biology teacher, one of the most exciting developments in recent years has been the mapping of the human genome. To help students figure out how it all works, you can order a 24x36-inch wall poster titled "Human Genome Landmarks: Selected Traits and Disorders Mapped to Chromosomes" from the Human Genome Project itself. Go to www.ornl.gov/sci/techresources/Human_Genome/posters/chromosome and click on "Order Poster" at the top of the page. Fill out the online form and allow three months for delivery (because of a "high volume of requests"). To find more Web resources on genetic disorders and traits linked to chromosomes, check out the five activities in the site's "Gene Gateway" section, which contains step-by-step instructions for new users.

Free Comics About How Money Works

Any social studies teacher can tell you that kids' eyes glaze over when you try to teach them how the economy works. Why not try a different approach—twelve different comic-style booklets from the Federal Reserve, free for the asking. Among the topics covered are the importance of saving, foreign trade, and inflation. One book explains the meaning and purpose of monetary policy, how the Fed makes that policy, and how the tools of monetary policy work. You can get up to 35 complimentary copies to distribute to the class. Order online at app.ny.frb.org. From the home page, click on "Publications Catalog," then on "Comics."

Other Free Resources for Teachers

FREE Federal Teaching Resources

Looking for a one-stop location where you can access hundreds of federally supported online teaching and learning resources? Look no more: In 1997, more than 30 federal agencies got together and created the Federal Resources for Educational Excellence (FREE) website (www.ed.gov/free). Here you'll find links to a vast array of lesson plans and other teaching aids from government agencies and organizations ranging from the Agency for International Development to NASA to the White House. The site is organized by subject matter—arts, languages, math, social studies, science, vocational education, and physical education, plus a section on educational technology—and it's updated monthly. Click on "New Resources" to check out recent additions.

Free Donated Items for Your School

If you need materials and supplies for your classroom, chances are there's someone who wants just as badly to give them to you. That's

Winning Cash for Teaching Excellence

Looking for some extra cash to keep your classroom running smoothly? Consider asking someone to nominate you or your instructional team (of up to four teachers) for *USA Today*'s annual All-USA Teacher Team. It's the paper's way of recognizing excellence in K-12 teaching. The 20 winning teachers or teams receive $2,500, with $500 for each teacher or team and $2,000 for the school. The winners are also profiled in the newspaper. To be eligible, you must be a currently teaching, full-time, certified K-12 educator (or team) with at least four years of experience at a public or private school in the United States or its territories. The nomination can come from students, their parents, or members of the staff, including administrators, but you cannot nominate yourself. Past winners have included a teacher of at-risk girls in a Virginia alternative middle school and a literacy and workplace skills teacher at a magnet high school in Tucson. Your nomination should emphasize your teaching situation, how you identify your students' needs, how you address them through your teaching practices, how well your practices work, and your impact on your students and the community. For information about applying, visit www.allstars.usatoday.com.

the premise behind the matchmaking service I Love Schools, Inc. (www.iloveschools.com). Some 26,000 teachers have registered on the site and asked for books, markers, even paper towels to help their classrooms run smoothly. Would-be donors can search for teachers by school, city, and state, as well as the specific needs the donor wishes to fill, from art supplies to toys and playground equipment. There's also a place on the site where like-minded donors can band together to help a particular school, teacher, or district. Once you register on the site, be sure to get the word out to inform the community that your needs are posted there. For a similar effort that focuses on matching schools in need with people who have computer and office equipment to donate, go to www.sharetechnology.org.

Free Art Images from Recycled Calendars

Teachers often have a hard time providing enough pictures for students to cut up and use in arts and crafts activities. Now there's a website that can help. Ecals.com sells calendars over the Web, but it also supports a recycling program that matches preschool through sixth-grade teachers who need old picture calendars with those who want to donate them. Once you register your school as a "recycling center" on www.ecals.com, you can request any number of old calendars. People who have them to donate find your "recycling center" listed on the site, and mail or deliver the calendars to you. You can specify the kinds of calendar images you want (for example, animals, nature) and don't want (swimsuit models). There's also a form you can print out and send to parents in your district asking them for old calendars. It's a simple, hands-on way to teach kids about the power of recycling. From the Ecals home page, click on "Recycle" to sign up.

Free Honor Certificates from Crayola

Why spend scarce classroom dollars on printed certificates to encourage and reward students for jobs well done? If you register at www.crayola.com and visit the Educators section, you can print out a variety of nifty color certificates for free. The Crayola company is very involved with children and offers many other teacher goodies on the site, including lesson plans you can search by subject, theme, grade, media, and the amount of time required to complete the activity. Art teachers may be particularly interested in tips about achieving interesting effects with crayons, markers, and watercolor pencils. Click "Special Offers & Events" on the home page for

Q What's the best way for teachers like me to keep parents up to date about what's happening in the classroom?

A A class website is a great—and free—solution. Create and customize your own class home page at the website of children's book publisher Scholastic Inc. (www.scholastic.com). Go to the teachers' section of the site, scroll down to "Tools," and click on "Class Homepage Builder" to register and set up the page. Your class home page allows parents and kids access to information on homework, class trips, and other topics, and can even provide answers to frequently asked questions. Parents can e-mail you from the home page, so communication between home and school is a lot more efficient.

special, limited-duration giveaways for teachers; a recent one offered free samples of Overwriters markers.

Browse Education Books Free

Stenhouse Publishers, a Maine-based business specializing in books by and for teachers, knows that it's hard ordering books without paging through them to see whether they meet your needs. Who wants to invest up to $25 on a volume that might disappoint when it arrives in the mail? So Stenhouse provides educators with an opportunity to "browse" its books online, chapter by chapter, for free, at www.stenhouse.com/pdfbooks.asp. The current season's books are available in their entirety; older books have a selection

---

National Education Association Resources

Do you belong to the National Education Association (www.nea.org)? If so, you've got a treasure trove of free help at your fingertips, including grants for professional development and discounts on magazines and rental cars.

- The "Grants & Resources" section of the NEA website (www.nea.org/resources/index.htmlx) lists dozens of sources of funding, such as a grant for science teachers to work in the field with other scientists and a $1,000 fellowship to study Abraham Lincoln at his Springfield, Illinois, presidential library.
- In the "Member Benefits" section (www.nea.org/mbhighlights/mb.html), follow links and punch in a code for varying discounts on rentals with Hertz and Alamo.
- The NEA Magazine Service provides a link to discounts of up to 85 percent off the cover price of nearly 600 magazines, including the most popular news and consumer publications; ask questions or order from a members-only toll-free number: 800-YOURMAG (800-968-7624).
- For hundreds of lessons on every conceivable topic, at every grade level, go to the "In the Classroom" section. You'll find creative plans for teams of students to compare the first draft of the Declaration of Independence with the final version, or put together charts to compare the price of gasoline with that of other liquids. Here you can also access curriculum resources provided by the Public Broadcasting Service. The monthly themed units and lesson plans link to online PBS resources, with recommendations for PBS programs that supplement the lessons.
- Finally, don't ignore this page on the NEA site: www.nea.org/resources/free-stuff.html; it lists some of the best deals for teachers.

of chapters available. Topics range from literacy to literature circles, social studies to dance.

Free Tips on Teaching Creatively

In 1991 filmmaker George Lucas established the nonprofit George Lucas Educational Foundation to "celebrate and encourage innovation in schools." On its website (www.edutopia.org), the foundation provides myriad resources for teachers looking for tips, research, case studies, and instructional modules for approaching teaching creatively. Educators can also get a free subscription to the foundation's magazine, *Edutopia*. To register, go to www.edutopia.org/magazine and click on "Subscribe to Edutopia magazine"; identify yourself as an educator and you'll be taken to the page for free subscriptions.

DEALS FOR CIVIL SERVANTS

Steep Discounts on Holland America Cruises

Looking for a little vacation from your important but stressful job? Active-duty police officers, firefighters, and teachers can get special prices on select cruises as part of Holland America Line's Community Appreciation Program. The cruise line conducts more than 500 cruises from 25 home ports and visits all seven continents. Offers vary by ship and sailing date, but discounts can be as much as 70 percent. You must show appropriate ID at the time of booking. Check with your travel agent for more details, or call Holland America toll-free at 888-425-9773.

Rental Car Discounts for FOP Members

If you're a member of the Fraternal Order of Police, you may be able to get discounts and special rates on rental cars. In 2006, Avis offered members a free third day in a weekend rental or $15 off a weekly rental of an intermediate- to full-size car. A link at the national FOP website sends you directly to the Avis reservation page with a discount code specifically for FOP members. For more information, check with your state lodge, or log on to the website www.grandlodgefop.org and click on "Service Providers." The organization lists a number of other discounts, such as 15 percent

Q How can I get a job teaching U.S. kids overseas?

A Both the Defense Department and State Department offer such jobs.

- The Department of Defense is responsible for the education of military dependents overseas. You can apply for openings by going to the current vacancies page (www.dodea.edu/offices/hr/employment/vacancies.htm) on the department's website and following the link to the USAJobs website.
- The State Department's Office of Overseas Schools offers assistance to nearly 200 schools serving the dependents of diplomats and other government employees in 135 countries. Its website (www.state.gov/m/a/os/) can point you to them by region so you can apply directly.

off at 1-800-flowers.com and a prescription drug program that lets you order lower-cost prescriptions directly from Canada.

Free Admission at Law Enforcement Museum

Normally it costs $12 for an adult to gain admission to the American Police Hall of Fame and Museum in Titusville, Florida. But, fittingly, the museum admits law enforcement officers for free and their guests at half price. The attraction, the first of its kind, is dedicated to officers who have been killed in the line of duty. It features interactive displays, simulators, and nearly 11,000 items that illustrate the history of law enforcement and showcase the latest trends. For a

Half-Price Homes for Teachers, Police, Firefighters, and EMTs

Teachers, law enforcement officers, firefighters, and EMTs willing to live in a revitalization area designated by the Department of Housing and Urban Development are eligible to buy a HUD home for half off the list price.

In an effort to encourage high-profile service providers to live in the communities they serve, the government has set up two programs: the Teacher Next Door Initiative (HUD Program 14.310) and the Officer Next Door Sales Program (HUD Program 14.198), which includes firefighters and EMTs.

Teachers must be full-time and state-certified in grades K-12 at a public school, private school, or governmental educational agency, and the home must be within the school district. Police officers must be employed full-time by a government unit or educational institution. Firefighters and EMTs have to purchase homes in the area served by their employers. Applicants cannot own another residence and must live exclusively in the HUD house purchased.

Single-family homes in these programs are listed and sold over the Internet. You bid the full amount—through a real-estate broker or independently—and get two mortgages: one for half the cost of the house, and a second zero-interest loan in HUD's name for the rest, discounted by half. A computer chooses the winning bid at random. If you stay for three years, the loan for the discounted half is forgiven; if you leave before that, you repay a pro-rated amount.

For details, contact the Teacher/Officer/Firefighter/EMT Next Door program coordinator at your local HUD Homeownership Center; at www.hud.gov/offices/hsg/sfh/hoc/hsghocs.cfm, or call toll-free 800-569-4287. Or see an overview of the programs by going to the Catalog of Federal Domestic Assistance at www.cfda.gov; click on "Search," then type "teacher next door" or "officer next door" in "Search Our Site."

discounted fee, you can also access the 24-lane indoor gun range. Visit www.aphf.org or call 321-264-0911 for more information.

Free Police and Fire Spanish Phrase Guide

If you'd like to learn enough Spanish to perform your job effectively in bilingual situations, check out the free samples of "workplace" Spanish geared to police officers and firefighters at www.spanishforpoliceandfire.com/freephrases.htm. The site is maintained by David B. Dees, who has taught more than 50 courses in Spanish for law enforcement situations and, with his wife, has written books on the subject. Dees provides Spanish equivalents for commonly used phrases that crop up in scenarios involving pedestrians, vehicles, and high-risk stops; Spanglish words; and slang/survival terms. With a little memorization, you'll be able to say everything from "You've got to fix the taillight" to "Stop, police. Everybody freeze." If you decide you want more in-depth training, you can order books and tapes on the site.

Housing Discounts for Government Workers

It pays to check for job-related discounts when you're in the market for a condominium or apartment. For example, in 2006, Florida-based condominium developer SunVest Communities USA (www.sunvestusa.com) offered police officers, firefighters, and educators a 3 percent discount on the 228 residences in its Mountain Canyon condo development in Phoenix, Arizona. Condos started in the mid-$100,000s, and all that was needed to qualify for the discount was a recent pay stub. Meanwhile, Chicago-based Equity Residential Properties' (www.equityapartments.com) Hometown Heroes program gave cops, firefighters, and teachers up to a 10 percent discount on rents for its 220,000 apartments in 34 states, with no application fee or security deposit. Check with your real estate agent or directly with any property you're interested in; such programs are not always advertised.

Legal Help for Accused Officers

When police officers face job-related legal difficulties, there's an organization they can turn to. The mission of the Law Enforcement Legal Defense Fund is to aid police officers who face criminal charges, or civil or administrative complaints stemming from actions taken in the line of duty. When you apply for assistance, a member of the board of directors (which includes such high-profile figures as former U.S. Attorney General Edwin Meese III), or his or her nominee, will interview you, the complainant's counsel, and potential witnesses to determine the facts of the case. The board must vote unanimously in each situation to provide aid that may cover some of the legal fees and living expenses while you fight your case. It might also include free co-counsel, help in finding your own counsel, a brief filed on your behalf, or free research. To learn more, go to www.leldf.org and click on "Assistance" and "Procedures."

It Never Hurts to Ask About Discounts

You can rack up substantial savings simply by asking about job-related discounts whenever you purchase a product or service. Companies that reduce the price for law enforcement officers, firefighters, and EMTs range from auto repair shops to exercise equipment retailers to cigar stores. There are so many discounts offered that it's impossible to list them all. Your best bet: Learn to be proactive. Don't be shy. Ask!

Check newspaper ads and the yellow pages. Call several different stores or local providers of the product or service you're interested in to find the ones that offer breaks for civil service employees. See whether the company's website sheds any light, though this kind of information won't always be advertised there. (Your chances of a discount are greatly improved if the owner of the business is a retired police officer or firefighter.) For ideas about what to look for, here are some offers from all around the country:

- Military and law enforcement officers, EMTs, and firefighters can buy Zippo lighters at a 40 percent discount at Cigar eXpress locations in Pennsylvania and Ohio. They also get 10 percent (or better) off the price of cigars and accessories. Visit www.cigarexpress.com/srvcs.htm or call toll-free 800-922-1233.
- Walt Disney World's Swan and Dolphin resorts offer varying discounts for local, state, and federal government employees. Call toll-free 888-828-8850 to check availability.
- At Jones Brothers Brakes (760-741-2373) in Escondido, California, firefighters get 10 percent off parts and labor.
- Precision Pool Tile Cleaning gives firefighters in Southern California a 15 percent discount. Call toll-free 888-300-8453.
- Police, firefighters, and teachers receive 25 percent off the service ticket at Affordable Mufflers in Houston. Call 281-496-4999.
- Eagle Rent-a-Car in Orlando gives military and police officers and firefighters a 12 percent discount. Visit www.eagle-rent-a-car.com/policies.php for the necessary code.

Civil Servants Save Big on Broadway

What would a trip to New York City be without a night at the theater? Yet tickets to a Broadway production can cost more than $100 each. One way to ease the sting is to become a member of New York's Theatre Development Fund (www.tdf.org). TDF is a nonprofit service organization for the performing arts, which, among other things, sells discounted same-day theater tickets at the TKTS booths at Times Square and South Street Seaport. Membership in the organization—open to teachers, civil service employees, and several other groups—entitles you to huge discounts on theater, dance, and music tickets ordered in advance through the website. As a member (the cost is $25 per year), you can get tickets to some Broadway shows for as little as $28-$32, even less for off-Broadway fare. For information on how to apply for membership, see "Special Deals for Special Folks," page 115.

Hotel Discounts for Government Employees

If you're traveling and considering a stay at a hotel chain, be sure to ask about its Government Program:

- Days Inn charges the best available rates within your per diem allowance (which means the room could cost less than the allowance) if you are a federal or state government employee. You will, of course, have to show the proper ID at registration, and some restrictions apply, including blackout dates. For more information, go to the website www.daysinn.com and click on "Programs."
- Choice Hotels' Government Programs offer federal, state, and local employees and military personnel a room rate equivalent to their per diem when they are on official business. (Government rates are available as well to military personnel enjoying leisure travel.) Choice owns Comfort Inn and Suites, Quality Inn, Sleep Inn, Clarion, Econo Lodge, and more. The offer is good at participating locations. For more information, go to the website www.choicehotels.com and click on "Offers & Programs."

APPENDIX

helpful resources

A selective listing of major government agencies and non governmental foundations, associations, and other sources that provide assistance, money-saving information, or free stuff.

GENERAL INFORMATION

CFDA
The Catalog of Federal Domestic Assistance
www.cfda.gov
Federal Citizen Information Center
Toll-free 888-878-3256
www.pueblo.gsa.gov

FirstGov.gov
The U.S. government's official Web portal
Toll-free 800-FED-INFO (800-333-4636)
www.firstgov.gov

Foundation Center
The leading U.S. authority on grant-makers and grants
Toll-free 800-424-9836
www.foundationcenter.org

Grants.gov
Toll-free 800-518-4726
www.grants.gov

U.S. Census Bureau
American Community Survey
301-763-INFO (301-763-4636)
www.census.gov/acs/www

CONSUMER

American Automobile Association
E-mail:
publicaffairs@national.aaa.com
www.aaa.com

AnnualCreditReport.com
Free credit reports
Toll-free 877-322-8228
www.annualcreditreport.com/cra/order

Better Business Bureau
The U.S. Council of Better Business Bureaus
703-276-0100
www.bbb.org

CarBuyingTips
www.carbuyingtips.com

Child Care Aware
Toll-free 800-424-2246
www.childcareaware.org

Cooperative Extension Service
202-720-7441
www.csrees.usda.gov/extension

craigslist
Classified ads of all types
www.craigslist.com

dealnews
Reports on best deals on computers, electronics, gadgets, and other consumer items
dealnews.com

Federal Trade Commission /Deter, Detect and Defend Against Identity Theft
Toll-free 877-438-4338
www.consumer.gov/idtheft

Find Legal Help
American Bar Association
Toll-free 800-285-2221
www.findlegalhelp.org

FirstGov for Consumers
Consumer information from the federal government
E-mail: gateway@ftc.gov
www.consumer.gov

Freecycle Network
An electronic forum for recycling unwanted items
E-mail: info@freecycle.org
www.freecycle.org

Legal Services Corporation
202-295-1500
www.lsc.gov

National Association of Child Care Resource and Referral Agencies
703-341-4100
www.naccrra.org

National Association of Insurance Commissioners
Gateway to state insurance department websites
816-842-3200
www.naic.org/state_web_map.htm

National Do Not Call Registry
Federal Trade Commission
Toll-free 888-382-1222
www.donotcall.gov

Overstock.com
Brand names at clearance prices
Toll-free 800-THE-BIG-O (800-843-2446)
www.overstock.com

U.S. Consumer Product Safety Commission
Toll-free 800-638-2772
www.cpsc.gov

U.S. Department of Transportation Citizen Services
202-366-4000
www.dot.gov/citizen_services

WorldWideWired
Links to online versions or websites of newspapers, magazines, and radio and television stations around the globe
www.worldwidewired.com

EDUCATION

To find your state's commission on higher education, search for "student aid" and your state's name in a search engine.

The Benevolent and Protective Order of Elks of the USA
Elks National Foundation
773-755-4732
www.elks.org

The Coca-Cola Scholars Foundation
Toll-free 800-306-COKE (800-306-2653)
www.coca-colascholars.org

Federal Resources for Educational Excellence
E-mail: free@ed.gov
www.ed.gov/free

The Federal Student Aid Information Center
Toll-free 800-4-FED-AID (800-433-3243)
www.studentaid.ed.gov

FinAid
Student guide to financial aid
E-mail: questions@finaid.org
www.finaid.org

The Gates Millennium Scholars Program
Toll-free 877-690-4677
www.gmsp.org

National Education Association
202-833-4000
www.nea.org/resources/free-stuff.html

Upromise College Fund
Toll-free 888-434-9111
www.upromise.com

EMPLOYMENT

America's Job Bank
Toll-free 800-833-3000
www.ajb.org

America's Service Locator
Directing employers and job seekers to essential local workforce services
www.servicelocator.org

Career One-Stop Centers
U.S. Department of Labor
Toll-free 877-348-0502
www.careeronestop.org

Equal Employment Opportunity Commission
www.eeoc.gov
Toll-free 800-669-4000

The Internet Job Source
E-mail: jobsource@aol.com
www.statejobs.com

Job Accommodation Network
U.S. Department of Labor
Office of Disability Employment Policy
Toll-free 800-526-7234
www.jan.wvu.edu

Job Corps
Toll-free 800-733-JOBS
(800-733-5627)
www.dol.gov/dol/topic/training/jobcorps.htm

Jobs.com
Toll-free 800-MONSTER
(800-666-7837)
www.jobs.com

State Offices of Apprenticeship
U.S. Department of Labor
Employment and Training Administration
Toll-free 877-US-2JOBS
(877-872-5627)
www.doleta.gov/oa/stateoffices.cfm

Studentjobs.gov
The federal student temporary employment program
www.studentjobs.gov

USA Jobs
Federal jobs and employment information
www.usajobs.com

FOOD AND HOUSING

AmeriDream, Inc.
Down payment assistance program
Toll-free 866-263-7437
www.ameridream.org

Community Food Projects Competitive Grants Program
U.S. Department of Agriculture
202-720-7441
www.csrees.usda.gov/fo/communityfoodprojects.html

The Federal Housing Authority Resource Center
U.S. Department of Housing and Urban Development
Toll-free 800-CALLFHA
(800-225-5342)
www.hud.gov/offices/hsg/sfh/fharesourcectr.cfm

Food Stamp Program
U.S. Department of Agriculture
Toll-free 800-221-5689
www.fns.usda.gov/fsp

Low-Income Home Energy Assistance Program
Toll-free 866-674-6327
www.liheap.ncat.org/sp.htm

Special Supplemental Nutrition Program for Women, Infants, and Children
Food and Nutrition Service
U.S. Department of Agriculture
703-305-2746
www.fns.usda.gov/wic

U.S. Department of Energy
Toll-free 800-DIAL-DOE
(800-342-5363)
www.energy.gov
Energy Efficiency and Renewable Energy
E-mail: fueleconomy@ornl.gov
www.fueleconomy.gov

U.S. Department of Housing and Urban Development (HUD)
202-708-1112
www.hud.gov
Directory of HUD regional and field offices:
www.hud.gov/localoffices.cfm
Home improvements:
www.hud.gov/improvements
HUD-approved housing counseling agencies:
www.hud.gov/offices/hsg/sfh/hcc/hcs.cfm

HEALTH

Administration on Aging
U.S. Department of Health and Human Services
202-619-0724
www.aoa.gov

American Cancer Society
www.cancer.org
Toll-free 800-ACS-2345
(800-227-2345)

American Diabetes Association
Toll-free 800-DIABETES (800-342-2383)
www.diabetes.org

American Heart Association
Toll-free 800-242-8721
www.americanheart.org

American Red Cross National Headquarters
202-303-4498
www.redcross.org

Ask the Pain Doctors
www.pain.com/sections/consumers/ask_the_dr

Cancer Legal Resource Center
Toll-free 866-843-2572
www.lls.edu/academics/candp/clrc.html

Centers for Disease Control and Prevention
Toll-free 800-232-2522
www.cdc.gov

Co-Pay Relief Program
Patient Advocate Foundation
Toll-free 866-512-3861
www.copays.org

DentalPlans.com
Toll-free 888-632-5353
www.dentalplans.com

Eldercare Locator
Toll-free 800-677-1116
www.eldercare.gov/Eldercare/Public/Home.asp

Medicare
Toll-free 800-633-4227
www.medicare.gov

MedlinePlus
U.S. National Library of Medicine and the National Institutes of Health
E-mail: custserv@nlm.nih.gov
www.medlineplus.gov

Merck Manual of Medical Information
www.merck.com/mmhe/index.html

National Association of Social Workers/Help Starts Here
The National Association of Social Workers consumer website
www.helpstartshere.org

National Cancer Institute
Toll-free 800-4-CANCER (800-422-6237)
www.cancer.gov

National Institutes of Diabetes and Digestive and Kidney Diseases
301-496-3583
www2.niddk.nih.gov

National Institutes of Health
301-496-4000
www.nih.gov

National Institute on Aging
Toll-free 800-222-2225
www.nia.nih.gov

National Library of Medicine Health Hotlines
Online database of health-related organizations operating toll-free telephone services
healthhotlines.nlm.nih.gov

Partnership for Prescription Assistance
Toll-free 888-477-2669
www.pparx.org

PDRhealth
Drug information from the Physicians' Desk Reference
www.pdrhealth.com/drug_info

Pregnancy and Newborn Health Education Center
March of Dimes Foundation
914-997-4488
www.marchofdimes.com

Prostate Cancer Foundation
Toll-free 800-757-CURE (800-757-2873)
www.prostatecancerfoundation.org

The Susan G. Komen Breast Cancer Foundation
972-855-1600
Helpline: 800-I'M AWARE (800-462-9273)
www.komen.org

U.S. Department of Health and Human Services
Toll-free 877-696-6775
www.hhs.gov

Vaccines for Children Program
Centers for Disease Control Information
Toll-free 800-232-4636
www.cdc.gov/nip/vfc

Yale-New Haven Hospital Nurse Advice Line
(Nationwide)
Toll-free 877-688-1101
www.ynhh.org

MILITARY AND VETERANS

AMVETS
Veterans services and advocacy
Toll-free 877-7AMVETS (877-726-8387)
www.amvets.org

e-Vets Resource Advisor
U.S. Department of Labor
Toll-free 866-4-USA-DOL (866-487-2365)
www.dol.gov/elaws/evets.htm

The Federal Web Portal for Veterans in Business
Toll-free 866-584-2344
www.vetbiz.gov

GI Bill
Toll-free 888-442-4551
www.gibill.va.gov

Home Loan Guaranty Services
U.S. Department of Veterans Affairs
Toll-free 800-827-1000
www.homeloans.va.gov

Military.com
Connecting service members, military families, and veterans to all the benefits of service
415-820-3434
www.military.com

Military OneSource
Toll-free 800-342-9647
www.militaryonesource.com

U.S. Department of Veterans Affairs
Toll-free 800-827-1000
www.va.gov
Facilities locator and directory: www.va.gov/directory/guide/home.asp
VA home loan guaranty program: www.homeloans.va.gov

Veterans Health Administration
U.S. Department of Veterans Affairs
Toll-free 877-222-8387
www.va.gov/health

MONEY AND TAXES

Federation of Tax Administrators
State comparisons and state tax holidays
202-624-5890
www.taxadmin.org

Independent 529 Plan
College savings accounts
Toll-free 888-718-7878
www.independent529plan.org

Internal Revenue Service
Toll-free 800-829-1040 (live telephone assistance)
www.irs.gov

Investing Online Resource Center
The facts about online investing
North American Securities Administrators Association
www.investingonline.org

IRS Free File
Free online tax preparation and electronic filing
www.irs.gov/individuals (click on "Free File")

Low Income Tax Clinics
Internal Revenue Service
Toll-free 800-829-1040
www.irs.gov/advocate (click on "Low Income Tax Clinics")

Morningstar, Inc.
Morningstar.com Investing Classroom
www.morningstar.com/cover/classroom.html

The Motley Fool
How-To Guides (money and investing)
www.fool.com/shop/howto

National Association of Securities Dealers
BrokerCheck
Toll-free 800-289-9999
www.nasdbrokercheck.com

Taxpayer Advocate Service
Internal Revenue Service
Toll-free 877-777-4778
www.irs.gov/advocate

TreasuryDirect
Purchase electronic Treasury securities direct from the U.S. Treasury
Toll-free 877-322-8228
www.treasurydirect.gov

NONPROFIT ORGANIZATIONS

National Association for the Exchange of Industrial Resources
Toll-free 800-562-0955
www.naeir.org

National Cristina Foundation
Giving used computer technology resources a second productive life
203-863-9100
www.cristina.org

VolunteerMatch
415-241-6868
www.volunteermatch.org

SENIORS

AARP
(Formerly American Association of Retired Persons)
Toll-free 888-OUR-AARP
(888-687-2277)
www.aarp.org

Benefits CheckUp
National Council on Aging
www.benefitscheckup.com

ElderLawAnswers
Toll-free 866-267-0947
www.elderlawanswers.com

Medicare Rights Center
Toll-free 800-333-4114
www.medicarerights.org

Pension Benefit Guaranty Corporation
Toll-free 800-400-7242
www.pbgc.gov

Pension Rights Center
202-296-3776
www.pensionrights.org

Senior Citizens Resources
FirstGov.gov
Toll-free 800-FED-INFO
(800-333-4636)
www.firstgov.gov/topics/seniors.shtml

Senior Community Service Employment Program
U.S. Department of Labor
Toll-free 877-US-2JOBS
(877-872-5627)
www.doleta.gov/seniors

Seniors4Hire
714-848-0996
www.seniors4hire.org

U.S. Social Security Administration
Toll-free 800-772-1213
www.ssa.gov

SMALL BUSINESSES

ACCION USA
Small business loans
617-625-7080
www.accionusa.org

Association of Small Business Development Centers (SBDCs)
SBDCs are supported by the U.S. Small Business Administration in partnership with the private sector and the colleges, universities, and state governments that manage SBDCs across the nation. To find your local office:
703-764-9850
www.asbdc-us.org

index

A

B

C

F

G

H

I

J

K

L

M

N

O

P

Q

R

S

U

V

W

Y